c Trust

...parts on Corruption

Betrayals of the Public Trust

Investigative Reports on Corruption

Edited by Sheila S. Coronel

Philippine Center for Investigative Journalism

Betrayals of the Public Trust
Investigative Reports on Corruption

Edited by Sheila S. Coronel
Book and cover design by Edgardo P. Legaspi

Photos from BusinessWorld library, PCIJ library, and by Alex Baluyut and Sonny Yabao.

This book was published with the help of a grant from the Asia Foundation.

National Library of the Philippines Cataloguing-In-Publication Data

Recommended entry:

Betrayals of the public trust : investigative reports
on corruption / edited by Sheila S. Coronel
– Quezon City : PCIJ, ©2000
1v

1. Government offices – Corrupt practices – Philippines.
2. Political Corruption – Philippines. 3. Exposure (Criminal law). 4. Investigative reporting – Philippines. I. Coronel Sheila S. II. Philippine Center for Investigative Journalism.
III. Title.

HV6306.P5 364.132'09599 2000 P001000030
ISBN 971–8686–27–4

Contents

Introduction

BY SHEILA S. CORONEL

The investigative reports in this book were written between 1990 and 2000, a decade that spanned the administrations of three democratically elected presidents: Corazon C. Aquino, Fidel V. Ramos and Joseph Estrada. During that period, the integrity of democratic institutions, which were re-established after the fall of Ferdinand E. Marcos in 1986, was challenged by charges of corruption and malfeasance. Virtually no office, including the Supreme Court and the Office of the President, was spared from accusations of wrongdoing and of abusing the public trust.

The media, let loose in 1986, has often subjected grafters to merciless scrutiny. And that, in many ways, has made a difference. During the Marcos era, a muzzled press could not expose the abuses of those in power. But the free press that emerged post-Marcos has exercised its watchdog role and has had some success in curbing the excesses of those in office.

Corruption is daily fare in Philippine newspapers; it also provides meat for the congressional exposés that keep the political mill grinding. A lot of the press reporting on corruption, however, has been on the investigations or revelations made by politicians or official bodies. While there are certainly outstanding examples of news organizations initiating their own investigations, these efforts have not been enough to uncover the widespread corruption in public life.

Many constraints hamper the media's ability to be a more effective watchdog. Intense competition in a crowded market means that news organizations often resort to the sensational in order to sell. Lack of skills and training restricts the capacity of journalists to do in-depth reporting. In most newsrooms, inadequate editorial, research and logistical support do not allow investigative journalism to survive. Ethical problems, including bribes to journalists and the impropriety of certain reportorial techniques, seriously impair the media's integrity and its reputation as a credible watchdog. In addition, libel suits, threats, harassment of media owners, the withdrawal of advertising, and in the provinces, the killings of crusading journalists, are very real deterrents.

The reports included in this volume show the range of corruption that can be found in various areas of governance: from high-level political corruption in Malacañang and Congress to low-level corruption in local governments. What we have found in the course of a decade's reporting on corruption is that there is no shortage of wrongdoing to investigate, whether one is a journalist working for a small community newspaper in Mindanao or a big broadcast network in Manila. The scale of the thievery may vary, but there is a sameness about the patterns of malfeasance.

This book shows how the Philippine Center for Investigative Journalism (PCIJ) has researched and put together investigative reports on corruption. All the articles in this collection come with an explanation of the research and reporting methods that were used by the journalists who wrote them. The documents that were obtained, the interviews conducted, and the other sources for the story are listed. The use of other techniques, such as computer databases or immersion in communities, is also explained. In addition, how stories are developed — by, for example, using case studies or establishing a pattern of irregularities — is discussed. When applicable, the impact of the reports, in terms of catalyzing policy or personnel changes, for instance, is also mentioned.

The reports are divided into five sections: services, the presidency and Congress, the courts, the environment, and local governments. In addition to the explanations for each article, each of the five sections of this book comes with an introduction that explains the peculiar difficulties that face (and faze) reporters investigating corruption in particular areas of governance. How these difficulties were overcome, and the techniques most applicable for uncovering corruption are discussed.

It is hoped that this collection will encourage more reporting on corruption and make it easier for others who are embarking on the challenging task of uncovering wrongdoing in public office, whether they are journalists, researchers, officials, activists or plain concerned citizens. The field is huge and wide open.

Following the Trail

Exposing malfeasance requires not only the nose, but also the doggedness, to sniff out wrongdoing and follow its trail. Patience and perseverance, especially with tedious detail, are needed. Other requisites are a basic knowledge of laws, the capacity to understand bureaucratic procedures, and the ability to chase documents that will provide evidence of malfeasance. Good journalists know where to find sources who will provide reliable information and help them piece together how wrongdoing was committed. Increasingly now, a familiarity with computer-assisted research tools (e.g. the use of computer databases and the Internet) is indispensable for investigative reporters.

All of these can be learned. Training on special skills, such as reading financial statements, constructing databases and Internet searching has proved useful in honing investigative skills. Reporting manuals, including those that provide tips on where appropriate documents can be found and the procedures for accessing them, arm journalists with the tools they need for conducting research. (The PCIJ has produced several reporting manuals and will soon come out with a manual on investigating corruption). In time, and with practice, journalists master these tools and sharpen the instinct for reporting on corruption. They are also able to develop a network of sources that will provide information on official wrongdoing.

The truth is that in the Philippines as in many countries, corruption is rarely hidden from public view. Petty corruption — policemen taking bribes from erring motorists or fixers who demand a fee in exchange for facilitating a permit or a license — is fairly easy to document. Reporters can interview victims or simply go through the processes themselves to see whether they are asked to make payoffs.

Corruption on a grander scale is harder to investigate, but not impossible. Many times, there are insiders in an organization who, for whatever reason, are willing to play the role of whistleblower. Often, they are only waiting to be asked the right questions by an inquisitive journalist. Sometimes, they don't even wait; a few of the stories in this volume, for example, were brought to the PCIJ's office by the whistleblowers or victims themselves. Otherwise, there are business or political rivals who can be tapped for information. Businesspeople who lose bids for government contracts may be willing to speak about how bribes have been extorted from them. Sometimes, police or other investigators are only to eager to share with journalists what they have found.

Evidence of actual pay-offs may be difficult to find, so journalists instead look out for lapses in established procedures or conflicts of interest. Sometimes, a pattern of irregular decision-making or awarding of contracts to favored firms can be discerned, even if proof of actual bribery is not available. One other area that is ripe for investigation is the lifestyle and public behavior of government officials. For example, it is difficult to show that judges are paid off, but reporting on judges meeting in private with litigants or lawyers with cases pending in their courts may be sufficient to demonstrate breaches in ethical conduct. Certainly, reporters who find tax examiners driving Volvos and sporting Rolex watches should start following the money trail.

Avoiding the Pitfalls

The more sophisticated types of corruption are the most difficult to report on, especially when they involve dummy firms and shareholders, corporate layering, overseas bank accounts and offshore companies. In an era of digital convergence, transnational money flows and international crime, investigating corruption becomes more challenging than it ever has been. Even the most talented investigative journalists can reach a dead end when investigating complex transactions that cross national borders and various legal jurisdictions. But even in these instances, it may be possible to get the cooperation of lawyers and accountants, as well as of official regulators and investigators. Otherwise, there are business rivals or company insiders who may have reason to blow the whistle.

Journalists should of course develop a certain skepticism about their sources. It is easy for corruption investigations to be manipulated. Reporters are often fed information by sources who have something to gain from an exposé. The challenge is to steer clear of partisan politics and to be independent of vested interests. Journalists must also behave themselves in a manner in which their autonomy cannot be questioned. But sometimes, no matter how careful they are, they will be accused of the basest motives. This is par for the course; reporters eventually learn to be patient and to realize that only after several exposés will they be able to prove their independence and develop a reputation for credibility and trustworthiness.

The public's trust is earned if journalists are careful about their methods. Investigative reporting has come under fire for sensationalism or for being too trigger happy with the use of undercover and surveillance methods. But if they are to have the public's confidence, journalists should be more self-critical about their methods and ethics. They must also be willing to disclose the methods they use in their investigations.

Outrage and Hope

The danger, of course, is that sustained reporting on corruption would lead to widespread cynicism about government. It is important that investigative reports make an impact in terms of policy reversals or personnel changes, or at least the initiation of official investigations of the wrongdoing that has been exposed. Otherwise, citizens will think that nothing can be done and they will view exposés as yet another distraction proffered by the media.

Some of the reports in this volume have succeeded in forcing the resignations of officials and in prompting official investigations. Some of them have had an impact on voting behavior and in shaping public opinion. Because of these exposés, the suitability of candidates running for public office and the capability of those already in office has been questioned.

But journalists alone cannot solve social ills. Citizens must do their part and eventually, the wheels of government have to be set in motion to fight malfeasance. At best, journalism plays a catalytic role. Investigative reports enrich public debate and put on the news agenda issues that should be of concern to citizens. By probing, for example, the consequences of corruption in terms of the quality of government services taxpayers get or the magnitude of the waste of public resources, journalists help readers to understand the problems of governance and to make decisions about who they should vote for and what changes they should demand. At their best, exposés should make people angry rather than cynical, and move citizens to action. Outrage makes change possible.

Ideally, investigative reporting should help raise the level of public discourse by bringing issues of corruption away from personal attacks or partisan politics to the level of policy, institutional or societal reform. Apart from the psychic rewards of exposing crooks, "naming and shaming" is important because it makes corruption visible and intelligible to the public. But investigative journalists should look at not only who is responsible for the wrongdoing they have uncovered and how it was done, they should also examine why it was possible and how it can be corrected.

For this reason, it may sometimes be good to feature the work of reformers, whistleblowers and organizations combating corruption. Citizens need to be informed about innovations that have worked or reforms that have been implemented — and what still needs to be done — so they can temper their outrage with a measure of hope.

(This book was published with the help of a grant from the Asia Foundation.)

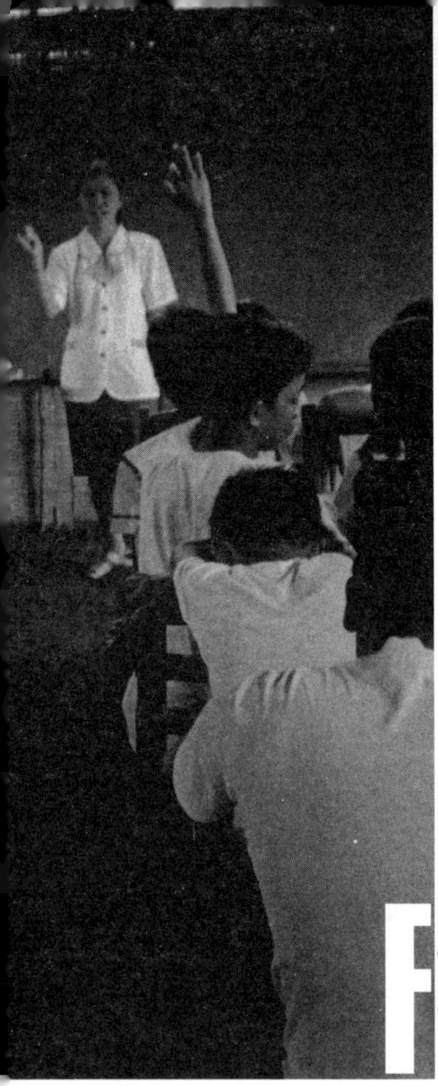

Services

For too long, citizens have suffered from the consequences of corruption in the delivery of basic services. Their complaints are legion: potholed streets, inadequate textbooks and broken chairs in public schools, expired medicines given out in government clinics. Very often, these problems persist for decades because of the systemic graft and corruption that lie at the core of bureaucracies tasked with providing for the fundamental needs of citizens. Certainly that is what we found in our investigations of among others, the departments of education, agriculture and public works.

In this section, we examine procurements and contracts by various government agencies providing frontline services. For most of the writers of the reports included here, this has entailed a thorough study of government procedures for buying supplies and equipment or contracting out work. It has meant reading procurement guidelines, bidding documents, project specifications, and contracts. After all, only when reporters know what the procedures and rules are can they discover whether these have been breached.

Many times, it was not possible to show that bribes have been accepted, but it was sufficient to prove that there were lapses in prescribed procedures or that rules have been violated either to favor certain firms and individuals or to cover up wrongdoing. Quite often, anomalous transactions are found out because they are full of procedural lapses or short-cuts. It is the reporter's task to discover those lapses.

This is where audit reports have been most helpful. Our reports have benefited from the cooperation of the Commission on Audit (COA), which has generally made it easy for journalists to obtain documents that show exactly how and where procedures were breached. COA is a good first stop for reporters who want to uncover bureaucratic corruption. (As will be shown in other sections, COA reports are less helpful in uncovering corruption in the courts or at the highest levels of government, such as the Office of the President). From the information and clues provided by COA reports, reporters can then proceed to search for other documents and sources. Gemma Luz Corotan's exposé on corruption in the National Food Authority, for example, would not have been possible without audit reports.

Court records, in instances where cases have been filed either in anti-graft courts or regular trial courts, are also a mine of information. In her report on corruption in the agriculture department, Prime Sarmiento used the number of cases filed, and the officials who were on the dock, as an indication of how pervasive graft was in the agency. She also used the information from these cases to show how the corruption takes place through such mechanisms as rigged bids and negotiated or "emergency" purchases.

These same tactics were used by grafters in education as well. Court documents were useful for Yvonne T. Chua's investigation of the long record of failed deliveries by a notorious supplier at the education department. In that investigation, Chua also examined bank records, particularly the use of letters of credit from a government bank, which was a novel way of skirting restrictions on advance payments for undelivered supplies.

Other documents that are routinely available—corporate and other business records, the certificates that suppliers or contractors submit to bid committees, business permits—provide further clues of malfeasance and help reporters piece stories together. Corporate records, for example, can give evidence of a common practice in many bureaucracies: the accreditation of contractors with records of unfulfilled obligations but who register new firms just so they can take part in biddings from which they have already been banned.

For sure, examining bureaucratic corruption is tedious work, and involves a familiarity with government rules and auditing procedures as well as some patience with numbers. But it also requires a sharp mind and a nose for malfeasance.

Investigating bureaucratic corruption, however, should not be limited to examining documents. Face-to-face interviews provide fresh information as well as background and context that cannot be gleaned from documents alone. In particular, information gathered from interviews with contractors and suppliers, even if they cannot be attributed by name, give insights about the prevailing "industry practice." It was amazing that entrepreneurs doing business with the government were willing to talk to reporters about pernicious practices, including bribery or collusion among bidders. Losing bidders were also more than willing to spill the beans; after all, they have legitimate gripes. It is necessary, however, to check the facts from these interviews with other sources that will attest to their veracity and to use only information that interviewees have first-hand .

Thus, Chua's interviews with over a dozen textbook suppliers helped her establish the standard bribes given to a host of government functionaries: in all, as much as 65 percent for supplementary texts. Similarly, Corotan's interviews with medical suppliers attested to how then Health Secretary Hilarion Ramiro was taking for himself up to 40 percent of the contracts at his department. Likewise, Chay Florentino-Hofileña's discussions with contractors involved in the rehabilitation of areas damaged by the Mount Pinatubo eruption showed that anywhere from 10 to 30 percent of government funds were lost to bribes, onerous contracts and irregular financial management. In these instances, having an estimate of how much is lost to corruption makes it easier for readers to appreciate the magnitude of the wrongdoing.

Sometimes, officials themselves acknowledge the extent of corruption in their agencies. This was the case in the education and agriculture departments. In these instances, officials were important sources of information. Indeed, reporters often find that reform-minded officials are willing to cooperate by releasing documents, providing leads, and making access to other sources possible.

But the journalists who wrote these reports did not limit themselves to officials. Lawyers and accountants are either in possession of crucial information or else have the expertise to help journalists understand procedures and numbers better. Government investigators, whether they are from congressional committees, administrative bodies, the courts or the police, already have many documents in their files that they are willing to share with reporters.

Often, however, there is no substitute for field visits for rounding out a reporter's understanding of the subject she is investigating. Florentino-Hofileña drove to Pampanga and interviewed Pinatubo victims to find out how government-funded reconstruction projects were responding to their needs. Chua went to Leyte and Samar to look at the impact of corruption on the quality of public school education in these areas. Corotan traveled to Baguio to see for herself the long lines of people queuing at the height of the rice shortage in 1995, and then to Nueva Ecija, to find out how farmers were being shortchanged by the government food agency.

Most times, it is necessary not only to explain how the wrongdoing was done and who was responsible, but also to show its impact in terms of the quality of services that citizens get. It is easy to get lost in the bureaucratic details, and in the course of their investigations, reporters have had to be constantly reminded of the big picture they were investigating: the thievery of public funds and its impact on the lives of people.

In many of these reports, the writers attempted to give both an overview of how malfeasance took place and specific instances that dramatize its extent and impact. We have found that the case study approach was useful in developing stories, as shown in Chua's exposé on corruption in the procurement of school desks, which zeroed in on the long list of crimes committed by a particularly notorious desk supplier. Sarmiento's focus on the Central Mindanao regional field unit of the Department of Agriculture showed the brazenness of corrupt officials and the courage of whistleblowers, making the case study one that inspires both horror and admiration.

All the work that journalists put into investigating bureaucratic corruption can be rewarding. Several of these stories have won awards. More important, some of them, like the stories on Ramiro, eventually led to investigations that prompted disgraced officials to either resign or to take the rap for the wrongdoing they have committed. Some of these exposés, particularly those on education and agriculture, have also pointed to where changes are needed and helped reformers clean up.

Public Works Mess

BY ERIC GAMALINDA

First published in *Malaya, Manila Times,* and *Manila Standard,*
November 28-29, 1990

Potholes happen. They are so ubiquitous and seem such an inevitable fact of Philippine life that they are deemed no longer worthy of media attention. But potholes are only the most visible manifestation of an entrenched system of graft in government road projects. This two-part report attempts to answer a fairly simple and obvious question: Who makes money out of potholes? The author, a fictionist, poet and occasional journalist, interviewed highways officials and academic experts for this report. He also looked at government audit reports.

What he found was an open acknowledgment that corruption is endemic in road building, permeating the entire life of road projects, from bidding to completion. Corruption persists in part because the system for disciplining erring contractors is weak. Officials and experts admitted the existence of pernicious practices: collusion among contractors bidding for a project, "ghost" deliveries, "ghost" projects, the use of substandard materials, the intervention of politicians, and the outright bribery of highways officials. It is a pattern of corruption that is evident not only in road projects but also in the procurement of other essential services, whether they are textbooks for schools or medicines for rural health clinics.

The PCIJ would examine these practices in more thorough detail in its subsequent reporting, using other investigative techniques, such as following the paper and money trails and actually visiting project sites. This article, by putting together information gathered from candid and revealing interviews and the studies done by NGOs and experts, sheds light on an everyday problem and the web of corruption that is at the root of it.

Who Makes Money out of Potholes?

First of Two Parts

CONTRACTORS do. Engineers do. So do some personnel employed by the Department of Public Works and Highways (DPWH). In fact, the process of road building and repair is so intricate that even the DPWH itself acknowledges the presence of syndicated graft and corruption within it, but can't tell where corruption begins.

"We cannot deny that that's happening," says Engineer Leonardo Nuñez, director for maintenance at DPWH.

"The problem is typical in any government office," says Raul Asis, assistant secretary for research and standards. "Contractors and government are equally liable."

According to studies conducted by nongovernmental organizations on the DPWH, road construction and repair involve project anomalies ranging from collusion among contractors to outright bribery of DPWH officials.

These anomalies include, among other things, the listing of more work programs than is required by the projects, ghost deliveries and ghost projects.

Cartels of contractors who are generally ill-equipped to handle projects have also been reported to corner bidding awards, while many contractors make up for the cost of "entertaining" DPWH officials by supplying substandard materials.

Payroll padding, nonpayment of rental of government equipment, nonconformity with quality control standards and bloated assessments of the value of land acquired through right-of-way have also been reported.

DPWH project engineers have also been reported to have hired dummy contractors for projects they themselves acquire.

Recently, the Philippine National Oil Company offered to dredge the Pasig river of debris left by contractors for the Metro Manila Light Rail Transit (LRT), but pulled out when the DPWH insisted on supplying their own contractors.

"Somebody wants to make money," said a PNOC official.

Calculating Losses

How much does the government lose in anomalous DPWH transactions?

While the DPWH information office gives an off-the-cuff figure of P80 million a year, Secretary Fiorello Estuar says "that is difficult to ascertain. Nobody will say how much he stole, would he?"

The pervasiveness of corruption within the department and the ineptitude of unqualified but favored contractors, coupled with implacable Philippine weather, garbage and drainage systems, are responsible for the country's potholed road network.

Lack of coordination between the DPWH and the Metropolitan Waterworks and Sewerage System (MWSS) has resulted in dug-up streets that are generally left unattended, while Estuar says the department is helpless against the conditions of local roads which do not fall under the DPWH's responsibility.

"There are opportunities for graft and corruption in the department," says Estuar, "because we are involved in procurement. The infrastructure program has P16.5 billion this year. That's a lot of money."

In a study made for the University of the Philippines, Dr. Ledivina Cariño said that corruption occurred from contract bidding up to payment for completed projects—in effect involving the entire road-building process.

"It's bigger than what we expect it to be," she says.

Her study, based on audits from 1987 to 1989, analyzed corruption involving about P1 million per project, which is peanuts compared to major multimillion-peso projects.

"It is easier in public highways because there are (fewer) people involved than in public works," she says.

Her study revealed that several projects were usually given to only one contractor who subsequently failed to meet deadlines.

"Even *pakyaw* contracts amounting to P8 million were given to licensed contractors (with the additional problem that some were not able to accomplish them). One contractor was given simultaneous contracts for 164 projects (that) were not accomplished on time," she reported.

But while some NGOs may have successfully uncovered some anomalies in road projects, many are not really technically equipped to assess these projects, she says.

Recently, the DPWH organized 15 teams of quality control inspectors to report on project deficiencies and anomalies throughout the country.

Many of these teams have reported not only deficiencies in construction but connivance between DPWH engineers and contractors as well.

While some regional offices have conducted their own inspections in anticipation of these teams, "*maraming naninibago*," says Asis. A lot of them are not used to it.

Some teams have been prevented from inspecting projects by local officials. Others either become the subject of black propaganda in provincial newspapers, or are offered bribes by project engineers and officials. "*Hindi nawawala ang offer* (We always get offers)," says a member of the DPWH Quality Assurance Unit.

Many of these inspectors have received threats from both DPWH engineers and local officials.

Their circumstance illustrates the extent of corruption involved in road projects—an entire web that may take some time to untangle.

Who Goes After the Crooks?

Conclusion

WHY can't the DPWH apprehend erring personnel? What happens to contractors caught in project anomalies?

Secretary Fiorello Estuar says that in 1989, there were about 12 instances where the department was able to break up contractor cartels.

These cartels had been maneuvering the bidding process so that one of their members would be granted certain projects.

The punishment for such collusion: suspension of the contractor for one year.

No charges have been filed against bidding officials, but there have been reshuffles, says a DPWH official.

Blacklisted contractors can simply be incorporated again and bid under a new name.

Contractors who complain that bribing DPWH personnel is standard procedure refuse to file their complaint "to protect their own interests," says Research and Standards Assistant Secretary Raul Asis.

Sofronio Ursal, Commission on Audit resident ombudsman, says there are cases filed against erring DPWH engineers pending at the Office of the Ombudsman.

The Office of Ombudsman Conrado Vasquez, however, says only cases adjudicated by the Sandiganbayan and the Office of the Special Prosecutor can be considered public records.

The COA has lodged cases against contractors and DPWH officials for noncompliance with plans and specifications and abandonment of projects, says COA Special Audits Director Fely Ona.

"The COA recommends the blacklisting of contractors, but it is up to the DPWH to do it," she says.

While anomalies occur in the bidding stage, the pressure to finish projects and shortcuts taken by contractors generally account for the poor condition of roads.

Leonardo Nuñez, DPWH maintenance director, says that asphalt roads have a general lifespan of 15 years. Many roads in Manila are more than 20 years old.

Funding and local politics are two other factors that cause poor roads.

"Sometimes (road improvement) is not possible because of lack of funding," he says. "Government officials also want their own programs, sometimes without technical consideration."

He says that potholes occur because of rain, the pressure to finish projects as soon as possible, and the wear caused by vehicles. Drainage also erodes the asphalt used on most roads.

"Some people actually induce flooding by plugging manholes and pumping stations, so that they can earn money by pushing stalled cars or ferrying people across floods," he says.

Who's Responsible?

Estuar insists that a distinction should be stressed between national roads, which fall under the responsibility of the DPWH, and local roads, which are managed by local governments.

While this is in line with the concept of decentralization, the capacity of local governments to cope with road repair, he says, "is spotty."

The DPWH is responsible not only for

national road conditions, but also for flood control and drainage.

Estuar's solution is a series of six circumferential roads for Manila and nationwide road networks utilizing existing roads, as well as a 15-year integrated flood control program for Metro Manila that is estimated to cost P15 billion.

Estuar recently organized 15 teams of quality assurance units (QAU) composed of "young, idealistic, competent engineers" who go around the country reporting on project anomalies.

One such project was the Ninoy Aquino Avenue near the Ninoy Aquino International Airport, where QAU teams found "deficiencies in construction."

QAU teams inspecting other projects have found cases of connivance between DPWH district engineers and contractors. Warnings are usually issued to district engineers for "negligence and laxity."

Their assessments are forwarded to the DPWH legal office and ombudsman, but contractors in question often hire lawyers and fiscals to badger QAU engineers.

Some of these engineers have been pulled out of their areas because of threats from local officials.

"It's politicians versus politicians," says one member of the QAU. "When we come in, we cannot fully implement our main purpose."

"Politicians still support their contractors," says Asis.

QAU teams have discovered that some DPWH district engineers have been acting simultaneously as engineers for private contractors.

Since January 1990, more than 50 district engineers and rank-and-file employees have been suspended for various anomalies, says this QAU member.

Members of QAUs have also received warnings from communist and secessionist insurgents who sometimes ask for commissions or even projects themselves. Recently, a DPWH vehicle was burned by irate rebels in Maguindanao.

Some engineers who have been overly strict about their inspections have been killed.

"The work is very challenging," says the QAU member. "We give them the message that they have to comply to the letter, unlike in the past when there was no check and balance."

Estuar admits that past programs of the department have dwelled on volume but have neglected quality control. "Now we are getting the real story," he says.

Aside from QAUs, he says he fielded "intelligence" persons in administrative offices. "What we want to do is to sound the message at the regional level," he says. But whether the message is taken seriously remains to be seen.

Money from Health

BY GEMMA LUZ COROTAN

These two reports on the unlamented former health secretary, Hilarion Ramiro, are examples of the use of investigative techniques for backgrounding officials. Ramiro was a little-known congressman from Mindanao when he was named by President Fidel V. Ramos to head the health department in 1995. Assigned to do a profile on Ramiro, whose qualifications for the post seemed questionable, Gemma Luz Corotan unearthed old NBI reports, traveled to Zamboanga where Ramiro was once regional health director, and talked to drug suppliers, former colleagues and health bureaucrats. Following the paper trail, she found that documents that would attest to Ramiro's tarnished past—including an audit report of his stint as regional director and a dossier on him compiled by the health department in 1987—were suspiciously missing. Interviews with disgusted health officials led Corotan to the discovery that just months into his new position, the secretary was already getting as much as 20 percent–commission from the department's purchases.

Five months after her Ramiro profile was printed, Corotan's follow up investigation was published. This time, going back to the officials who were her original sources, she delved more deeply into the anomalies that were taking place in the health department under Ramiro's leadership. She found that the secretary had issued a secret order that centralized all financial transactions in his office and gave undue power to other officials who had a record of graft. This order removed the checks-and-balances in the department's financial transactions and made it easier for Ramiro and his men to make deals.

Corotan got a copy of that order; she also found audit reports that attested to the questionable record of those that Ramiro had appointed to sensitive posts. In addition, she talked to suppliers, including the agent of a drug company, who said that the secretary asked him for a car in exchange for a contract. Based on such interviews, she found out that Ramiro was taking for himself as much as 40 percent of the contracts signed by his department. As a result of this investigation, and of a congressional inquiry that revealed other allegations of corruption, Ramiro was forced to resign two weeks after Corotan's second report was published.

"DOH Hounded by Corruption Charges" was among the 10 finalists in the 1996 Jaime V. Ongpin Awards for investigative reporting.

Ramiro's Record of Sleaze

First published in *Today* and *Philippine Star*, November 9-10, 1995

IN 1986, Hilarion Ramiro, then regional health director for western Mindanao, left the Department of Health (DOH) in disgrace, hounded by charges of corruption, profligacy and abuse of authority.

Today, almost exactly 10 years later, Ramiro stands at the helm of the DOH, his appointment to that post approved by Congress.

A former congressman and staunch member of the ruling Lakas-NUCD, Ramiro had lobbied intensely for his confirmation. At one point, congressmen said, he even dangled to members of the House of Representatives the possibility of allotting P100 million per congressional district from the DOH budget.

The secretary had reason to be worried. In 1986, he resigned from the DOH when the allegations against him surfaced and were investigated by a screening committee formed by then health secretary Alfredo Bengzon.

Those accusations hound Ramiro to this day. "There were charges, yes, but no convictions. Any administrator is a target of these allegations," he said. He claimed these charges were politically motivated and used against him in his 1987 congressional campaign. "These cases were dismissed by the Ombudsman," the secretary said in an interview.

But in its hurry to approve Ramiro's appointment, the Commission on Appointments failed to query the health secretary about these charges or to obtain government records that attest to these allegations.

The commission also did not examine Ramiro's three-month stint as health secretary, during which he was accused by drug suppliers and members of the DOH staff of sitting on lucrative procurement contracts while his aides demanded fat commissions from suppliers.

In 1987, the National Bureau of Investigation (NBI) Region 9 office reported that Ramiro connived with four suppliers from Zamboanga, Cebu and Manila to obtain supplies, medicines and equipment which were overpriced by as much as 40 percent.

It also discovered that Ramiro authorized the "ghost" deliveries of P19-million worth of supplies and equipment which were intended for government hospitals, but never really delivered.

The NBI report said that the bulk of the supplies came from Cebu City, naming two favored suppliers, Cebu Medical Supply Services and Medicor, which were suspected to be partly owned by Ramiro.

The report was forwarded to the investigative services department of the NBI's Central Office in Manila, an NBI official based in Zamboanga City who took part in the investigation said in a recent interview.

According to that NBI official, the report contained the testimony of a health official based in Ozamis City who had worked closely with Ramiro and had intimate knowledge of what he described as "wide-scale hanky-panky" in the regional office during Ramiro's tenure.

Indeed, the 1987 NBI investigation showed that there was sufficient basis to file charges, and the official recommended Ramiro's prosecution in court. But the case never prospered, said the NBI official, because the investigation was inexplicably squelched when the report reached the central office. (The NBI official asked not to be identified for fear of getting into trouble with his superiors.)

Serious Charges

When the Aquino government took over in 1986 and a new health secretary was named, similar charges were made against Ramiro, who was asked by Bengzon to choose between having to face serious administrative charges and resigning from his regional directorship. He chose to resign.

Bengzon refused to be interviewed for this article, saying he did not want to be involved in the dispute. But in a press conference in 1986, when he announced the resignation of Ramiro and six other regional directors, Bengzon revealed the reasons for the latter's ouster: several cases of corruption, including instances when Ramiro, as administrator of a government hospital in Ozamis City, personally followed up fraudulent Medicare compensation claims of "ghost" patients.

In fairness, however, Ramiro was credited for the effective delivery of basic services in the far-flung provinces in his region. But, said a DOH official, he also demanded a cut of up to 25 percent of contracts awarded to suppliers. "He may have been an effective administrator but he was expensive," the health official said in a recent interview.

This is corroborated by a supplier in Zamboanga City who charged that a 25-percent cut was the norm in dealing with the DOH during that period. These unauthorized commissions were, he said, given out of goodwill more than anything else. "After adding a hefty increase to the market price, it still allows us a huge margin of profit. *Ano ba naman yung* 25 percent?"

Tirso Abag, Jr. of the DOH regional office in Zamboanga City, who was Ramiro's financial officer in the early 1980s, said that overpricing was impossible under the Direct Order Payment System (DOPS), which sets the ceiling for the prices of medical supplies and equipment. "*May* DOPS *na, may* bidding *pa*," he said. "Then, we remove another 10 percent from the lowest bid. *Paano mo masasabing may* (How can you say there was) overpricing?"

But another DOH official insisted that DOPS prices which were set in Manila were often changed as Ramiro ordered his staff to replace the authorized prices with a new set of prices that had been agreed upon between the DOH and their suppliers.

"Remember we don't get the original copy of the DOPS from Manila, xerox *lang kaya kayang-kayang baguhin* (we only received xerox copies so it was easy to tamper with the documents)," revealed the official, who worked with Ramiro during his stint as regional director. "There is really no bidding to speak of. If you're willing to pay the price, you're in."

"*Ang maganda kay* Ramiro, *lahat pinagbibigyan niya* (The good thing about Ramiro was that he accommodated everyone)," said a drug supplier in Zamboanga City. "That is why a lot of suppliers welcome his appointment. He does not go by the rules. There was really no bidding to speak of during his time as regional director because it is normal practice for these suppliers to meet and agree among themselves on who will win the bid on a particular drug or equipment while the other suppliers get the chance to bid the lowest price on other drugs or equipment."

Aside from charges of overpricing, the dossier prepared by the DOH screening committee in 1986 included complaints that Ramiro dipped his hands into public funds to satisfy a gambling addiction.

The dossier also contained charges that he paid a Malacañang official to secure his appointment as DOH regional director when he was still administrator of an obscure government hospital in Ozamis City.

Missing Files

This dossier on Ramiro is just one of many incriminating records that have mysteriously disappeared from the DOH archives. Its contents, however, were revealed by a member of the screening committee who asked not to be identified. Commission on Audit (COA) reports during Ramiro's term as regional director are also missing, suggesting either incompetent record-keeping or a deliberate attempt to conceal information or wipe Ramiro's record clean.

Our requests to the NBI and the DOJ to gain access to investigative reports on Ramiro were refused, but their contents were revealed to us by officials who had written these reports or had thoroughly read them.

"A Cabinet member is considered to be a member of the First Family and in deference to them, we cannot release those records without their clearance," NBI Director Mariano Mison said.

The Commission on Appointments also had pending requests for access to those records, but it confirmed the appointment of the secretary in undue haste even before obtaining them.

Not one of the members of the commission made a motion to subpoena witnesses or records on these charges.

Playing Politics with Health

Conclusion

HEALTH Secretary Hilarion Ramiro, his friends say, had his sights set on the top health post to redeem himself from the ignominy he suffered when he was accused of corruption and booted out of his position as regional health director in 1986.

But, only three months after he became health secretary, his critics say he is back to his old form.

Interviews with Department of Health (DOH) officials, insiders and suppliers show that the corruption which marred Ramiro's term as regional health director for Western Mindanao continues "in unprecedented magnitude."

In an interview, the secretary laughed off these charges. "These are rumors that can't be confirmed," he said.

Since his appointment to the top DOH post, however, Ramiro has centralized the approval of purchase orders and the processing and release of checks in his office and that of his trusted chief of staff, Undersecretary Manuel Roxas.

A member of Ramiro's staff who asked not to be identified said that this setup has made a tidy profit for consultants in the secretary's office. These consultants call suppliers who are then compelled to fork out as much as 20 percent of their contracts to get Ramiro's signature on the dotted line.

A member of the DOH bids and awards committee complained that some 200 contracts worth almost P1 billion are being held up in the secretary's office, awaiting his signature. Such a bottleneck, said the DOH official, had never happened in the department before. (Many of the DOH bureaucrats interviewed for this series refuse to be identified for fear of repercussions.)

"In the past, the chief of staff and the secretary were the final signatories of all checks released by the department to suppliers, but their role was mainly ministerial," said the DOH official. "Once a supplier has gone through the process of accreditation and evaluation and has been approved by the bids and awards committee and given their purchase orders, the chief of staff and the secretary automatically sign the check without much ado. This is the first time it has happened that checks are being held for as long as three weeks, effectively delaying the delivery of medicines and supplies to end-users."

The power of the secretary and his consultants to hold the checks for as long as they can, said the official, in effect overrules decisions made collegially by the bids and awards committee, which is tasked to review the qualifications of suppliers who bid for government contracts.

The official added: "*Kung ayaw nila sa* supplier *na in*approve *na namin, hindi lang nila pipirmahan ang tseke* (If they disagree with the supplier we had approved, they simply refuse to sign the checks) . At the same time, they can pressure us through this method to approve the bids of the suppliers whom they favor."

Bending the Rules

In one case, the DOH chief of staff pressured the committee to change the supplier for mannequins intended for the DOH's Stop Death Program in favor of another supplier who they claimed had a better product.

"Legally, you can't do this," said the member of the bids committee. "They gave the specifications. The technical evaluation committee had decided that the product of this supplier meets the specifications they set and this supplier is the lowest bidder. After a product has been approved by the bids and awards, they (Ramiro's aides) suddenly come here saying that they have changed their specifications, favoring another supplier whose mannequins were significantly more expensive.

They threatened not to sign the checks of the supplier we originally approved if the technical evaluation committee did not change its recommendations. We did not give in. The check is still on hold."

In another instance, Ramiro's office instructed the committee on inspections to go easy on BDM Trading, a favored supplier of cadaver bags which the committee, in a resolution, had decided to ban from the bidding process because of repeated noncompliance with DOH standards.

"*Laging palpak ang* delivery that we felt it was an attempt by the supplier already to fool DOH and cheat taxpayers of their money," said a member of the committee on inspections.

The committee banned the firm the fourth time it delivered substandard products. After that, one of Ramiro's aides approached the committee head and promised her a promotion if she withdrew the ban. She refused. Until now, the ban has not been imposed because Ramiro refused to endorse it, said a committee member.

Such behavior has not endeared Ramiro to honest DOH officials. Apparently in response to their concern, Ramiro announced in a recent speech in Legazpi City that he was terminating the services of his controversial consultants.

Two of these consultants, who were responsible for holding suppliers' checks in the secretary's office, were simply farmed out to potentially lucrative agencies under the DOH. In an interview, Ramiro said he transferred these two men to "less controversial posts."

One was appointed to the board of directors of Chemfields, a sequestered drug company manufacturing antibiotics. The other was assigned to the Employees Compensation Commission, one of the more graft-ridden departments inside DOH.

The secretary also plans to appoint his son Gerard, a medical student, to the Chemfields board.

Ramiro confirmed that the Presidential Commission on Good Government is planning to nominate Gerard to the board. He said having his son in the board could be an advantage because Gerard will serve as his alter ego in the company and so could "better serve the interests of DOH." But he added that if his son were nominated, he would decline the appointment.

Extravagant Lifestyle

Departing drastically from the spartan lifestyle set for DOH employees by his predecessors, Ramiro is accused by his critics of using DOH funds for expensive, unnecessary junkets for his people.

"The hallmark of his administration is its extravagance," said a long-time DOH bureaucrat who took part in one of the junkets. "We used to hold these meetings only in the DOH office and only among top and middle-level officers. But he brought 80 of us to Legazpi City where we were billeted in the top hotel and dined on expensive food and wine. The subject of the meeting was over in three hours, but we were there for four days and the activities consisted mainly of sightseeing.

"The ladies were given small bags where they expected to find the agenda of the meeting. Instead the bags contained a guide on what to eat, where to go, and what to buy in Legazpi City."

In an interview, Ramiro insisted that these were not junkets but "medical missions."

His birthday party, however, provides proof of extravagance not previously seen in the DOH.

Interestingly, Ramiro held the celebration of the department's Foundation Day on his birthday. One of the parties was held at the Diamond Hotel, the bill paid for by funds solicited from DOH suppliers, a health official revealed.

"The food was overflowing—75 percent of it went to waste," recounted one of those who attended the party.

Indeed, Ramiro's lifestyle leaves many unanswered questions. His 1992 statement of his assets and liabilities attests to a financial base that went far beyond his earnings as DOH regional director and congressman.

Ramiro, according to the statement is worth at least P10 million. He bought a multimillion-peso house in posh New Manila, Quezon City, six months after he became congressman. The value of the house was declared in his statement as P8 million. Ramiro, however, claimed that he got the house by swapping it with his parents' home in Magallanes Village, Makati.

But veteran DOH bureaucrats are more cynical. "In the last three months, the DOH has been turned into a tool for personal profit, effectively eroding the culture of excellence started by Ramiro's predecessors like (Alfredo) Bengzon and (Juan) Flavier," said a DOH official.

The corruption is so blatant that it has plunged the department into a state of lethargy, attested many career professionals who cited, among others, the case of a presidential appointee who returned his appointment as financial services director and opted to be demoted instead because he refused to swing an anomalous transaction worth P25 million.

The infectious energy and passion of former secretary Juan Flavier, who kept out of the financial transactions of the agency because he was too obsessed with its programs, is sorely missed in the department, the same sources said.

"Many have lost their idealism and their pride. Now, they call the DOH the Department of Hobbies because many are cross-stitching instead of working. No one really cracks the whip because management has set the pace for the rest of us. Most days are declared half days. *Konting ulan,* half day. *Kaya ang tawag namin sa* DOH, Department of Half-day. *O kaya,* Department of Housing because the first time Ramiro talked to us, he did not outline his health policies which was what we expected. He promised us housing as if we were children to be wooed and bribed. He is first and foremost a politician and he acts like one," recounted one disgruntled doctor.

Proof of Ramiro's savvy as a politician is his refusal to be drawn into a running war with the Catholic Church on the family planning issue.

With members of the Commission on

Ramiro's lifestyle leaves many unanswered questions.

Appointments, he played the role of persistent suitor with a sincere handshake and earnest small talk. He is described by congressional staffers as a backroom dealer who has overcome the lack of excitement in his personality through his connections to the powers that be.

Ramiro's closeness to President Ramos, who has taken a see-no-evil stance on most of his political appointees, has shielded him from the barbs of public ridicule and is perceived to be his greatest strength.

Representing the district of Misamis Occidental, Ramiro was one of three congressmen who bolted the Laban ng Demokratikong Pilipino to join the Ramos camp in 1992. He is one of the Lakas originals, who include Speaker Jose de Venecia, Agusan del Norte Rep. Edelmiro Amante and former Rizal congressman Francisco Sumulong.

Ramiro has been amply rewarded for his loyalty. He is candid enough to admit that he was promised the post of health secretary, the reason he convinced his wife to run in the 1995 congressional elections.

In Manila's political circles, he is perceived to be a supporter of de Venecia's presidential bid, in which the DOH and its grassroots network are expected to play a crucial role.

DOH Hounded by Corruption Charges

First published in the *Manila Standard* and *Malaya*, March 11, 1996; and *Manila Times*, March 11-12, 1996

ONE morning in February 1996, a sales representative of a multinational drug company was invited to jog with Health Secretary Hilarion Ramiro near his home in New Manila, Quezon City.

According to the sales representative, who had to jog along in leather shoes, he was bluntly told that the health secretary wanted a new car in exchange for signing a contract.

Ramiro does not deny the incident took place. "The issue about the car was just a joke I made to a supplier," he said in an interview. The company representative, however, took the joke seriously. He reported the incident to his superiors, who were then instructed to negotiate with the secretary's wife, Misamis Occidental Rep. Hermina Ramiro.

Career health officials see the incident as only one of a number of recent events that show how, under Ramiro's leadership, corruption is apparently being institutionalized in one of the government's largest bureaucracies.

Ramiro denied there was anything irregular in the way he runs the Department of Health (DOH). But health officials and employees say that in his eight months in office, the secretary has left a trail of questionable decisions and transactions that threaten to derail the effective delivery of health services.

The DOH has a substantial budget: For 1996, it was allotted P9.2 billion, of which over P2.5 billion, or roughly a third, was supposed to go to supplies and medicine. The opportunities for graft are plentiful, especially in the purchases of drugs and supplies.

But Ramiro's recent actions, among them the decision to clear Lloyd Laboratories, a local company accused of manufacturing fake drugs, sent signals that the secretary was not about to put in order a multibillion-peso health industry that has resisted government regulation.

The case of Lloyd's was reported to the National Bureau of Investigation, which raided the company and seized a haul of fake drugs and incriminating documents in July 1995. Ramiro, however, cleared Lloyds in January 1996. In exchange, according to rumors in the drug industry, he received a Pajero van and 12 suits. Weeks later, Ramiro was photographed cutting the ribbon during the launching of Lloyd's new manufacturing plant.

But he denied the pay-off. "As for Lloyd, I signed something from their PR person who was here everyday," he said, referring to the clearance given the company. "I think I signed it by accident because there was a lot of paperwork on my desk. But I am ordering another investigation to rectify this matter."

"As for the Pajero, I am still using my old Pajero," he added. "I've been asking my consultants to get me a new one from the foreign projects, but so far, no one has delivered."

Career health officials claim Lloyd's case is only the tip of the iceberg. Members of Ramiro's staff, they say, have been known to call suppliers who were then compelled to fork out as much as 40 percent of their contracts to get the secretary's signature.

DOH insiders say that Ramiro has set the tone of corruption in his administration by personally getting involved in the financial transactions, unlike his two predecessors. A former congressman and a stalwart of the ruling Lakas-NUCD party, Ramiro was a DOH regional director during the Marcos era who resigned in 1986 amid allegations of graft.

In an interview, Ramiro said that the problem of corruption has already been addressed by the creation of a committee on financial transactions, which will review all financial transactions of the department before they are presented to the Office of the Secretary for his signature.

Secret Order

But the move, say critics of the new system, will not remove corruption but merely centralize it. DOH officials interviewed for this article say Ramiro has in fact consolidated his control not only over purchasing but over the most sensitive operations of the DOH, by virtue of Department Order 245-1, a secret department order he issued shortly after he assumed his post in July 1995.

Ramiro has set the tone of corruption in his administration by personally getting involved in the financial transactions.

The order, which is marked confidential, created "a top-level sub-committee responsible only to the Executive Committee which will cut across organizational authority and functional lines."

This sub-committee is allowed to overrule any of the decisions made collegially by the DOH's regulatory bodies such as the accreditation, inspections, and bids and awards committees which review the qualifications of suppliers who bid for government contracts.

Under the old system, a supplier's bid must be approved by the accreditation committee, the bids and awards and technical evaluation committee, the committee on inspections and various other committees whose decisions carry weight.

An examination of Ramiro's order shows that the secretary has in effect eliminated the checks and balances that has traditionally existed in the health department and which act as a check against graft.

The order gives the sub-committee control over sensitive departments such as the Cashier and Disbursement Section, the Financial Operations and Frontline Service Audit, and the Office for Legal Affairs, which are tasked with overseeing and monitoring various transactions entered into by the DOH.

Moreover, three of the four members of this powerful but secret committee have been tainted with allegations of graft: Undersecretary and Chief of Staff Manuel G. Roxas, Undersecretary Teresita de la Cruz, and DOH consultant Antonio San Juan. Only the fourth member, Assistant Secretary Manuel Dayrit, has not been accused of anomalies by DOH officials and employees.

To this day, Ramiro has not made public the sub-committee's existence. A DOH official says the order was circulated only within Ramiro's close circle because of the controversy it was expected to generate.

When interviewed, Ramiro expressed surprise that its existence had leaked out and was vague about its functions. In a later interview, he denied the committee exists. "As far as I know, there is only the executive committee, composed of the undersecretaries and the assistant secretaries," he said.

Centralizing Control

Since its creation, this committee has reshuffled personnel in key places in the DOH, moves that insiders say are calculated to squelch opposition and control the financial and administrative sector of the DOH.

A series of department orders reveals that the group has placed its own people in the Finance Service, the Financial and Operation and Frontline Service Audit, the Cashier and Disbursement Section, the Procurement and Logistics Service, Accounting, Budget, Personnel, and the Office for Legal Affairs.

"Under this set-up, no irregularity committed by Ramiro's people will be reported and no charges filed," said a DOH official. "The agenda is the protection and provision for their future, even covering the period beyond their retirement."

Indeed, committee members have covered up for their men. In one case involving P100,000 missing from a canteen in the DOH operated by the Health Employees Association of the department, they transferred the investigation to two offices headed by committee appointees to save another of their men from a serious probe.

Investigation of a similar financial anomaly in the Philippine Public Health Association formerly headed by Undersecretary Manuel Roxas was also transferred to a friendly body.

Moreover, to ensure that the secret committee has a steady supply of funds at its disposal, P50 million in Primary Health Care funds was transferred from the Health Manpower Development and Training Service to the Office of the Chief of Staff headed by Undersecretary Roxas.

Under the law, these funds can subsidize any community-based project using the primary health care strategy and are therefore the least likely to be questioned.

Tainted But Trusted Deputy

Ramiro's main man, Roxas, his chief of staff and undersecretary, is himself involved in some questionable transactions. "He is an expert in holding on for months and sometimes over several years official documents, particularly contracts and purchase orders like toilet bowls, DDT and many more for bargaining purposes," said a DOH insider who was privy to these negotiations. "He is too shy to demand for his share so he holds on to the papers until the interested party starts to offer."

He has been accused, for example, of postponing the signing of a purchase order for some P68 million worth of anti-tuberculosis drugs in the hope that the winning bidder would make him an offer. Roxas denied this charge. "Our goal here is to facilitate transactions, not to delay them," he said.

But DOH insiders point to other allegedly questionable actions:

• Using his position as regional director, and later undersecretary for public health service, to influence chiefs of hospitals to purchase their equipment from his brother, the registered owner of V.G. Roxas Enterprises. In 1991, he wrote a letter to the chiefs of government hospitals directing them to buy x-ray units and other hospital equipment from the company.

Audit documents show that V.G. Roxas is notorious for overpricing. A comparative statement of costs of medical supplies for a Bohol hospital in 1986 reveals that V.G. Roxas had transactions in Bohol with an 89 percent overpricing. Another audit report showed that the same company sold oral thermometers overpriced by 200 percent and KY jelly by 240 percent.

Roxas claims, however, that his brother's company has stopped doing business with the DOH Central Office since 1986. "It is dealing with the regional health units, but that is entirely my brother's own business, and I have nothing to do with that."

But a copy of an introductory letter from Roxas to the chief of one hospital in the Visayas showed he used his influence to get that hospital to purchase x-ray units and other equipment from his brother's firm.

• Awarding the contract for 200,000 toilet bowls to the second lowest bidder, a marketing company that was buying its supply from a manufacturer of PVC pipes, not toilet bowls, in March 1993.

The supplier delivered the toilets for the World Bank-funded project only in 1995, two years after it was awarded the bid, but was not penalized. Yet the DOH paid some P1.2 million more to the supplier than it would have had it granted the contract to the lowest bidder.

Roxas claimed that the instruction to suspend the bidding and award the contract to the second-lowest bidder came from Malacañang.

• Purchasing 1,000 sets of malaria spray guns which were supposed to be U.S.- made. According to the Bidding, Evaluation and Awards Committee, the contract went not to the lowest, but the highest, bidder: Lamgar, a Cebu City-based establishment.

Lamgar was declared winner, according to a DOH insider, after eight months of manipulation by disqualifying the other bidders who gave much

Three members of the secret committee are tainted with allegations of graft.

lower bids. Upon the delivery of the items, it was also observed that the box containing the complete set of spray guns had a marking of "made in Taiwan" in tiny letters.

Moreover, the item was priced at P5,305 per set. An independent check in a store in Quezon City showed that the same item was selling at a retail price of only P1,595. This means an overprice of P5.3 million for the entire transaction.

Roxas, however, denies this transaction ever took place.

Another committee member, Undersecretary Teresita de la Cruz, has also been accused of irregularities. These include purchasing 412 ambulances at a cost of P111.3 million in 1995.

According to a DOH source, it was de la Cruz who drew up specifications for the ambulances which would fit only one vehicle currently available in the market, the Besta vans distributed by Columbia Motors. De la Cruz's husband is the vice-president for marketing of Columbia Motors.

In addition, the purchase of cars by the Philippine Health Development Program was also allegedly personally followed-up by de la Cruz. "This transaction was the talk of the town for almost a month," said a DOH insider.

Antonio San Juan, one of Ramiro's consultants and also a member of the secret committee, is similarly tainted. San Juan has allegedly used his position as Roxas's confidant and assistant secretary for personnel management to demand that chiefs of hospitals buy medical supplies from his son, the owner of AJ III Enterprises of Malolos, Bulacan.

In addition, documents show that San Juan is owner of a newly registered Cebu-based drug and hospital equipment supplier, Sanjo Medipharma Philippines. As owner of a company that could have transactions with the DOH, San Juan is in a clear conflict-of-interest situation.

The Rice Scam

BY GEMMA LUZ COROTAN

First published in the *Manila Times* and *Manila Chronicle*, September 8-11, 1995; *Manila Standard*, September 8-10, 1995; and *Today*, September 11, 1995

This story was written during the 1995 rice crisis when a drought-induced shortage drove rice prices sky-high and saw Filipinos lining up for hours to buy government-subsidized grain. This three-part report offered a fresh angle on the rice shortage, tracing it to large-scale graft and corruption in the National Food Authority (NFA), the government agency set up to ensure a stable grain supply at an affordable price.

Using interviews with NFA officials, farmers, traders and consumers, and combining these with audit reports and academic studies, Gemma Luz Corotan wrote an investigative profile of the NFA, an agency she described as "tailor-made for corruption." She found that corruption, mismanagement, and the cozy relationship between the agency and profiteering grain traders were the reasons why the NFA was short of funds to buy a sufficient amount of rice as a buffer against shortages. Based on audit reports and court records, she drew up a long list of anomalies at the NFA, ranging from anomalous shipping and warehousing agreements to the awarding of lucrative contracts to favored businessmen. She also went to Baguio to see the rice queues for herself and to Nueva Ecija, one of the largest rice-producing provinces, to find out how rice farmers were coping. This report was one of 10 finalists in the 1995 Jaime V. Ongpin Awards for investigative reporting.

Inept and Corrupt, NFA Can't Assure Stable Rice Price

First of Three Parts

BAGUIO CITY — A culture of ineptness and corruption—revealed by a string of anomalous transactions ranging from inflated shipping contracts to questionable rice sales—reigns within the National Food Authority (NFA), impairing its ability to assure consumers of a steady rice supply at affordable prices.

Documents and interviews with NFA insiders, rice farmers and traders reveal a web of cozy relationships among NFA officials and unscrupulous traders and shed light not only on a few cases of graft, but on an entire system that seems tailor-made for corruption.

Our investigation also shows that the agency deliberately engaged in policies that created huge profits for itself while putting the food security of millions of Filipinos at risk.

NFA administrator Romeo David denies these charges. "I have always been against graft and corruption," he says. "My initial activities were of housecleaning and putting the house back in order."

But documents, including Commission on Audit (COA) reports, paint a picture of the NFA as a loosely run ship which lost hundreds of millions by violating its own standard operating procedures and practicing generally unsound management practices.

As the government's grains and marketing arm, the NFA is supposed to guarantee that farmers have a ready market for their *palay* and make reasonable profit for their produce. It is also mandated to ensure that cheap rice is available all year round.

In Baguio City, as in many parts of the country, long queues demonstrate how miserably the NFA has failed to live up to its mandate.

At 6 a.m., Jose Pagadian, 76, sits on his haunches at the public market here, his back hunched wearily as he waits in line for the local Bigasang Bayan to start dispensing rice at 10 a.m.

The line, consisting mostly of women with their babies and children in tow, started forming at midnight the day before and now extends from inside the market to the street outside. Buyers come here as early as they can, often sleeping among the markets' produce to catch the supply of cheap rice before it runs out.

"In my whole life, I've never done this before," whispers Pagadian, who remembers waking up to the fragrant smell of upland rice. Today, that kind of white, fluffy rice sells for more than P25 a kilo and is just a painful memory to the old man.

Soaring Rice Prices

Three weeks after the government assured that grain prices would stabilize, poor Filipinos, who comprise about half of the country's population, are still routinely queuing up for a limited supply of cheap rice—and the end is not in sight.

NFA statistics show that the price of rice increased by 126 percent from June 1992, when the Ramos government took over, and the third quarter of 1995. Between January and August 1995, rice prices increased by 21.4 percent for regular milled rice and by 31 percent for well-milled rice, a record high.

In 1991, a kilo of well-milled rice was

sold at about P10. By September 1995, it was selling at P20 to P22.

David insists that the crisis was mainly brought about by the El Niño drought that hit farmers in 1995. He says that traditionally, the price of rice is higher during the lean months and the problem will ease once the October harvests come in.

Others, however, see no relief in sight. Historically, an examination of rice prices show that prices stay up even after a bumper harvest. Despite reassuring pronouncements by Agriculture Secretary Roberto Sebastian that the crisis will pass once the market is flooded with the grain, rice prices have not decreased.

In many provinces the supply of imported rice still comes in trickles. Much of it, our investigation shows, is still hoarded, some with the connivance of NFA agents and unscrupulous traders; the rest is still stuck in transit.

NFA insiders confirm the top-to-bottom presence of grafters within the agency, severely affecting its delivery of services to farmers and consumers.

"It is pervasive and rampant, ranging from petty to big-time graft," says Romano Sanchez, head of the NFA Employees Union.

The corruption, according to Marcelo de Guzman, head of the National Farmers Action Council, is rooted in the low levels of the NFA's present support prices.

"This situation is fertile ground for laziness and graft, with some NFA officials resisting any increase in the NFA support prices so that they can avoid undertaking procurement operations and so that their friends among unscrupulous traders could continue to exploit farmers who are being offered low prices for their produce," de Guzman adds.

In 1994, COA issued two reports which chided the NFA management for its "leniency and failure to adhere strictly to the law and regulations."

As a consequence, the government lost P1.225 billion in 1994 because of anomalous contracts executed by NFA officials, COA said. This is money that NFA officials could have otherwise used to increase the support prices of *palay*, one factor farmers always blame for the rice crisis.

Anomalous Contracts

The anomalous contracts ranged from shipping and trucking privileges granted to a favored few and import contracts detrimental to the Philippines, the COA report said. It also recommended the filing of charges against responsible officials whom it did not name.

David says the NFA and COA are trying to retrieve more than P1 billion that various NFA officials have failed to account for. He also cites 39 administrative cases filed against these officials for "civil service violations."

But Sanchez says that no high-ranking official has been punished for graft and that officials involved in questionable transactions continue to enjoy the perks of their position.

COA reports, court records as well as interviews with NFA insiders paint a picture of an agency so ridden with corruption and so ineptly managed that it cannot perform its tasks. The charges against the agency include:

• **Unnecessary losses incurred from failure to buy *palay*.** COA's 1994 preliminary report says the food agency lost more than P42 million when it borrowed P323 million from banks for the

Cereal Procurement Fund (CPF). The amount was never used, and the P42 million represented interest payments the NFA had to pay for the undisbursed funds.

The CPF refers to the money the NFA allots for the purchase of rice and corn that it sells to consumers at subsidized prices. The CPF, which was set at Pl.2 billion in 1994, is borrowed, with interest, from local banks.

The NFA bought only 68,635 metric tons of rice in 1994, its third lowest procurement level since 1980, thus missing its procurement target by as much as 80.05 percent.

The 1994 rice purchases by the NFA represent only 0.6 percent of total rice production. The government needs to corner at least 24 percent to effectively intervene in the market prices of rice.

David blames high *palay* prices, more than the P6-per-kilo government support price, for the NFA's failure to buy more of the grain. The agency, however, has been criticized by farmers for buying *palay* only when the prices dip to exploitative levels, even if it had the funds to purchase rice at a higher price.

• **Unfunded rice purchases.** In 1993, the government lost P100 million when officials and implementers of the government's *palay* and procurement programs in Nueva Ecija connived with some *palay* traders in the issuance of "postdated unfunded checks as payment for *palay* stocks."

The transactions were irregular, according to Nueva Ecija Regional Trial Court Judge Cecilio Wycoco who acquitted a rice mill operator for issuing a bouncing check. In the first place, the judge said, "These transactions are not covered by sufficient bond to answer for any act of defalcation."

In dismissing the complaint, Wycoco said that there was apparently prior knowledge between the traders and the NFA officials that the checks were unfunded.

Wycoco recommended to the justice department the filing of administrative and criminal actions against the people who are implementing the procurement scheme.

In addition, a January 1994 COA report said the government lost millions from contracts awarded by NFA officials which were not covered by surety bonds. In one case, P535 million was lost on the sale of corn grains which were not backed by such bonds.

• **Anomalous contracts.** A COA report dated January 10, 1994 confirms widescale hanky-panky and incompetence within the organization. Among others, this report noted that contracts for the sale of grains done by the NFA-Manila office throughout 1991 as well as the first half of 1992 "were onerous as these favored the feed-users to the disadvantage of the government."

There was no uniformity in the terms and conditions of the contracts, it said. In some cases, discounts were given when none were called for, and in others, the NFA actually provided shipping gratis to a favored few.

NFA Entangled in a Web of Graft

Second of Three Parts

A MONTH after the rice crisis hit the headlines, the National Food Authority (NFA), the government's grain procurement and marketing agency, has failed to put down soaring rice prices.

To critics, such failure is symptomatic of an agency that is so riddled with graft and so badly managed that it cannot deal with the current crisis.

Commission on Audit (COA) reports, court records and interviews with NFA insiders, farmers and NGOs accuse the agency of a long list of violations and anomalies. Despite these, the NFA and its leadership have remained unscathed even as they stand at the center of the worst rice crisis to hit the country in 20 years.

The charges against NFA include:

• **Profiteering from rice imports.** Philippine Confederation of Grains Associations (CONFED Grains) executive vice-president Pablo Pablo confirms that unscrupulous traders through contacts inside NFA are able to get huge rice allocations of imported rice which are resold at unreasonably high prices.

Rice traders and dealers in Metro Manila and the provinces say this is one of the reasons why, when the government imported rice in July 1995, the NFA recorded a fast turnover of stock, but the cheap imported rice was not visible in the market.

In its latest report, the COA took the NFA to task for its defective importation contracts. The NFA, it said, lacked provisions to enable the agency to reject infested stock from abroad or, at least, to reduce the buying price.

Rice importations, says Rafael Mariano of the Kilusan ng Magbubukid ng Pilipinas (KMP), create opportunities for grafters within NFA.

COA, for example, cited the case of the rice imports from Thailand in 1993 which it said was "detrimental to the country."

The imports were meant to ease a predicted shortage during the lean months of July to September in 1993. It turned out that the stocks were not disposed of until March 1995, meaning there was no lack of rice in 1993.

It would seem that NFA's intent was not to stabilize prices during lean months, but to make fat profits, which it was not supposed to do. Thai rice was bought for P4.86 a kilo, but was resold by the NFA at almost double the price—from P8.50 to P9.50.

Once NFA sells at a high price, traders follow suit. In the end, the NFA earned a whopping P680 million from the transaction.

But it also lost, by COA's reckoning, at least P25 million from the pilferage and rotting of grain in its warehouses.

• **Bribery and hoarding.** Rice wholesalers and retailers speak of bribing NFA officials in order to buy imported quality rice.

Traders admit to hoarding their stocks for as long as six months, on the advice of their NFA friends, in order to push up prices. Aware of the traders' price manipulation, wholesalers and retailers themselves hoard their stocks in anticipation of inevitable price increases.

A long-time rice retailer admits that

weeks prior to the August 1995 crisis, rice sellers knew that prices were going to soar. Supply was never a problem, he insists.

The raids conducted by various government agencies were a joke, he adds, because the stocks were in Isabela and they decided to raid Binondo. Any NFA official worth his salt knew this, the retailer says.

• **Overpriced shipping and trucking charges.** An NFA insider confirms the millions lost by the government from illegal transactions between NFA officials and private shipping and trucking companies.

In one instance, a former chief of the internal audit department discovered an irregularity committed by Francisco Garcia, NFA director for Region 12, in connivance with Pedro Hernandez, marketing operations officer at the NFA central office in Quezon City.

According to the internal audit, the government lost P482,000 in overpriced freight charges for a shipment of corn from Mindanao to Manila. It blamed Hernandez for authorizing Garcia to ship the corn at P24 a bag, despite the fact that another grains shipment which was on the same boat to Manila was being sent over at only P19 a bag.

David claims appropriate actions were taken against erring officials. But the two officials mentioned in the internal audit report were not charged and were merely asked to explain their involvement in the anomaly. They are still with the NFA because, says David, "the explanation of the officials plus their supporting documents were accepted and were considered satisfactory."

• **Questionable rental of warehouses.** Despite the availability of its own storage facilities, the NFA opted to rent private warehouses, a 1994 COA report said. In one case the NFA was found to have leased a private warehouse for more than four times the amount the authority charged to rent out its own facility. Rental expenses, according to COA, could have been reduced by P1.2-million had the NFO used its own facilities.

The National Farmers Action Council's de Guzman also accuses the NFA of leasing out its warehouses at a profit to softdrinks, garments and other private firms instead of using them to store rice that would cover for the lean months.

In several instances, the NFA was found by COA to have leased out the facilities to big-time rice millers with whom they are supposed to compete in the first place.

In his 1993 decision, Nueva Ecija Judge Wycoco recommended that the practice of storing *palay* stocks in private warehouses be stopped, considering that NFA houses are vacant.

"One is wont to speculate that the government agents in charge of such a high financing scheme have seen to it that a system or device has been put in place for them to benefit from such a defalcation," Wycoco said.

Financial Mismanagement

• **Erroneous bookkeeping.** A 1994 COA report said NFA's anomalous bookkeeping practices overstated shrinkage and spillage costs by P11 million in 1991 and 1992.

• **Abuse of farmers.** Romer Pascual, farmer and a small-time rice trader in San Leonardo, Nueva Ecija, says NFA field agents extort money from farmers by abusing the agency's power to classify grains according to purity and moisture content. The lower the classification, the lower the buying price.

Without a scientific method of classifying a certain type of *palay* stock, the agents can say a certain farmer's stock is of low quality valued at only P2 per kilo. If the farmer wants to sell at the maximum price of P6, he would have to pay the NFA agent a commission.

An NFA insider says this practice enriches NFA agents and officials who later resell the quality rice they had acquired from farmers or else trade this for the inferior rice brought to NFA by traders and millers.

Through this method, blackmarketeers are able to corner NFA rice, which later ends up being sold in the markets at higher prices.

• **Commissions from license fees.** The licensing of retailers and wholesalers who sell NFA rice is done by in-house notaries who charge illegal "facilitation fees."

Commissions are also involved in nearly every transaction, say NFA sources, including the simple purchase of official signboards declaring that NFA rice is sold at a particular store.

• **Questionable leadership.** At the highest level, NFA administrator David himself has two graft cases in the Ombudsman and various cases in different trial courts. But he dismisses these charges as the handiwork of his enemies.

One complaint charged David with electioneering, as a result of an ill-advised "quick count" conducted by the NFA following the May 1995 elections. The activity was deemed illegal and unauthorized by the Commission on Elections.

David is also facing civil cases filed by security agencies who felt they were cheated in the bidding process conducted in 1994 by the NFA. The contract involved the hiring of some 3,600 security guards for NFA operations nationwide. This is more than half of the NFA's workforce of 6,200.

For security services alone, the NFA will have to pay P16 million a month. The Commission on Audit has asked David to justify the huge allocation for security services.

The NFA chief has also been charged with illegally donating more than P250,000 worth of rice to various government, media and private sector personalities.

Another scandal involves NFA's alleged payment of P18 million as advanced rental to the owners of the two buildings housing the NFA's main office on E. Rodriguez Ave., Quezon City.

David says there is nothing irregular about this, but Section 83 of the Auditing Code of the Philippines expressly prohibits advance payments of any kind by any agency for any service not yet rendered or supplies not yet delivered. His critics charge that the interest that such an amount could earn from the banks could substantially boost its procurement funds.

• **Weak internal controls.** All told, irregular practices remain rampant in the NFA, according to a June 30, 1994 COA report which says "weak internal control systems mark certain areas of operation by NFA."

This was caused by the management's failure to strictly implement prescribed internal control standards and procedures.

Much of the report may be garbled in terms understood only by accountants, but it does state among others that for the 1993 calendar year:

- Verification of the consolidated contingent assets account were highly deficient to the extent that its integrity was under question. A 25-percent increase amounting to some P206 million was noted.

- Cash, inventory and fixed asset accounts were unverifiable due to unreconciled accounts showing a variance of P103 million.
- Booking, error and or unrealized valuation cast doubt on the validity of its miscellaneous account amounting to P223 million.
- Losses arising from avoidable causes deprived the agency of close to P23 million in one year of operations alone.
- One contract of sale amounting to P535 million was unsecured.

Rice Policy Follows a Formula for Crisis

Conclusion

GUIMBA, Nueva Ecija — Pete Mina, 45, surveys his fields in barangay Nagpandayan here, trying to remember the last good rain he felt on his face.

In 1994, he enjoyed a bumper harvest. But in 1995, he watched as his seedlings took root in the slight rains of El Niño and then simply stopped growing. His yield is down from 90 cavans per hectare to only 15. His dreams for himself and the small cooperative of 45 farmers that he heads have turned to dust.

Mina is used to seeing his dreams crumble. Drought, crop failures, farm bankruptcy and high costs of inputs are among the many battles farmers like him fight all year round.

But he is bewildered at how last year's rice harvest, which he sold for P7 a kilo, is now selling for P22 in the local market. If rice prices are that high, why does he feel so destitute? Why are farmers going hungry, unable to buy the same grains they planted and nurtured last year?

Mina says the local National Food Authority (NFA) deliberately did not buy their *palay* in order to give private traders control of more than 90 percent of the farmers' produce.

"*Inutil ang* NFA *dito. Pinabayaan nilang ang* cartel *ang magdikta ng presyo, kahit na tagtuyo. Kung bumili sila noong mataas ang ani, hindi ganito kataas ang presyo* (The NFA is useless here during the dry season. If they had only bought at a good price during the harvest season, prices today wouldn't be this high)," he says.

Mina adds that the high rice prices severely hit landless agricultural workers who earn starvation wages of only P35 a day. He believes the prices will stay at their peak levels.

In nearby Muñoz, farmers' groups threaten to block the delivery of grains to Metro Manila if the government through the NFA does not increase support prices for *palay*.

Amid the national frenzy generated by the rice crisis, legislators are calling for a major revamp of the agency tasked to ensure adequate grain supply and stabilize rice prices.

"The NFA has simply become a rice-importing agency intent on earning profits for its operations," said Senator Orlando Mercado in a privilege speech.

The NFA was mandated to directly intervene in the market through the purchase and sale of *palay* or rice at predetermined levels. It sets a *palay* support price and a rice release price. It also attempts to defend these prices through procurement and distribution programs.

The *palay* support price is supposed to assure farmers of reasonable profits from *palay* production, while the release price is expected to control prices during lean months by assuring consumers of the availability of rice at affordable levels.

Dismal Performance

On both counts, it is clear that NFA has performed dismally. According to a 1989 study by the Philippine Peasant Institute, the NFA controlled only 6.14 percent of farmer's total production between 1980 and 1987.

In 1989 and 1990, it procured only 2.2 and 4.5 percent of total production, respectively. And in 1994, the government controlled only 0.6 percent of total production, a record low.

To be able to effectively intervene in market prices, the government should buy at least 24 percent of total production. It should also have an accessible rice inventory equivalent to a 90-day supply on July 1 of each year.

But, according to the PPI study, traders simply let NFA buy up to its maximum financial capability. Then traders bought the remaining surplus production at a price lower than the support price.

A study conducted by the PPI in Mexico, Pampanga indicates that a rice farmer earns only P40.45 a day every cropping season, assuming that the produce was sold to the NFA. If sold to traders or middlemen, which is often the case, farmers' incomes go down to P7.12 a day.

A 1989 study by Dina Umali of the University of the Philippines, Los Baños shows that despite the NFA's paddy procurement, much of the rice was actually sold below the NFA support price.

Umali cited the following factors as the primary reasons behind NFA's failure to influence rice prices:

- Budgetary problems, which limited NFA's procurement targets to 10 to 15 percent of the country's total production.
- Bad timing, which resulted in rice not being bought during the peak harvest season when supply is high and prices are low.

According to the study, NFA easily lost out to traders who depress prices.

Because of these deficiencies, the NFA's share in the market stocks plummeted from 22.41 percent in 1979 to only 4.03 percent in 1989. In Metro Manila, for example, the NFA could supply only about 10 percent of daily demand.

Delayed arrival of imports is attributed to lengthy decision-making. But rice imports usually arrive during the harvest season and not during the lean months, further depressing *palay* prices.

Farmers here say that they are forced to sell their produce immediately after harvest even at a low price to meet their consumption and production needs, as well as to pay off debts.

According to the PPI study, farmers were drawn to traders who are already well-entrenched in the community and could easily be approached for cash in times of need and emergency. Among the various marketing agents, the big-time trader, together with the usurer-trader and the landlord-trader, quoted the lowest *palay* prices at P2.82 a kilo.

Woes of Farmers

Farmers have complained that the NFA's procurement system also inhibited them from selling to the agency, the PPI study said. The NFA requires farmers to have procurement passbooks, three copies of tax declaration of filed rice cultivation, an information sheet, three copies of pictures and a P2 fee before buying their produce.

Despite early projections of an impending shortfall, the NFA refused to purchase *palay* in sufficient quantities.

Said the PPI: "Ordinary rice farmers have found these requirements cumbersome. Another disincentive to farmers is the check payment system since most farmers need cash. Moreover, the agency's stringent requirements of a 14-percent moisture content and 90-percent purity have been criticized by rice farmers as favoring only big farmers and traders who own post-harvest facilities. While the support price is P6 a kilo, the average farmgate price of *palay* is only P4 a kilo. During harvest times, the farmgate price can fall to as low as P2.80 to P3.50 a kilo."

In most cases, the study said, the NFA offered the highest price at P3.50 a kilo. Despite its higher buying rate however, the NFA is niggardly about buying *palay*. Last year, it had a P4-billion budget for *palay* procurement. The NFA used only P300 million of the amount, belying claims that the NFA did not have enough funds.

In a hearing of the House Appropriations Committee, NFA Administrator Romeo David admitted that the agency has not been buying *palay*. Of the P850 million allotted to the agency from January to June 1995, only P26 million has been allotted to NFA regional offices for buying *palay*.

The bulk of that amount, David admitted, has been used to pay off old debts. With no other buyer for their produce, farmers were left with no choice but to sell to the traders in the community.

David says it is unfair to assess the NFA's success according to the amount of *palay* it procures. "At the present support price for *palay*, we were able to influence the farmgate price to move to price levels that provide the farmers with reasonable profitable returns on their investments. We were able to encourage traders to offer better prices than the government support prices."

The same policy, however, allowed traders to control as much as 50 to 80 percent of the total 1995 production, enabling them to let prices soar to dizzying heights.

Despite early projections of an impending shortfall, the NFA refused to purchase *palay* in sufficient quantities, even if it had enough money to buy as much as 600,000 metric tons of *palay* annually. The agency purchased a little more than 10 percent of this total in 1995.

According to David, importation is resorted to only when the rice buffer is very much less than the country's 90-day requirement. As a last resort, the NFA announced that it would import some 500,000 metric tons of the commodity only in the second quarter of 1995.

More than just sufficient, the volume of these imports, had they arrived on time, would have caused a glut in the market which would have depressed the farmgate price.

This strengthens suspicions that the move to import may not be due to a local shortage but to a deliberate plan by NFA and agriculture officials to increase imports by not buying *palay* from farmers.

Farmers in Nueva Ecija say they sold their *palay* to traders in 1994 and early 1995 because the NFA simply stopped buying *palay*. To discourage farmers from selling to the NFA, agents still quoted *palay* prices of P6 a kilo while traders, to corner the rice supply in a year of predicted shortages, were buying at P7 to P8 per kilo.

At P6.50 per kilo, the farmer earns P97,500. The cost to produce a kilo of *palay* is no less than P5. To harvest 15,000 kilos, a farmer spends about P75,000, giving him a net profit of P22,500 for one year or Pl,875 per month.

At a time when its buffer stock was already very critical, the NFA nonetheless frittered away time and resources to conduct an unofficial quick count of the May 1995 elections.

Elections, Not Rice

The NFA union said: "In many of our provincial offices, official activities were very much affected because of the quick count. Quite a pity because during the month of May, rice prices had been steadily rising."

As a seller, the NFA's profit and loss statement says it all. In 1994, the agency sold only 119,581 metric tons of rice compared to 486,339 metric tons in 1993 and 688,989 metric tons in 1992. The 1994 sales volume is only 30.24 percent of the targeted 395,485 metric tons.

In the private sector, such inefficiency would result in the sacking of responsible officials. This variance from the projected targets would have been considered inexcusable.

If the NFA could have avoided the present rice crisis, what are the prospects for the future? The answer: Not good.

David has announced that the government will slowly withdraw from direct market intervention and concentrate on providing marketing support services to farmers. The shift in policy is allegedly done in pursuit of deregulation in line with the General Agreement for Tariffs and Trade (GATT).

But Senator Orlando Mercado pointed out that because the rice industry produces a staple grain, GATT entitles it to a 10-percent government support.

This means the government can even double its present support for rice, which has been calculated at only five percent.

What the Philippines is doing contrasts sharply with the experience of India. Like the Philippines, India's rice production is one of the most inefficient in the world, producing 2.6 tons per hectare, close to our 2.8-ton average.

Despite this, India, with 910 million people, has more rice and wheat than it knows what to do with.

Already, it has a two-year stockpile of grain and every square inch of its silos and warehouses is occupied.

Unlike the Philippines, India's government buys 70 to 90 percent of all crops produced by the villages. Farmers sell because the government buys at high prices. As a result, agricultural productivity has increased.

In contrast, the NFA buys at a lower price than private traders and in the long term, plans not to buy any more grain at all.

Profits from Disaster

BY CHAY FLORENTINO-HOFILEÑA

First published in the *Manila Times*, *Manila Standard*, *Manila Chronicle*, and *Malaya*, September 2-3, 1996; *Evening Paper*, September 3, 1996; and *Abante Tonite*, September 6, 1996

Few disasters in this calamitous country can match the scale of the 1991 Mt. Pinatubo eruption and its aftermath. To deal with the consequences of the disaster, the Mt. Pinatubo Commission was formed in 1992 and over P10 billion in public funds was set aside for its operations. Four years later, it was becoming increasingly clear that a good portion of the money meant to rehabilitate the lahar-ravaged areas of Central Luzon was going instead to private pockets, to the detriment of the victims of the disaster. The misuse of Pinatubo funds was a story of wide public interest, but we were not too sure that our investigation would yield evidence of malfeasance.

It did. This report—which was researched in the course of several months and involved interviews with government contractors, officials and disaster victims—estimates that anywhere from 10 to 30 percent of the funds allocated for reconstruction projects was lost to illegal commissions, onerous contracts and irregular financial management.

The investigation found evidence of rigged bids, routine padding of costs, extravagant spending on unnecessary equipment, and grand—and criminal—waste. Journalist Chay Florentino-Hofileña also discovered that a clique of retired military officials monopolized resettlement projects for Pinatubo victims, in the process getting a cut of the funds for themselves. This two-part investigation was put together from facts gathered from documents, especially government audit reports, and interviews with knowledgeable sources (road contractors, highways officials and insiders in the Mt. Pinatubo Commission). It won for the author the third prize in the 1996 Jaime V. Ongpin Awards for investigative reporting.

Millions Lost in Mt. Pinatubo Projects

First of Two Parts

ANGELES, Pampanga — For nearly a year, two amphibious trucks, which cost the government close to P50 million, lay idle in a military warehouse at the Clark Special Economic Zone here. They are probably the most expensive—and so far, useless—trucks anywhere in the world.

Intended for disaster operations in areas devastated by the Mount Pinatubo eruption, the trucks have remained unused. Two years ago, the Commission on Audit (COA) questioned their purchase, saying that the disbursements were of "doubtful validity" and had inadequate documentation.

The trucks also appear to be grossly overpriced. A Finnish company had offered to supply the Mt. Pinatubo Commission (MPC) a similar, but slightly smaller, vehicle for only P5.6 million each.

How the price became inflated is a story of inefficiency, corruption and waste. And it is a story that repeats itself in the disaster-control and rehabilitation efforts that have been undertaken by the MPC, a government body created in 1992 and which, in the four years since then, has received over P10.3 billion from the public coffers.

A review of public records and interviews with officials, auditors, contractors and politicians revealed that the government has lost anywhere from 10 to 30 percent of the amounts given to the MPC because of shady deals involving commissions, onerous contracts, and irregular and faulty financial management practices.

Our investigation shows that government officials, retired military personnel, politicians and contractors have made quick profits from the disaster, skimming off large amounts of money from allocations for government infrastructure and resettlement projects. Since 1992, the MPC has been administered by a succession of retired generals and colonels appointed by President Fidel V. Ramos.

"Easily 10 to 30 percent is lost," says former Public Works secretary and MPC technical advisory board member Jose de Jesus. Although this is common in most public works projects, such corruption in a disaster zone—where human misery is of epic proportions and available funds cannot meet existing needs—makes the situation even more tragic.

Wheeling-Dealing

The case of the trucks is a classic example of the complex deal-making that goes on behind these anomalous transactions. As early as 1992, some military officials lobbied with congressmen to include a special provision in RA 7637, the law that created the MPC and allocated funds for its operations.

"They wanted a provision for the purchase of amphibious trucks," says a congressman who asked not to be identified. "The military wanted to buy them and found the budget deliberations the fastest way to do it."

The congressmen obliged. Thus, the curious provision in RA 7637: "Funds shall be allocated in the first year for the acquisition by appropriate government agencies of special equipment, such as amphibians and other equipment designed for use in the affected areas in an amount not to exceed fifty million pesos (P50, 000, 000)."

With the law behind them, these military officers, some of whom were in the MPC, quickly went to work. It helped that the MPC's top and middle levels were stacked with retired generals and colonels.

No bidding was conducted, with the emergency used as excuse to shortcut the procedures. In September 1993, the MPC entered into a contract with the London-based Glover Webb Limited for the purchase of the two amphibious vehicles for a total of $1.78 million, or close to the P50 million which RA 7637 had allocated.

A retired colonel, Arturo Alabanza, who was the Philippine representative of Glover Webb, signed letters to MPC after the contract was signed.

The following year, COA questioned the purchase, saying that "documents evidencing cost reasonableness, mode of award, papers relative to the deposit in the opening of letter of credit and escrow deposit as described from the respective vouchers, and authority for effecting advance payment were not attached."

Despite these questions, the transaction proceeded. In December 1994, Glover Webb asked for an additional P12.9 million to cover shipping and spare parts for the two units. Then in July 1995, the Bureau of Customs demanded P26.9 million in duties and taxes which, up to now, the MPC has not paid. All in all, the transaction could cost the government P89.8 million.

But a check with Sisu Defense, a Finland-based company, revealed that its NA-140 all-terrain vehicles, which are similar to the amphibious trucks bought from Glover Webb, costs about $200,000 or P5.6 million each—roughly one-fifth of what the MPC had spent.

In 1995, the Glover Webb vehicles were formally unveiled in ceremonies in Camp Olivas in San Fernando, Pampanga but one became unoperational not long after, because it got entangled in lahar and wires. "(Are they) providing P50 million worth of services?" asks a ranking MPC official. "I don't think so."

MPC Executive Director Antonio Fernando admits that the trucks "have not been tested for lahar. I am not very sure they were cut out for lahar situations. It still has to be proven." He says that when he assumed his post, the purchase was already a done deal.

Moreover, for each day that the trucks are left idle, the government is losing money. "*Igarahe mo lang iyon, gumagasta ka na* (You spend money even if you just store them in a warehouse)," the ranking MPC official says.

No bidding was conducted, with the emergency used as excuse to shortcut the procedures.

Questionable Transactions

But the purchase of these trucks are only among countless other questionable transactions. The breaching of the P2.7-billion FVR megadike, allegedly because of the use of substandard construction materials, is the latest example of money literally down the drain. Intended by the government to be a symbol of the heroic efforts to fight the forces of nature, the dike has instead become another symbol of government corruption and deceit.

Contractors and officials say that the megadike construction merely replicated the pattern of rigged biddings and commissions for officials and bureaucrats that has marked other infrastructure projects in the Mount Pinatubo area.

Extensive interviews revealed that the standard operating procedures for these projects are so marked by graft that even the highest MPC officials have expressed their frustration at being unable to do anything about them. MPC chair Salvador Enriquez says, "I am already happy if I am able to reduce them."

Public works officials, contractors and auditors say that the usual procedures followed for these projects are the following:

• **commissions:** anywhere from 10 to 20 percent commissions are given to local officials who may include the congressman, governor or the mayor, and officials or personnel of the implementing agency contracting them. The overhead is incorporated into the total project cost that is charged against government, leaving enough profit for the contractors.

A five to 10 percent commission for government officials is affordable for contractors, but 20 percent or higher will result in the contractor cutting corners and using substandard materials to recover his expenses. One contractor says some of them scrimp on the cement that is supposed to be poured for roads, for instance, or shorten them altogether.

The "losing" bidders are assured by the winning bidder of a "three to five percent" share of the contract cost.

• **rigging of bids:** Public works department insiders—sometimes "for as low as P10,000"—are willing to leak the approved agency estimate (AAE) which is an important basis for choosing the winning bid. Contractors then offer bids that are very close to the AAE to get the most out of the available money.

The "winning" bidder agrees to shoulder, at the very least, the administrative costs of preparing a bid, ranging from P20,000 to as much as P100,000, depending on the size of the project and the value of the contract. At times, a contractor even offers to prepare a supposed competitor's bid, leaving only a blank for the latter's signature to be filled in.

The "losing" bidders are assured by the winning bidder of a "three to five percent" share of the contract cost. Desilting contracts usually carry a five percent share—higher because there are more opportunities to recover the cost in the course of the project. "*Kasi malaki ang daya* (Because they can cheat more)," says one contractor.

The "RTG" or "Round the Game" person also receives part of the three to five percent. Acting as a fixer who has connections inside, the RTG who is neither an

MPC or DPWH employee, nor a contractor, convenes the contractors and facilitates the collusion.

"Bidding *pa lang, namumuhunan ka na* (You start giving out money at the bidding stage)," says one contractor. Bidders are left with not much choice but to "cooperate" because even if one wins without agreeing to the collusion, he may either have a difficult time collecting or be unable to obtain the cooperation of the other bidders the next time around, an MPC insider says.

• **padding costs:** Contractors resort to "variation orders, either change orders or extra work orders" that allow them to charge higher than what they had originally bid to recover the costs of having to pay commissions to various government officials and employees. Others resort to "front-loading" or doing substantial work only at the beginning, only to abandon the project later.

The rigging of bids was especially evident in the megadike project, allege MPC insiders. The project was broken up into 45 contract packages with three to five contractors bidding for each package. This facilitated the rigging of bids since it became easier for a few contractors to talk and negotiate among themselves. Some contractors even used several licenses to hide the fact that several contracts were awarded to them, MPC officials say.

Enriquez had proposed "internal controls" and suggested that a set of contractors work on the lahar embankment, while a different set work on cementing or the armoring. This way, those who do cementing end up checking on those supposed to do the work before them. But this proposal was not followed. Breaking up the project into packages clearly contradicted Enriquez's intention.

The Department of Public Works and Highways (DPWH), which administers the Mt. Pinatubo infrastructure projects, appears helpless to stop such rigging. Former Mt. Pinatubo Rehabilitation-Project Management Office (MPR-PMO) director Florante Soriquez has conceded that the department "cannot resort to police power" to continuously put the contractors under surveillance. The National Bureau of Investigation's efforts to probe a previously reported rigged bid have faced a blank wall as contractors have refused to speak up.

"Investigations reach a dead end because no one wants to talk. So when we bid new projects we cannot ban those contractors whom we suspect of wrongdoing, because the NBI was unable to turn up evidence against them," Soriquez said, referring to the first round of bidding for the megadike contract packages in early 1996.

Messy Finances

The problem, however, is that erring contractors have not been disciplined by either the DPWH, which contracts out the infrastructure projects, or the MPC, which is in charge of resettlement and livelihood.

A 1994 COA report has reprimanded the MPC for assigning projects to contractors whose capabilities were not commensurate to the jobs required. It added that the MPC awarded bids to contractors who had earlier been blacklisted; had been identified as having inadequate, poor or leased equipment; or had submitted bids higher than the approved agency estimates.

COA also pointed out other financial irregularities in the MPC. In 1993, for example, COA cites unliquidated cash advances worth P8.5 million released to Soriquez, P500,000 released to the mayor of Olongapo City, and P532,233.84 released to MPC planning officer Teresita Salud.

Current MPC Comptroller Wilson Solis says the frequent changes in directorships from 1993 to 1995 and the inadequate training of personnel in government accounting procedures partly explain the messy financial history of the MPC.

Brig. Gen. Antonio Venadas was the MPC's first executive director appointed on December 8, 1992, and replaced by retired Col. Jaime Venago on November 16, 1993. Venago served until his death in November 1994 and was succeeded by retired Col. Antonio Fernando who acted as officer-in-charge until his formal appointment in January 1995. Enriquez became chairman of the MPC only in 1995.

The MPC is among the agencies of government that have been or are currently being managed by retired military officers, among them Brig. Gens. Venadas, Jaime Muyargas (former comptroller), and Napoleon Angeles (former resettlement administrator); Colonels Pacito Nefulda (resettlement consultant) and Generoso Basilio (site manager) of the Air Force and Reynaldo Melosantos of the Army (former director for plans and programs); the late Col. Venago; and current executive director Col. Fernando.

Army Clique Enriched by Pinatubo Resettlement Funds

Conclusion

MABALACAT, Pampanga — In the early evenings, the more than 3,000 residents of the Mauaque Resettlement Area here brace themselves for faucets that will remain dry for at least the next 11 hours. On bad days, power cuts occur twice or thrice in a day and the water that flows, if there is any, is foul-smelling.

Many of the residents here, all victims of the Mt. Pinatubo eruption and lahar flows, work as sales clerks, caddies or maintenance men in the Clark special economic zone, earning the P120 a day minimum pay offered by most establishments. In a month, they can take home a little over P3,000.

The others, however, do have not jobs. "*Magugulat ka, kahit na walang trabaho ang mga tao, kumakain pa rin kahit papaano* (You just wonder how people somehow manage to eat even if they have no jobs)," says barangay captain Adolfo Dizon.

But for many of those who have made their homes here, Mauaque is a blessing, compared to the cramped and miserable evacuation centers where they had lived for two years.

This blessing consists of 90-square-meter houses with glass jalousie windows and wooden trusses; cemented roads; street signs; four 30,000-gallon water tanks; a school, market, hospital and day-care center. The site is impressive, much better than resettlement areas previously constructed under the supervision of the National Housing Authority (NHA) and local governments.

Beneath the gloss, however, is scandalous corruption involving a clique of military officers and former NHA officials who have monopolized major construction work in Pinatubo resettlement projects.

About P3.26 billion or one-third of the P10.398 billion that government has given the Mt. Pinatubo Commission (MPC) since its creation in 1992 has been set aside for building new communities for people displaced by the disaster. In Pampanga alone, some 22,000 lost their homes after a series of lahar flows. Of these, 13,000 are still in evacuation centers, awaiting resettlement.

> **A substantial chunk of the resettlement budget may have been siphoned off to the pockets of officials.**

Of the P3.26 billion for resettlement, as much as P1.3 billion in cash advances from July 1993 to July 31, 1996 has been paid to the commander of the AFP Corps of Engineers Task Force Mt. Pinatubo for various construction work ranging from land survey and site development to construction of bunkhouses and electrification.

But officials, contractors and auditors interviewed for this series say that a substantial chunk of the resettlement budget assigned to the Task Force may have been siphoned to the pockets of officials who have managed to run circles around the MPC's financial management system. Some of these officials, these sources allege, include men who were, or still are, in the military service.

"Where one has a monopoly, he can do anything and it can be disadvantageous to the government," says a ranking MPC official familiar with Pinatubo resettlement projects. "It is big money laid on the table. All the vultures, creative ones, are looking at that money—*lahat ng klaseng tulisan, negosyante,* (all kinds of crooks, businessmen), politicians."

In fact, MPC chair and Budget Secretary Salvador Enriquez had attempted to bring in the 51st Engineering Brigade of the Army to break the firm grip of the Task Force on resettlement projects, but did not succeed.

Gift-giving

The alleged point man of the resettlement clique, according to sources in and out of the MPC, is the Task Force Mt. Pinatubo commander, Navy Capt. Pastor Ramos, Jr. By giving their imprimatur to Ramos, retired Col. Antonio Fernando, MPC executive director, and Angelito Lazaro, MPC resettlement administrator—both formerly of the NHA—are, according to MPC insiders, also among those who have benefited from the resettlement operation. There is no direct evidence linking them, however, because their "tracks are well-covered," the sources say.

Fernando denies the accusations. "If people are suspecting that we are making money, that is not true." Because the Armed Forces community is such a small one, he says, such money-making deals cannot be kept secret. "*Kung kikita ang isa, hihingi iyong iba* (If one makes money, the others will ask for their share). How can you make everybody happy?"

Ramos has resorted to giving gifts to officials keeping tab of the MPC. According to sources who have personal knowledge of at least one verified transaction, Senator Gloria Macapagal-Arroyo, chair of the Senate Joint Congressional Oversight Committee (JCOC) monitoring the MPC, was the beneficiary of P100,000 worth of Christmas calendars in 1994, prior to the May 1995 elections.

The calendars were run in a small printing press based in Angeles and were paid for in cash. Though the amount is small, MPC sources question the propriety of the contribution, especially since Arroyo chairs the Senate JCOC, which has initiated investigations against the MPC.

Cozy relations between a staffer of Arroyo, a certain Ranulfo Albao, and the contributor are also being questioned by the MPC sources. The contributor stood as one of the sponsors in Albao's wedding in February 1996, sources present during the event confirm.

The MPC resettlement group was set up to establish "new and viable communities for the displaced victims of the Mt. Pinatubo eruption" and the AFP Corps of Engineers was tapped to speed up the process.

The construction of at least two of the largest resettlement sites in Pampanga—Mauaque and Madapdap in Mabalacat—was awarded to the AFP Task Force headed by Ramos. It is in the construction of these resettlement areas that "creative liquidation," according to MPC insiders, is said to play a critical role in the siphoning off of funds.

Documents say that Ramos spent P46,000 per housing unit in Mauaque and finished the job in six months, but MPC sources close to contractors allege that he actually got contractors to do the job and paid them only P39,000 per unit. Another three percent is said to be deducted, supposedly for government auditors, leaving the contractors with P37, 830 per unit.

This translates to a balance of P8,170 per housing unit or as much as P25 million (eight percent for the entire project) going elsewhere, presumably to MPC officials in cahoots with the contractors. Mauaque's 3,050 housing units cost the government P320 million. MPC insiders allege that the money is "distributed among members and patrons of the resettlement clique."

The clique allegedly involves not only Ramos but also Lazaro, who, as resettlement administrator, is in charge of drawing up agency estimates, and Fernando, their immediate supervisor. Both Fernando and Lazaro have allowed the major contracts to be "funneled" to Ramos, according to one MPC insider, allegedly facilitating the division of shares.

Fernando, a graduate of the Philippine Military Academy, is described as a hard worker, a good administrator and manager. He is said to be thorough and can work for long stretches. Even before he became executive director, the unspoken rule in the inner circles of the MPC was "You watch my back, I'll watch yours," says one insider.

Formerly NHA assistant general manager, Fernando has two pending cases with the Office of the Ombudsman, one of them filed by the COA. The nine cases also filed against him when he was with the NHA were consolidated into one, which was subsequently dismissed.

Despite the pending cases against him, Fernando was appointed by President Ramos as MPC executive director in January 1995, reportedly through the intercession of a close friend who sought the endorsement of First Lady Amelita Ramos.

The use of contractors for the

Money is "distributed among members and patrons of the resettlement clique."

Mauaque project is also contrary to the AFP Corps of Engineers' directive that units are "not allowed to enter into contracts" and violates the "project by administration" provision of the project agreement between MPC and the Task Force.

Project by administration means the MPC is dispensing with public bidding and is instead contracting the naval construction brigade Task Force, which is part of the AFP Corps of Engineers, to administer the project and provide personnel, equipment and materials or supplies at cost. Furthermore, a government-to-government contract prohibits any one side from making any form of profit since the relationship is not a business transaction.

Contractors privy to the project say they were asked to provide supplies as well as labor, as in any "direct contract"; others were subcontracted to provide labor alone and were paid P4,800 per unit on a "*pakyaw*" basis, as stipulated in the project agreement. Assuming only six working days for the construction of one unit and six laborers, the workers each ended up with P792 a week.

The contractors say they were paid "in cash" every Saturday afternoon for distribution to their workers. This makes it more difficult to trace the actual value of transactions, but Ramos justifies paying in cash, saying that since the daily pay that workers received was small, cash payments were more convenient.

Since the agreements between the subcontractors and Ramos were "verbal" and were in no way formalized in writing, the contractors say, no trace whatsoever of the transaction between them can likewise be found in MPC books. The source also says that Ramos has told several contractors, "*Alam niyo naman, iyong 20* percent, *iyon ang pinamimigay namin sa itaas* (As you all know we give 20 percent to the higher-ups)."

Ramos however denies the accusations, saying that the housing units have been "properly turned over and accepted by the MPC" and that he has "liquidated cash advances with certification from the COA" or the Commission on Audit.

Because the money is siphoned elsewhere, contractors are, in turn, unable to pay laborers—many of whom are lahar victims themselves—higher wages.

Asked why contractors agreed to do the work for only P39,000 per unit without documents to hold on to, the contractors say "there was not much work" available.

"*Kung wala silang puhunan, si Pastor ang nagbibigay ng materyales tapos ibabawas na lang sa kanilang* collection (If they have no capital, Pastor would advance the construction materials and later deduct the cost from the collection)," one contractor says.

Because the money is siphoned elsewhere, contractors are, in turn, unable to pay laborers—many of whom are lahar victims themselves—higher wages.

The MPC has built a total of 25 resettlement areas in Zambales, Tarlac, Olongapo, Pampanga and Nueva Ecija. More than half of these sites or 13 are in Pampanga, the most devastated by lahar.

Insufficient Controls

Insufficient controls within the MPC may have encouraged corruption. The AFP Corps of Engineers office says that because of the emergency nature of its work, the Task Force is a "special case" and as such, enjoys some "autonomy."

Internally, however, the defense department is tightening its controls over the disbursement of funds to engineering units undertaking civil works projects. A March 21, 1996 memorandum issued by Defense Secretary Renato de Villa specifies that the "funds allocated for the project shall be remitted to the concerned Major Service in appropriate check(s) which will be transmitted through the Office of the Secretary of National Defense and the General Headquarters..."

It has been the practice of the MPC to remit the checks directly to the Task Force commander. Citing the "emergency nature of the relationship" between the MPC and the Task Force, Fernando says he prefers to maintain the status quo "in the interest of time and delivery of housing units." Besides, he says, the practice had never been questioned by the COA in the past.

Ramos boasts that the quality of the resettlement areas they have built is far superior to the earlier resettlement areas built by private contractors under NHA supervision. Those housing units even cost higher at P52,000 each, he says.

At Madapdap for instance, steel rafters and steel windows with glass are being used, while at Mauaque they used glass jalousies with aluminum frames and wooden jambs, and bolted wooden rafters. The housing units built by other agencies do not have columns, have wooden frames covered with *lawanit* on the outer side for windows, and nailed rafters that cause "poor rigidity," according to a comparison by the Task Force.

What is curious, however, is that while the quality of those units are admittedly poor, they were accepted by the MPC, and none of the officials from the MPC, NHA and local government units, even contractors involved in the projects, have been made to account for them.

Stealing from Public Schools

BY YVONNE T. CHUA

First published in *Philippine Star* and *Manila Times*, November 30-December 3, 1998; *Manila Standard*, *Malaya*, *Sun Star Daily*, and *BusinessWorld*, November 30-December 2, 1998; *Dyaryo Uno*, November 30-December 5, 1998; and *Leyte Samar Weekly Express*, November 28, December 4-18, 1998

The PCIJ's Yvonne T. Chua, who covered the education beat in the 1980s, began her investigation of corruption in the edu cation department with this three-part series examining the procurement of school desks. What she found was a bureaucracy where the norm was ghost deliveries, rigged bids, contracts for dummy companies, and collusion between officials and suppliers and among suppliers themselves. Using as case study one particular supplier with a long record of irregular contracts, this series shows how deeply embedded the corruption is at the education department, and how difficult it is to root out.

This investigation (as well as Chua's subsequent report on textbook procurements, which is also included in this collection) shows that corruption takes place wherever the discretionary authority lies: bureaucrats who have the power to request for supplies, to sign contracts, to monitor delivery, and to release payment. She found payoffs taking place from the beginning of the procurement process—in the accreditation of suppliers—up to the time the supplies are delivered (or not delivered) and paid for. This investigation was based on interviews with education officials, government auditors, suppliers and former education bureaucrats. It also relied heavily on public records, including audit reports, court documents, and stacks of files from the education department. The information from these documents was painstakingly pieced together until it was obvious who the culprits were and where the gaps in the system had to be plugged.

What gave this series the human drama was a visit to Samar and Tacloban, where the impact of the corruption in the procurements of school desks was starkly evident. This series was one of ten finalists in the 1998 Jaime V. Ongpin Awards for investigative reporting.

A Pattern of 'Ghost' Deliveries Plagues DECS

First of Three Parts

GUIUAN, Eastern Samar — Every school day, 13-year-old Cristina Quijano walks four kilometers to Guiuan National High School, the only public high school in this 404-year-old Visayan coastal town. It takes her some 30 minutes to make the trip, burdened as she is with a schoolbag—and a plastic stool.

The stool is Quijano's insurance that she would not be sent home by the principal who instructed the school's 937 students to bring their own chairs when classes opened last June. But she cannot leave it in school because her own home is also lacking in chairs.

Most students at the school are luckier than Quijano, since they don't have to return their chairs home each day; their parents had made or bought them an armchair especially for their use, or allowed them to borrow an extra chair or stool from home. The children have all been sensible enough to put their names on the backs of the chairs to ensure no one else can claim these for their own.

But the chairs are now falling apart. Constructed crudely from coconut lumber in assorted styles and sizes, nearly all the students' chairs have lost an armrest, a backrest, a portion of the seat or a leg, or, in some cases, all four.

Still, the children make the most of what is left, even if it means turning their laps or window ledges into writing tables or balancing precariously on a wobbly chair all day long. It beats having to stand, sit on the floor or share a classmate's equally battered chair while lessons are given, as some students do. The children are also only too grateful that the days of sitting on tree trunks while holding classes under coconut trees as they did in June and July 1998 are over.

Converted into a national high school in 1994, the responsibility of meeting Guiuan National High School's classroom and armchair requirements falls squarely on the Department of Education, Culture and Sports (DECS). These days, however, that has unexpectedly been shifted to parents. Of the school's six three-classroom buildings, three are makeshift *nipa* structures that parents and students assembled hurriedly after the principal, Corazon

Obsequio, appealed for their help. But because they had made the classrooms the priority, many parents, mostly poor fisherfolk, had no money to spare for their children's chairs.

Perennial Shortage

Guiuan National High School is by no means the only public school that is reduced to waiting in vain each year for chairs from DECS. Like textbooks, classrooms and teachers, school desks and armchairs are in perennial shortage at the country's 40,000 public elementary and high schools. DECS statistics place the current shortage at 3.3 million pieces in elementary schools and 226,621 pieces in high schools.

The shortage exists despite the huge sums allotted each year to DECS for desk and armchair procurement. Since the late 1980s, the yearly budget for these items has averaged P250 million, peaking to P500 million in 1995 and 1996 when Ricardo Gloria was education secretary. Theoretically, the amount can buy at least 400,000 each year and roughly keep pace with the projected three percent annual increase in enrolment.

But the DECS budget seems outdated, considering that Congress nationalized all local high schools in 1989 and made the national government responsible for all their needs, and that DECS itself lowered to six years old the admission age for Grade 1 beginning 1994.

It hasn't helped that Congress has never thought of setting aside funds to repair about 300,000 dilapidated desks and armchairs that are retired each year. DECS gives desks and armchairs an average life span of three to four years.

The current shortage of school desks and armchairs, however, also stems partly from a string of bad and irregular transactions DECS has entered into with suppliers, and which have caused the government to lose millions of pesos every year.

A case in point is an P81.7-million contract with CKL Enterprises, a long-time supplier that was fully paid before deliveries were ever made. Indeed, it exemplifies a host of problems, including overpricing, delays and even ghost deliveries, that have besieged procurement contracts of the education department, as well as many other government agencies with sizable procurement budgets.

The case also demonstrates how rules are bent, procedures ignored, and checks and balances removed in favor of a supplier who has chalked up a disreputable track record in fulfilling government contracts.

Obsequio recalls the last time DECS delivered armchairs was in 1996, when the school division in Borongan, the provincial capital, sent 29 plastic and steel armchairs. By then, however, Guiuan National High School already had 500 students.

Obsequio was still optimistic enough to expect a delivery of 500 all-plastic armchairs the following year. The chairs never came. The following schoolyear, no chairs came as well. Meanwhile, the student population has climbed to 937.

Obsequio and other public school officials say the lack of chairs has taken a toll on the students' learning. According to Obsequio, classes are disrupted when a student, tired from standing or sitting on the floor, causes trouble by grabbing a schoolmate's chair. She also points out: "Because our students can't sit comfortably, they can't listen well to the lecture."

Officials in other schools also blame the high absenteeism among students partly on the shortage of chairs. At the

Leyte National High School in Tacloban City—the biggest and supposedly best-equipped high school in Eastern Visayas—officials and teachers say scrambling for a seat each day has become a "disincentive" for some students to attend classes.

Incomplete Deliveries

To be sure, that lack of school chairs can be traced back largely to CKL Enterprises that is owned by 53-year-old businesswoman Jesusa T. de la Cruz.

Two years after bagging the biggest contract to supply armchairs and being paid in full, CKL Enterprises has supplied only 40 percent of the 185,086 armchairs it pledged to deliver by April 24, 1997. It has not shipped a single armchair to Eastern Visayas, Western Visayas and Western Mindanao. Even in Metro Manila, where the chairs are made and shipped from, only 10 percent of the supposed beneficiaries have gotten their share.

The incomplete delivery has intensified the dearth of armchairs in public high schools nationwide because CKL's contract accounted for 41 percent of high school armchair requirements that DECS was scheduled to fill for schoolyear 1997-98.

For DECS and the Commission on Audit (COA), the transaction was not just a simple "fast break"—full payment, no delivery—but it ingeniously employed a form of payment that government rarely resorts to for domestic suppliers: documentary letter of credit.

Who are behind what appears to be an anomalous arrangement is unclear. But in a move that has baffled the new set of education officials, Ombudsman Aniano Desierto in August 1998 cleared ex-Education Secretary Ricardo Gloria, former Education Undersecretary and now Western Samar Rep. Antonio Nachura, and DECS chief accountant Blanquita Bautista of any criminal and administrative liability in allowing CKL Enterprises to be paid before deliveries were made.

Bautista had certified that funds were available for the transaction. Nachura, then chairman of the Pre/Post Qualification Bids and Awards Committee on the 1996 Desk/Armchair Project, entered into the contract with de la Cruz, allowed the payment by letter of credit and signed along with Gloria the disbursement voucher that transferred the money to Land Bank of the Philippines to cover the transaction. Gloria approved the contract and signed—even before deliveries were made—acceptance of the draft that became one of the bank's bases for paying CKL in full on December 24, 1996.

According to the Ombudsman, DECS made no lapses in judgment, but Land Bank may have. "The bank concerned," said the resolution from the Ombudsman, "being a government banking institution, could have taken a vigilant role so as to obviate any attempt to defraud the government." The judgment astonished education officials and people familiar with bank practices.

But more to the point were questions as to how and why a company owned by de la Cruz, who had acquired a notorious reputation in DECS, got accredited, joined the bidding, and clinched the P81.7-million and several other multimillion-peso contracts before that—and then allowed an uncommon form of payment.

Portrait of a Supplier

Jesusa T. de la Cruz of Binalonan, Pangasinan, owner of CKL Enterprises, used to be a small-time businesswoman in the 1970s. But until her latest caper attracted attention, she was one of the DECS's biggest contractors, supplying teachers' uniforms, school desks, office furniture and instructional materials. She was also into the construction of schoolbuildings in the early 1990s.

Bautista, chief accountant of DECS since the mid-1970s when Juan Manuel was education secretary, remembers that de la Cruz's first few contracts covered curtains for Teachers Camp and the education department. De la Cruz had transacted business mainly under a company named Giomiche—a combination of her three children's names.

At that time, De la Cruz chased contracts for teachers' uniforms and, occasionally, furniture. The budget for teachers' uniforms by then was running at about P50 million a year.

Giomiche's contracts for uniforms grew rapidly, allegedly with the help of a relative of de la Cruz in the administration division at the DECS central office. Department insiders say this DECS employee was closely related to the wife of an education undersecretary.

In the early 1980s, however, DECS discontinued the awarding of contracts for teachers' uniforms when it found that massive graft and corruption attended most transactions, says a former education undersecretary. Instead, the government released clothing allowances directly to teachers.

But de la Cruz was not one to give up easily. DECS old-timers recall that when then Education Minister Jaime C. Laya asked for proposed designs for teachers' uniforms, his administrative people got him to approve a set of designs prepared by Giomiche. They then sent the minister for his signature a circular awarding Giomiche the contract to supply the uniforms. Suspecting something irregular, Laya refused and ordered DECS to pay Giomiche the cost of the designs.

That was the last that was heard of de la Cruz at the DECS central office. By then, the economic crisis had also shrunk the procurement budget and the government began decentralizing purchases.

De la Cruz reportedly ran into financial problems in the months that followed. "At one point," Bautista recalls, "*bumagsak ang negosyo niya* (her business went into decline)." But a contract to renovate the Bureau of Treasury in Intramuros in the twilight years of the Marcos regime soon reinvigorated her company.

Post-EDSA education officials knew nothing about de la Cruz or Giomiche until they requested the National Bureau of Investigation (NBI) to discreetly run a check on its National Capital Region office. They were dumbfounded when the NBI reported how procurement rules had been modified to allow one supplier to provide the lumber used for school desks. The supplier: de la Cruz.

According to a former assistant secretary, education officials acted quietly to cut de la Cruz's umbilical cord to DECS-NCR by not extending the terms of retiring regional officials. In place soon was a new set of officials who, having seen what became of their predecessors, were wary about awarding contracts to de la Cruz. It was already the 1990s, and de la Cruz relocated most of her operations to Davao City. She opened an educational supply store and rented a factory that produced wooden furniture, including school desks.

At about that time, Venancio Nava, assistant director of DECS-NCR, was appointed director DECS-Region 11 based in Davao. Today, Nava, de la Cruz and a number of regional and division officials face criminal complaints before the Ombudsman, as well as charges in regional trial courts and the Sandiganbayan, for transactions made in 1991 and 1992 that COA calls "irregular."

Pattern of Irregularities

The P81.7-million contract that de la Cruz was to obtain from the DECS central office in 1996 is reminiscent of these transactions. COA-Region XI director Jimmy Naranjo notes, "The cases follow the same pattern: They (DECS) start paying before she makes full deliveries." This despite a strict prohibition in Presidential Decree 1455 on advance payments for procurement of supplies, materials, equipment and services without approval of the president.

Among the transactions questioned by COA is one involving Business International Wood Products Inc., a firm owned by de la Cruz and run by her son Michael. In February 1992, the firm was paid the full amount of P1,033,450 but delivered to DECS-Region XI only P525,600 worth of office furniture. COA also says the purchase was done without public bidding, adding that no contract existed to justify the release of public funds to the company.

Nine months later, the DECS regional office again gave Business International Woods Products full payment of P2,081,700 despite getting only 1,176 of 3,084 graders' desks stipulated in the contract, COA reported.

Pending before the Ombudsman in Mindanao, meanwhile, is a complaint against DECS regional officials and Giomiche for the full payment given to de la Cruz before construction of elementary school buildings in Davao City, Davao del Sur, Davao del Norte, Davao Oriental, General Santos City, South Cotabato and Surigao del Sur was completed.

A number of purchases by DECS Region XI from de la Cruz's firms were also found to have questionable price tags. In 1991, auditors noted, Giomiche supplied the Davao City school division construction materials that were overpriced by as much as 695 percent. COA said the government was shortchanged by P512,967.70.

The following year, the same DECS regional office bought from Giomiche 14,671 dictionaries for P184 per copy. According to COA, the overprice was some 131 percent that translated to a loss of P1.5 million from the government. The state auditors also noted that the purchase was made without the benefit of public bidding.

But while the filing of the cases forced de la Cruz to lie low in Davao, she apparently became busy in neighboring Regions X and XII, where she managed to land government contracts. Not long after, de la Cruz was staging a big comeback, this time at the DECS central office under a new company name, CKL Enterprises.

Laments Naranjo: "These people have not learned their lessons."

For 25 Years, Notorious Supplier Did Business with DECS

Second of Three Parts

JESUSA "Susie" T. de la Cruz registered the business name, CKL Enterprises, with the Department of Trade and Industry in 1992, at about the time that the Commission on Audit (COA) began uncovering her questionable deals at the education department's Region XI office in Davao.

But de la Cruz took three years before activating CKL Enterprises in both Davao City and Quezon City. Registered as a wholesaler, her Quezon City office lists monobloc plastic chairs as its principal product.

In 1995, CKL—which represented itself as the exclusive distributor of LKD World of Chairs, a marketing arm of a plastic furniture maker—was accredited in the all-plastic category by the Pre/Postqualification Bids and Awards Committee (PBAC) of the Department of Education, Culture and Sports (DECS).

The following year, CKL was accredited anew in the same category by PBAC, which by then was headed by undersecretary for legal affairs and legislative liaison Antonio Nachura, now a congressman representing Western Samar.

That was also the year CKL clinched the controversial P81.7-million contract to supply 185,086 all-plastic armchairs to public high schools.

CKL has since been paid in full for the armchairs. But education officials say the company managed to deliver only 40 percent of the armchairs as of the April 24, 1997 deadline stipulated in its contract with DECS. (CKL says it has delivered 63 percent of the chairs.)

The DECS has called in some P98 million in performance and surety bonds posted by CKL. It has yet to get the money, though, and its lawyers are not too optimistic.

But DECS Secretary Andrew Gonzales is unrelenting, and has asked de la Cruz to return P49.4 million representing the undelivered desks, and pay damages equivalent to P46.4 million or a total of P95.8 million. Gonzales also confirms: "We're definitely pressing criminal charges."

Centralizing Procurements

De la Cruz declined to be interviewed for this story. As it is, the DECS chief has prohibited all DECS offices nationwide from doing business with her firms—CKL Enterprises, Business International Wood Products, Giomiche Inc. and Tashi Garment—on pain of disciplinary action.

But the damage has already been done, as hundreds of thousands of public school students make do without chairs during classes. DECS veterans are also unsure that lessons will be learned from the CKL fiasco so long as politics and the *padrino* mentality pollute the system.

They note that CKL's formation came at a time that Education Secretary Ricardo Gloria was recentralizing procurement of school desks and armchairs.

Gloria had cited the need to standardize the design, quality and price of school desks and armchairs nationwide as chief reasons for letting the DECS central office regain its active role in procurement. But his decision took many education and audit officials by surprise.

Centralized procurement had been

abandoned since 1986, when DECS allowed regional directors and division superintendents to buy desks. The central office limited itself to issuing guidelines, including price estimates, and scrutinizing and approving big contracts exceeding field officials' signing limits.

"The concept today is regionalization," says Eufracio Rara, DECS auditor from 1994 to 1998. "The region is a mini-central office and regional directors are like combat officers, you just need to give them guidelines. When you centralize, you reverse the process of development."

But as a result of the Gloria directive, the central office for two years joined its regional offices in buying the desks and armchairs that public schools needed nationwide. Purchases done at the central office consumed 50 percent of what had become a P500-million pie in 1995, rising to 80 percent in 1996.

CKL was among the first few suppliers that qualified under Gloria's procurement guidelines. It joined the 1996 bidding for 298,126 all-plastic armchairs for public elementary and high schools nationwide. Had CKL won the contract to supply all these at the initial price it submitted, the transaction could have run into P241.78 million. But Allied Moulding Corp., a large plastic furniture manufacturer accredited by DECS for the first time, kept beating CKL in pricing.

In the end, PBAC split the contract between CKL and Allied Moulding: CKL got 62 percent while Allied Moulding got the rest.

DECS officials got COA to agree to negotiated purchases of school desks.

Accrediting a Crook

Then PBAC chair Nachura admits he and other education officials had heard about the criminal cases against de la Cruz and her firms. But he says accreditation of de la Cruz's CKL was a collective decision. "This was not," he says, "an individual decision." Yet an order issued by Gloria shows that the job of PBAC's accreditation group was largely recommendatory, with the chair making the final approval.

Accreditation allowed CKL to bid for contracts of all-plastics chairs. In 1995, the firm would also benefit from two of Gloria's several directives on procurement.

In a September 11, 1995 memo, Gloria set the prices for seven categories of chairs and desks that DECS was buying. Two months later, he amended the memo to allow price increases in four of seven categories citing "representations of the different manufacturers."

The increases ranged from P35 to P65 each, except for monobloc plastic chairs, of which CKL was an accredited supplier. For those, DECS raised the price from P450 to P650 each for plastic armchair and from P895 to P1,105 for a plastic graders' desk.

Gloria now says PBAC then headed by undersecretary Alejandro Clemente had recommended the adjustments. Later, on Nachura's recommendation, Gloria also approved negotiated purchases as the mode of procurement for school desks and armchairs in lieu of public biddings.

Nachura and other education officials had gotten COA Chairman Celso Gangan and Rara to agree to negotiated purchases by citing, among other reasons, the danger of the procurement money reverting to the national treasury at the end of the year and the urgency of bidding out the contracts.

The impact of the memo was felt nationwide. One after another, DECS regional offices canceled or indefinitely postponed public biddings that were already scheduled for desks and armchairs. When 1995 drew to a close, de la Cruz had picked up, through negotiated procurement, P109 million in contracts to supply desks and armchairs at the higher prices approved by Gloria. A review of a contract entered into the same month by DECS with another supplier shows that the armchairs at the time could be had for P450 apiece.

Then came the 1996 bidding for the all-plastic student armchairs.

Rigging Bids

A public bidding requires at least three qualified suppliers or it would be declared a failure. In the 1996 bidding for school chairs, DECS had accredited only two, CKL and Allied Moulding, but pushed on with the public bidding anyway. When a failed bidding was declared, PBAC negotiated with the two companies.

At the time, Allied Moulding had thought it would easily win the contract to supply all the needed armchairs. When the initial bids were opened, it had priced the chairs at P669 each or P142 lower than CKL's P811. It also expected PBAC to disqualify CKL, whose armchairs came with book tray and footrest, two features that were not in the original specifications.

But in what Allied Moulding charged as an "unexplained display of compassion" to de la Cruz, PBAC met with CKL's proprietor on August 20, 1996 and allowed her firm to resubmit on August 22 at 10 a.m. a proposal for armchairs without book tray and footrest. Allied Moulding, which was excluded from the meeting, was also told to submit a new proposal.

Although CKL submitted its proposal at 4:05 p.m., or way past the deadline, PBAC failed to disqualify it, prompting Allied Moulding to file three letters of protest. Despite the pending protests, Nachura sent the companies a notice for the final submission of proposal on August 30.

Although CKL submitted its proposal at 4:05 p.m., or way past the deadline, PBAC failed to disqualify it.

Allied Moulding says it joined the final round "for fear of technical disqualification." CKL also submitted a proposal and, this time, several samples of chairs. Allied Moulding, which was not invited to attend the durability tests run on the chairs, learned later that CKL's samples broke when tested. It also learned that CKL's final proposal quoted prices that exactly matched its own.

Documents show that Allied Moulding protested the conduct of the biddings from beginning to end. But according to Nachura, Allied Moulding "is stopped from making any complaints anymore" when it accepted the arrangement that gave CKL the P81.7-million contract to supply 185,086 secondary armchairs and Allied Moulding a P49.8-million deal covering 113,040 elementary armchairs.

Nachura insists, though, that awarding the contract to CKL "was not completely my responsibility. I was merely chair of PBAC, and PBAC consisted of a number of members."

Gloria, however, says Nachura, as

chairman of PBAC, was empowered to suspend proceedings and recommend a rebidding if he disagreed with the committee for valid reasons. "That is expected of him. It is his responsibility as chairman of the committee," he says.

Nachura says he and Gloria would have been the last persons to favor de la Cruz since the businesswoman had filed a graft case against them before the Ombudsman in Mindanao earlier that year. Gloria and Nachura have since been cleared of those charges.

Still, Nachura admits that continuous representations by de la Cruz convinced him to give in to her odd request that entailed an abrupt departure from normal government practice: payment by letter of credit (LC).

In lobbying for an LC, de la Cruz had complained about frequent delays in the release of payment by the DECS accounting division, as well as cited the large amount covered by the contract, Nachura recalls.

Letter of Credit

Nachura, by his own admission, is vaguely familiar with LC transactions. He also concedes that opening an LC for local purchases by the state "is not an ordinary course taken... (it is) not the normal procedure." Indeed, it was the first time in the education department's 100-year history that it would be paying a local supplier by LC.

A former budget official says: "Letters of credit don't make sense in government purchases. Funds are supposed to have been earmarked so there's no reason to resort to an LC. Cash releases are made to pay suppliers during the anticipated delivery time."

While government agencies sometimes run out of cash to pay suppliers, says the official, delays in payments have also been due to the failure of suppliers to present to government accountants all the proofs of delivery and acceptance.

> Nachura admits that continuous representations by de la Cruz convinced him to give in to her odd request that entailed an abrupt departure from normal government practice: payment by letter of credit.

Strangely, the DECS accounting division was excluded from the preparation of the LC for CKL. Chief accountant Blanquita Bautista, who certified the availability of funds, says DECS legal officers instead took charge.

On December 23, 1996, through a disbursement voucher, DECS transferred to Land Bank of the Philippines P81.7 million to cover the transaction.

Auditor Rara learned about the transaction only in April 1997, during a post-audit of DECS, when he came across the disbursement voucher without documentary support. He wrote Nachura for a copy of the contract, a distribution list of armchairs, delivery receipts and acceptance reports, and the performance and surety bonds. He also questioned why a domestic LC was needed.

Seven months later, Rara's findings formed the basis of graft charges filed against Gloria, Nachura, Bautista and de la Cruz before the Ombudsman. The three DECS officials were charged with paying de la Cruz in full on December 24, 1996 for a non-existing contract and in the absence of proof of deliveries.

The date on the contract was December 31, 1996. But Ombudsman Aniano Desierto junked the charge that a contract was non-existent when CKL was paid on December 24. Nachura and Bautista were cleared after telling investigators they had signed the contract on December 19 and had even written that date beside their signatures. Gloria was also cleared after he produced two witnesses, including a legal consultant he had hired, to testify that he, too, signed the contract on December 19.

Desierto also cleared the DECS officials of any liability for allowing de la Cruz to get paid in full before making any deliveries. Instead, he ordered an inquiry into possible lapses by Land Bank where the LC was opened and negotiated.

But Gonzales says, "The bank is not at fault." That view is shared by people well versed in LC transactions. Under such arrangements, the supplier gets paid by a bank to which the buyer has transferred the money, provided that he submits all the documents set down by the buyer in the letter of credit. If the documents are in order, the bank automatically releases the payment.

A safeguard, therefore, is for the buyer to put down in the LC as many documents as he deems necessary to prevent fraud. In the case of CKL, Gloria and Nachura issued a clean LC, listing only the minimum requirements: a sales invoice and a duly accepted draft.

Land Bank international trade department head Zenaida Dayao says de la Cruz presented the two documents in requesting payment on December 24, 1996. Dayao recalls Gloria had already signed acceptance of the draft, which she says is tantamount to "an approval for payment of the negotiation." At that time, though, CKL had not made any deliveries because DECS had just issued the notice to proceed with its contract on December 23.

Land Bank officials say they saw no need to check with DECS before releasing payment.

Payment Before Delivery

Nachura never gave Rara an explanation as to why Gloria signed the draft before deliveries of the desks. "Perhaps," Nachura says now, "it may have been because Secretary Gloria did not know so much about letters of credit."

But Gloria says he depended on the recommendations of Nachura, PBAC and DECS lawyers for a transaction he knew little about. He says he signed the draft after this cleared with Nachura. Says the ex-DECS head: "I thought deliveries were made because that's what they told me."

Nachura, meanwhile, insists that "a draft per se is not payment." Yet in commerce, a draft is a bill of exchange or a bank check that can be drawn at sight or demand. In effect, Gloria had issued CKL a draft that became payable the moment he signed its acceptance.

Nachura also shifts the responsibility to the Land Bank, which he says should have demanded proof of delivery, including the sales invoice, delivery receipts, inspection report and acceptance report which were written into the contract.

Dayao, however, invokes international rules on LCs set by the International Chamber of Commerce (ICC). These rules say that letters of credit are transactions separate from contracts. Banks, therefore, are not required to examine contracts even if these are mentioned in LCs.

Besides, the Land Bank says, DECS never furnished it a copy of the contract. But then DECS could not have done so at the time, as the contract was notarized on December 31, 1996—at least on paper. A check showed that CKL actually notarized the contract on January 2, 1997 but had asked the notary public to antedate the notarization date to December 31. No copy of the contract, however, can be found at the notary public and the Quezon City regional trial court.

Land Bank officials say they saw no need to check with DECS before releasing payment because two DECS representatives had accompanied de la Cruz on December 24 to file the application for the LC at its Pasig Capitol branch.

De la Cruz, for her part, wrote then Education Secretary Erlinda Pefianco in April to explain that the delay was caused by the overheating of her manufacturer's machines because of El Niño and its difficulty to buy the spare parts due to the currency crisis.

But El Niño and the financial crisis had not set in at the time of the contract's April 1997 deadline, both having begun only during the second half of that year. An executive of CMC, a plastic furniture maker from which CKL sources the armchairs, also says he has no recollection of a massive breakdown of his machines that year.

The CMC executive adds that he did not know about the contract to supply 185,086 armchairs. He stresses that his company is capable of producing and delivering what DECS had needed within 120 days. But, he says, de la Cruz did not place orders totaling that many armchairs and has been inactive since late 1997.

And while de la Cruz in her letter complained that the 120-day delivery period was too short, the other supplier, Allied Moulding, managed to deliver all the 113,040 chairs under its P49.8-million contract in 51 days.

DECS turned down de la Cruz's request for an extension. On October 21, 1997, in another attempt to convince DECS to overlook her shortcomings, de la Cruz wrote Gonzales offering to deliver the remaining chairs within 180 days. Gonzales's reply reads in part: "For us to agree to an extension under the circumstances will be contrary to law and will make us criminally liable under the Graft and Corrupt Practices Act for granting you undue benefit and advantage to the detriment and damage."

Corruption is Embedded in the DECS Culture

Conclusion

IT IS the country's biggest bureaucracy and it is guaranteed the biggest chunk of the annual budget by the 1987 Constitution. These two factors, say observers, have helped make the Department of Education, Culture and Sports (DECS) one of the most corrupt state agencies in the Philippines.

But the new administration at DECS wants to change that image. DECS secretary Andrew Gonzales says he hopes to build a "culture of excellence" where administrators will be people of integrity.

"There's talent in DECS," says the erstwhile president of De La Salle University. "There are good people in DECS and there are honest people."

Gonzales is actively scouting for these people to eventually become the principals, supervisors and superintendents. "Hopefully, over the generation, we will have a more competent, more dedicated, more honest group of middle-level managers for the entire system," he says. "This is the work of a generation; it can't be done overnight."

DECS insiders and former officials say many suppliers have acquired the knack of rigging public biddings.

Gonzales is under no illusion that graft and corruption can be licked, but takes exception to criticisms that DECS is among the dirtiest of government agencies. "Clearly, on a scale of five, if your were to rank DECS, the integrity of DECS would probably be three, which doesn't make it very far from the other departments," he argues. "The larger the department and the more funds available to run the department make, the problem (of graft and corruption becomes) more difficult."

Former top education officials, however, wonder how far the new set of education officials will get in breaking the culture of corruption at DECS. Observes an ex-DECS official: "The regional director, *galing sa pagka*-superintendent *na galing sa* principal *na galing sa* teacher—most rose from the ranks and have been exposed to a corrupt system. Corruption begins the moment that teacher goes to the congressman or the principal to get a job, (because later he would) need to do them a favor."

Indeed, the annals of DECS are replete with stories of how millions of pesos in taxpayer's money earmarked for the education of the needy has been lost to suppliers and government employees who collude to permit overpricing, short deliveries or ghost deliveries.

Litany of Graft

In the 1980s, for instance, desks bought under a P30-million World Bank-funded project were found to be grossly overpriced or made of cheap wood, forcing many of the state employees involved to flee the country.

In the early 1990s, the House education committee ordered an inquiry into the delivery of thousands of termite-infested, substandard desks to schools to the two Negros provinces.

In 1995, a year before DECS awarded the controversial P81.7-million contract to Jesusa T. de la Cruz's CKL Enterprises, the Commission on Audit (COA) uncovered irregularities in four regions. The worst cases were detected in Cagayan Valley. Of 49,308 tablet armchairs bought for P34 million by the regional office, 11,140 pieces never got delivered, 21,486 arrived unassembled, and 2,400 lacked parts like writing pads, backrests and seats. The armchairs were made of inferior plastic and undersized GI pipes. COA placed the losses at P8 million. In addition, over 8,000 chairs intended for public elementary schools ended up in high schools, a private school, and even *barangay* halls and daycare centers.

Enlisting the help of some DECS officials and employees, many suppliers expertly exploit loopholes in the law and government rules to turn the procurement process to their favor. When they fail there, they unabashedly resort to money, politics, kinship, legal tactics or the media—sometimes a combination of these—or play on the vulnerabilities of officials who hold the key to purchases.

DECS insiders and former officials say many suppliers have acquired the knack of rigging public biddings. At the DECS central office not too long ago, a supplier who had the backing of a legislator formed 16 dummy companies that joined in nearly all the bids for DECS purchases. Says a former education secretary: "*Kahit sino ang manalo, panalo pa rin siya* (Whoever wins the bidding, that supplier still gets the contract)."

A special audit done in 1993 by COA, meanwhile, discovered that 17 firms that cornered multimillion-peso contracts at the Quezon City school division actually belonged to just one group. Auditors found that only one person had collected and cashed the checks for all 17 companies.

There have also been cases when some suppliers colluded with each other to force a failure of public bidding or take turns at winning contracts. And when newcomers emerged as a potential threat to their business, they tried to buy them off.

According to an executive of Allied Moulding Corp., CKL's de la Cruz offered to buy the rights of his firm when Allied Moulding looked as if it would win the 1996 bidding for the all-plastic school chairs. "I never entertained her offer at all," says the Allied Moulding official. "We wanted to get into DECS because it was a new market for us."

De la Cruz declined to be interviewed for this article. Secretary Gonzales, though, describes her company, CKL, as "a chameleon" because "it comes in different forms under the same owner and the same group to hide their identity." But Gonzales concedes that de la Cruz is only one among many suppliers who have resorted to lying low after getting into trouble and then resurrecting their businesses under new names. After all, he says, "there's no preventing companies from appearing under a new name because it's so easy to incorporate."

Buying Officials

By far, however, insiders say buying off government officials and employees has been the quickest way for suppliers to gain their cooperation. The offer of money is often made to government personnel given signing authority—those who requested the allocation (to ensure the items get included in the quarterly procurement), those in the procurement committee (to award the contract), those who monitored deliveries (to fake acceptance and inspection reports), and those who released the payment (to ignore the spurious reports).

In government parlance, this money is "SOP" or standard operating procedure. In cruder terms, however, it is a commission, a kickback, or bribe money.

Former Budget Secretary Salvador Enriquez once said "commissions" ate up 45 percent of government purchases. But a former resident DECS ombudsman says these reached as high as 70 percent for big contracts at the education department.

What Enriquez failed to compute, he says, was the money suppliers gave up front just to be accredited, to make sure purchases were lumped so they involved bigger sums, and to get the items they were offering included in the quarterly allocation. This easily added up to 25 percent of the contract, he says, while noting that part of the money went to people in the budget department, which authorizes the releases of public funds.

"That's the entry free, *parang* toll gate," says the ex-DECS resident ombudsman. "Whether you win or not, you pay. It's like lotto: *tumaya ka muna* (you make a bet first)."

Officials directly involved in the awarding of contracts were then normally offered eight to 10 percent of the contract. According to one former regional director, the commissions he was being offered began at a low of five to 10 percent.

Politicians also poke their fingers in the DECS procurement pie.

"*May mga tagabulong diyan*, usually DECS insiders connected to the supplier. All transactions are done in cash," says a former DECS undersecretary for operations.

The exchange of money was made in different places. One ex-DECS official who was in the department in the 1980s says a supplier delivered to his house a briefcase that held P1.2 million in exchange for a contract. He says he refused the money.

The former ombudsman says some regional directors met up with Metro Manila suppliers when they came to the capital for their monthly meetings at the central office.

One regional director was notorious for his "kitchen conferences." According to an ex-aide, he and his suppliers would meet quietly at the kitchen of the regional office where money would change hands.

The Chain of Corruption

Because of the fat commissions they had to cough up, suppliers apparently found it only justified to overprice their goods or resort to under-deliveries, delivery of substandard or defective items or, worse, "ghost" deliveries. A COA study conservatively estimates that a tenth of the total P50-billion procurement budget in 1994 was lost to overpricing. Quips the former DECS undersecretary: "If you have to do it right, how can you still make money?"

In truth, while COA has blown the whistle on the irregularities, some DECS insiders say there have been government auditors who were also involved in their cover-up. With advice from DECS and COA personnel, the suppliers would place markings on batches of goods without defects. "When the auditor does a spot check, he just does a sampling. He doesn't pick something without markings," says the former DECS ombudsman. "If the auditor doesn't like what you gave, be prepared for a special audit."

DECS insiders and former officials also say politicians are not content with meddling in the appointments and promotions of teachers. They say some—including members of Congress who hold the power over the purse and can block appointments and initiate investigations—also poke their fingers in the DECS procurement pie.

One DECS undersecretary was only weeks into his job when a congressman phoned to call his attention to a supplier who was in danger of losing in the bidding. "He told me, *Pare, akin yan. Meron ako diyan* (That's mine. I've interest there),'" says the official. He was to get many similar calls during his six-year DECS stint, which has now ended.

In the case of special allocations like the pork barrel funds of lawmakers, DECS people rarely got a cut, says the former

DECS ombudsman. "It's purely an arrangement between the politician and the supplier. DECS was just the implementing agency."

Gonzales suspects de la Cruz was among those who enjoyed strong political backing. "Definitely," says the secretary who is bent on hauling CKL's owner to court, "they have been able to get away with these things because of political protection of some people upstairs who seem to thrive on this kind of influence peddling."

Unfortunately for de la Cruz, Gonzales is not the only person at DECS she has irked.

Susana Cabahug, DECS-Region XI director, believes de la Cruz filed a graft complaint against her after she awarded a desk contract to another supplier. "She attempted to influence me into deciding in her favor but I declined...I refused to accede to her unlawful requests," says Cabahug in an affidavit before the Ombudsman. "The complaint is nothing but an act of vengeance, harassment and sour graping."

De la Cruz has filed cases against other DECS officials. But complaints like these are not the only ways suppliers try to get back at officials and employees who failed to award them contracts.

Exploiting Vulnerabilities

According to another ex-DECS undersecretary, one supplier resorted to using the country's top columnists to attack the department when a contract did not land on his lap. "*Hindi kami tinigilan* (They wouldn't stop)," says the former official. "One columnist even met me at a hotel to ask me to just give the contract to (the supplier) *para matapos na* (to end the hassle)."

Suppliers are also known to study closely the habits of education officials and capitalize on their vulnerabilities. A friend of a former high-ranking education official says the latter's weakness for high-stakes poker was his undoing. "He would lose hundreds of thousands pesos at games his deputy and a supplier helped arrange and would sign his IOUs at the back of his calling card," he says. The supplier then named his price: contracts at DECS.

These days, the new DECS administration thinks occasions for graft and corruption can be minimized partly by strengthening internal controls and checks and balances in the procurement process.

Undersecretary Antonio Valdes, who now chairs the Pre/Postqualification Bids and Awards Committee (PBAC), has ordered a new round of accreditation of DECS suppliers. He has imposed tougher conditions. Among other things, the company's chief executive officer must sign the documents that are submitted for accreditation and board members must include additional information such as their taxpayer identification number and home addresses.

The new DECS administration thinks occasions for graft and corruption can be minimized partly by strengthening internal controls and checks and balances in the procurement process.

"This is to prevent them from just using dummies or shell companies before they bid," says Valdes. "(They) must be honest-to-goodness legal entities whom we can run after in case there is a discrepancy or there is something anomalous."

Valdes has scrapped the old setup where procurement committees were formed for the different items DECS needed to buy. "We consider that a flaw because then that person (in the committee) is easily identified by possible suppliers and he becomes a target of all kinds of proposals," he explains.

Instead, only one PBAC is taking charge of procurement of all items. Valdes says the committee is composed of people who are not end-users and are not familiar with suppliers. It also includes a representative from the Philippine Institute of Certified Public Accountants to ensure transparency.

The number of PBAC members has been increased from six to 18, from which seven are selected by raffle to handle the procurement only the day before the bidding.

The biddings are currently held at the DECS central office, but will be devolved to the regions "as soon as we're satisfied with the quality of the people in the regions in terms of their integrity," says Valdes. Public biddings will be the rule, he adds, and payment by letters of credit has been ruled out.

On top of the post-audit that is done by COA, DECS is paying big private accounting firms—except the Carlos J. Valdes group which the undersecretary's father owns—to perform spot checks on deliveries. "We can't do this on all deliveries," admits Valdes. "It's (also) going to be very expensive, but we can at least leave it hanging like a Damocles sword."

Former DECS officials wish Valdes and company well. But they confess that it is difficult to stay clean in a graft-ridden environment. While some joined and left the department pure, say the ex-officials, others fell on the wayside.

It is difficult to stay clean in a graft-ridden environment.

To be sure, many education secretaries and undersecretaries had gone to DECS with cleaning a dirty house as their first order of business. Some began their term by going after the corrupt elements, says one ex-DECS official. "But," he says, "what happens to the cases? It's difficult to make the charges stick or the wheels of justice turn very slow. People soon succumb to being practical, they succumb to the system. They become involved in irregularities then rationalize when they're caught with the hands in the cookie jar."

Resisting the lure of dishonest money at DECS is simply herculean, says one former assistant secretary. As he puts it, "It's like going to a beach party and not taking a dip, or going to a department store full of toys and not touching one."

The Plunder of Textbook Funds

BY YVONNE T. CHUA

First published in *Business World, Philippine Star, Manila Standard, Philippine Daily Inquirer, Manila Times, Today,* and *Malaya,* March 3-6, 1999

Over 20 people were interviewed for this three-part series on the corruption that takes place in the procurement of textbooks. These included textbook publishers, agents, education officials and government auditors. Published in the wake of a scandal that rocked the government after the discovery of a delivery by a textbook agent of a box containing P3 million to the head of the budget department, this series revealed the massive payoffs that are made in the awarding of government textbook contracts. Based on interviews with textbook suppliers who requested anonymity for fear of endangering their business with the government, this report showed that the bribes could be as high as 65 percent for supplementary textbooks. That is why much of the funds, especially those from legislators' pork barrel, is siphoned off to buy supplementary materials rather than the basic textbooks that schoolchildren need more urgently.

This report, published simultaneously in six Manila dailies, showed how the chain of corruption extends from the textbook supplier all the way to the presidential palace. The account of how a publisher made her payoffs on a visit to a regional office of the education department with P1.17 million in bribes in her handbag demonstrated in graphic terms the trail of bribery that accompanies a routine business transaction with the government. While Chua's earlier story on the procurement of school desks focused on a case study of one supplier, this series takes a more "global" approach, establishing the "industry practice" for commissions and payoffs and how exactly the corruption pie is shared.

This report also discussed the damage caused by corruption on public school students who suffer from an acute shortage of textbooks. These investigations on corruption in desk and textbook procurements formed the foundation for Chua's book, *Robbed: An Investigation of Corruption in Philippine Education,* which was published by the PCIJ in 1999.

Up to 65% of Textbook Funds Goes to Bribes

First of Three Parts

WHEN A medium-sized book publisher based in Quezon City set out in 1998 on a trip to a regional office of the Department of Education, Culture and Sports (DECS), she carried a bag bulging with wads of cash.

That afternoon, she needed to thank 10 people for the P20-million contract for the purchase of supplementary educational materials that her firm produced. The deal was funded by the "pork barrel" money of a Luzon congressman who was then running for the Senate.

Inside the room of the DECS supply officer, her first stop, she pulled out a brown envelope from her bag and casually handed it over. She ran into some clerks on her way out of the room and handed each of them a crisp P500 bill for *"merienda."*

The publisher then made her way to the accountant who obligated the fund. Another brown envelope was produced. The next stops were the chief accountant, four accounting clerks who helped prepare her check, and the cashier. Out came six more envelopes.

There was one more person to visit before her final stop at the regional director: the auditor, who also gladly took the brown envelope she proffered. At the regional director's office, she waited awhile before she was ushered into the room. When they were alone, she handed out the last and fattest brown envelope.

In all, the envelopes held P1.17 million—P1 million or five percent of the contract for the regional director; P50,000 for the supply officer; P15,000 for the accountant who obligated the money; P40,000 for the chief accountant; P5,000 each for the accounting clerks; P10,000 for the cashier who released the check; and P20,000 for the auditor. Adding other "thank you's" to other officials, including the 40 percent for the congressman who provided the funds, the payoffs ate up more than 50 percent of the contract she had landed.

But the publisher was relieved that the DECS people had not demanded more. Perhaps, she surmised, it was because three other publishers were doing the rounds that same afternoon.

Bribery has become a way of life for DECS suppliers, who say the P3-million bribery attempt at the Department of

Budget and Management (DBM) on January 19, 1999 was just one link in the chain of corruption so deeply embedded in the procurement of textbooks and supplementary materials.

They also say the payoffs take place wherever some sort of discretionary power is exercised, from top to bottom—from as high up as Malacañang as the botched bribe try shows, and as low as the clerk cashier who prepares the check.

Over 20 people interviewed for this series, including executives of publishing houses, government suppliers, textbook authors and former and current DECS officials and employees, confirmed the blatant and sophisticated cheating in government purchases of educational materials.

They say it has come to a point that much of the money is being channeled away from textbooks, of which there is a serious shortage, to the purchase of "supplementary materials," from which bigger cuts can be made. Supplementary materials include books, charts, maps, videos and the like supposed to enrich a child's learning.

But most of those interviewed, especially the suppliers and publishers, spoke on condition of anonymity, fearing their disclosure would cost them their business with the government.

Agents who have been supplying the DECS since the 1970s speak longingly of the days when bribes were smaller and bribe-takers were fewer. "People in the old DECS were nicer," recalled an agent-turned-publisher. "You'd just bring them to a nice restaurant and give them a little. The employees were happy with token amounts."

But as the funds available for textbooks increased, monetary needs of DECS workers grew and word of the generosity of suppliers spread, DECS officials and employees began clamoring for bigger cuts in government contracts. Even non-DECS people began asking for a slice of the pie. "They grow demanding by the day," the publisher lamented.

Staggering Bribes

A September 1998 Social Weather Stations survey ranked DECS as the sixth most corrupt state agency in the eyes of the public, after the Department of Public Works and Highways, Bureau of Internal Revenue and the police.

But a former high-ranking DBM official said that as the Ramos administration ended, DECS overtook the DPWH. So staggering were the bribes from DECS suppliers that many congressmen and senators suddenly shifted their pork barrel (Countrywide Development Fund and Congressional Initiative Allocation) from DPWH to DECS, he said.

The bribes or kickbacks go by the now familiar term "SOP (Standard Operating Procedure)." Agents and publishers, however, prefer to call them "*tapon*" ("throwaways") that they automatically budget when they sell their books to the government.

In their meetings, various associations of book suppliers and publishers openly discuss the sums that are set aside for "*tapon*." And although they jealously guard the identities of their connections—the "*tirador*" who negotiates and collects on behalf of a state official, and "fixers"—they generously warn peers to stay away from the "*matatakaw*" or greedy officials.

DECS suppliers work within a range for the "*tapon*"—from a low of 20 percent to a high of 65 percent of a contract. The commission that agents actually kept for themselves—five to 10 percent—fell outside the range.

"The range is very fluid," said a member of the Book Suppliers Association of the Philippines who has been supplying DECS since 1982. Much, she said, depends on the number of DECS offices, government agencies and go-betweens that are involved and how greedy they were.

Bribes also vary according to the source of funds that are used for purchases and the type of materials supplied to schools, said another publisher who once worked for DECS.

The lump sum appropriations that Congress sets aside each year specifically for textbooks and other instructional materials are by no means the only funds available to public schools for these items. Within the DECS system, savings from the Maintenance and Other Operating Expenses (MOOE) at the central and field offices are added to the pot for textbook purchases.

For years, millions of pesos had also found their way to DECS for books from pork barrel funds until these were abolished by the Estrada administration. Local governments also help in the purchase of schoolbooks through contributions from the local school board fund.

Normally, suppliers deal only with the DECS division, region or central office, or two offices at most, at any one time. In these transactions, government auditors inevitably have to be included in the "*tapon*" to ensure they look the other way when irregularities or lapses are committed.

But when transactions require a realignment of the DECS budget, pork barrel funds and the local school board fund, the chain of corruption extends to the DBM, Malacañang, Congress and local government units.

Sharing the Loot

Long before the Quezon City-based publisher went on her afternoon "appreciation" trip, for instance, she had already handed a broker P5 million or 40 percent of the contract for the congressman who had used part of his pork barrel to buy her materials. She had been told that amount included the five percent that the lawmaker's chief of staff was to give DBM officials and employees for releasing the SARO or special allotment release order for the transaction.

Weeks before she showered her thanks at the DECS regional office, the publisher had also gone to the school divisions to distribute "cuts" to superintendents who had received the books. This came up to three percent of the contract. The publisher had also taken care of the administrative officer (P7,000 each) and auditor (P10,000 each) in every division.

But she has no regrets about having to give so much grease money. For that particular transaction, she still stood to gain P3 million even after paying the printer and forwarder.

Suppliers said supplementary materials are actually where they and government officials make a killing and not on textbooks, as many believe.

Thus, despite the severe textbook shortage, which has caused textbook to pupil ratio to worsen to 1:6 in elementary and 1:8 in high school, the bulk of purchases for public schools has been used for supplementary and reference materials, from which bigger cuts can be made.

"*Manipis lang ang tapon diyan* (The 'throwaway' isn't much from textbooks)," said the agent-turned-publisher of textbooks contracts. "It's 20-all." She meant the bribes given to the regional office and schools divisions under it add up to 20 percent of a contract.

In contrast, kickbacks for supplementary materials start at a low of 40-all and hit a high of 60-all to 65-all, suppliers themselves said.

In the case of textbook purchases, regions transact directly with the private sector, and the regional director takes five to 10 percent, said suppliers. The region's supply, finance and budget, accounting, and administrative officers and auditor, meanwhile, each expects 0.5 to one percent. The allocation of the division superintendent who receives the textbooks is three percent while the staff gets two percent.

"There are division superintendents who complain about the three percent," said the publisher, "but they know that we can't go any higher because they know our profit margins are small."

The lean margins are due to the price caps and other rigid conditions, including paper specifications and door-to-door delivery, imposed by DECS on textbooks.

While supplementary materials are covered by price ceilings as well, they are allowed a bigger markup. On average, supplementary materials cost 20 to 30 percent more than DECS-approved textbooks because their pricing is based on a print run of only 5,000 copies instead of the 50,000 copies used for textbooks. DECS also does not prescribe the type of paper for supplementary materials.

When sold directly to a DECS regional office, suppliers are prepared to throwaway "40-all" for supplementary materials. At least 15 percent would go to the regional director and another 15 percent shared by division superintendents under him.

Cuts from 'Pork'

In the case of supplementary materials offered to congressmen and senators, publishers often budget "50-all" as "*tapon*." As much as 30 to 35 percent usually go to the legislator and his staff, five percent to DBM, and the rest to the DECS office that receives the pork barrel. But there have been instances when kickbacks reached 60 to 65 percent because the lawmaker kept the 30 or 35 percent for himself or demanded 40 percent.

An ex-staffmember of several lawmakers said suppliers went directly to legislators to offer their books. The lawmaker's chief of staff or a relative acted as the "*tirador*" and negotiated with the suppliers.

"The practice was *kaliwaan*," said the staff. The supplier gave half of the SOP as soon as the lawmaker signed the letter to the DBM identifying the titles he wanted to purchase with his pork barrel. Either the supplier or the chief of staff followed up the release of the SARO from DBM. When the SARO was released, the supplier went back to the legislator to pay the balance of the SOP.

The staff noted that some suppliers even got legislators to sign requisition issue vouchers, which is against auditing rules. And since the titles were already specified, it was futile for DECS to hold public biddings.

Division superintendents and district supervisors enjoy one privilege that their regional bosses do not: They have at their disposal the Special Education Fund (SEF) or the local school board fund.

The fund is drawn from proceeds of the one-percent real property tax a city, town or province collects. It is intended for teachers' allowances, construction and maintenance of schoolbuildings, instructional materials and school supplies. In some rich Metro Manila towns and cities, the SEF reaches P500 million each year.

Only the local school board, co-chaired by the governor and school superintendent or the mayor and the district supervisor, has control over the SEF. It is what many book suppliers run after these days, offering SOP of "20-all" to "40-all," depending on how powerful the school superintendent or district supervisor is. If the school official is co-equal with the governor or mayor, then the SOP rises to "40-all," because the two would split the kickback in half. If the school official is subordinate to the local official, his share is normally cut to five percent.

To be fair, not all state officials demand SOP. One ex-Central Luzon governor, for example, refused the 15 percent share offered her, asking that it be used to buy more books. What she didn't know was the superintendent got five percent of the contract. One former congressman also often asked that his share be used for supplies that public schools needed.

But the former governor and the former congressman are exceptions. Said a supplier: "The majority of them are spoiled and greedy."

Aside from payoffs, DECS suppliers have resigned themselves to doing extras for school officials, especially when they come to Manila. Said a publishing house executive: "Suppliers fetch them at the airport, billet them at an expensive hotel, give them pocket money, chauffeur them around town and buy the *pasalubong* that they would bring back to their provinces."

But what irk suppliers are state officials and employees who wangle for more money or break their word. One supplier said she was forced to cough up 20 percent instead of the agreed upon 15 percent after a DECS regional director threatened to give the contract to someone else. "I had no choice," said the supplier. "Right behind me were people willing to take over."

A broker who cornered millions of pesos in pork barrel funds also said some lawmakers became greedier as the years went by. On his first term, a popular Southern Luzon congressman settled for 20 percent. But on his second term, he demanded no less than 40 percent.

One ex-DECS official asked an agent to turn over to him the entire 20 percent intended for the central office, promising to take care of the shares of "helpful" employees. But the agent later had to shell out another five percent for DECS employees because the official kept all of the money.

Suppliers are also finding out that clinching contracts from the local school board is not that simple, especially in Metro Manila. Publishers now shun one city after several agents were told to first see the mayor's wife, who asked them pointblank, "Can you give a car?" They were then told that the car was on top of the SOP they were to give to the mayor.

Government should run a lifestyle check on DECS officials and employees.

Some suppliers suggested that if the government is serious about curbing corruption, it might want to run a lifestyle check on DECS officials and employees.

According to the suppliers, one high-ranking education official who resigned last year now has a posh resort in Mindanao. A retired regional director, meanwhile, owns a house in Ayala Alabang and Xavierville. Another ex-regional director operates a big private school in Luzon. Remarked the agent-turned-publisher: "They're so corrupt, it makes you cry."

The Chain of Corruption in Textbook Purchases

Second of Three Parts

UNTIL now, no one in Malacañang admits to have had an acquaintance with Maryann Maslog prior to January 19, 1999, when she was accused of having brought a P3-million bribe, arranged neatly in a box, to the Department of Budget and Management (DBM). But while education department suppliers interviewed for this piece said that they also found it strange that she was there, they said it was only because they knew her "turf" to be Congress.

Maslog, they said, was a freelance agent who worked for several publishers in securing lucrative contracts covering textbooks and educational materials. She was known to work the legislative halls to land these deals.

Still, when she went to Malacañang that day, it was at the behest of a "consortium" of suppliers; she may not have been familiar with the venue, but it should have been business as usual. Maslog, said suppliers, was to hand over the "SOP," or kickback, for the DBM's release of a Notice of Allocation (NCA). This NCA, released four days before Maslog turned up in the Palace grounds, was the suppliers' assurance that they would be paid for a contract covered by a P200-million Special Allotment Release Order (SARO).

In separate interviews, suppliers said the consortium had budgeted a "20-all" for DBM, the Office of the President, the fixers and the go-betweens, meaning the bribes made up 20 percent of the contract. With the bungled operation, however, no one will now say who were supposed to receive the SOP. Said one publisher: "Who's gonna tell? I'm not gonna tell."

Although the bribery attempt was a fiasco, it is nevertheless telling of how far corruption has reached when it comes to contracts involving requirements of the Department of Education, Culture and Sports (DECS). The result of such large-scale corruption is tragic: Today millions of Filipino schoolchildren don't have textbooks and those that do are often using substandard texts.

The problem is that multimillion-peso book contracts at DECS have been clinched for years by suppliers who are more interested in the illicit earnings that they can make than they are in providing quality reading for students. In separate interviews, these suppliers revealed how they have divided the spoils by forming groups and appropriating specific areas in DECS as their respective "territories."

To the new set of DECS officials, the typical book supplier is a sales agent masquerading as a publisher who operates either at the central office or in the field. Sometimes though, they say, a supplier can also have several agents working to corner contracts for his or her company.

These notions may well hold for smaller contracts. But for those involving millions of pesos in the division, region or central DECS office, it is often not a case of supplier versus supplier. Instead, suppliers—whether agents or publishers—join forces to run after these big contracts.

Forming Syndicates

Suppliers prefer to call their groups "consortia," but DECS insiders use the more derogatory term "syndicates" to refer to these alliances, which they say began in the late 1980s.

The alliances were inevitable, suppliers explained. Most of them had begun as agents trying to supply the needs of DECS offices as much as they could. But as their business grew in the 1980s and they saw how especially lucrative the sale of supplementary materials was, many became publishers themselves and began hiring writers to develop titles for them.

The titles were submitted to DECS for adoption as textbooks for public schools. When they were rejected, the agents-turned-publishers instead got the titles approved as "supplementary materials" so they could still offer them to schools. By 1997, when the government began adopting several titles instead of just one from the private sector for use as textbooks in each grade level subject, many of these agents-turned-publishers successfully got into the list of DECS-approved textbooks.

Because their operations were small, most agents (now publishers) could only produce a limited range of titles, unlike the established publishing houses. The vastness of the DECS market—45,000 public schools in all—also proved too much for each of them to take on alone. By forming themselves into a consortium, suppliers were able offer even more titles and cover more ground in their marketing.

Each consortium has cut up DECS into territories and assigned a group or groups of agents whose full-time job was to woo principals, supervisors, superintendents and regional officials to buy their titles. This arrangement suited field officials because they did not have to deal with too many agents or publishers. The field soon began dealing only with these agents, making it very difficult for a newcomer. "You'd have to say who recommended you," said one publisher. "If you don't drop the right name, you're out."

One big Pasig-based publishing house discovered this harsh truth when it tried getting a share of the huge DECS market in 1997, shortly after DECS had approved several of its titles for use as textbooks in public schools.

The company's general manager recalled her optimism when their in-house sales representatives first tried to offer titles to school principals. Under the procurement guidelines issued that year, principals were to order books from the list of DECS-approved titles and relay their preference to the district supervisors, who in turn gave the schools' choices to division superintendents. These superintendents then were supposed to consolidate the lists from the districts and forward the orders to the regional office.

"No one wanted to talk to them," the general manager said of her company's sales reps. "At schools, they were given the runaround by principals. They were also given the runaround by the superintendents. One sales representative tried to see the regional director; but he never got to see him. They (DECS people) just wanted to talk to people they knew."

The publishing house eventually hired agents who belonged to the consortium and paid them 30 percent in commission. Said the firm's marketing executive: "It's a temporary marriage of convenience."

Greasing the System

Suppliers explained the system this way: One agent or publisher is armed with authority from several publishers to promote and distribute their titles and collect payment. Each group under the consortium is headed by a "captain ball" who runs after big contracts. It often falls on the captain ball to advance the "*padulas*" (grease money), which he or she later collects from the rest of the members whose titles were included in the package he or she fashioned for DECS field offices.

Two publishers and one broker said the consortia have their respective contacts in different government offices, all of them well placed. They include people at both the DBM and DECS who tip them off about funds that have been requested and funds that were available.

At DECS, the contacts are often with the budget office, a DECS official said. At DBM, they were usually budget analysts assigned to the DECS desk. "They alert the suppliers about what items are in the budget," said the insider.

Every piece of information carries a price. Some government employees even resort to selling advice of allotment (AA) or the SARO for P1,000 apiece.

Suppliers then work for the release of the SARO or the NCA. At the Malacañang compound, the office involved is always the DBM. But when funds need to be realigned or SAROs cover big amounts, approval of the President is needed.

Suppliers said they employ fixers in these offices and strike up agreements with officials. But they also engage the services of powerful go-betweens as their link to the Palace. During the Ramos administration, one consortium often sought the help of the daughter of a high-ranking Malacañang official for the release of SAROs and NCAs.

When a SARO is finally released to DECS, which can now enter into transactions with suppliers, DECS officials already know to whom the contracts were to be awarded because, one supplier said, "agreements had been forged way back."

The two publishers and the broker said that this was what was supposed to happen with the P200-million SARO that wound up in the headlines in early 1999, along with a very unflattering mug shot of Maslog.

They said the consortium had gotten wind from their usual contacts at DECS and DBM that Education Secretary Andrew Gonzalez and his undersecretary, Antonio Valdes, had written DBM requesting the release of P260 million and P410 million from the 1998 budget for the purchase of textbooks. The consortium then sought the help of two people close to Malacañang to act as go-betweens to obtain the approval of President Joseph Estrada for the SARO's release.

It had been a common practice of the consortium to hand over the "SOP" when the SARO was released. But although the P200-million SARO was released to DECS on December 15, 1998, no payoff was made because the group had wizened up. In the dying months of the Ramos administration, SAROs were released, purchase orders were issued, but many suppliers remain unpaid to this day because NCAs have not been released. This was why the consortium waited until the DBM issued the NCA before sending off Maslog to Malacañang, said the publishers and the broker.

Other suppliers confirmed just how well entrenched the consortia have become at DECS and other government offices. According to an ex-supply officer of a Metro Manila school division, these groups sometimes even carried the sub-allotment advice to the regional offices.

Some regional directors, in turn, have been known to send the sub-allotment advice along with a favored supplier to a division, a publisher said, adding: "The message was clear: Buy from this supplier and split the SOP with the regional director."

Flouting the Rules

The SOPs dangled by suppliers are often huge enough to entice DECS officials to skew decision-making process or flout the rules. A common violation is the purchase of supplementary and reference materials that are not in the list of titles approved by DECS. Surprisingly, violations are committed not only by the field offices, but by the DECS central office itself.

This was so in 1997, the last year when Ricardo Gloria was DECS secretary. The Commission on Audit (COA) estimated that the DECS central office could have saved P7.7 million had it not bought three titles—*DECS Today* published by Dane Publishing, *FVR through the Years* by Pacer and *Education into the 21st Century* by JOER Printing—that had not been approved by the department. COA noted that DECS accounting office nevertheless made the payments because of the marginal notes of then President Fidel Ramos and Gloria.

Interestingly, too, *Education into the 21st Century* was written by then DECS Undersecretary Alejandro Clemente. The title eventually made it to the list of approved reference materials—a month after DECS had already bought and paid the publisher P1.19 million for 6,998 copies.

On many occasions, DECS also bought overpriced supplementary materials, COA said. For example, in 1995, DECS Region II bought drill cards and flash cards from five firms for a whopping P4.423 million. The COA computed the items' total value to be only P893,454.

Like basic textbooks, supplementary materials are covered by price ceilings. While many suppliers stick to ceilings, some, with the help of the National Printing Office (NPO), have found a way to jack up the prices.

All that was needed, suppliers said, was to get a school principal or divisions superintendent to request the NPO to quote the price of the book that they were offering using a lower print run of, say, of 500 or 1,000. "In reality, we tell the NPO, 'This is the price I want,' and they accommodate," said one supplier, adding that the helpful NPO personnel usually get P5,000.

Oversupply of supplementary materials is also commonplace. Metodio M. Gapasin, division superintendent of Negros Oriental, has been charged administratively with buying from Philflex Trading and General Merchandise in 1996 a total of 16,265 flipcharts—thrice the number of teachers in the divisions. The flipcharts were part of the 35,555 flipcharts he had bought for P17 million, a grossly bloated total, according to DECS. Not only that, the purchase was done with no public bidding and no authority, said the department. Gapasin has also been charged with splitting the payment into several checks.

DECS is investigating ghost deliveries of supplementary materials in Muslim Mindanao by another publisher as well. Yet COA reports indicate that in numerous cases, supplementary materials bought by regional directors were not responsive to the needs of schools.

At the close of 1995, the COA found P17.9 million worth of reference materials lying idle in the warehouse of DECS Region XIII. The materials, it said, had been bought without consulting principals and division superintendents, who preferred textbooks and workbooks. The COA also described the materials as being "of poor quality."

That same year, the director in Region V spent P1.89 million to buy 1,000 copies of a dictionary that was not on the list of approved reference materials and was not requisitioned by the schools. It was also not included in the procurement program. The purchase, COA declared, was unnecessary because the division had purchased 20 units of Colliers Dictionary the year before. In addition, the dictionaries were delivered earlier than the preparation of the requisition issue voucher, purchase order and disbursement voucher, and the payment was split into seven.

Aggressive publishers donate school buses, even school buildings.

Meanwhile, most book publishers say even private schools are beginning to act like DECS and are no longer content with the discounts they enjoy.

For years, standard discounts given to private schools averaged 15 percent with an additional five percent given to schools that pay promptly. Many publishers also agree to give schools donation equivalent to five percent of total sales.

In recent years, however, the cut-throat competition in a small market of only 9,000 schools has led some publishers to undercut each other and breach agreements made within their associations. Some offer discounts of as high as 30 to 35 percent.

And as private schools witness how publishers spoil the public schools, the word "commission" has already found its way to their vocabulary. An executive of one of the biggest textbook publishers said an association of private schools has recently asked publishers for commissions of 40 to 45 percent.

"Since the private schools have heard of what some publishers give to public schools, they decided they might as well ask for the same arrangement," she said.

She added that most publishers balked at the request, with one even calling it "blackmail." But two publishers were open to the suggestion, one of whom said he was willing to offer a 50 percent commission, related the executive.

"It's indeed high time," she said, "(that) we come up with a code of ethical standards for the book publishing industry."

Can DECS Stop Textbook Scams?

Conclusion

IT HAS been no secret to the new bosses at the Department of Education, Culture and Sports (DECS) that the procurement of textbook and supplementary educational materials had for the last 20 years or so yielded fat dividends for a significant number of the department's officials and personnel.

But DECS Undersecretary Antonio Valdes, who has barely warmed his seat at the department, said they have just made it harder for such people to profit from these procurements, and are warning DECS suppliers to unlearn their old tricks—or else.

Suppliers themselves agreed with some former and current government officials that the dirty deals had not only led to hundreds of millions of pesos of public funds going to the pockets of corrupt individuals, but also to a critical textbook shortage. They add that it is likely that the dismal quality of many textbooks can also be traced to corrupt practices, which puts a premium on little else besides profits.

In an interview, Valdes said that the various internal controls DECS recently adopted in textbook purchases will double the number of books for the country's 45,000 public schools.

But he also admitted that no system is foolproof and that there are just some things they cannot undo, even if they wanted to.

If the new DECS officials could only have their way, for instance, they would bid out contracts for textbooks covered by the P200 million released by Department of Budget and Management (DBM) on January 15, 1999 and which is now at the center of controversy because of an alleged bribe attempt. But, said Valdes, in this case, public bidding is out of the question.

The money, he explained, is drawn from the 1998 DECS budget and must therefore be used according to the guidelines that prevailed that year. "Our hands are tied," he said.

Approved by then DECS Secretary Ricardo Gloria, these guidelines eschew public biddings in favor of "school empowerment" in purchase of the books. But they have led to huge payoffs given the many levels of DECS personnel involved in the purchase and whom publishers and their middlemen needed to entice with kickbacks or "SOPs" to ensure orders. More often than not, said the publishers, the merits of a book had not been prime considerations in the decision over which to buy.

The school principals chose titles from the list of DECS-approved textbooks developed by the private sector. While publishers agree that principals ought to be the best people to judge what their schools needed, this was hardly so in public schools. Pointed out one publishing house official: "For 25 years, they never chose the books they used."

Indeed, since the 1970s DECS had dictated which titles public schools should buy. Until 1995, each subject per grade level had just one prescribed title. Following the enactment of Republic Act 8047 that year, however, DECS decided to have multiple titles per subject per grade level. But all the textbooks still needed DECS approval.

Another executive of a publishing company also noted that DECS had failed to prepare the principals to select the textbooks that they needed. "The educational seminars for principals didn't push through because there was no money," he said.

Principals can also be easily dictated upon by their superiors like the district supervisor and the division superintendent, the two executives said.

Publishers have also discovered that even if the principals requisitioned certain titles, the selection can still be changed—without their knowledge or consent—by their higher-ups. When publishers or principals presented their Requisition Issue Vouchers (RIVs) to show the titles they had ordered, regional officials often whipped out their own RIVs covering a different sent of titles supposedly submitted by the principals. "It's a case of my RIV against your RIV," said a marketing executive of a publishing house.

Because of abuses of the school empowerment policy for textbook purchases, DECS is torn between giving the money to regional offices to order the books or keeping the money at the central office and ordering the books directly from publishers, Valdes said. No decision has been made.

Return to Public Bidding

But he said that for sure, textbooks to be purchased using the 1999 budget would be done by public bidding. The P504-million lump sum appropriations are initially estimated to buy 7.4 million textbooks.

The biddings of each regional office will be done at the DECS central office in Pasig so DECS can closely watch the proceedings. Membership of the bidding committee will change for each bidding, with most of them chosen by drawing of lots immediately before the bidding date from the 18 members who now compose the DECS Pre/Post-Qualification, Bids and Awards Committee or PBAC.

According to Valdes, the new bidding system will cut out the middleman who has made DECS purchases expensive through SOPs. "It would be illogical for a publisher to go through the bidding process using agents and brokers because they would have to incur additional marketing expenses," he argued. "Why make an agent bid for them when they can bid for themselves?"

Yet despite his optimism that it will work, he conceded that the system "is only as good as the people who will implement them." He is also not 100 percent sure of the integrity of all the members of the bidding committee. "But," he said, "what you can do is to keep them off-balance, make it uncomfortable and make it more difficult for them to cheat."

Valdes said that PBAC members will serve for only six months to a year, but not one of them knows exactly when they will be replaced.

Notwithstanding the stricter procurement guidelines, certain DECS officials and suppliers have not given up their merry old ways. Suppliers returning from the regional offices said some officials have demanded an additional 10 percent in kickbacks because it is much more difficult to rig contracts now. Some officials have also informed suppliers they need the extra money to buy off their colleagues in PBAC.

A PBAC member said one supplier has already offered him a brown envelope stuffed with cash and another has promised to give him a 20-percent cut of the contract.

On top of a new bidding process, DECS has required suppliers to reapply for accreditation. This has worried some small publishers who said the qualifications DECS demands appear to favor big and established publishing houses.

Among other things, DECS expects publishing activity to go on when they look up the addresses that publishers declare in their application to ensure they are not fly-by-night operations or mere agents.

But some small suppliers said that while they may not have printing facilities and work out of their homes, they are nevertheless legitimate publishers who commission the titles they develop for DECS and hire other firms to print these books. They also enjoy credit access that has allowed them to meet orders from DECS over the years, they said.

At this stage, though, bidding already appears unlikely in a number of subject areas in certain grade levels.

While DECS has approved 312 titles for use as textbooks in elementary and high school, 20 subject areas in different grade levels—one core subject in elementary and six core subjects in high school—have only one title each. Public bidding is also unlikely in five subject areas with no approved titles.

Many publishers blame the failure of DECS to approve enough titles for certain subject areas chiefly on the evaluation process supervised by the DECS Instructional Materials Council Secretariat (IMCS). Of 610 titles submitted by the private sector for use as textbooks in public schools in the last two years, 50 percent were rejected, IMCS records show.

On the surface, that does not look like a bad batting average at all. In truth, authors and publishers said they would not be complaining were it not for what they perceived as inconsistent evaluations of the books they had submitted.

Problems with Evaluation

According to one publisher, some books got conditional approval even when they failed to cover some learning competencies required by DECS while other books were disapproved outright over a mere illustration, a selection or an exercise. Several publishers also noted that evaluators tended to reject textbooks that exceeded the minimum learning competencies or did not carry buzzwords familiar to them.

A DECS textbook evaluator is supposed to be a master teacher, subject area specialist or curriculum expert for one subject area or more, with at least five years of relevant experience in the said subject. Yet in the last two rounds of evaluation, IMCS relied on regional textbooks coordinators to nominate evaluators. During a consultative workshop with publishers, IMCS executive director J. Arthur Fernandez admitted nominations were occasionally based on friendships rather than merit and there was not enough time to orient the teachers on the evaluation process.

Some publishers said there has also been a possible leakage of the evaluators' identities, which are supposed to be confidential. Although they offer no proof, they cited publishers who claimed or appeared to know the results of the evaluation even before the results came out.

Fernandez, for his part, said he is certain there were no leaks in the first batch of textbooks. But he did not discount there might have been some the second time around. According to Fernandez, this was inevitable because some textbook writers came from

DECS who naturally learned about events scheduled for evaluators. "They knew each other," he said. Still, he said, the IMCS adopted safeguards to ensure the confidentiality of the whole process.

While a decision still has to be made in the case of subjects areas with no approved titles, Fernandez and Valdez said DECS might have to continue allowing commercial reprints of DECS-owned titles in these subject areas.

DECS had ordered a stop to commercial reprints beginning December 1998. RA 8047, which was aimed at ending the government monopoly of textbook development and production, had given DECS three years to phase itself out of these tasks, and the education department was therefore anticipating finally turning them over to the private sector.

But giving a go-signal once more to commercial reprints may be risky since publishers and DECS officials said that in the past, abuses had attended the issuance and use of authority to reprint. Printers or publishers are supposed to secure authority from the education secretary to reprint a specified number of DECS-owned titles within one year and pay a royalty of P1 for every copy printed.

One publisher recalled paying P10,000 to facilitate the release of an authority to reprint because, she said, DECS personnel had sat on her application. In another instance, education officials stumbled upon a publisher carrying an authority to reprint with the forged signature of the DECS secretary. There have also been printers who just produced commercial reprints without approval of DECS or with expired authority. Some also sold commercial reprints intended for the general public back to DECS.

Cases of principals and superintendents procuring commercial reprints from unscrupulous firms have also been documented. A special audit of the Quezon City schools division found that in 1991, Superintendent Bienvenido Icasiano bought P1.2 million worth of textbooks from commercial printers who used permits that had expired five years before. The Commission on Audit (COA) also found that Icasiano bought commercial reprints from companies that had no authority from DECS but were merely "authorized" by another supplier with existing rights.

Reforming the System

But Valdes is so confident about the new anti-corruption controls they have installed at DECS that he says even the procurement system of World Bank is no comparison. "Our system is more stringent than World Bank," he said. "For example, they don't have inventory checks. They also go for bidding, but their agency estimates are one-figure estimates rather than a range of high and low."

The World Bank has required DECS to adopt its procurement system for a Bank-funded purchase of textbooks. At least P200 million will be used to buy books from the private sector for schools in 26 poor provinces.

Valdes said DECS will follow the Bank's system for the project, but will ask that the department be allowed to adopt safeguards, including inventory checks, even if it means the expenses have to come out of DECS's own pocket.

The education undersecretary said that DECS is dead-set about cracking down on corruption. The department has already blacklisted several suppliers, including Dane Publishing Corp., whose representatives were found carrying a letter purportedly from President Joseph Estrada directing DECS to give business to the company. "They can't do business with us until the outcome of the (National Bureau of Investigation) investigation," Valdes said.

In December 1998, Education Secretary Andrew Gonzalez also ordered DECS offices not to buy the *Diksyunaryo ng Wikang Filipino, Sentinyal Edisyon* from Merylvin Publishing House after ascertaining that there was no contract between the firm and the Komisyon ng Wikang Filipino (KWF), owner of the copyright to the dictionary, to print and distribute the book.

It would be difficult to determine to what extent the new anti-corruption measures regarding textbook purchases will work.

By then, however, Merylvin had sold 1,336 copies worth a total P2.9 million to the DECS National Capital Region using a certification issued on May 3, 1998 by then KWF Chairman Ponciano Pineda that company owner Esmeralda Malapit was the exclusive distributor of the hardbound dictionary. Sales were apparently helped by the fact that Merylvin had printed a picture and message of President Estrada on the back cover.

Pineda, who retired in January 1999, has denied having anything to do with Merylvin. Yet to get him off the hook, several KWF commissioners have suggested entering into an antedated contract with Merylvin, minutes of the KWF's meetings and exchange of letters among the commissioners show.

Meanwhile, to cut down on abuses in the purchases of supplementary materials, DECS has banned schools from buying supplementary and reference materials until the year 2000. It is reviewing the list of supplementary materials to discard titles that do not meet DECS standards and adjust prices of certain materials to remove overpricing. At present, a total of 1,248 titles appear on the list.

Some titles were never submitted for evaluation but were ordered included in the list by Gloria. The authors were mostly former DECS officials, including secretaries Isidro Cariño and Onofre D. Corpuz, undersecretary Alejandro Clemente and assistant secretary Ulpiano Sarmiento. Gloria made the exception, saying they were eminent persons, according to a DECS employee.

Valdes acknowledged that the ban on supplementary materials would apply only to money that comes from DECS and not money from the local school board fund. "We don't have control over them (local school boards)," he said.

He also said that it would be difficult to determine to what extent the new anti-corruption measures regarding textbook purchases will work. But he added he would like the new system to be judged by how effectively money has been used for purchases. Said Valdes: "If you have maximized its (money) use, gotten the number of books you can buy, then you can safely conclude that you have minimized cheating."

The Burdens of Agriculture

BY PRIME SARMIENTO

First published in *BusinessWorld* and *Ang Pahayagang Malaya*, January 24-25, 2000.

Like corruption in the education department, graft in the delivery of agricultural services has been going on for decades yet it has remained largely unreported upon, except for occasional reports about scams being uncovered. In this two-part series, Prime Sarmiento, who covered the agriculture beat for the *Manila Times* before going on to report on commodities for Dow-Jones, goes beyond individual instances of graft to probe systemic corruption in the Department of Agriculture.

What she found was that corruption is rooted in the department's regional field units which are given tremendous power and resources with little monitoring and accountability. This has resulted in the widespread misuse or diversion of funds intended to provide support for farmers in the form of planting materials, machinery and breeding animals. In interviews, officials attested to the existence of a culture of "corruption and waste" which is partly responsible for the lackluster performance of Philippine agriculture.

This investigation established a pattern of graft by examining graft cases filed in various agencies, audit reports, as well as voluminous documents from the agriculture department itself. In addition, Sarmiento interviewed former and current agriculture officials. To see for herself how agriculture projects were being implemented, she traveled to Sultan Kudarat and Cotabato. The second part of this series examines the Central Mindanao regional field unit and found that corrupt agriculture officials have resorted to arson, murder and intimidation to silence whistleblowers. We found this case study approach useful in dramatizing not only the extent of the corruption, but also the lengths to which those who would expose it risked their lives and their safety. The case study, along with interviews with farmers, also put a human face to the story which would otherwise be only a lengthy chronicle of bureaucratic malfeasance.

Weighed Down by Corruption and Waste

First of Two Parts

PUROK SAN ANTONIO, TACURONG, SULTAN KUDARAT—Jaime Gatchalian, a 42-year-old tenant-farmer rues the day in April 1999 when he accepted a sack of *palay* seeds from the Department of Agriculture (DA).

Because the seeds were given out free as part of a government program to boost rural productivity, Mang Jaime thought he would be able to save at least P600. He usually spends P3,000 every cropping season to buy farm inputs like fertilizers, pesticides and seeds.

But when harvest time came that October, Mang Jaime's one-hectare field yielded only 19 sacks of grain, while his neighbor, who bought *palay* seeds from a private supplier, harvested 60 sacks per hectare.

Mang Jaime thinks he should have known better. He was hesitant to use the seeds that came from the DA's provincial office. But this was the first time in his 20 years of tilling the land that farmers in his area had been offered government assistance.

The fertile, river-fed plains of Sultan Kudarat are among the most productive rice-growing areas of Mindanao. Farming is the main livelihood of two-thirds of the province's over 500,000 residents. This is an area that should be a major beneficiary of government assistance for agriculture.

But in interviews in three major rice-growing towns in this province, farmers complained about the kind of support they had been receiving from the DA: low quality planting materials, unhealthy farm animals, and undelivered farm equipment. Farmers say that if they get DA assistance at all, it is usually too little too late, or as in Mang Jaime's case, it brings more harm than good.

At the root of these problems, both former and current DA officials say, is an agriculture bureaucracy that is mired in what DA consultant and once DA undersecretary for policy and planning V. Bruce Tolentino calls a culture of "corruption and waste."

Analysts say that this culture is partly responsible for the lackadaisical performance of Philippine agriculture, which has been growing at an average of one to 1.7 percent from 1980 to 1997, compared to 2.8 to 5.9 percent in other Asian countries.

Agriculture and food security are supposed to be the centerpiece of the Estrada government's poverty reduction program.

For 2000, the proposed budget for the agriculture department is a hefty P21 billion, up from P14.9 billion in 1999. But this investigation shows that unless the prevailing culture in the DA is reformed, the delivery of agricultural services will remain problematic, and a big chunk of the funds set aside for raising rural productivity will end up wasted or stolen.

Pattern of Graft

Complaints filed at the DA Resident Ombudsman's office and reports submitted to the Commission on Audit (COA) and the Office of the Ombudsman as well as interviews with agriculture analysts, farmers in Sultan Kudarat, and regional and national DA officials, attest to a pattern of graft, corruption and inefficiency in the DA that has resulted in the misuse or diversion of funds intended to provide support for farmers in the form of planting materials, machinery and breeding animals.

In the 1970s, under the tenure of Secretary Arturo Tanco, implementation of DA programs was devolved to Regional Field Units (RFU), in an effort to make delivery of services more efficient and responsive to local needs.

Every year, the DA allots big sums to subsidize the production costs of farmers. Depending on the program of the current DA secretary, these subsidies come in the form of either dole-outs or soft loans. For these, RFUs get funds from a nationwide productivity program such as "Makamasa" or "Gintong Ani" on top of their annual allocations from the central office. RFUs also have the power to decide how the money is going to be used and when it will be released.

The theory is that RFUs know the situation on the ground, and can implement programs as they see fit, without having to go through the DA bureaucracy. Farmers' lives are dependent on weather patterns and delays in the delivery of farm inputs can have disastrous consequences.

But Tolentino and other DA officials say that the discretion given to RFUs has only made them notorious for graft and inefficiency. Because the DA bureaucracy is "weak, fragmented and uncoordinated," Tolentino adds, there is no effective monitoring of regional units.

"There's a huge amount of waste," he says. "For example, December *na*, people in the RFUs are worried *hindi ko pa nagastos ang pera ko* (we haven't spent our funds). So they'll do all kinds of weird things just to close the books by December. They'll commit money to half-finished projects, or half-thought projects, or weird and crazy ideas."

Based on complaints and cases filed against DA employees, the most common method used by corrupt officials is to divert funds meant for farm inputs into buying costly and worthless items. In auditing parlance, this is known as "technical malversation."

> **The most common method used by corrupt officials is to divert funds meant for farm inputs into buying costly and worthless items.**

This was the case in the DA's Regional Field Unit in lahar-ravaged Central Luzon, where P1.5 million meant to buy corn for distribution to farmers was used to buy 4,000 document keepers instead. The DA legal division has found that these document keepers were overpriced by 50 percent; no public bidding was held to buy them; and the supplier delivered only 70 percent of the contract he had been paid for.

Another method is to rig the bidding process. The DA central office has required that procurements must go through public biddings to ensure the government of quality purchases at the cheapest prices. Suppliers are also required to post a bond prior to taking part in the bidding to ensure that they will not renege on their commitments.

Bending the Rules

But RFUs and other DA bureaus and agencies are given leeway to bend the rules. As a result, they have managed to do away with bids in favor of negotiated purchases from favored suppliers. Or, even if public biddings take place, officials allegedly maneuver behind-the-scenes to ensure that certain suppliers bag coveted contracts.

For example, from 1990 to 1992, the DA Central Office used P100 million meant to buy fertilizers for the Rice Production Enhancement Program and to fund land reform-related projects to print information manuals instead. In a report, the DA Resident Auditor said these transactions were "not only highly anomalous but tainted with fraud, collusion and deceit." He said that the manuals were contracted without public bidding; they were three times more expensive than they should be; and there was no immediate need for them.

At the RFUs, anomalies related to rigged bids have resulted in substandard and overpriced farm inputs or worse, "ghost" deliveries of much-needed seeds or fertilizers. Corrupt DA officials look the other way because they get "commissions" ranging from 10 to 50 percent of the total contract, DA officials and employees allege.

This was apparent in the Cordillera Administrative Region (CAR), where the private suppliers themselves confessed that they were compelled to fork out grease money so they can get contracts from the RFUs.

In an affidavit, Martina Yodong, owner of the Salidummay Construction and Merchandise, alleged that "on several occasions, we have to beg for the mercy (of the CAR regional finance chief Beatrice Odsey) for the release of POs (purchase orders), which she withholds ... and our papers are only released when she is promised a certain amount."

Corrupt practices continue because of the collusion among the highest officials of regional units.

Yodong said that Odsey demanded from her P30,000 as grease money to facilitate the payment of a contract to construct a fence and supply plastic bags. The same official had already been accused of purchasing farm machinery and banana and pineapple suckers in 1989 and 1990 without public bidding and paying suppliers even before deliveries were made.

Meanwhile, in the Western Visayas, DA Regional Director Arturo Pescayo has been in hot water for a "ghost" contract in which P1.2 million was disbursed to build cemented basketball courts used for drying grain, but which were never constructed.

Corrupt practices continue because of the collusion among the highest officials of regional units, making it difficult for the central office to track down the anomalies, admits former DA Secretary Salvador Escudero III.

An examination of cases filed against

RFUs in Central Luzon, the Cordillera, Central Mindanao, Western Visayas and the central office itself shows the connivance among ranking officials. In all these cases, the evidence showed that the regional finance chief colluded with either or both the regional director and assistant regional director to divert funds and to cover up the tracks of their malfeasance.

To their credit, all DA secretaries have tried to rein in the abuses committed by regional units, but the anomalies persist. In 1997 and 1998, Escudero ordered the investigation of the operations of the DA's field operations in Regions 3 (Central Luzon) and 12 (Central Mindanao). But just a few years before, his predecessor, Carlos Dominguez had already probed the operations of Region 12.

In 1990, then DA secretary Senen Bacani cracked the whip on Cordillera officials. But 10 years later, the problems there seemed to have remained unresolved, prompting the current DA secretary Edgardo Angara to relieve Cordillera regional director Faustino Maslan and suspend finance officer Odsey for their involvement in several anomalous transactions.

The burden of monitoring field operations lies on the DA central office in Quezon City. Usually, such monitoring is based on reports filed by the field units themselves or by people sent to the regions by the central office. This means that complaints from the field rarely get to the DA office in Quezon City.

"The beneficiary is unable to communicate his problems," says Tolentino. "If he wants to file a complaint, he has to go to the municipal, provincial and regional, then national office, where his problem has to go through the assistant secretary, then the undersecretary and eventually to the secretary. By then, a year would already have passed."

Tolentino, who was commissioned by the Asian Development Bank to study the agriculture bureaucracy, instead suggests "multiple layers of monitoring" to include NGOs, cooperatives, local officials and the DA's clientele—farmers, fisherfolk and livestock raisers. He also advocates that other functions currently exercised by the central office, such as policy planning, monitoring and accountability, be taken over by the RFUs in coordination with local governments and communities.

With such reforms, the complaints of farmers like those in Sultan Kudarat might be heeded. "We got nothing from DA, not even seeds," gripes a barangay captain in Isulan, the capital. " The only time we got something from the DA was last year when they gave us rat poison."

She complained that even at the height of El Niño in 1997, farmers in her village did not receive much needed seeds and water pumps, even if the DA had disbursed P1 billion for irrigation facilities, including dams and small irrigation pumps, and P173 million for seeds, fertilizer and pesticides.

Farmers complain that they get no help from DA.

Farmers in nearby Esperanza town said they did get seeds, but only in September 1998. "By then, El Niño was over," says an officer of a local farmers' group. "We just milled the seeds to get rice." She also complained that the goats they received from a DA program in 1998 were all sickly.

Roger Chio, DA's Regional Director for RFU 12, which has jurisdiction over

Sultan Kudarat, says that not all the farmers' needs could be accommodated because of limited funds. There is no assured budget to purchase seeds, for example. He also advises farmers to reject low-quality inputs that they are given.

Measuring Graft

Just how prevalent corruption is at the DA is a matter of debate. In 1998, the Congressional Commission on Agricultural Modernization noted that while the DA has been occasionally figured in high-profile cases of graft, it has not been, as an institution, "the subject of research on graft and corruption, nor has it been singled out as an extremely graft-ridden department." Escudero concedes that corrupt DA officials exist, but asserts that these are a minority.

But last year, Ombudsman Aniano Desierto, citing the number of cases filed from 1996 to 1999, included the DA among the top 10 graft-prone government agencies. During this period, he said, 64 DA-related graft cases were filed at the Ombudsman's office. These cases involved high DA officials, among them a former secretary, undersecretary, and several heads of attached agencies, bureau chiefs and regional DA official.

Similarly, a Sandiganbayan survey of cases filed against 24 agencies from 1990 to 1995 showed 483 cases involving P86. 3 million against DA officials or employees pending at the anti-graft court.

A former undersecretary who was at the DA for more than 10 years believes that while the money lost from "systemic" corruption at the DA may not be as big as that in other government agencies, "the persistence (of corrupt practices) and the (DA officials') inability to act on them, definitely puts the DA in the (graft-prone) league."

Ridiculous Waste

COA has made similar observations. The 1997 COA audit on "Gintong Ani," Escudero's banner program intended to provide farm inputs through soft loans, provided evidence of delayed/lack of funds, non-adherence to implementing guidelines and lack of coordination among the DA central office, the RFUs and local government units.

COA also pointed to several instances when the DA central office, some RFUs, attached agencies and bureaus undermined accounting rules by not submitting necessary papers like disbursement vouchers and contracts and paying ridiculous amounts for obviously overpriced items and services. Such was the case of the RFU in the Eastern Visayas, which COA accused of "wasteful spending of government funds" because it purchased *bangus* fry overpriced by 45 percent.

After Gintong Ani's lackluster performance, the new DA secretary, William Dar, introduced a new farm productivity program called "Agrikulturang MakaMASA." In its 1998 report, the COA reported the same pattern of anomalies that befell previous DA programs: questionable emergency purchases, advance payment for supplies and negotiated procurement instead of public bidding.

COA cited the case of the Western Visayas RFU, which awarded a P10-million contract for livestock purchase without a public bidding. COA also found several instances of "irregular, unnecessary, excessive and extravagant expenditures." The DA central office itself was guilty of this offense, according to COA, when it "unconscionably incurred the amount of P3.9 million for newspaper and magazine advertisements."

The prevalence of corrupt practices is further attested to by complaints filed before the office of the Resident Ombudsman at the DA, where some 20 complaints have been lodged, including a charge that one Mindanao regional director used DA money to build a P100-million house.

Other complaints were filed against a regional director in a Luzon province whose favorite supplier is allegedly notorious for delivering bad seeds. RFU officials in another Luzon province were accused of giving farm loans to local officials instead of to farmers and fisherfolk.

Bienvenida Gruta, who became the DA's Resident Ombudsman last November, says her office has received anonymous complaints against two RFUs in Mindanao, one RFU in Visayas and one Manila-based DA bureau, all of them involving either ghost or incomplete deliveries of farm machinery. Gruta intends to form a task force to probe these complaints.

In Cotabato, Arson and Murder Fail to Silence Whistleblowers

Conclusion

COTABATO CITY—When the Department of Agriculture's (DA) regional office here was torched on May 7,1998, most people dismissed it as just another mishap in a city known for its homegrown mayhem.

But the story behind the fire that razed the 500-square meter plot where the DA office once stood is one that witnesses say involves not just arson, but assorted crimes, including murder, malfeasance and the thievery of public funds.

It is a story that shows that exposing corruption in places like Cotabato may be life threatening because grafters can go to great lengths to protect themselves.

But this story also attests to the courage and persistence of those who expose wrongdoing despite the threats to their lives and careers.

The story begins in 1990 when chemist Marlene Esperat took on the job of chief of the Regional Chemical Analysis Laboratory (RCAL) for the Livestock Division of the DA's Regional Field Unit in Central Mindanao (RFU 12). The laboratory was then located in the Sultan Kudarat municipality of Maguindanao, about eight kilometers from Cotabato City.

"There was a cobra inside the laboratory, which was surrounded by tall grass," Esperat recalled. "There was no water, no air-conditioning and the lab equipment was covered with dust."

For the next six years, Esperat, an energetic woman determined to do her job well, hounded RFU 12 for funds to buy the equipment she needed and to construct a new building to house the laboratory. While following up on her request, she accidentally saw the regional unit's 1991-1992 financial report, which said that there was an annual allocation for her laboratory of P400,000. "But I was receiving only P175,000," she says. "That's when I became suspicious."

In 1996, Esperat took part in the DA's National Chemistry Congress in Iloilo

City. There, she learned that other RFUs had set aside P1 to 2 million each to construct buildings for their laboratories as part of the DA's overall plan to boost livestock research.

Esperat then confronted Assistant Regional Director for Livestock Mustapha Ismael and asked for a new building. But Ismael told her that the funds meant to build the proposed laboratory had been channeled to other livestock-related facilities like breeding stations. Ismael, RFU finance officer Osmeña Montaner and other regional officials promised that by 1997, the laboratory would get all the funds it needed.

But not long after, Esperat came across the RFU 12's official logbook, and discovered that in March 1997, Montaner had disbursed P1 million to a certain Jettie Construction supposedly as payment for the construction of a laboratory building. The fund release was highly irregular since the construction had not even started.

Later, in June 1997, Esperat went to Manila and checked the disbursement report of the RFU 12 at the Department of Budget and Management. She was aghast when she saw records saying that the livestock division of the regional office, to which her laboratory belonged, had already been given P8 million to construct a building for the lab.

Esperat returned to Cotabato City and demanded that Montaner explain why so much money had been released for a nonexistent building. She went on to file formal complaints at the Office of the Ombudsman in Mindanao and at the Legal Division of the DA-Central Office. She accused Montaner of being the mastermind of the various irregularities in the region.

She also accused 16 regional officials and employees, including former regional directors Alejandro Yadao and Bienvenido Almirante and incumbent Assistant Regional Directors Ismael and Abusama Alid, of diverting funds intended to build a laboratory to buy useless and overpriced office supplies. She further charged that these office supplies were just "ghost" purchases.

Arson and Other Threats

When then Agriculture Secretary Salvador Escudero III learned about the case, he ordered an investigation, and in February 1998, revoked Montaner's authority to sign checks for the regional director.

Ismael, the assistant regional director, wrote a letter to Escudero denying all of Esperat's charges. Tagging Esperat as a "very liar woman," Ismael explained that the proposed laboratory building was not constructed in 1997 because Esperat insisted on a new design for a three-story building instead of the original two-story building that she had earlier proposed.

In public, Esperat and Montaner traded barbs. She reported Montaner's supposed anomalies to the local press and told reporters that suppliers who dealt with the DA in the region had confessed to her that "they have to resort to substandard deliveries because RFU 12 officials were demanding 10 to 20-percent commission." These suppliers, Esperat said, were afraid to issue affidavits for fear that Montaner would get back at them.

In an interview, Montaner denied these charges. "No such thing happened in Cotabato. *Kung totoo yan, ba't wala pang nagrereklamo* (If these allegations are true, why has no one come forward to complain)?"

Gutted by Fire

On May 7,1998, amid the heat of these arguments and while Escudero's probe on Esperat's allegations was making progress, the DA's office in Cotabato City was gutted by fire. Because the incident took place just a few days before the presidential elections, the fire was dismissed as just another election-related event.

But one year after the fire, two witnesses, regional property custodian Pembain Sangcopan and security guard Carlo Carulasan, swore in written affidavits that Montaner and his friends burned down the DA office to destroy evidence of their wrongdoing.

Carulasan narrated that on April 30 and May 4,1998, he saw Montaner's driver bring two gallons of gasoline and flammable substances to the accounting office of RFU 12.

Then, at mid-afternoon on May 7, the guard was called to a meeting with Montaner, four other RFU officials and two local policemen. In that meeting, Carulasan said he was told that "something" would happen to him if he did not cooperate with the group.

An hour later, Carulasan said he found out that a fire had started in the DA's accounting room. He ran to the accounting office, hoping to help quell the fire. Instead, he came upon Montaner's driver, who poked a gun at him and ordered him to stay put.

Carulasan said he saw the driver and his companions pour gasoline in the other offices and then turn on electric fans and air conditioners to fan the flames. Three days after, he said, the same group burned other DA offices, including the livestock and personnel division and the auditors/ cashier's office.

As the fires raged, Sangcopan, the property custodian, managed to save some documents from burning. These included the list of P7.9-million worth of office supplies which were supposedly bought by RFU 12 in 1996, but which Sangcopan testified were never delivered.

Both Carulasan and Sangcopan had earlier signed affidavits absolving Montaner of involvement in the arson. But the two witnesses retracted their statements after fleeing Cotabato City and being placed under the protection of the government's Witness Protection Program.

> Two months after he reported the anomaly, Geronimo was gunned down in his own home by two unidentified men.

Charges Dismissed

In November 1999, the Department of Justice (DOJ) recommended the dismissal of the arson charges against Montaner. DOJ Prosecutor Carlos Pormento said that the witnesses were not credible, although he recommended that several of Montaner's associates, including his driver, who was seen by these same witnesses pouring gasoline in the building, be charged with arson.

The DOJ prosecutor also relied on the certification of RFU 12's auditor that audit reports that would attest to Montaner's alleged wrongdoings did not perish in the fire as the DA's audit office was not severely damaged by the blaze.

A recent visit here, however, showed that the entire DA regional office has been reduced to ashes, except for a few bricks and wooden posts. Moreover, despite repeated requests, Montaner could not produce the audit documents that supposedly survived the fire.

Esperat fled Cotabato on May 10,1998, after she learned from Carulasan that Montaner planned to have her killed.

She took the murder plot seriously, learning from the experience of Estelita Jardino, assistant chief accountant at the Agriculture Training Institute (ATI), an attached agency of the DA. Jardino, who has one blind eye and partly deaf ears, alleges she was the victim of Montaner's failed murder attempt in 1982.

At that time, Jardino was RFU 12's accountant and was imposing strict accounting and auditing rules on Montaner, then the regional budget officer. She became suspicious that anomalies were taking place after she had visited the Central Mindanao Integrated Agricultural Research Center (CMIARC) in Kidapawan, North Cotabato, and learned it didn't receive any planting materials even if the funds for these materials had been disbursed.

According to Jardino, the DA's suppliers told her that they were forced to deliver substandard farm inputs or not to deliver anything at all because Montaner was demanding commissions ranging from 20 to 50 percent. But neither the suppliers nor the CMIARC officials were willing to issue affidavits for fear of Montaner.

Montaner was demanding commissions ranging from 20 to 50 percent.

As the months passed, Jardino said Montaner was becoming increasingly upset with her for demanding proper documentation for releasing funds. Jardino said that she also had to brush off Montaner's earlier attempts to bribe her. When he realized that she could not be bought, Montaner asked her to leave Cotabato City, she testified. She also began getting anonymous threats on the phone and by mail.

In September 1982, Jardino was shot near her left eye while she was at the Bureau of Agricultural Extension compound in Cotabato city. She went into a coma for some time and was bedridden for over two years. In 1985, when she had recovered, she was reinstated and assigned to the ATI's office in Metro Manila.

More Harassment

But still, Montaner did not leave her alone, she said. Jardino claimed she was forced to drop the graft charges and frustrated murder attempt that she filed against Montaner at the DA-Central Office and the National Bureau of Investigation because in August 1998, Montaner threatened to kill her if she refused to do so.

"When I returned to Cotabato City to get my salary, Montaner cornered me," recalled Jardino. "He said, 'Lita, sign this document. It's a statement of desistance. Sign it or you will not get out of Cotabato alive.'" She signed the document and never set her foot in that city again.

Jardino considers herself lucky to be alive. In February 1989, Regional Seed Coordinator Geronimo Provido reported that RFU 12 officials had purchased P291,000 worth of overpriced palay seeds meant for land reform beneficiaries and paid for the products in advance of delivery in December 1988.

Two months after he reported the anomaly, Geronimo was gunned down in his own home by two unidentified men. In November 1989, Provido's widow Victorina asked then Agriculture Secretary Carlos Dominguez to investigate the killing.

In March 1990, the DA's Board of Personnel Inquiry (BOPI) verified Geronimo Provido's report. The BOPI recommended that several regional officials, including Montaner, be slapped with "charges of dishonesty and conduct prejudicial to the best interest of service." But these charges were never filed. The BOPI logbook says that that the case was dropped because no one was pursuing it.

Only 10 years later would more facts about Provido's murder come out. In his July 1999 affidavit, RFU 12 security guard Carulasan alleged that Montaner told him that it was his henchman, Berting Salipada, who killed Provido.

Montaner finds this allegation preposterous. *"Kung totoo yan, bakit wala pang naikakaso sa akin* (If these were true, how come no one has sued me)?" he asked.

But there were findings that attested to anomalies pinned on Montaner. In 1987, the Commission on Audit (COA) reported that for 1985 and the first semester of 1986, several financial transactions of RFU 12 were riddled with irregularities. These included disbursements made to CMIARC which were either not received or remained unaccounted for or else were used for purposes other that for which they were intended.

While then COA Chairperson Eufemio Domingo recommended to the DA to further investigate these irregularities, the case never prospered because no one filed charges. Montaner, however, denied that he had anything to do with the irregularities discovered by COA.

Escudero, who had ordered a probe of RFU 12, says that Montaner has a lot of explaining to do, but insists that the anomalies in RFU 12 are isolated cases.

But an examination of cases filed against other RFUs shows that the same pattern of anomalies takes place in other regions. The only difference is that in other areas, there is none of the macabre drama that has taken place in Central Mindanao.

The Water Thieves

BY LUZ RIMBAN

First published in *Manila Standard*, *BusinessWorld*, and *Freeman Daily*,
March 6-7, 2000

Unlike the other stories in this section, this report examines corruption in two private companies rather than in a government agency. The corruption that takes place in these firms abets the pilferage of water by big companies and housing estates that have installed illegal water connections with the connivance of former employees of the government-run Manila Waterworks and Sewerage System (MWSS), which was privatized in 1997.

This article shows how Metro Manila's two water concessionaires are suffering from the legacy of corruption bequeathed to them by the MWSS. From court records and interviews with the concessionaires, the author found the companies suspected of water pilferage. She also traced the layers of collusion—between MWSS employees and big firms, between local governments and water pilferers—that account for the large-scale theft of Metro Manila's water.

This series shows the impact such thievery has on small consumers: they not only have to pay more for their water but also risk their water supply being contaminated by pilferers who pierce water pipes to put up illegal connections.

Big Companies Steal Water

First of Two Parts

MOST people think that the biggest water thieves are squatter communities often pictured in broadcast and newspaper reports as stealing water through illegal connections.

They are not. The biggest water pilferers are large commercial, industrial and residential users that consume huge volumes of water daily, among them some big corporations, malls, hotels, motels, condominium owners, and real estate developers.

A culture of corruption in what used to be Metro Manila's sole water utility firm—the Metropolitan Waterworks and Sewerage System (MWSS)— abetted this big-time water thievery. Corruption in local bureaucracies condoned it.

Two-and-a-half years since the privatization of the MWSS—the largest water privatization project in the world—this very culture of corruption is preventing the two new water concessionaires, Maynilad Water Service and Manila Water Company, from solving the problem.

Among the big corporations where Maynilad has found illegal water connections are Coca-Cola Bottling Company, Unilever Philippines, and Merville Park Subdivision in Parañaque. Manila Water's records yield such names as Loyola Grand Villas and the San Juan Slaughterhouse.

Maynilad and Manila Water, and before them the MWSS, have been losing billions of pesos each year to these big water pilferers. Coca-Cola's arrears arising from a discovered illegal connection believed to have been installed in its Pandacan bottling facility in 1984 amounted to P27 million. Unilever's unpaid accounts were assessed at P19 million, Merville Park at P18 million.

Unilever and Coca-Cola admit to the discovery, near or within their premises, of illegal connections. But officials deny their corporations used illegally drawn water. These connections, they say, have either been plugged long before their time or were never in use. Still, Republic Act 8041 states that the existence of illegal connections constitutes prima facie evidence of water pilferage. The cases are being settled amicably.

Manila Water has so far filed cases against four customers for violation of Republic Act 8041—which penalizes water pilferage—one of them the San Juan Slaughterhouse whose arrears are estimated at P3 million.

Documents also show a dispute between the concessionaire and V.V. Soliven, developer of Loyola Grand Villas. Water had to be cut off from portions of the exclusive village after V.V. Soliven failed to pay debts of over P600,000 arising from an illegal connection.

Small Customers Bear the Brunt

But it is not only the two concessionaires who lose out from water pilferage. Small, law-abiding water customers also bear the brunt of water theft. Thieves puncture water lines that result in the contamination of the water supply.

Water pressure drops in places where thieves divert water supply for their own use. Among these thieves are water sellers, some of whom go as far as turning off water valves that result in no-water situations in some areas. Consequently, ordinary consumers are forced to buy water from these water sellers for a price 13 times higher than the amount that both concessionaires charge.

And because the concessionaires are losing revenue, they would have to seek price adjustments to recover losses, resulting in ordinary consumers paying the price for other users' misdeeds.

"We must change the perception that it is the poor people who do this (steal water)," says Yves Bories, a French water utilities expert and vice-chairman of Maynilad's management committee.

Unfortunately, Maynilad and Manila Water have themselves to blame for such a perception. Most of their publicized raids against water thieves have been directed at squatter communities in Metro Manila, which have been easy targets of the two concessionaires' campaign against water theft.

True, the number of illegal connections in these communities is high, but the total volume of water they steal is low. It is the thieves among the big entities—those that illegally siphon off huge volumes of water from both concessionaires—which are actually causing them enormous losses.

The registered big water users account for a huge chunk of the concessionaires' incomes. They are those classified as Large Meter Accounts. These include condominiums and subdivisions that consume huge volumes of water and are billed rates for residential users. Then there are industrial and commercial customers, which are charged higher rates.

Maynilad's Large Meter Accounts comprise only 0.5 percent of its customer base, while its industrial and commercial customers make up around six percent of its total of nearly 500,000 customers. Combined, they contribute some 32 percent to the company's income.

At Manila Water, the combined Large Meter Accounts and industrial and commercial users are likewise estimated to be less than 10 percent of its 300,000 or so customers, but they contribute 40 percent of the company's collections.

The Full Force of the Law

Not surprisingly, both Maynilad and Manila Water have hesitated to use the full force of R.A. 8041 against those among their big customers who violate it. "They are good customers and we are not here to prosecute them but to settle with them," said Maynilad corporate communications director Bertrand Pesayco. In recent months, spiraling losses have forced the firm to take a more aggressive stance against water thieves.

"We discourage the filing of cases," says Manila Water staff lawyer Jovencio Fulgeras. The objective, he says, is not to send big water thieves to jail but to make them pay for what they stole.

> The bureaucratic requirements for water service connections have left many potential water customers with no other recourse but illegal connections.

When Manila Water, a consortium operated by Ayala Corporation and British-American International Water Ltd, won the concession to take over Metro Manila's east zone in August 1997, it discovered 11,000 illegal connections in its service area. But thousands more were surfacing every quarter.

Maynilad, owned jointly by Benpres Holdings and the French Suez Lyonnaise des Eaux, disconnected 700 large and small illegal connections in December 1999 alone. It is harder hit by the problem. Maynilad handles the west zone, the bigger and older section of MWSS's water service area.

It is in the west zone where the MWSS, first known as Carriedo Waterworks, then the National Water and Sewerage Authority (NAWASA), began operations 120 years ago. An aging pipe network and a huge customer population have contributed to higher incidences of thefts and leakage.

"There are a lot of illegal connections turning up everyday. The more you look, the more you find," Bories reveals.

But in search of the roots of this problem, the water concessionaires will have to point the finger at themselves. Most of the employees of both Maynilad and Manila Water are former personnel of the MWSS, a government corporation riddled with corruption, where it was common knowledge that illegal connections could be had for a price and officials could be bribed to ignore such offenses.

Corruption in the Bureaucracy

The other side of the problem is corruption in the bureaucracy whose cooperation is essential in providing water service connections to customers, and in rehabilitative measures such as repairs of leaks and detection of illegal connections which are mostly found underground.

Excavation permits issued from barangay level up to local government units, traffic enforcement units and even the Department of Public Works and Highways are necessary before any digging—whether for water service connection, detection of illegal connections or leak repair—can be done.

Florencio Cayco, executive assistant to Maynilad president Rafael Alunan says excavation permits are easy to get if one pays or bribes his way through. The bribe amount varies depending on the type of road to be excavated—whether barangay roads, municipal roads or national roads.

If the excavation is to be done on busy streets, a permit has to be secured from traffic enforcement offices. Even in small barangay roads, which Cayco says present the least problems, barangay officials ask for "donations" before allowing engineers to excavate.

In some cities and municipalities, the processing of excavation permits are centralized in the mayor's office, contributing to long delays which force potential water customers to resort to quick, but illegal, water connections.

"In Makati," wrote Cristina David and Arlene Inocencio in a paper for the Philippine Institute for Development Studies in 1996, "it is common knowledge that such connections can be obtained for cost of about P25,000 in contrast to P2,300 for a legal connection."

Admittedly, the bureaucratic requirements for water service connections have left many potential water customers with no other recourse but illegal connections. Apart from the excavation permit for which an applicant must shoulder a fee of as much as P4,000, the applicant must also present proof that he or she owns the property where the connection is to be made.

Before the MWSS privatization, impoverished families who squatted on other people's properties were automatically disqualified from MWSS service. As a result, the most number of illegal connections is found in squatter communities.

With privatization came remedies that included changes in the requirements for water service connections. Squatter families now need only to present barangay clearances to secure legal water connections. Both Maynilad and Manila Water have also provided public faucets to contain water theft in blighted communities.

"Whilst the highest number of illegal connections are within depressed areas, we are having good success in identifying these through our Barangay Sweep Program. We have given depressed communities an opportunity to register as new connections and pay their arrears since August 1997," says Manila Water corporate communications chief Joel Lacsamana.

Identifying illegal connections in these depressed communities has been easy. But doing so among the big water users has been a perennial problem. "*Malalaking kumpanya yan* so basically, *mayroon yang paraan maitago, kasi nga malaki. At hindi mo basta-basta mapapasok. Alangan naman papasukin ka alam nilang nagnanakaw sila ng tubig* (They are big companies so they have ways of hiding it. And you cannot just go in. They wouldn't let you in because they know they are stealing water)," says former MWSS administrator Angel Lazaro III, who presided over the MWSS for two years at the time the government was preparing to privatize the water utility.

"We are in a difficult position," says Nestor Gabot, an engineer with the now-decentralized Task Force on Illegal Connections at Manila Water. Thieves, he says, will always find ways to outwit the water concessionaires, who often learn of illegal connections through tips either from within the concessionaire or the erring establishment. But by the time his group obtains the necessary permits, Gabot laments, the suspected water thieves would have done away with the evidence.

Engineers investigating illegal connections and leaks verify tips with sonar or sound devices meant to detect such underground problems. Cayco says it is difficult to use these devices during the day when traffic and noise are heavy. They usually wait till late evening or early morning when there is minimal traffic on the road. This contributes to delays that allow suspects time to dispose of evidence.

Water Thieves Operate with Impunity

Conclusion

ENGINEERS of Metro Manila's water concessionaires say that investigating water pilferage is a long drawn-out, tedious and dangerous undertaking often hounded by political pressure.

There is also no guarantee of success: in fact few of the water thieves are nailed in the end. Although the law states that the mere existence of illegal connections constitutes prima facie evidence, the courts usually demand stronger proof.

"Kailangang makitang sila ang nagkabit (We have to prove that it is they who installed it)," says Manila Water staff lawyer Jovencio

Fulgeras. And because the water concessionaires are unable to prove beyond reasonable doubt that the suspected water customer installed the illegal connection, anti-pilferage cases are usually dismissed.

The impossibility of finding the actual culprits also affects the settlement of cases. Where water concessionaires manage to dig up illegal connections, water users would normally reason out that the connection happened before their time, or that the management of erring establishments was not aware of the offense.

This makes it even more difficult for water concessionaires to settle arrears resulting from pilferage. Still, says Florencio Cayco, executive assistant to Maynilad president Rafael Alunan, the company's priority remains making the pilferers pay for the water they consumed and avoiding lengthy legal disputes.

Among those who have shown a willingness to settle is Unilever Philippines, a top producer of soap and shampoo, whose assessed arrears from an illegal connection amounts to P19 million.

Unilever's general manager for corporate development Chito Macapagal admits an illegal connection was unearthed inside the company premises. It was likely, he said, that the connection was installed long ago before the present management took over what used to be the Philippine Refining Company. Investigations showed that the connection led to a water line that had been plugged and remained unused for years.

Macapagal maintains that it would be unfair to penalize the present management of Unilever for an offense it did not commit. "We are a responsible company and it was we who immediately sought out Maynilad to resolve this issue," Macapagal says. Still, he concedes that Maynilad is only trying to enforce the law, and Unilever is willing to settle, but for much less than it is being billed.

Coca-Cola, Too

Down the road from the Unilever factory in Pandacan, Manila is Coca-Cola Bottling Company, another establishment where Maynilad has unearthed an illegal connection. The firm was initially billed P 27 million for drawing water illegally since 1984. The basis for the assumption is that the road over the underground connection was paved that year, although the connection may have been there earlier.

Coca-Cola Bottling Company external relations manager Arnie Dy admits an illegal connection was found, but doubts whether it was used at all. "I can't say categorically that it was not used at all but all I can say is that management will never tolerate an illegal practice like that just to earn a little more profit," Dy says. The company's Manila production plant was closed down last year.

Coca-Cola settled for P 2 million under an agreement that made no mention of illegal connections, and classified the payment as "unpaid water consumption." The agreement also called for Maynilad to assist Coca-Cola in checking wastage and correcting systems faults.

Not all suspected water pilferers though would take to settling the dispute amicably. Manila Water engineer Nestor Gabot narrates the case of an establishment where a bypass connection was discovered.

> Influential protectors can sometimes shield big water pilferers.

A bypass is a water service connection to a main pipe bypassing the water meter.

When a team of Manila Water engineers raided the firm, the owner offered them a bribe of P100,000 rather than settle his arrears, which were estimated to have reached P3 million. The Manila Water team rejected the offer, Gabot says, and asked him to settle his obligations. Despite several notices and demand letters, the owner refused to pay and instead filed a temporary restraining order in court to stop Manila Water's closure of his water supply.

Influential protectors can sometimes shield big water pilferers. Former Manila Waterworks and Sewerage System (MWSS) Administrator Angel Lazaro III says he would get calls from powerful people interceding when big water thieves were caught. "I would just say yes, but then go ahead with the investigations," says Lazaro. "*Meron talaga.* Yes *na lang ako ng* yes. *Pero pagka alam nilang may nag-aalaga, natatakot rin ang mga tao ko* (There are really people who intercede. I just say yes. But once they know a suspected water pilferer has a protector, my people get scared.)."

The practice continues to this day. Cayco says calls from protectors of big water thieves are passed on to Maynilad president Alunan. Sometimes the requests come from people whose power and influence are no match even for Alunan. These cases are passed on to Maynilad's owners, the Lopez family.

Armed and Dangerous

Big water thieves are not only rich and influential, they are often armed and dangerous. Former MWSS employees and executives interviewed for this article, including Lazaro, say it is not uncommon for water utility personnel investigating pilferage by big firms to be threatened by the companies' armed guards.

Both concessionaires admit that water theft would not take place without the connivance of corrupt contractors and MWSS insiders. But the best-kept illegal connections are those made by MWSS personnel themselves.

Common knowledge within both Maynilad and Manila Water is the practice by former MWSS employees of accepting bribes to install illegal connections. Common knowledge too is the so-called "*alaga* system" where water thieves give corrupt officials and employees regular bribe money to ignore their offenses. Under the "*alaga* system," it is the bribe-taker who is usually directly involved in installing the illegal connection.

Lazaro believes only a small fraction of MWSS employees was involved in water theft during his time. Still, the corruption may have reached management levels. A former MWSS engineer now connected with Manila Water says several cases of water theft ended up nowhere after being turned over to the legal department of MWSS.

Another former MWSS employee recalls that several years ago, an anti-pilferage team pounced on an apartment building with illegal connections, only to be told after they made their report to back off from the case. The row of apartment buildings, he said, belonged to the then MWSS administrator.

The practice goes all the way down. A former MWSS employee says personnel laying pipes that pass through depressed communities would offer to install illegal connections, charging anywhere from P10 to P12,000 for a cluster of four to five homes.

When MWSS was privatized in August

1997, the concession agreement called for the two concessionaires to absorb the water utility's employees who numbered some 5,000 that time. Most went to Maynilad, which covers a bigger concession area.

Because the company continues to suffer huge losses from water pilferage and leaks, these former MWSS employees have been under suspicion and have complained of a virtual witch-hunt.

Non-Revenue Water

Maynilad's problem is that it has not been able to bring down its rate of non-revenue water or NRW—the amount of water produced and unbilled—which now stands at a high 67 percent. Manila Water's NRW, on the other hand, is almost half of Maynilad's at 39 percent. Under the concession agreement, the water concessionaires are supposed to bring NRW down to 25 percent in 10 years.

At 67 percent, this means Maynilad loses two-third of its revenue and earns only 33 percent. A high NRW is an indication of inefficiency in water distribution, one of the reasons the MWSS was privatized in the first place. The Philippines' NRW remains one of the highest in Asia. Among the lowest is Singapore, with an NRW rate of 20 percent.

At the height of the El Niño problem in the summer of 1998, both concessionaire's NRW dropped considerably but it was an artificial reduction caused by the low water supply. When the water supply is low, there is little water to steal or lose to leaks, hence the low NRW.

NRW is water lost to both theft and leakage. But it is difficult to say exactly how much of the NRW is lost to theft and how much to leaks. There are those who say theft predominates, otherwise all the water gushing out from leaks would have flooded Metro Manila. The contrary view is that more water is lost to leaks since most of the MWSS pipelines are old, brittle and prone to punctures.

This debate has been raging within Maynilad. On the one hand are engineers and other employees who say that most of the non-revenue water is lost to leaks. Management, on the other hand, has maintained that the greater volume is lost to theft.

Bienvenido Gaurino, former chief of the anti-NRW Task Force of the Maynilad Water Service, Inc, says it has never been established which of the two is the bigger determinant of NRW. "That remains one of the biggest debates within Maynilad," says Gaurino, who admits he espoused the view that leaks, more than theft, comprise the bigger percentage of NRW.

> Maynilad officials promise to prosecute at least one big fish among water thieves to show the rest they mean business.

Sadly, he says, management has come to suspect those like Gaurino, with opposing views, of involvement in illegal activities. A number of middle-level employees have been removed from previously sensitive assignments, demoted or were otherwise forced to retire, himself included, Gaurino laments. Talk has it that more of them will be retired or fired.

Lazaro takes this view: "*Kung alam mo kung gaano karami ang ninanakaw ibig sabihin puwede mong pigilin. Kaya di mo mapigil kasi di mo alam kung saan* (If you know how much water is being stolen that means you can prevent it. But you can't because you don't know where it is). So by definition, pilferage, you don't know."

But Yves Bories, vice-chairman of Maynilad's management committee, says it would not matter which of the two—leaks or theft—is the more rampant problem. "Whatever the figures, the action plan is still the same. You translate one kind of loss to another. You repair leaks, then there is more water to steal. All causes are linked together," he insists.

Michel Versmerch, NRW specialist at Maynilad, points out that impunity, the absence of punishment, is what makes water thieves commit the crimes. "When there is impunity, it could spread out all over." Maynilad officials promise to prosecute at least one big fish among water thieves to show the rest they mean business.

A parallel move is being undertaken against corrupt Maynilad employees. At least five employees have been dismissed from the service, although not all cases were related to complicity in water theft.

Both Maynilad and Manila Water are also upgrading their systems to detect water theft without having to go through the process of securing excavation permits from concerned government agencies. One of these measures is the replacement of water meters.

Both concessionaires are also strengthening the territorial units which directly oversee water distribution. The concessionaires have divided their zones into business areas to closely monitor the inflow and distribution of water. Technical measures have been instituted to allow concessionaires to compare actual consumption with the users' requirements, especially those using huge volumes of water.

The Presidency and Congress

Corruption at the highest reaches of government, which usually involves the abuse of the prerogatives of high office, is not easy to document. In bureaucratic corruption, where procedures and functions are clearly defined, it is relatively easy to find a paper trail to show lapses in procedure and the overstepping of the bounds of an official's powers. Not so with the presidency and Congress.

As head of state, the president is given vast powers and has discretion over appointments, contracts and policy. He or she also has the run of the entire bureaucracy. Congress has the power to make laws, to define how government money is going to be spent, and also to conduct investigations that make officials in other branches of government quake in their *barongs*. The stories in this section show that such tremendous powers are so easily abused, and that despite documentary proof that such abuse has taken place, it is very difficult to make high officials accountable for their actions or their lapses.

The investigative techniques used for the reports in this section vary widely. The first article in this section, which examines the proprietary and family interests of members of the House of Representatives, was put together by constructing a computer database. This report was based almost exclusively on routinely available public records, primarily the statements of assets of congressmen.

From the database, it was fairly easy to show that members of the House were in thorny conflict-of-interest situations as they often authored bills that would benefit their or their family's business and other interests.

The other reports used techniques outlined in the previous section: looking at bidding rules and procedures, studying bid documents, corporate records and contracts, and obtaining audit reports. The series on the misuse of hundreds of millions of public funds to build the Centennial Exposition employed these methods. So did the report on the Amari land scam.

But investigating corruption in high places invariably involves a political—not just a financial—dimension. The exposés on Amari and the Centennial Exposition, for example, linked the large-scale diversion of funds to the need by the ruling party of the day to raise money for elections. In the case of Amari, hundreds of millions of pesos were funneled to officials from commissions from the sale of government property just before the 1995 local elections. To fund its 1998 presidential campaign, the Lakas party diverted money intended to build the Centennial Expo and solicited contributions from the project's contractors.

In both these cases, high-profile congressional investigations were undertaken. Documents from congressional inquiries provided the baseline information for journalists who later undertook more far-reaching investigations. They discovered that the congressional probes fell short of linking the misuse of public funds that they discovered to high officials of the executive and legislative branches, and to the need by political parties to build up a war chest for elections.

Congress can subpoena records and compel witnesses to testify in its inquiries, that is why congressional investigations can uncover information that journalists may have difficulty obtaining. On the other hand, journalists have the edge because they can talk to witnesses more privately, without the glare of publicity, and without fear of exposure. Moreover, journalists, unlike politicians, are not bound by a political agenda or by party loyalties.

Other documents that have proved useful were court records, particularly in the case of the preferential loans supposedly obtained by former House Speaker Jose de Venecia with the help of Ferdinand Marcos. De Venecia faced several lawsuits for the nonpayment of these loans as well as probes by various government bodies and government banks that provided loans or loan guarantees to his company. There was therefore a long trail of paper that attested to his failure to pay for loans obtained at the behest of Marcos.

The de Venecia story highlights the links between business and politics in the Philippines. When investigating political corruption, it is the ties that bind people that reporters have tried to uncover. The de Venecia loan investigation looked into the history of the relationship between the former Speaker and Marcos. The probe of the contract for the rehabilitation of the North Luzon Expressway examined the political connections of the two firms that were bidding for the contract and their use of the political arena—congressional investigations, bribery of congressmen, and the media—to advance their business interests.

Thus, although documents were valuable in investigating corruption in high office, interviews with knowledgeable people, frequently insiders of an organization, provided invaluable information the reporters needed to establish telling linkages. In fact, the investigation on presidential paramour Rosemarie Arenas relied almost exclusively on interviews to assess what influence she wielded over the appointments and policies of the Ramos government.

Stories on the influence-peddling by powerful individuals who are not accountable because they do hold official posts must invariably rely on interviews. This was the case with the Arenas story, for which over 50 people were interviewed, and with the article on President Joseph Estrada's "midnight Cabinet." The challenge for reporters is to get sources to talk and afterward, to check and counter-check the information they have been given. Documents are sometimes useful for counter-checking information, but when these are not available, reporters have no choice but to interview other sources who have first-hand knowledge of what they are investigating. Sometimes journalists reach a dead end, and judicious judgment is required to decide whether they have enough substantiated information to go through with a story.

Those who report on political corruption are frequently beset with ethical and other dilemmas. One of these is the use of unnamed sources, an issue that is discussed in greater detail in the introduction to "The President's Paramour." Another is the potential for an exposé to be used by the rivals of the officials whose malfeasance reporters were able to uncover.

Writing about political corruption can be emotionally satisfying to reporters who are determined to nail crooks in high office. These stories generally also get much more publicity and prominent play on newspapers than stories of bureaucratic corruption. They can also have an impact. The Amari exposé, for example, raised doubts about de Venecia's character and questions about the land scam hounded his presidential campaign.

But writing about corruption in high places can also be like treading on a minefield. Some of the writers of these stories have been attacked either by the officials they exposed or by fellow journalists. Their motives and methods were questioned, even their integrity was opened to public scrutiny. Reporters can protect themselves by making sure they get their facts right and can defend the journalistic methods they have employed to write a story, by not being beholden to their sources in any way, and by behaving in a manner in which they cannot be reproached for their partisanship or lack of integrity.

A House for the Elite

BY ERIC GUTIERREZ

First published in *Malaya, Manila Times, Business World,* and *Manila Standard,* August 9-11, 1993; and *Pacific Daily News,* September 30-October 2, 1993

This three-part series on the business interests and family ties that influence legislation in the House of Representatives marked the first time that the PCIJ built its own computer database to analyze data gathered from public records. Political researcher Eric Gutierrez worked many months on this series, a collaboration between the PCIJ and the Institute for Popular Democracy, which was expanded and published in book form in 1994 as *The Ties that Bind: A Guide to Family, Business and other Interests in the Ninth House of Representatives.*

Using Lotus software, Gutierrez put together in a grid information on congressmen that was available from public documents, particularly legislators' statements of assets, their official resumés and property (land, corporate, etc.) records. He used this grid to match congressmen's proprietary interests with the kind of bills they authored and their committee memberships. What he found was a House marked by conflicts-of-interest, where legislators proposed bills that would benefit their businesses. Put together and analyzed, the data on congressmen's business interests also yielded new information on the changing class composition of Congress, away from landowners to entrepreneurs and professionals.

Digging into the family backgrounds of each member of the House and then putting the information together in a database, Gutierrez also found that an astonishing number of congressmen—two in every three—belonged to political families that had been in public office for over two decades. Overall, from Gutierrez's research, the portrait that emerges is that of a House of Representatives drawn from an elite that has wealth, education and political pedigree.

This series won for Gutierrez first place in the 1993 Jaime V. Ongpin Awards for investigative journalism.

Congressmen Legislate for Themselves

First of Three Parts

SEVERAL members of the House of Representatives have filed bills that could benefit their business enterprises, but many have avoided sanctions because of legal loopholes in the conflict-of-interest rule.

Republic Act 6713, known as the Code of Conduct and Ethical Standards for Public Officials and Employees, states that a conflict of interest occurs when "an official is a substantial stockholder, director or officer of a corporation; owner or substantial shareholder in a business; or a partner in a partnership."

Many representatives are stockholders of firms or owners of business enterprises. Several of them have filed bills that could benefit their interests. But the Code does not say what legislators should do in case of a potential conflict of interest.

The House ethics committee chairman, Rep. Mariano Yulo, asserts that no conflicts of interest occur if the bills benefit not only the congressmen but their constituents as well.

Representatives who file bills on behalf of particular sectors or industries do not violate the conflict-of-interest rule—even if they may personally profit from those bills—because they represent certain constituencies, he says.

But former Senator Rene Saguisag, once chairman of the Senate ethics committee, opts for a stricter interpretation of the law. "My own strict view is that if members of Congress engage in a particular business, they should at least inform the House," he says. "Besides, should they be advocates of measures that benefit themselves?"

These representatives may also have violated Section 12, Article VI of the Constitution that requires members of Congress "to notify the House concerned of a potential conflict of interest that may arise from the filing of a proposed legislation of which they are authors."

Whose Benefit?

The following are some members of Congress in potential conflict-of-interest situations. They have filed bills that would benefit both their businesses as well as certain constituencies they represent.

Congressional records show that none of them have notified the House of such possible conflicts, in apparent disregard of the Constitution.

- Twenty-seven Mindanao representatives led by Davao City Rep. Manuel Garcia, all landowners, filed House Bill 1967 providing for the suspension of agrarian reform in Mindanao until the year 2020.

- Ilocos Sur Rep. Eric Singson filed House Bill 5074 which allows locally made cigarettes with foreign brand names to be exported and also provides tax rebates for tobacco manufacturers and traders. Singson's wife, Candon Mayor Grace Singson, runs a tobacco trading and hauling business.
- Zamboanga City Rep. Ma. Clara Lobregat authored House Bill 554 which orders the soap and detergent industry to shift to 100 percent-use of coconut-based chemicals. The Zamboanga representative is chairperson of the Lobregat Family Milling Corp. and was once on the board of seven coconut oil mills.
- Sugar planter Romeo Guanzon of Negros Occidental filed House Bill 628 which bans the importation of cheap foreign sugar, except in an actual shortage, in which case only sugarcane planters and millers will be authorized to import.
- Davao del Sur Rep. Benjamin Bautista filed House Bill 1507 which excludes "commercial livestock, poultry, swine-raising, aquaculture including saltbeds, fishponds and prawn ponds" from the coverage of the agrarian reform law. Rep. Bautista operates a fishpond in his province.

Loopholes in the Law

These representatives say that their constituencies, not their personal coffers, will gain from these proposed measures. Lobregat adds that the bill she proposed is primarily intended to phase out the use of ecologically harmful non-biodegradable chemicals in soap-making.

Members of Congress have raised conflict-of-interest issues when examining presidential appointees to the executive branch, particularly to the Cabinet.

Executive officials are required to divest themselves of their business holdings to avoid possible conflicts of interest. But there is no such requirement for members of Congress.

The rules of the House of Representatives do not contain any guidelines to enforce the constitutional provision on notifying Congress of a potential conflict of interest.

Neither do these rules have any provisions to ensure that members of the House make a full and accurate disclosure of their assets and liabilities, as mandated in the Constitution.

Congress also seems to ignore the possible ethical problems that may arise when representatives sit on committees whose deliberations may have a direct impact on their business interests.

For example, landowners are members of the agrarian reform committee and bankers sit on the committee on banks and financial institutions.

This is not necessarily bad: It can be argued that bankers may be able to contribute more to discussions on the financial system. Moreover, legislators have been known to vote against their own interests.

But the many and varied business, family and land interests of the members of the House of Representatives pose real and urgent questions about conflicts of interest that Congress has to resolve.

Ethics committee chairman Yulo recognizes the problems posed by these conflicts, but offers no solutions. "We would like people from the outside to recommend measures for the ethics committee," he says.

In his State of the Nation address, President Ramos asked the Ninth Congress to be "the instrument to free and democratize our economy."

But given the many proprietary interests of the majority of the members of the House, Congress is severely constrained as an effective instrument for democratization.

Very few representatives come from non-propertied social sectors; thus, the interests of the lower social strata are seldom articulated and the will of the propertied rich often prevails.

The best example of this were agrarian reform debates in 1987 and 1988 when the landlord majority in the House watered down a bill that provided for large-scale land redistribution.

Cornering Committees

Committee memberships are full of potential conflicts of interest. For example, two of the most vocal spokespersons of landed interest in the House—Negros Occidental Rep. Hortensia Starke and Cebu Rep. Pablo Garcia—sit in the committee on agrarian reform.

That 29-member committee also includes two ranch-owners (Kalinga Apayao Rep. Elias Bulut and Bukidnon Rep. Jose Zubiri); two first-term congressmen with landholdings worth several million pesos (Laguna Rep. Rodolfo Tingzon and Capiz Rep. Vicente Andaya); three fishpond operators (Davao del Sur Rep. Benjamin Bautista, Sr., Antique Rep. Exequiel Javier and Tingzon) and three agribusiness executives—Nueva Ecija Reps. Pacifico Fajardo and Victorio Lorenzo and Bulacan Rep. Angelito Sarmiento.

The committee has received 10 bills that seek to limit the scope of agrarian reform, many of them filed by legislators who own land or operate fishponds.

The committee on agriculture is similarly structured: only six of its 41 members have no interest in agriculture. The committee includes agribusiness entrepreneurs like Lorenzo whose family owns Lorenzo Farms, Inc., one of the biggest agribusiness firms in the country; Zamboanga City Rep. Ma. Clara Lobregat who chairs a coconut oil milling company; and Tarlac Rep. Jose Cojuangco, Jr. whose family owns a sugar refinery.

Similarly, 10 of 21 members of the committee on housing and urban development have interests in real estate firms. These include Muntinlupa Rep. Manuel Villar, known as the dean of Philippine real estate, whose Manuela Corporation is the ninth largest real estate development firm in the country.

Other committee members are Manila Rep. Amado Bagatsing, founder of a real estate and construction business; Malabon Rep. Teresa Aquino-Oreta whose husband's family runs the real estate, insurance and management firm, AM Oreta and Co. Inc.; and Cavite Rep. Renato Dragon, a former realtor and consultant to four realty companies.

In the committee on banks and financial institutions, 19 of 40 members were once or are still presently involved in banking. Reps. Ciriaco Alfelor, Allen Quimpo and Jose Villarosa own stocks in rural banks.

Reps. Rolando Andaya, Lualhati Antonino, Renato Dragon, Felicito Payumo, Ricardo Silverio, Rodolfo Tingzon and Jose Villarosa were directors or executives of commercial banks. Reps. Eric Acuna, Al Francis Bichara and Rafael

Lopez-Vito headed Savings and Loan associations. Several others were stockholders or executives of investment and finance houses.

One of the most sought after committee chairmanships—that of the committee on trade and industry—belongs to Iloilo Rep. Alberto Lopez, scion of the Lopez family which runs one of the biggest business conglomerates in the country.

Ten of the 50-member trade and industry committee are corporate executives or belong to families operating business enterprises. Only 14 members of the committee have no business involvement.

Among the members of this committee are: shipping magnate James Chiongbian; Ramon Durano III, whose family runs a chain of enterprises in Danao, Cebu; Pampanga Rep. Carmelo Lazatin whose companies are involved in construction and real estate; and Negros Occidental Rep. Marcial Punzalan, an agribusiness entrepreneur.

Rich Dominate the House

Second of Three Parts

SOME of the country's biggest landowners and wealthiest businessmen are members of the House of Representatives.

The family of Tarlac Rep. Jose Cojuangco, Jr. runs the 6,000-hectare Hacienda Luisita. Negros Occidental Rep. Hortensia Starke owns sugar and rubber plantations while Rep. Manuel H. Puey has four haciendas in northern Negros Occidental. Laguna Rep. Rodolfo Tingzon declared landholdings worth P140 million.

The most prominent legislators are also business tycoons and industry leaders. These include the likes of shipping magnate James Chiongbian of Saranggani; cousins Rogelio and Angelito Sarmiento who own an agribusiness, logging and construction conglomerate; and Iloilo Rep. Alberto Lopez whose family runs an investment house and broadcasting, agribusiness and public utility companies.

The conflicts of interest in Congress can be traced to the web of interlocking family, business and professional connections that link the members of the House to one another and to other sections of the country's political and economic elite.

Data culled from the statements of assets and liabilities filed by members of the House show that the link between wealth and political power remains strong.

The data show that only 16 representatives are not millionaires. Of these, 13 are white collar workers or self-employed businessmen.

Ninety-eight representatives—nearly half of the total—are well-placed professionals, bankers and executives of large firms.

Slightly less than half—88 representatives—are part of the uppermost social strata: they own major businesses or land more than 100 hectares in size or declared net worth of more than P10 million.

Congress has traditionally been controlled by the wealthy. Such a composition has meant that legislation tended to favor the rich. "You cannot expect Congress to pass bills imposing an affluent consumption tax since in effect they would be taxing themselves," says former Nueva Ecija Rep. Edno Joson.

But while many of today's representatives appear to be as wealthy as their predecessors, the sources of wealth are more diverse.

In 1940, only 10 percent of the members of Congress were entrepreneurs. By 1970, the number had risen to 30 percent.

In the present House of Representatives, 36 percent were full-time business people or corporate executives prior to their election to Congress; 15 percent more were involved in various business concerns even as they held public office.

Landholding is no longer the major source of wealth for most, as it was in earlier legislatures, although 116 of 199 members of the House own agricultural land.

Landholding is no longer the major source of wealth.

The representatives' statements of assets and liabilities show the diversity of their sources of wealth (see table).

Representation in the House has traditionally been denied the poor. None of the elected representatives belong to the lower class. Even the appointed sectoral representatives for the farmers and workers are actually middle-class professionals. Poor people have been denied public office because they do not have the tremendous resources needed to win an election campaign. And, once in office, a representative must meet the demands of his or her constituency for jobs, doleouts, medical services and other forms of patronage.

The business interests of representatives, however, do not always have a direct bearing on their policy preferences. For example, some landowners in Congress favor land reform.

Cagayan Rep. Juan Ponce Enrile, who operate huge logging concessions on Samar island and Agusan del Sur, advocated a total logging ban. But critics say that this change of heart comes at the twilight of the logging industry. Moreover, logging companies comprise only a small portion of Enrile's business empire.

Different motives determine how representatives vote. The most basic are motives based on economic interests. But there are other powerful motives, such as the desire to please Malacañang, as the voting on the debt cap bill showed. That proposal was defeated after the Palace asked the House leadership to kill the bill.

Sometimes, congressmen trade a vote on an issue in exchange for support on another issue, or even to appear before the public as crusading progressives or grandstand before the press, says former Rep. Florencio Abad.

House members may also vote in order to build alliances or bring down political rivals. Such cavalier attitude toward lawmaking is encouraged by the lack of party discipline and insufficient public scrutiny of the legislative process.

The absence of well-organized lobby and interest groups makes it easy for legislators to vote as they please. There appear to be only few instances when House members voted solidly on the basis of their intellectual convictions, observes Rep. Bonifacio Gillego, a leader of Congress' progressive bloc.

Landholding and Agriculture

Nearly two-thirds of House members own agricultural land. Others do not declare any landholdings, but they are shareholders in family-run agribusiness firms. For example, Iloilo Rep. Alberto Lopez owns stocks in at least two family corporations that own vast tracts of land.

Most representatives also own real estate: about a fourth are involved in real estate and realty corporations.

Half of the House—101 representatives—own three or more pieces of land. Fifteen members of Congress own only one or two pieces of real estate but hold controlling interests in enterprises involved in real estate development.

These include Vicente Andaya of Capiz who owns four family-run firms involved in real estate and construction; Manuel B. Villar of Muntinlupa, the acknowledged dean of real estate and controlling stockholder of at least six big real estate companies; Enrile, whose JAKA Group of Companies includes eight firms involved in real estate and construction; and Luz Bakunawa of Masbate whose Hi-Tri Development Corp. was the fifteenth biggest construction company in 1988.

Traders, Bankers and Loggers

A significant number were entrepreneurs who started out as traders of products ranging from agricultural produce to industrial machinery. Others operate retail outlets.

At least 45 representatives once ran or are currently involved in trading companies. Many of these companies are also part of larger business conglomerates.

Reps. Lualhati Antonino, Jose Cojuangco, Jr., Samuel Dangwa, Rodolfo del Rosario, Ramon Durano III, Juan Ponce Enrile, Rafael Lazatin, Edward Matti, Dominador Nazareno, Ricardo Silverio and Danilo Suarez are stockholders of trading firms which are part of a chain of companies owned or controlled by their families. Some of these trading firms market the products of their sister companies.

Many representatives are also rural bankers while some were once top executives of big commercial banks. Twenty members of the House are controlling stockholders of rural banks and loan associations in their districts. Appropriations committee chairman Rolando Andaya was once assistant vice president of the Bank of the Philippine Islands. Nineteen members of the House committee on banks and financial intermediaries have interests in or were once employed by the banking industry.

Seventeen representatives were once or are still presently involved in logging. These include:

- Davao del Sur Rep. Alejandro Almendras who set up logging companies in southern Mindanao.
- Rep. Lualhati Antonino who is stockholder of MILUDECO and WEMILCO, two logging firms owned by the Antonino family. MILUDECO operates a concession in South Cotabato covering 32,575 hectares.
- Rep. Victorico Chaves who is chairman of the El Labrador Lumber Company, which operated concessions in Agusan del Sur and Bukidnon.
- Rep. Junie Cua who is vice president of Luzon Loggers Inc., which operates a concession in Quirino, and stockholder of Isabela Lumber Industries.
- Rep. Rogelio Sarmiento who took over Sarmiento Industries from his father. The company was one of the biggest logging concessionaires in Mindanao;

its timber license agreement recently expired.

- Rep. Faustino Dy, Jr., once president and general manager of Isabela Wood and Development Corporation, who was linked to illegal logging activities by environmental groups in the Cagayan Valley. He represents Isabela, the province with the largest remaining reserves of virgin forests.

Mining, Transport and Construction

Other representatives have invested heavily in the mining industry. Rep. Antonio Cuenco owns P20 million worth of mining rights and a mining company that bears his name. Majority Floor Leader Ronaldo Zamora is director of the Rio Tuba Nickel Mining Corporation in southern Palawan. Speaker Jose de Venecia headed the Landoil Group that engaged in oil exploration.

Five representatives have interests in small-scale mining. Another five are stockholders in the country's biggest mining firms—Philex, Atlas Consolidated and Benguet Corporation.

Some members of the House are also involved in the export of Filipino workers abroad, especially to the Middle East and Taiwan. Isabela Rep. Rodolfo Albano, for instance, owns the Romar Employment Agency.

Other members of the House figure prominently in the construction industry. Samar Rep. Rodolfo Tuazon owns RT Tuazon Inc. Reps. Bensaudi Tulawie, Oscar Garin and Antonio Kho, all engineers, operated construction firms before their election to Congress.

Some representatives have invested in the transportation industry. Rep. Samuel Dangwa was president of Dangwa Transit Corporation until 1990. James Chiongbian, Crisologo Albines and Manuel Puey are all shipping tycoons.

INDUSTRY / BUSINESS	NUMBER OF REPRESENTATIVES
Agriculture and Landholding	132
Real Estate	45
Construction	18
Fishing	26
Logging	17
Mining	14
Tourism and Travel	11
Hotels and Restaurants	12
Trading and Retailing	50
Transportation	4
Shipping	7
Banking	42
Finance and Capital Investment	36
Insurance	4

All in the Family

Conclusion

IN THE House of Representatives, politics is all in the family.

More than two-thirds of the members of the House come from families that have held public office and maintained political influence for at least one generation.

One of every three representatives comes from a family that has been in power through several generations despite changes in presidents and regimes.

Another 30 percent are from families who have been in power only since 1972, after the declaration of martial law, or even as late as 1986, after the EDSA revolt.

As far as the data gathered in this study show, only 54 of 199 representatives have no close relatives in politics. These tangled family ties may directly influence at least one important piece of legislation—the proposed bill banning "political dynasties."

Political families are marked by their capacity to influence political decision-making and deliver substantial votes to favored candidates. At the core of every successful politician's organization are relatives that maintain and expand the family's political and economic influence, oftentimes across generations.

Usually, several members of the same political family hold national or local office. These clans are also financially affluent, especially in the context of the localities they control.

An examination of government records and interviews with congressional staff reveal that at least 145 representatives belong to families that may be considered "political."

The phenomenon of political families makes the distribution of political power less than ideal. Many scholars say the Philippines is an oligarchy where only a few rule. Others call it democracy for the elites.

An entrenched oligarchy makes it difficult for newcomers and deserving candidates from less-privileged sectors to break into mainstream politics.

The growth of program-oriented and community-based political parties is also seriously impaired when elections are reduced to contests between families rather than issues.

Rep. Bonifacio H. Gillego says that the families' control of economic resources makes it easier for them to win public office. Many wealthy families also tend to back politicians they can trust to protect their interests.

Many rich families prefer to support their own relatives' bid for public office, says Gillego, because they are more loyal defenders of the families' interests. Through time, the families develop well-oiled political machines which guarantee their continued control of elective office.

Former Nueva Ecija Rep. Eduardo Nonato Joson cites his own family's experience. In his province, only candidates allied with political families have won elections.

Joson believes that his own success as a politician is due largely to his father's influence. "It was easy to benefit from his prestige and influence, especially because people believed '*kung ano ang puno, siya ang bunga.*'"

The people's perception of the family is important, Joson continues, since the dynasty issue can be used against a family if it has become unpopular or abusive. A family cannot maintain itself in power through terrorism and cheating alone, he says.

But in recent years, the power of the families has been diminished by the entry of new aspirants to political office like military officers, middle-class reformers and newly affluent businessmen. Some families are also weakened by infighting.

The politicization of grassroots communities by Church, nongovernmental organizations and the radical Left have also challenged the families' continued dominance. So have the mass media and the growing urbanization of the country.

The families remain a dominant force in the House of Representatives.

Still, the families remain a dominant force in the House of Representatives.

Records show that at least 30 representatives are third- or fourth-generation politicians in their families. Some examples:

- Venice Borja-Agana of Bohol is the daughter of former Ambassador Jacinto Borja, the son of Candelario Borja, Bohol representative from 1907 to 1916.
- Antonio V. Cuenco of Cebu descended from Manuel Cuenco, former governor of Cebu and Mariano Jesus Cuenco, former congressman and Senate President.
- Jose "Peping" Cojuangco, Jr. of Tarlac descended from Jose Cojuangco and Melecio Cojuangco, both former Tarlac representatives.
- Conrado Estrella III of Pangasinan is the son of the late Robert Estrella, Pangasinan congressman in 1969, and the grandson of Conrado Estrella, Sr., a former governor, assemblyman and Marcos Cabinet minister.
- Milagros Laurel-Trinidad of Batangas descended from Jose B. Laurel, Jr., former Speaker of the House, Jose P. Laurel, former President, and Sotero Laurel, a member of the 1898 Malolos Congress.
- Alberto Lopez is the son of Fernando H. Lopez, a former senator and vice-president who is the son of Benito Lopez, a former Iloilo governor.
- Ferdinand "Bongbong" Marcos, Jr. of Ilocos Norte descended from former President Ferdinand Marcos and Mariano Marcos, Ilocos Norte representative from 1925 to 1931.
- Rosenda Ann Ocampo of Manila is the daughter of former congressman Pablo V. Ocampo, a grandson of the 19th century politician Pablo Ocampo, secretary of the 1898 Malolos Congress and first Philippine Resident Commissioner to the United States.
- Ralph G. Recto of Batangas is the son of former Batasan assemblyman Rafael Recto and grandson of Claro M. Recto, one of the country's best-known politicians during the American and post-war periods.
- The late Gerardo A. Roxas, Jr. of Capiz descended from Gerardo Roxas, a former senator, and Manuel Roxas, the post-war President. On his maternal side are Araneta relatives who have dominated Western Visayas politics since the 1850s.
- Mariano M. Yulo of Negros Occidental is the son of former Bacolod Mayor Alfredo Yulo and the grandson of the original Mariano Yulo, a senator from 1928 to 1931.

Fathers, Sons and Daughters

At least 64 representatives are children of renowned political figures in the provinces they now represent. This validates the observation that political office can be passed on from parent to child and inherited like property. Of this group, 20 are children of former legislators. They are:

- Rodolfo Albano of Isabela
- Teresa Aquino-Oreta of Malabon
- Amado and Ramon Bagatsing, Jr., both representing Manila
- Antonio Cerilles of Zamboanga del Sur
- Renato Diaz of Nueva Ecija
- Ramon D. Durano III of Cebu
- Juan Ponce Enrile of Cagayan
- Wilfrido Enverga of Quezon
- Tito Espinosa of Masbate
- Arnulfo Fuentebella of Camarines Sur
- Carlos R. Imperial of Albay
- Carmelo Lazatin of Pampanga
- Ma. Carmela Lobregat of Zamboanga City
- Cirilo Roy Montejo of Leyte
- Victor Ortega of La Union
- Amadeo R. Perez, Jr. of Pangasinan
- Manuel H. Puey of Negros Occidental
- Rogelio Sarmiento of Davao del Norte
- Margarito Teves of Negros Oriental
- Licurgo Tirador of Iloilo

The Children of the House

On the other hand, some representatives' children are now into politics themselves. Mario Ty and Glenda Ecleo of Surigao, Benjamin Bautista and Alejandro Almendras of Davao del Sur, Santiago Respicio of Isabela, Francisco Mamba of Cagayan and Pablo Garcia and Antonio Cuenco of Cebu, have children currently holding elective posts.

The young daughters of Jose Cojuangco, Jr. of Tarlac and Crisologo Abines of Cebu were named youth sector representatives in the provincial boards after they won the Sangguniang Kabataan elections. Abdullah Dimaporo, son of Rep. Mohammad Ali Dimaporo and a former representative himself, is now the governor of Lanao del Norte.

Jose Yap of Tarlac, who ran and won as mayor of Victoria in 1951 but was disqualified by the Supreme Court for being underaged, has two children in public office. Jose Jr. is mayor of newly created San Jose town, carved out of the provincial capital of Tarlac. His brother Victor is the vice-mayor of Victoria.

Husbands and Wives

In addition, 23 representatives have spouses who either occupy, once occupied or contested important government positions. Representatives whose spouses are incumbent mayors or governors are:

- Crisologo Albines of Cebu
- Edelmiro Amante of Agusan del Norte
- Luwalhati Antonino of South Cotabato
- Jose Aspiras of La Union
- Jose Cojuangco of Tarlac
- James Chiongbian of Saranggani
- Pacifico Fajardo of Nueva Ecija
- Katherine Gordon of Zambales, whose husband Richard was until his resignation in June 1993, mayor of Olongapo
- Alberto Lopez of Iloilo
- Pedro Romualdo of Camiguin
- Eric Singson of Ilocos Sur
- Niel Tupas of Iloilo

Siblings in Office

Forty-six members of the House have brothers and sisters active in politics. Representatives with more than one sibling who ran for office in May 1992 are:

- Crisologo Abines, whose brother Apolonio Jr., is vice-governor of Cebu. A second brother, Emiliano, is mayor of Oslob while a third, Regino, is vice-mayor of Oslob.
- Ernesto Amatong, whose brother, Isagani, is Zamboanga del Norte governor. Another brother, Prospero, is Davao del Norte governor.
- Luis Assistio, whose brother Macario Jr., was re-elected Calookan City mayor. His sister, Aurora Henson, is the other representative of Calookan in the House.
- Ramon Durano III, whose brothers, Jesus and Thaddeus, are mayors of Danao City and Sogod, respectively.
- Faustino Dy, Jr., whose half-brother, Benjamin, is governor of Isabela and whose brother, Faustino III, is Cauayan mayor.
- Bensaudi Tulawie, whose brother, Kimar, was Sulu vice-governor while his other brother, Benhajar, is Talipao mayor.

The circle of families stretches wide. In all, 58 representatives have uncles, nieces, nephews and cousins who are currently or were once in public office. Thirty-three have either married into other political families or have in-laws in public office.

A Web of Relatives

Finally, the intertwined family trees within Congress itself are best illustrated by the following:

- Ramon Bagatsing, Jr. and Amado Bagatsing, both representing Manila, are brothers.
- Calookan Rep. Luis Asistio is the brother of the other Calookan representative, Aurora Asistio-Henson.
- Rogelio Sarmiento of Davao del Norte and Angelito Sarmiento of Bulacan are cousins.
- Jose Sumulong Cojuangco and Emidgio Sumulong Tanjuatco of Rizal are cousins.
- Alejandro Durano Almendras of Davao is a cousin of Cebu's Ramon Durano III.
- Celestino Espinosa Martinez of Cebu is a nephew of Masbate Rep. Tito Espinosa.
- Renato Yap of Quezon City is a nephew of Tarlac Rep. Jose Yap.
- Malabon's Tessie Aquino-Oreta is a niece of Herminio Aquino of Tarlac.
- Rodolfo del Rosario of Davao del Norte is the brother in-law of Manuel Garcia of Davao City.
- Herminio Aquino is the son-in-law of Romeo Guanzon of Bacolod City.
- Rodolfo Albano and Manuel Garcia have children married to each other.
- Five Visayas congressman—Reps. Alberto S. Veloso, Eriberto Veloso Loreto, Antonio Veloso Cuenco, Ramon Duterte Durano III and Raul Veloso del Mar—are relatives.
- Hortensia Starke of Negros Occidental, Alberto Lopez of Iloilo, Rafael Lopez-Vito of Iloilo are relatives.

The President's Paramour

BY MARITES DAÑGUILAN VITUG AND GLENDA GLORIA
First published in the *Philippine Daily Inquirer*, October 11-12, 1993

This two-part story on Rose Marie 'Baby' Arenas, President Ramos's former mistress, is one of the most controversial investigations undertaken by the PCIJ. Publication of the story by the *Philippine Daily Inquirer* set off a discussion about investigative methods, particularly the use of unnamed sources. It also stirred a hornet's nest about whether the media should probe the private lives of public officials. The President was understandably mad about this report, and three days after it came out, a disputed one-third of the *Inquirer's* shares were put under receivership by the Securities and Exchange Commission, which was then headed by one of Arenas's friends.

Although Arenas had been featured as a "socialite" and "philanthropist" in the lifestyle sections of newspapers and referred to in blind items in columns, this report marked the first time a newspaper printed the worst kept secret in town: that Baby Arenas once had a relationship with the President. What this investigation found out was that she played a key role in Ramos's presidential campaign and that she tried to wield influence— with varying success— over government appointments and policies after Ramos had been elected.

Knowing the sensitivity of the subject matter they were delving into, the writers checked land, birth registry and corporate records. But their more important sources were people. Marites Dañguilan Vitug and Glenda Gloria interviewed 50 persons over several months, including former and current military officers, businesspeople and former members of the Ramos presidential campaign staff. Most of these persons have had first-hand dealings with Arenas. They included people from the various Malacañang factions, some of Arenas's dearest friends and some of her worst enemies. While most of the interviews were on the record, most of the interviewees asked not to be identified by name. Arenas herself refused to be interviewed.

To guard against false leads and story feeds, the writers checked every piece of information they were given. No information from a single source was used unless it was corroborated by others. They took every effort to find sources who had first-hand knowledge of supposed deals and requests. Twice, the reporters waited outside the Arenas home on a Wednesday to check whether the weekly meetings involving high government officials were indeed being held there.

Despite the preponderance of unnamed sources, the PCIJ board of editors decided to release the story because of the lengths to which the writers had gone to corroborate the information they had and the quality of their sources, among them high government and military officials who spoke about what they had witnessed, rather than what they had heard from others. The PCIJ also felt that as Arenas's actions were taking place in the arena of politics, which is a very public realm, then journalists had the right to report on them.

Ironically, this report indicated that Arenas was likely less influential than what the gossip in Manila coffee shops made her out to be. It also shed light on the influence that private—and therefore unaccountable—individuals have on the affairs of state. What the report lacked—and what would probably have helped cool down the furor a bit—was sufficient explanation of the method of the investigation, the number and types of sources used, and the manner in which the information gathered had been confirmed.

A Past Relationship Impinges on the Present

First of Two Parts

A PHOTOGRAPH of President Fidel V. Ramos in white duck uniform is prominently displayed in the luxurious living room of 2056 Lumbang Street in Makati's posh Dasmariñas Village. This is the residence of Rose Marie 'Baby' Jimenez Arenas, where some of the country's most powerful officials regularly meet.

Arenas, a wealthy former beauty queen and fashion model, is said to have had a relationship with President Ramos. At least two persons close to Mr. Ramos have asked him about this, and they say the President dismissed it as part of the past, a tacit admission of the liaison.

Similarly, Jose Almonte, national security adviser, once referred to it as "something that happened in the past...a matter between two persons." Aides of the President as well as Cabinet members we interviewed consider the relationship common knowledge.

When, then, does the President's private life become public concern?

Indications are the private past is impinging on President Ramos's present official affairs. While Arenas does not shape policy, her actions affect the credibility of the President. Talk of her influence is pervasive, even if the reality is she does not get her way all the time.

Although Mr. Ramos has on occasion given in to Arenas' requests, presidential aides say he is also discreetly trying to curtail her influence and to contain the potential damage she can cause the presidency. Almonte, the president's close friend from their days together as Philcag officers in Vietnam, has apparently been assigned to handle this delicate situation.

Arenas is known to have sought favors on behalf of a number of business interests and to have influenced a few appointments in government. "She asks for jobs, concessions but these are low level—not the PLDT (Philippine Long Distance Telephone Co.) or Cabinet posts," a friend of Arenas says.

A Cabinet secretary admits that because of Arenas's actions, "some people are beginning to doubt the sincerity of the President. His credibility is getting adversely affected." Others in the Ramos government think she is hurting Mr. Ramos, even "eroding the effectiveness of the presidency."

Arenas's power is both real and perceived. She draws strength from her association with Almonte, who is probably the president's closest and most trusted adviser.

She also projects a power image, flaunting her access to the Palace. She is not shy about making known that she is close to the top official of the land. Recalls a former Ramos Cabinet member, "She says she calls the President directly." Arenas has also shared this information with other people.

The case of Arenas may be unique, compared to experiences of past presidents. Manuel Quezon had reported liaisons, but these apparently did not affect official matters. Ferdinand Marcos's affair with Hollywood actress Dovie Beams had no impact on the affairs of state, although others now say the former First Lady, Imelda Marcos, started building her domain after her late husband's relationship with Beams.

But Arenas's role as a wielder of influence is not uncommon. Says Felipe Alfonso, president of the Asian Institute of Management: "She reflects a highly personalistic society and a protectionist system. Here, protection of industries means protection of families, individuals and power blocs."

Cabinet Worry

Perceptions that Arenas uses her access to Malacañang to boost certain businesses or place people in government has worried some Cabinet members. "It is not getting out of hand but it is getting to be a problem," a Cabinet secretary said.

As a result, two unofficial meetings of some Cabinet members were held in April 1993, one in Beijing during the President's state visit, and another in Hong Kong, following the China trip. The agenda focused on what to do about "the problem."

Those who attended were: Foreign Affairs Secretary Roberto Romulo, Defense Secretary Renato de Villa, Trade and Industry Secretary Rizalino Navarro, Interior and Local Governments Secretary Rafael Alunan, then Press Secretary Rodolfo Reyes. The Hong Kong meeting included Angel Ramos Jones, the President's daughter who lives in the Crown colony.

These Cabinet members thought it was important that the President be informed about the growing concern about Arenas's activities and the disturbing talk about her influence on the Palace.

"The problem needed to be met head-on," said one former ranking government official. Assigned to take on the difficult job of telling Mr. Ramos was de Villa, a close friend of the president's. It is not known whether de Villa accomplished his mission. (He declined to comment.)

Almonte's role in all this baffles Cabinet members and political observers. He is constantly with Arenas in public gatherings as well as in private functions—attending Sunday mass and weekly meetings in Arenas' residence. "He's the official nanny, the handler," remarked one government official. (Almonte did not respond to requests for an interview.)

A retired general believes that Almonte is supposed to "soft pedal" the situation. "But he and the President are riding the tiger," warned the former military officer.

Almonte's closeness with Arenas sends confusing signals to the business community.

Rather than defuse the situation, Almonte's association with Arenas seems to perpetuate the perception that she is indeed powerful and has access to Malacañang. "It appears that it is important to be on the side of Baby. Because the perception is: To be on the side of Baby is to be on the side of the President," a former Malacañang official said.

Almonte's closeness with Arenas sends confusing signals to the business community. He and legal counsel Antonio Carpio are believed to be part of a group within Malacañang that is drafting Mr. Ramos's populist program to break monopolies and level the economic playing field. In the process, this group has crossed swords with big business.

The group ostensibly wants to rid the country of the clubbiness and cronyism that characterized previous administrations. But, observes former Tourism Secretary Narzalina Lim, once a member of the Ramos Cabinet: "The President says it's a level playing field. But it ain't so when one has to go to persons like Mrs. Arenas. We can close our eyes to the relationship. But once it affects the way business is done, it demoralizes people."

Mr. Ramos has indeed given written instructions to government officials not to grant special treatment and favors to his friends and relatives. (We asked presidential spokesman Jesus Sison for an interview, but he declined.)

Discreetly, the President has also been blocking Arenas's attempts to use her links to Malacañang to seek favors, aides to Ramos say. They insist Arenas has no influence on the President.

"This is definitely not a hostage situation," a Malacañang source said, dispelling the impression that President Ramos is unable to act for fear of what Arenas might do.

Opposing Blocs

The President thrives in seeking advice from various groups which are not necessarily familiar with each other's work. This situation, explained Ed Joaquin, Philippine Tourism Authority chairman, makes it difficult for any single group to control the presidency. In the battle for primacy, it is like that opposing blocs stifle each other's bid for favors.

Still, the President, some say, may not be capably handling the situation. Observes an Army officer: "He's (Ramos) acting like a fireman, putting out the fire wherever it is."

According to government officials and presidential aides, Arenas, on two occasions, was about to go public with the relationship. During the presidential campaign, she visited Ramos' headquarters on Pasay Road, Makati and nearly raised hell because campaign staffers who did not know her denied her request for stickers.

Visibly mad, Arenas threatened to call the media, a member of the campaign staff recalls. She was later placated.

"If Baby (Arenas) gets angry, she can do a lot of trouble. The President needs trouble like a hole in the head," says a retired general.

Our investigation has shown that Arenas has, on occasion, intervened on behalf of business interests. (Arenas declined to be interviewed despite repeated requests.) Not at all times, however, did the intervention lead to desired results, such as in the case of the unification of the stock exchanges.

In March 1993, when the Makati and Manila Stock Exchanges were engaged in a furious battle over the site of the unified Philippine Stock Exchange, Arenas invited stockbrokers representing both exchanges to her Dasmariñas Village home for a meeting.

Government officials like Securities and Exchange Commission Chairperson Rosario Lopez, national security adviser Jose Almonte, and presidential legal adviser Tony Carpio were also present.

Arenas pitched for an agreement to move to Tektite Towers in Ortigas Center, a proposal favored by the Manila Stock Exchange. She asked the Makati Stock Exchange representative to compromise. That would be a birthday gift to the President, she was quoted as saying. (Ramos's birthday is on March 18.)

President Ramos was then in Japan for a state visit. Upon learning of the incident, a stockbroker informed then Finance Secretary Ramon del Rosario, who was with the President in Tokyo.

Earlier, in February 1993, Mr. Ramos had appointed del Rosario chairperson of the committee to oversee the unification of the stock exchanges. But unknown to del Rosario and the President, Arenas was campaigning for a transfer to Tektite.

When Mr. Ramos found out, he was, sources said, "very upset." Furthermore, these sources say, he made clear he did not authorize Arenas's campaign.

Eddie Lim, chairman of the Makati Stock Exchange, who, sources say was present, denied the meeting ever took place. However, other sources stand by the story.

Questions have been raised in the business community: Why did Arenas intervene in the fight of the stock exchanges? In what capacity did she do so? Why were ranking government officials—two of them from the Office of the President—present in the meeting unauthorized by their boss? Both also know that an oversight committee had already been formed to deal with the issue. Carpio declined to be interviewed.

Despite Arenas's intervention, however, Carpio said he pushed for a vote among the stockbrokers. "It was the democratic thing to do given the contending parties," he told a journalist.

In the end, the stockbrokers voted for a functional unification, but the squabbling between the two exchanges continues.

No Clear Signals from Ramos

The incident is indicative of the President's leadership style. Sources in government say Mr. Ramos has not given clear signals to his Cabinet about how to relate to Arenas. Neither has the issue been discussed in meetings with the President.

Wrote former executive secretary Peter Garrucho, Jr. in his *Manila Standard* column in July 1993: "There have been proxy battles such as the Tektite versus the Makati Stock Exchange. The fight over control of the Office of the President continues as well...If you have allowed factions to thrive, you do not really choose and decide; you balance."

One of Arenas's more important links to government is through her friend Rosario Lopez, who was appointed SEC chairperson by former President Corazon Aquino. Lopez is accused of graft by former SEC commissioner Armando Gonzales who has filed charges with the Ombudsman and the Senate Blue Ribbon Committee. Lopez dismissed these charges as sourgraping by Gonzales, whose term at the SEC expired in March 1993.

In early 1993, then Finance Secretary del Rosario wrote Mr. Ramos, recommending that Lopez be replaced, supposedly because she was a source of disunity, which harms the capital market.

Despite the graft charges and despite del Rosario's recommendations, Lopez remains in office. Complains one SEC official, "The perception is she can't be touched because of her friendship with Arenas."

Arenas also seems to have successfully used her influence in the case of a logging company in desperate need of government help in fighting off an attempt by a rival firm to grab part of its concession.

The logging concessionaire approached a Malacañang official to complain, but got nothing until he tried an alternative power venue: Arenas. Apparently through her intercession, a senior Malacañang official called the Department of Environment and Natural Resources (DENR). As a result, the attempt to encroach into the concessionaire's turf was foiled.

Among some members of the Chinese-Filipino community, Arenas is seen as a "facilitator." Explains one Chinese-Filipino: "Many see nothing illegal in asking her to speed up a bureaucratic process. In Philippine politics, whom you know counts. What would prevent us from asking her help?"

For example, this source cites, Arenas, through her representative, is known to "facilitate" release of shipments from the Bureau of Customs: "It makes matters easier."

Rose Marie's brother-in-law, Vicente Arenas, is president of Wellspring International Corporation, a trading company that recently approached the Bureau of Customs with a proposal.

Asked about the proposal and whether it was illegal, Customs Commissioner Guillermo Parayno answered: "All I can tell you is that I said no (to Arenas)." He added that he has no information about "facilitation" of shipment release by Mrs. Arenas or her representatives.

In two meetings, the President instructed Parayno "not to be influenced" by people claiming to be close to him. Mr. Ramos mentioned specific reports he received about influence peddling in the Bureau. "I have no problem saying no," stressed Parayno.

Duty Free Philippines, it is said, is also one of the establishments Arenas does business with. Initially, Jojo Barreiro, Duty Free corporate communications officer, agreed to provide a list of local suppliers of Duty Free. However, after several follow-ups, his office refused to release the list.

One of Arenas's friends says she tries to get Duty Free concessions for friends. Arenas also offered a journalist a shopping trip to the Duty Free shop to gain goodwill.

Barreiro said they had indeed received offers from friends of Arenas to supply goods to the company. One of these is the Benjamin, the Favored Son Jewelry shop located at the Shangri-la Hotel in Makati. It is owned by Benjamin Yap, son of the chairman of the board of *The Manila Bulletin*, Emilio Yap.

Arenas, Barreiro said, tried to arrange a meeting with Benjie Lim, manager of Duty Free, but nothing came of it. Barreiro said all these died a natural death: "There is no shadow of a company of Baby Arenas or friend of hers doing business with Duty Free."

Battle for Spoils

Arenas has not kept away from the battle for spoils. On a few occasions, she promised government appointments to some, including a retired general. "She (Arenas) told me that I was the subject of her conversation with the boss (referring to Mr. Ramos) and that I was going to be given work," the general said. The job never came.

Arenas, sources say, has influenced a few official appointments. Mita Pardo de Tavera, chairperson of the Philippine Charity Sweepstakes Office, is said to be one of them. She was an early appointee and reported to the PCSO without official appointment papers. The board of trustees was supposed to have nominated the chairperson.

Pardo de Tavera is the mother of Josine Elizalde, known to be a close friend of Arenas and one of those who regularly attend the Wednesday meetings at her home.

Initially, it was thought that former President Corazon C. Aquino was responsible for the appointment because Pardo de Tavera was her former social services and development secretary. Mrs. Aquino, however, has made known that she has not requested any government appointments.

A source from the PSCO said, however, that Pardo de Tavera was appointed because of her reputation, "not because of connections."

Ramon Arenas, former assistant treasurer and now member of the board of directors of Manila Electric Company (Meralco), is Rose Marie's husband. They are known to live separately but remain friendly to each other.

While Arenas is related to the Lopezes of Meralco, there was something unusual in the circumstances surrounding his selection. Felipe Alfonso, president of the Asian Institute of Management, was the management nominee. However, Almonte called and visited a Meralco official to ask that a switch be made: Ramon Arenas will be named representative of management while Alfonso will be the government nominee.

Rose Marie Arenas has other relatives in government. Among them are Ed Joaquin, chairman of the Philippine Tourism Authority, and SEC Commissioner Perfecto Yasay, Jr. Joaquin is Arenas' cousin. He was active in the Ramos campaign. Yasay is married to Cecile Joaquin, sister of PTA's Ed Joaquin.

There are failed attempts to push for government appointments as well. Two former Ramos Cabinet members say Arenas lobbied for Manuel Elizalde's nomination as ambassador to Mexico.

Elizalde is known to be a donor to the Ramos campaign. He is also the brother-in-law of Arenas's bosom friend, Josine Elizalde, and was one of Arenas's select guests during her private birthday dinner in Dasmariñas Village in July 1993.

Before Elizalde's nomination, Foreign Affairs Secretary Roberto Romulo had already informed Louie Garcia, former trade attaché to North America, that he was the department's choice for envoy to Mexico. Garcia said he "got caught in the shuffle." The position is still vacant.

Seeking Legitimacy: Arenas's Links to Ramos

Conclusion

AS EARLY as 1989, Rose Marie (Baby) Jimenez Arenas was hosting weekly meetings, usually held on Wednesdays, attended by friends and supporters of then Defense Secretary Fidel V. Ramos. At that time, Ramos was already being talked about as a potential presidential candidate.

A year later, when Ramos emerged as a likely contender, these meetings evolved from social gatherings into "informal strategy sessions" aimed at boosting Ramos's chances in the elections. Some of those who joined the initial meetings later formed the inner core of a team for candidate Ramos's presidential campaign.

At the same time, Arenas joined a group of Gen. Jose Almonte, then chief of the Economic Intelligence and Investigation Bureau (EIIB), in closed-door meetings at the EIIB office in Camp Aguinaldo. She fretted about rumors of a coup and joined planning meetings to launch Ramos's candidacy.

"We all felt there was a deferential attitude towards Baby—even Joe (Almonte) was deferential," a member of the core group said. Ramos did not attend these initial meetings.

The "Wednesday Club," as some have called it, remains to this day a remnant of the Ramos campaign. But an aide to President Ramos says the meetings stopped in July 1993 since most of Arenas's usual guests already "decided to withdraw from her."

Close to 20 people belonged to the inner circle of Arenas's Wednesday meetings. Recently, as persistent controversy surrounded the meetings, the number of those attending has declined to at least 10.

Early in 1993, Arenas invited a journalist to dinner in her Dasmariñas Village residence. On that Wednesday evening, the journalist saw 50 or more guests, including some government officials, retired military officers and foreigners.

To other government officials and some businessmen, the "Wednesday Club" appeared more like a "kitchen cabinet," an alternate power center. It took place a day after the Tuesday Cabinet meetings, giving the impression that issues discussed in the Cabinet were likewise talked about.

It was also seen as a "court of last resort" for those seeking favors and wishing to influence presidential decisions—because key advisers of President Ramos were present.

The Wednesday Group

Among those who attended the Wednesday meetings were: National Security adviser Jose Almonte, presidential legal counsel Antonio Carpio, Philippine Olympics Committee chief Rene Cruz, former presidential spokesperson Annabelle Abaya and husband Anthony, Philippine Communications Satellite Corporation board member Antonio Lukban, Philippine Veterans Investment and Development Corporation (PHIVIDEC) head Col. Cesar Pio Roda, PLDT senior vice-president for electronic data processing Ed de Leon, and Josine Elizalde.

Lukban, a retired general, was assistant secretary for logistics when Ramos was defense secretary. He and Col. Roda belong to class 1956 of the Philippine Military Academy.

Pastor Saycon, who worked for Ramos during the presidential campaign, and newspaper columnist Teodoro Benigno were reported to have joined the meetings in the early period. Saycon is currently deputy secretary-general of the Lakas-EDSA-NUCD. Arenas also invited at least two Cabinet members to the meetings, but they declined.

"Baby likes to arrange things, to broker meetings," says a friend. "A lot of people seek her out thinking she would make a difference."

A retired military officer who attends the meetings admits the discussions sometimes tackled serious matters such as governance: "We provide inputs to the President if there is a decision he (Ramos) has to make."

But he dismisses suggestions that the meetings indicated intervention in state affairs: "It is not a power bloc because our goal is pure—to help the President." He stresses that the Wednesday group knows Ramos does not depend solely on one source of advice for critical decisions.

Still another source who was active in the campaign says the Wednesday meetings were meant mainly for Arenas: "She was a reality to contend with and it was one way of making her feel she belonged."

But a government official who is a "Wednesday Club" habitué says that the meetings have recently turned into venues for "*hingahan ng sama ng loob* (ventilating sentiments)," particularly on the part of Arenas who feels her actions are being restricted.

In its hey-day, the "Wednesday Club" fit Ramos's style of leadership marked by centralized decision-making. "The more he (Ramos) arrogates to himself what should be the decision of others, the more people depart from the normal channels and instead find individuals who can influence him most effectively," wrote former executive secretary Peter Garrucho, Jr. in the *Manila Standard*.

Campaign Fund-raiser

Arenas's bigger role in the campaign, sources say, was in helping fill up the coffers. She is said to earn generous sums from renting out her houses in exclusive villages in Makati.

Arenas wants it known that she contributed heavily to the Ramos presidential campaign. She has told a number of people that she sold anywhere from two to seven of her 21 or so houses, aside from jewelry, for the campaign.

Arenas wants it known that she contributed heavily to the Ramos presidential campaign.

Arenas's actual property holdings, however, remain a mystery. A check with the Makati Registry of Deeds shows she owns a 1,179 square-meter lot in Dasmariñas Village. The Lumbang Street house, where the Wednesday meetings are held, is not registered in her name. In the Dasmariñas Village homeowners list, that property is listed in the name of a certain Freddie Go.

Arenas's Registry of Deeds record gives as her address a home in North Forbes, Makati. The Makati condominium where she actually lives is also not listed in her name. There was likewise no recorded sale of her Makati property during the campaign period.

But an aide of Ramos who dealt with Arenas during the campaign estimates that she may have donated P50 million. This includes campaign paraphernalia such as stickers, hats, fans, umbrellas and pins, which she may have solicited from her businesspeople friends.

Arenas comes from an upper-middle class family with no substantial wealth. Her father worked with the Bureau of Internal Revenue and her mother was the soprano Remedios Bosch, who taught for many years at the University of the East. In the late 1970s, her now-estranged husband, Ramon, was in the shipping business. Ramon, who comes from a wealthy Negrense family, was recently appointed to the board of the Manila Electric Company.

Arenas was, by some accounts, one of Ramos's more aggressive campaigners. "It is this aggressive drive on the part of Baby and her group that contributed a lot to the decision of Ramos to run for the presidency even after his defeat in the LDP convention. Those in the know credit Baby for the hard work done by this particular group to make Ramos win," wrote *Inquirer* columnist Julie Amargo, a close friend of Arenas.

What remains a mystery to this day, even to those who worked closely with him during the campaign, is Ramos's trip to Zurich, Switzerland in March 1992. While he claimed he met with Christian Democrat-supporters, he admitted in subsequent press briefings that the trip was "private in nature."

In Switzerland, the secretary-general of the Swiss Christian Democratic Party, Iwan Rickernbacker, said there was no official contact with candidate Ramos or any other Filipino, the Associated Press reported at that time.

Even his principal backer, former President Aquino, considered the trip a "purely private endeavor." A confused campaign staff gave different versions of the trip, including one that hinted of a bungled meeting with the Pope.

In a meeting, Ramos's aides queried him about the trip "to be able to defend him more easily," recalls one of his campaigń managers. This time, Ramos contradicted his earlier admission that the trip was private.

Instead, he repeated the line that he met with Christian Democrats. "We read signals from him that it was something that we should not pursue...that we should just stick to the official line which was really hard to believe. It was an illogical trip," says the campaign manager.

A source close to Arenas insists that the President made the trip to Switzerland to visit Mrs. Arenas's youngest son, Roberto. Roberto currently goes to an elite boarding school in England, but Arenas said in a 1992 interview with *Graphic* magazine that her son plays soccer in Switzerland.

During his confirmation hearing as defense secretary in 1988, then Senator Aquilino Pimentel asked Mr. Ramos if he had a son by another woman. Pimentel had received an unsigned document containing this information.

In an executive session of the Commission on Appointments, Ramos was said to have emphatically replied: "It is not true." Recalls Pimentel, "I left it at that. I did not know about Arenas then."

Roberto Jose Pio Antonio Arenas's birth certificate shows he was born on February 19, 1978 in Makati to parents Ramon Lopez Arenas and Rose Marie Bosch Jimenez.

Charity Work

Although she had already been involved in charity work for soldiers, Arenas began to take a high profile after the 1986 uprising. In the early 1980s, she was fundraising for the Philippine Constabulary, then headed by Mr. Ramos. The V. Luna Hospital, now renamed Armed Forces of the Philippines Medical Center, was also a beneficiary of her work.

Col. Catalino Guevarra, AFP Medical center head, says Arenas was a frequent donor of groceries for wounded soldiers confined at the hospital. She visited the hospital at least three times a year.

A retired general recalls having met her in Camp Crame shortly after February 1986. "(Jose) Almonte called me to refer her. She inquired about charity work for soldiers. In the course of our conversation, she also practically told me about her relationship with my boss (Ramos)." Eventually, this officer did errands for her.

Arenas's main charity organization is Padre Pio Lend a Helping Hand Foundation which she claims her mother founded. As of early October 1993, Securities and Exchange Commission records showed that the Foundation is not registered with the SEC. As such, it has no legal personality, giving rise to problems of accountability for donations received and funds raised.

In March 1993, the Foundation raised funds by mounting a concert to pay tribute to Arenas's late mother, soprano Remedios Bosch Jimenez. The concert was later aired on television; its sponsors included PLDT, EDSA Shangri-la Hotel, Fortune Tobacco and Philippine Amusement and Gaming Corporation. Arenas also donated to her Foundation during her birthday in July 1993.

Noemi Reyes, president of the Foundation, declined to be interviewed.

Arenas is a generous donor to other charity organizations. In August 1993, she donated P100,000 to the RAM Foundation, Inc. which is headed by former Army Lt. Col. Gregorio Honasan. The RAM Foundation is currently raising funds for its Orphans Scholarship Program.

She is also one of the incorporators of the Mt. Pinatubo Hidden Temple Shrine and Community Foundation which was founded in 1992 to build a shrine and rehabilitate a village for dislocated victims of Mt. Pinatubo. She donated P500,000 to the Foundation.

"I know Baby to be very generous and charitable," says a newspaper editor. Arenas, one of her friends says, finds it hard to say no to requests or favors: "She accommodates anyone who calls on her."

It was not long before such high visibility was criticized in the press. Immediately after Ramos won the presidency, Arenas decided to tap the services of public relations experts to counter media criticism against her.

In June 1992, she was reportedly agitated by a blind item in the defunct *Daily Globe* that referred to her as "Imeldific Part 2" allegedly because she got VIP treatment at the Ninoy Aquino International Airport.

Months later, Arenas went on a media binge, meeting with journalists, granting interviews and having her photos published in newspapers and magazines. Almost all of the full-length feature articles written on her were lavishly positive. Pleased with one of these articles, she gave a gift check worth thousands of pesos to the author.

But she was less kind to the bearers of bad news about her. In a speech before the Makati Rotary Club in June 1993, she lashed at the media: "The things that have been attributed to me have been largely nasty and nastiness is always good fodder for news. Besides these speculations being absurd...they question my motives, yet they have been aired through an institution powerful enough to assign blame while itself escaping blame."

More recently, Arenas made it to the front pages when Senator Ernesto Maceda alleged that she has been consistently seen escorted by policemen. Arenas denied the claim, as did the Philippine National Police, which said it has not assigned any bodyguards to her. Interior and Local Government Secretary Rafael Alunan said in response to a questionnaire that he had no knowledge of Arenas's security men.

Yet, four uniformed bodyguards were seen accompanying Arenas during her birthday party at the Shangri-la Hotel in Makati in July 1993. A senior defense department official said some of her guards were formerly with the Armed Forces.

Arenas may raise another storm if reports are true that she intends to run for a seat in Congress to represent Makati, a plan that worries some presidential aides. Public office will give Arenas a mantle of legitimacy and propel her from the backroom to center stage.

"People expect her to vanish after long years of relationship (with) and help for the President?" asks a friend of Arenas. "She will not do that."

De Venecia's Debt Trail

BY STELLA TIROL

First published in the *Philippine Daily Inquirer, Manila Chronicle* and *Business Star*, August 18-19, 1992

This three-part series, published just after Jose de Venecia was elected Speaker of the House of Representatives, documents how a well-connected individual was able to build a business empire by getting favorable loans and loan guarantees from government banks. When this story was published, most Filipinos hardly knew anything about the congressman from Pangasinan who had taken over the reins of leadership in the House. But Stella Tirol, who once reported on the stock market for a business newspaper, heard stories about the unpaid loans and controversial business transactions that the Speaker had entered into as head of the Landoil conglomerate in the 1970s. After an initial check to find out whether there was basis for these stories, she set out to do a full-scale investigation of de Venecia's business dealings.

In the course of several months' research, she found that the House Speaker had chalked up as much as P5 billion in unpaid loans that taxpayers were still paying for. The loans were backed by minimum collateral and had apparently been used for purposes other than that for which they were supposedly intended. Tirol found evidence that funds from the loans were diverted into multiple layers of banks, which hid where the money went.

She put this series together by examining records of court cases filed against de Venecia by two government financial institutions from which the Speaker had obtained loans or loan guarantees, and by 150 Landoil workers who had not been paid their salaries. In addition, she also obtained documents from the Blue Ribbon Commission and found, among others, letters written by de Venecia to the Development Bank of the Philippines, which were accompanied by an endorsement letter from Marcos himself. From interviews with the Speaker's former associates, lawyers, businessmen and government investigators, Tirol traced de Venecia's ties to the former president and concluded that these ties served him well in making Landoil grow to become one of the country's top construction firms.

This report shows how information from government records and interviews with knowledgeable sources can be woven together to produce an investigative profile that reveals how business and politics are so tightly intertwined. De Venecia's successful use of political connections—first to further his businesses, and then, to throw a monkey wrench at investigations of his past business transactions—provides a classic example of the primacy of politics in the Philippines.

One week after this series was published, the Senate began an investigation of Landoil. But like previous probes into de Venecia's past, this effort eventually fizzled out. This series was a finalist in the 1992 Jaime V. Ongpin Awards for investigative journalism.

Government Banks Say They Were Gypped

First of Three Parts

HOUSE Speaker Jose de Venecia, Jr.—for more than 15 years the head of a business empire that spanned construction and oil exploration—has left a string of bad debts and questionable loan transactions that have not been resolved since 1986.

His flagship company was Landoil Resources Corp., which formed the core of a conglomerate that at its peak spanned 26 affiliates and subsidiaries.

While he was at the helm, from the mid-1970s to the early 1980s, the company and its subsidiaries borrowed millions of dollars and pesos from government banks, which up to now remain unpaid.

These unpaid loans—amounting to more than P5 billion as of 1987—have become obligations of the national government and are being serviced at the Filipino taxpayers' expense.

The way the loans were obtained and used have been questioned since 1986 by state financial institutions. It is alleged that de Venecia used his close relationship with deposed President Marcos to obtain huge loans with minimum collateral and to get other concessions from government banks.

For example, a 1979 loan transaction is alleged by the Development Bank of Philippines (DBP) to have been approved because of pressure from Marcos.

According to a pending case filed by the DBP with the Tanodbayan in 1988, Landoil managed to cancel P98 million worth of loans granted and guaranteed by DBP in exchange for parcels of rural land worth only P13 million.

Another government institution, Philippine Export and Foreign Loan Guarantee Corp. (Philguarantee), alleged findings of fraud and loan diversion.

In a report, it said that three Landoil subsidiaries diverted loans worth a total of $70 million to other projects not approved by Philguarantee in the 1980s.

The ultimate destination of these loans could not be determined because of Landoil's use of as many as four layers of banks. Philguarantee said Landoil subsidiaries tried "to purposely keep the loan proceeds away from the control of Philguarantee."

Originally created in 1973 for land development and oil exploration, Landoil cashed into the booming Middle East construction market in the late 1970s, eventually becoming the 91st largest construction company in the world in terms of value of contracts.

To fund its multimillion-dollar projects, the company borrowed heavily from government banks. It also took out from foreign banks at least $100 million in loans, which were guaranteed by the Philippine government.

When the Middle East market crashed with the outbreak of the Iran-Iraq War, the company went bust. By 1983, it was near collapse and the government was left holding an empty bag because in many cases, Landoil loans were not backed by sufficient collateral.

Of the $100 million in loan guarantees extended by Philguarantee, only about five percent was secured by physical assets, according to a government official.

Links to Marcos

De Venecia's close association with the late President Marcos has long fueled talk in the business community about these transactions.

A former newspaperman and a Liberal Party member, de Venecia was tapped by Marcos in 1966 as minister to Vietnam. He later ran and won in 1969 as an independent congressman in Pangasinan's second district, and became part of the Northern Luzon bloc that was closely identified with the former president.

But de Venecia, who retired from politics in 1972 to concentrate on business, said he was a victim, rather than a crony, of the deposed dictator. He accused Marcos, who ended up owning 45 percent of Landoil, of seizing a significant block of Landoil shares through a front company, Piedras Petroleum, in 1977 after Landoil struck oil in Palawan.

De Venecia, who ranks fourth in line to the presidency, also denies that he or his company enjoyed financial privileges or engaged in fraud or loan diversion.

He branded these as old allegations that have been resolved by the Presidential Commission on Good Government (PCGG) and the Sandiganbayan in 1988.

But an examination of documents and interviews with government officials indicate that these allegations—especially those dealing with financial transactions—have never been resolved.

The DBP case is pending before the

Tanodbayan after more than five years. Philguarantee's most damaging findings were not addressed in a compromise agreement entered into between the PCGG and Landoil in 1988.

That compromise agreement was signed on July 19,1988 and has since been questioned by Philguarantee, subsequent PCGG commissioners, Landoil's former lawyer and the company's overseas workers.

The PCGG agreement states two things: First, it says that Landoil had submitted proof that showed the company and its officials were victims, rather than cronies, of Marcos.

Second, it asserts that Philguarantee had conducted an investigation that cleared Landoil and its officials of allegations regarding behest loans and the cause of its business reverses.

This assertion, however, is false. Philguarantee questioned the compromise agreement, informing the PCGG in a letter soon after the agreement was signed that it had never cleared Landoil and de Venecia.

In 1986, Philguarantee had sent the PCGG its preliminary findings of fraud and loan diversion and asked the commission to continue the investigation in preparation for the possible filing of charges against Landoil and de Venecia.

While the compromise agreement was not binding on Philguarantee or DBP as they were not signatories of the agreement, de Venecia cites the settlement as proof that he was cleared of fraud, loan diversion, and financial impropriety.

Despite Philguarantee's letter pointing out the error, the PCGG never corrected the agreement. Instead, the settlement was implemented.

Government Shortchanged

Landoil pledged to give the PCGG P13 million as part of an insurance payment obtained by the company from Lloyds of London. It also promised to pay the PCGG 45 percent of other insurance claims and all other company receivables.

In exchange, the PCGG agreed to drop the graft and corruption charges filed at the Sandiganbayan against Landoil and de Venecia.

David Castro, who was appointed PCGG commissioner after the deal was struck, said the government was shortchanged. In newspaper reports, Castro, who was a former lawyer for Lloyds, said the PCGG was not informed of the amount of the total insurance payment, which was $5.3 million or more than P100 million.

The P13 million that Landoil turned over represented only about 10 percent of the whole settlement, he said. He said the government should get more.

A former lawyer for Landoil, Manuel Camacho, also raised questions on where the rest of the $5.3 million had gone.

Hired by Landoil to settle the case with Lloyds, Camacho wrote the PCGG in 1988 that the insurance proceeds were diverted abroad, to the detriment of government and former Landoil overseas workers who have not been paid for more than five years since the company collapsed.

Camacho alleged that de Venecia had handpicked and illegally convened a new Landoil board of directors to approve the diversion of these funds to a New York law firm.

Originally, Landoil itself was to receive funds and use it to pay overseas contract workers, Landoil employees, Camacho's lawyer's fees, Landoil's operational expenses and Philguarantee, according to documents.

In a case filed at the Office of the Ombudsman in July 1988, more than 150 Landoil overseas workers attacked the diversion of the money abroad "for questionable and still unexplained purposes." They pointed out that Philguarantee, the wholly owned government institution that was to receive a portion of the settlement, was similarly gypped.

Since then, the workers have been partially paid. Philguarantee, however, did not get anything from the settlement.

House Speaker had Close Relationship with Marcos

Second of Three Parts

ALTHOUGH Jose de Venecia, Jr. is better known as the Speaker of the House of Representatives and the man who enjoys President Ramos's confidence, he spent more than a decade of his life in business as president of Landoil, the construction and oil exploration conglomerate.

The son of a Pangasinan judge and the grandson of a Dagupan mayor, he rose to prominence through business as well as through politics.

But de Venecia began his professional life as an 18-year-old reporter for Pan Asia Newspaper Alliance, where he is remembered for his eagerness to get people to like him. "He would flatter you to death," said his contemporary, Tony Gatica, a former reporter. "His asset was his charm."

When he left journalism, de Venecia tried public relations and broadcasting. Later, with the help of a stockbroker friend, he became vice-president of Redeco, a speculative oil exploration firm.

De Venecia's first marriage to Victoria Perez, daughter of the late Speaker Eugenio Perez of Pangasinan, helped pave his entry into politics. (That marriage has since been annulled and he is now married to Gina Vera-Perez).

He was a great favorite of his mother-in-law, Consuelo Perez, then Liberal Party treasurer. Through her influence, de Venecia became a spokesman for President Diosdado Macapagal during the 1961 election campaign.

In 1965, however, he quarreled with Macapagal. This clash torpedoed his first bid to represent Pangasinan's second district in Congress and pushed him to the camp of newly elected President Marcos, a man he would be linked to more than a decade later.

De Venecia says that it was Marcos who asked him to go to Vietnam where he spent four years as a minister at the Philippine Embassy in Saigon. At night, he visited Filipino soldiers, occasionally singing army ballads with military officers, among them Capt. Fidel Ramos.

In 1969, de Venecia returned to the Philippines to run a second time for a seat in Congress. He won overwhelmingly as an independent candidate but martial law cut short his term. Instead, he concentrated on business.

In 1973, de Venecia helped put up Landoil with capital from Taiwanese tycoon Tan Yu. Later, he bought out Tan Yu and built up Landoil to become his flagship company.

Risky Ventures

As a businessman, de Venecia was attracted to high-risk ventures. He was one of the oil-drilling pioneers, and is credited for the consortium's discovery of the country's first commercial oilfield in Palawan.

He took Landoil overseas, presiding through its go-go years when it became the 91st largest construction company in the world in terms of value of contracts.

But it was also de Venecia who pushed for the development of a million-dollar hotel and resort in Mariveles, Bataan, which ultimately faltered. And it was also he who presided over the company's fall when the Middle East construction market collapsed in the early 1980s.

In business circles, de Venecia became known as a master persuader, famous for convincing strangers to leave jobs to join his firms or even to invest huge sums in his ventures.

"Joe is the type of guy who can sit beside a stranger in an airplane and charm him into making a deal. By the time the plane touches ground, he has a preliminary agreement in his hand," Manuel said.

But others are not as generous. Conrad Andres, a stock market analyst who saw Landoil's rise and fall, doubts whether de Venecia has the ability to lead during times of crisis. "Landoil is a basket case and I think it reflects on de Venecia," he says. "You should do well not only during the good times, but also when the situation becomes difficult."

In de Venecia's view, Landoil was destined to become one of the country's most successful companies until Marcos came in 1977. De Venecia claims that Marcos took 30 percent of the company's stocks "illegally and forcibly" through a front company, Piedras Petroleum. Later, Marcos is believed to have acquired another 15 percent.

De Venecia wrote the Presidential Commission on Good Government in 1987 that Marcos demanded the shares after the company had struck oil and landed $70 million in contracts in Saudi Arabia. In exchange, Piedras gave land in Mariveles, Bataan that the company did not need.

But financial records show that, contrary to de Venecia's claims, Landoil's star began to soar only from 1977 after Marcos got into the company. Before that, the firm was not even listed among the country's top 1000 corporations. But by the end of 1977, Landoil was ranked 889 in the top 1000. Four years later, it became the 147th largest company in terms of revenues.

Behest Loans

The first allegations of a close relationship with Marcos would arise out of a series of loan transactions with DBP on the Bataan resort. These transactions were made after Marcos had seized control of the company.

DBP sent details of these transactions to the Presidential Blue Ribbon Commission created by Mrs. Aquino in 1987 to look into "behest loans," those given by government banks supposedly because of pressure from Marcos.

In 1988, DBP filed a case against Landoil at the Tanodbayan. It charged that Landoil had gypped the bank by trading in barren Bataan land worth only P13 million in exchange for canceling P98 million in loans. That case is still pending.

A Blue Ribbon Commission member said that the behest nature of the loan was well known within the bank. De Venecia's proposal to DBP was accompanied by a letter written to Marcos.

Landoil borrowed P23 million from DBP to develop a resort in Mariveles, Bataan. Later it also got a $10-million loan for the project from a syndicate of foreign banks. That loan was guaranteed by DBP in 1978.

The P23 million loan was subject to several conditions. But over time de Venecia, through several letters to the DBP, managed to change and even waive these conditions.

He got the bank to waive the requirement that he and other Landoil subsidiaries act as co-signers of the loan. This "left the loan partially secured only," to the prejudice of the bank, DBP said in its complaint.

But de Venecia went a step further. In 1979, he managed to cancel the P23 million loan and to convince the bank to assume Landoil's $10 million debt, in exchange for land in Bataan.

The DBP gave the court a May 27,1979 letter written by de Venecia to Marcos saying that since the government was interested in acquiring land in Mariveles anyway, Landoil could turn over some of its properties there in exchange for the cancellation of its loans.

Three months later, the board approved Landoil's proposal even if it knew that the Mariveles properties were undeveloped. But it required the company to put up a fund to develop the land so its value would rise to the value of the loan. In the next meeting, however, the DBP board members decided to waive that requirement as well.

In 1986, the DBP estimated that the properties were worth only P13 million. The bank appraiser's report described the Mariveles land as "raw" and "barren," accessible only by boat or foot trails.

Today, the Asset Privatization Trust has been tasked with selling off the land but despite more than five biddings since 1988, most of the lots have had no takers. The land was offered to the Department of Agrarian Reform but DAR rejected it because it was barren.

De Venecia is Not Yet Cleared

Conclusion

LANDOIL'S rise to become one of the world's biggest construction firms was financed by government loans and loan guarantees.

By the late 1970s, the company became bolder and entered into contracts with Middle East governments to build roads and manage ports. To do this, it borrowed heavily so that by the early 1980s, its debt was three times that of its equity.

About half of these loans or about $100 million were granted by local banks or guaranteed by the Philippine government through Philguarantee.

By 1985, Landoil's debt to Philguarantee had grown so huge that even the country's finance officials criticized it during a Cabinet meeting, according to a *Manila Bulletin* report.

By then, the Landoil Group had become Philguarantee's largest borrower, outpacing Marcos crony Rodolfo Cuenca's Construction Development Corp. of the Philippines (CDCP).

Most of these guarantees were not backed by sufficient collateral. In an interview, de Venecia pointed out that ambitious projects require such huge financing that a company may not have enough assets to mortgage.

When the Iran-Iraq war erupted and recession hit the Middle East, Landoil's fortunes plummeted. It could neither collect its receivables nor pay its debts.

As of September 1987, six companies in the Landoil group owed Philguarantee P5.2 billion. None of this has been paid.

Moreover, in a 1986 letter to PCGG, Philguarantee alleged the company committed fraud and "serious irregularities" in the use of these loans.

It cited three subsidiaries of Landoil as having diverted loans worth a total of $70 million in the 1980s. These were Philippine-Singapore Ports Corp., Philippine Hospitals & Health Services Inc., and Greater Manila Land Corp.

Landoil subsidiaries diverted the loan proceeds to other projects and purposes that were not approved by Philguarantee, thus violating its guarantee agreements, a Philguarantee report said.

In interviews, de Venecia insisted that no diversion took place because many of the loans were corporate loans that could be freely used by different subsidiaries.

Documents, however, showed these were project-specific loans. When told this, de Venecia said, "The Middle East was in flames. The whole thing had to be reviewed. You are not doing business in Escolta."

Loan Diversions

A Philguarantee investigation alleged that a Landoil subsidiary, Philisinports, may have diverted a substantial portion of a.$30 million loan.

Although Philisinports claimed that the loan was used for other Middle East projects, Philguarantee said in a report that it doubted that claim as the money was coursed through European and Hong Kong banks.

Another Landoil subsidiary, Greater Manila Land Corp. claimed that it used a $27-million loan to pay advances made by Landoil on two Middle East projects. In a report, Philguarantee said that its investigations showed that the projects were nonexistent. One of them was even supposed to have been in a war zone.

And even if such payments were made, Philguarantee said that this would have violated the terms of the loan guarantee that prohibited the funds from being used for projects other than those stated in the original agreement.

The agency also doubted whether another Landoil subsidiary, Philippine Hospital and Health Services, actually needed a $5-million loan as working capital for its projects. Philguarantee claimed that the subsidiary seemed to have enough funds to finance its undertakings.

Philippine Hospitals deliberately diverted funds to Landoil's Hong Kong affiliate, despite being aware of Philguarantee's condition to have the funds deposited with a government bank, from which the company could draw when needed.

Where all these diverted funds went remains a mystery. Philguarantee noted that tracing the ultimate destination of the loans was difficult because Landoil used as many as four conduit banks. The subsidiaries also purposely kept the loan proceeds away from the control of Philguarantee, the report stated.

FLAWED COMPROMISE

De Venecia, who became angry when asked about these allegations, repeatedly insisted he was cleared by the PCGG, which he said had investigated him for three years.

The PCGG compromise agreement is often cited by de Venecia as having cleared him of financial impropriety but interviews indicate that the accord had controversial and anomalous provisions.

It also appears that the agreement was hastily signed because of pressure from Landoil and from de Venecia himself who by then had been elected to Congress and headed the House's monetary and credit policy committee.

Two requests for the PCGG to provide its records on the case were denied. The commission said it was undertaking inventory.

The compromise agreement was signed in July 1988 during the 30-day tenure of Adolfo Azcuna when the PCGG was in the middle of a political storm.

The PCGG and the Office of Solicitor General were trading accusations on graft and corruption that were draining the commission's energies and deflecting the attention of most officials from their work.

From what could be gathered, the push to sign the agreement was strong. PCGG Commissioner Quentin Doromal remembers being given the impression that "time is of the essence."

Landoil claimed that the outcome of the PCGG investigation would affect its case on its insurance claims filed abroad, according to several PCGG sources. "My impression was that if we did not act, government would lose more," Doromal said.

Doromal said the agreement was supported by a commission resolution but could not remember who else, aside from him, was present during the vote.

PCGG commissioner Jose Laureta, who handled the agreement, said it was a unanimous decision. But PCGG Commissioners Ramon Rodrigo and Orlando Romero said they do not remember having approved the resolution and may have taken a leave at the time the agreement was approved. PCGG Chairman Azcuna declined to comment on who was present at the deliberations.

The compromise agreement clears Landoil and de Venecia of being Marcos cronies. It also clears the company of having used Marcos connections to contract loans.

But a PCGG official who asked not to be named said there was dissatisfaction among the rank and file with the agreement, which was the most concessional granted during that period.

De Venecia's testimony did not respond to all the allegations against him and the amount turned over was contingent, said the official. "PCGG violated its own policy of granting immunity established in 1986 that asked for full disclosure, full testimony, and restitution," he said.

Because of that dissatisfaction, the agreement was reviewed. It was approved a few months later. "We were never allowed to fully investigate," an official claimed.

Squeeze Play on the Expressway

BY SHEILA S. CORONEL
First published in the *Manila Standard* and *Manila Times*, March 4-5, 1996

This story begins with a P250,000-bribe given to a young congressman who was questioning the award to a business conglomerate of a contract to rehabilitate the North Luzon Expressway. On the surface, it would seem that this was a clear and simple case of a company trying to squash an investigation of its behavior. But this was far from a simple story, as it involved the intense rivalry between two giant firms—the Lopez-owned Benpres and Ital-Thai, a Thai construction conglomerate—that was fought with the use of political connections, smear tactics and well-funded media campaigns.

This two-part series also demonstrates the use of congressional investigations as a way to put the squeeze on business competitors. No doubt, business rivalries can be dirty, but they become even dirtier and murkier once they enter the political arena. This report was based on a pile of documents, including contracts, correspondence between officials and the firms involved, records of a congressional investigation, and internal documents from the Philippine National Construction Corp., which had the franchise over the expressway, and the Toll Regulatory Board, the government body that oversees the country's tollways. These documents showed the procedural lapses and the shortcuts that accompanied the awarding of the expressway contract to Benpres.

Interviews—with the businessmen involved, their political allies, government regulators, and the congressmen who were perhaps unwittingly led to investigate Benpres by the House Speaker, who was on good terms with Ital-Thai—provided the political context in which events took place.

Benpres's actions—including the bribery of congressmen and the use of the company's media clout as owner of broadcast giant ABS-CBN to put down critics—indicated the lengths to which the conglomerate would go to secure a lucrative contract. Ital Thai's behavior, including the mobilization of congressional allies to push for a probe of its rival, was equally brazen.

This story is instructive as it sheds light on how companies wield the weapons of power against their competitors. It also shows the need to go beyond the surface of events—such as a bribe given to a congressman—and examine the motives and actions of key individuals and companies who are part of the drama. This series was a finalist in the 1996 Jaime V. Ongpin Awards for investigative journalism.

A Clash of Giants

First of Two Parts

A few days before Christmas of 1995, a representative of Benpres Holdings Corporation gave Quezon City congressman Michael T. Defensor a brown envelope containing a thick wad of crisp P1, 000 bills.

In a taped interview with journalists on February 22, 1996, Defensor says he took the money—P200,000 in new notes—and returned it to a member of the Lopez family which owns Benpres, the conglomerate that includes broadcast giant ABS-CBN and the power firm Meralco. The Lopez kin accepted the money, but denied any knowledge about its source.

Benpres, too, denies the bribery charge, and Defensor himself, fearing reprisal from the Lopez family's powerful media network, fudged the details of the payoff in a congressional hearing on February 27. "I have just started my political career," he explained afterward. "I cannot go against ABS-CBN."

Without his knowing it, the 26-year-old congressman—an idealistic, former student leader whose independent thinking has impressed his older colleagues in the House—has found himself caught between powerful business and political forces interested in an infrastructure project that is expected to yield revenues of over half-a-trillion pesos in 25 years.

At stake in this controversy is the future of the North Luzon Expressway, the dilapidated highway that links Manila to

Central Luzon. The battle for the expressway shows how a high-stakes corporate dispute is fought in the Philippines and displays the weapons of power that can be wielded by the players: money, media clout, congressional investigations.

In July 1995, a company jointly owned by Benpres and another Lopez firm, the First Philippine Holdings Corp., signed an agreement with the government-owned Philippine National Construction Corporation (PNCC) to rehabilitate and extend the tollway to Subic and Clark.

But another company, the Italian-Thai Development Public Company Ltd., was also interested in the project, and presented an alternative proposal to rebuild and extend the highway to Pangasinan.

Ital-Thai had a champion in House Speaker Jose de Venecia, who not only suggested that the firm bid to build the highway to his home province, but also interceded for the company, when it looked like Benpres was going to get the deal.

"I suggested to Ital-Thai that they should take a look at extending the highway to Pangasinan," de Venecia admitted in an interview. "They presented a proposal. So I told (public works secretary Gregorio) Vigilar to defer the agreement with Benpres and to see whether Ital-Thai had a better proposal."

De Venecia said he was interested in the project because it would benefit his home province of Pangasinan. But there were also persistent rumors, which the Speaker has denied, that Ital-Thai contributed to the Lakas campaign kitty in the May 1995 elections.

Vigilar, however, refused the Speaker's request. In two memos to the President in June and July 1995, he insisted the Benpres proposal was "more advantageous to the government" and that it was far too late to consider another proponent.

Congress Intervenes

Weeks later, several congressmen began making privilege speeches hitting the Benpres agreement with PNCC. Subsequently, de Venecia ordered the House committee on public works to investigate the deal.

There appeared to be reason to investigate: the agreement was a negotiated contract with a government corporation whose leadership had opposed the terms as onerous, because it would give a private company near-total control of its biggest asset—a tollway franchise. Moreover, critics maintained there were procedural and legal lapses in the negotiations, which were conducted with a seeming lack of transparency.

> The battle for the expressway shows how a high-stakes corporate dispute is fought in the Philippines and displays the weapons of power that can be wielded by the players: money, media clout, congressional investigations.

Nueva Vizcaya Rep. Carlos Padilla, for one, said the agreement was marked by "falsification" and "criminal subterfuge." Batanes Rep. Florencio B. Abad argued that it should have been more thoroughly evaluated and reviewed.

Defensor received a comparison of the Ital-Thai and Benpres proposals from a senior congressman allied with de Venecia. He used this information in a privilege speech in November 1995, when he said the tollway agreement smacked of "highway robbery." He also grilled public works and PNCC officials who testified in the committee on public works, of which he is a member.

He says he was not aware, till later, of the machinations behind the scenes. "When I found out the real score, two or three weeks after I made my speech, I was very disappointed," confessed Defensor. "I felt bad. After I gave my speech, money was flowing. It seemed there were people (in the House) brokering for Ital-Thai."

And then came the offer of money from Benpres, which was made not only to Defensor but to at least one other member of the public works committee. The bewildered congressman found himself caught in a battle of the giants.

This whole affair raises questions about the conduct of business and politics in this country. It shows how corporate battles can be fought not only in boardrooms but in the halls of Congress and the offices of executive departments.

It also reveals how the public, and Congress for that matter, can be kept completely clueless about a multibillion-peso transaction that involves a government firm with a congressional franchise.

From the beginning, Benpres's entry into the North Luzon Expressway project sparked controversy. Questions about the wisdom of the company's proposal were raised in a series of internal government memos.

These questions were apparently legitimate ones, but they would probably not have been publicly aired, and certainly not brought up in the House, had de Venecia and Ital-Thai not entered the picture and encouraged an investigation.

"I had been warned by Benpres that it was possible we were only being used, that it was the Speaker who was instigating the investigation," said Batanes Rep. Florencio Abad, who was one of those who castigated the Benpres deal in the earnest belief that it was a questionable transaction. "I started thinking about it, and after a while I had the feeling *na mukhang naiisahan ako rito* (that I was being had)."

Flagship Project

Benpres became interested in the project in November 1993, after its chairman, Oscar Lopez, met with the President, who encouraged the company to participate in the government's "flagship" infrastructure projects.

At that time, the PNCC was already negotiating with a Malaysian company that was interested in extending the expressway from San Fernando to Subic. "Suddenly, Vigilar's chief-of-staff said we have a better partner, the Benpres group," recalled Ramoncito Abad, who was then PNCC president. "We met with Geny (Eugenio Jr.) and Oscar Lopez. Vigilar said, they are your partners for the Subic project. What else could I do? Here was a Filipino company with Vigilar's blessings."

When interviewed, Vigilar said he does recall telling PNCC this. "We did not champion anybody," he said. "What we championed was a method by which PNCC could get itself out of its present situation."

Financially, PNCC was in dire straits. It was heavily indebted, as it had to absorb all the bad loans incurred by Marcos crony Rodolfo Cuenca who owned the company when it was still called the Construction and Development Corporation of the Philippines (CDCP).

PNCC had no money to rehabilitate, much less extend, the tollways. Moreover, the Toll Regulatory Board (TRB) headed by Vigilar refused to grant an increase in tolls unless the company shaped up.

"We suggested to them, that since they could not work their way out of their difficulties, they should go into a partnership with a company that has financial clout," explained Vigilar. That company was Benpres.

The PNCC leadership, however, resisted. Abad argued that Benpres and First Philippine Holdings, which are mainly in telecommunications and power generation, had no track record in road construction.

"They also wanted our franchise," he said. "When we said no, they said they wanted the usufruct of the franchise, which is the same thing, because the usufruct would give them full control. They wanted the entire North Luzon Expressway. They wanted everything, including the businesses and commerce on the side. They wanted free right of way for their phones, their water, power and transmission lines."

Toward the end of 1994, the negotiations were reaching an impasse. On November 25 that year, Eugenio Lopez, Jr., Benpres president and chief executive officer, wrote President Ramos, accusing the PNCC management of "intransigent, unprofessional and deceptive behavior."

He also asked for "fundamental changes in PNCC" and warned that the project cannot proceed "unless some action is taken immediately to professionalize the management" of the government company.

Three weeks later, on December 20, 1994, Vigilar seconded Lopez's observations in a memo to the president that accused PNCC of discouraging investors. Nine days afterward, he put more pressure on the company by asking the Toll Regulatory Board, which he heads, to pass a board resolution warning that PNCC's franchise could be cancelled if its financial state was not improved and if it insisted on resisting possible business partners.

"The company was in trouble," explained Vigilar. "We told them you run the risk of having your franchise cancelled, that's the equivalent of clobbering them on the head... But we were merely offering a government corporation a way out of its dilemma."

Benpres's lack of experience, he said, was not an obstacle as it was being called in mainly for its financial clout and managerial expertise, which PNCC sorely lacked.

Still, Abad and PNCC chairman Leonides Gonzales resisted. In a letter to the President on January 10, 1995, they said that PNCC's "acquiescence to such an agreement will not endure the scrutiny of a congressional investigation nor the Tanodbayan."

In the end, both Abad and Gonzales caved in to pressure. Sensing that they had lost Malacañang's support, they resigned from PNCC in January 1995, paving the way for a new leadership more inclined to enter into a partnership with Benpres.

"All these happened just before the (May 1995) elections," said a congressman who asked not to be named. "And no one could afford to go against the Lopezes and ABS-CBN."

Benpres, however, insists that its proposal was approved on its own merits and that it was the government who set the negotiating rules. "Toll road projects are not easy to do," said J. Xavier Gonzales, the firm's chief operating officer. "They are risky. We preferred a public bidding, but it was the government which decided to do it this way."

On July 26, 1995, PNCC signed a joint-venture agreement with the Benpres group in Malacañang. The agreement gives the Lopez companies 80 percent control over a new company that would rehabilitate and operate the expressway and extend it to Subic and Clark by 1999. The company will spend close to P20 billion for the project, which is expected to generate revenues totaling P585 billion for 25 years.

"The agreement is onerous to PNCC and the riding public," Abad insisted in an interview. "And the way it was negotiated smacks of irregularity."

Vigilar disagreed. "PNCC gets a percentage of the gross revenues and a 20 percent share of the remainder," he said. "What better deal can you find?

Whatever the case, Benpres seemed to have won. But the battle was far from over.

Deception on the Highway

Conclusion

The NORTH Luzon Expressway is a bumpy, 100-kilometer stretch of road that has seen better times. Night and day, vehicles choke its lanes, which are now too narrow to absorb the volume of traffic. Entire segments of the road are covered with potholes or chunky asphalt that wears out the tread of tires and tries the patience of motorists.

The expressway is a showcase of decay, an exhibit of the sad state of Philippine infrastructure. In November 1996, dignitaries heading for Subic for the Asia-Pacific Economic Community (APEC) summit will have to pass through this sorry highway.

In July 1995, the Benpres Holdings Corporation got the multibillion-peso contract to repair and extend the expressway to the former base lands of Subic and Clark as part of a joint venture agreement with the government-owned Philippine National Construction Corporation (PNCC).

Benpres rushed the approval of the agreement and convinced both the President and Public Works Secretary Gregorio Vigilar to approve it by invoking APEC. In a note on the margin of a November 1994 letter written by Benpres president Eugenio Lopez, Jr., Ramos ordered Vigilar to ensure that the project is on track in time for the APEC meeting. He reiterated this order in another note he wrote on the margins of a memo submitted by Vigilar in December 1994.

The secretary, a West Point graduate and former military officer like Ramos, followed these marching orders. In a series of memos to the President in 1995, he justified skipping certain procedural and administrative requirements in negotiating the joint venture agreement with Benpres by saying that APEC could not wait.

The result, critics say, is an agreement that is not only onerous but also procedurally and legally infirm.

Moreover, a close examination of the agreement reveals that the project's impact on APEC will be minimal. The only segment of the road that will be finished in time for the summit is an 8.5-kilometer stretch that cuts through the mountains of Bataan, and which will reduce travel time from Subic to Manila by 20 minutes.

In a memo to the President on January 9, 1995, then PNCC chairman Leonides Gonzalez and president Ramoncito Abad accused Benpres of deliberate deception. "What Benpres is 'downplaying' is the fact that it could only deliver an insignificant eight-kilometer stretch" of road in time for the APEC Summit, they said.

The rest of the expressway—in all its glorious decay—will remain as is by the time the APEC summit takes place in November 1996. The 40-kilometer San Fernando-Subic segment, which will connect the existing expressway to Subic, will not be operational until the year 2000.

Indeed, controversy has stalked practically all aspects of Benpres' agreement with PNCC. Even the date of the contract's signing is controversial. Everyone who signed the agreement agreed that the signing took place in the presence of President Ramos in Malacañang on July 26, 1995. But the copy of the agreement itself puts the signing date as August 29, 1995.

Benpres chief operating officer J. Xavier Gonzales said that all that was a clerical error. He said the agreement was notarized by a lawyer only on August 29, which was also mistakenly put as the date of signing.

Others claim it was not such an innocent mistake. "This is falsification pure and simple," Rep. Carlos Padilla said in a privilege speech in the House.

When the signing took place on July 26, the PNCC board had just approved the guidelines for choosing prospective partners for the North Luzon expressway project. The guidelines were submitted to the Toll Regulatory Board, the government agency supervising tollway projects, which approved them on August 11.

In other words, the joint venture agreement was signed a month before the guidelines for such an agreement were actually approved. Thus, Padilla accused Benpres of "criminal subterfuge"—changing the date of signing in the final agreement to cover up the fact that the contract preceded the guidelines.

Vigilar saw nothing irregular about this. "Even when we were discussing (with Benpres), we were already evolving the guidelines," he said in an interview. "We had no signed guidelines, true, but we were not operating blind because we had drafts. And we were going by the BOT (Build-Operate-Transfer) law."

The BOT law, however, provides for public bidding. Benpres itself wanted a competitive bidding, but the Department of Justice (DOJ), in a June 1994 opinion, said this was not necessary because the PNCC franchise allows it to enter into joint ventures even without a bidding.

Gray Area

In a sense, many of the problems that hound the contract have to do with the fact that both the government and Benpres were negotiating in a gray area covered by conflicting laws and provisions.

For this reason, the agreement has become vulnerable to legal scrutiny in a country where there is no shortage of legal experts. This vulnerability was heightened by the fact that the government took some "short cuts" on established procedures. Because of these, interested parties can actually take the case to court and delay the project.

The DOJ opinion, for one, said that the joint venture agreement had to pass through the Government Corporate Monitoring and Coordinating Committee (GCMCC), an inter-agency body that screens transactions made by government corporations.

But Vigilar asked the president to do away with this requirement as well. "We were in a hurry to get these things going," he explained. "If we went through the GCMCC, it would have delayed the project for at least two to three months."

The secretary also argued that the agreement did not fall within GCMCC's purview, which is to ensure that government involvement in the private sector is minimized.

He reasoned that although Benpres had no track record in construction, as the guidelines required of a joint venture partner, it had the financial clout and the managerial skills that PNCC needed.

In similar fashion, Vigilar brushed aside other objections to the contract put forth by other government agencies.

For example, both the Department of Justice and the Office of the Government Corporate Counsel (OGCC) had objected to transferring the usufruct—or the right to use and benefit—from the PNCC franchise to the joint venture company to be formed by Benpres and PNCC.

PNCC has a franchise to operate both the North and South Luzon Expressways until the year 2007. That franchise was granted by presidential decree to Rodolfo Cuenca's Construction and Development Corp. of the Philippines (CDCP) in 1977. When the government bailed out the heavily indebted CDCP in 1983, the government became the company's majority shareholder and CDCP became PNCC.

In an April 1995 opinion, Justice Oscar Garcia, the government corporate counsel, who happens to be a protégé of House Speaker Jose de Venecia, wrote that transferring the usufruct "was nothing short of an abdication of PNCC's franchise over the North Luzon Expressway."

"It is our view," he added, "that such abdication should not be allowed." Garcia also said that "the proposed agreement is so encompassing in scope as to exceed normal joint venture proposals."

He noted that since 80 percent of the joint venture company to be formed was to be owned by Benpres, PNCC would also be abdicating its "mutual right to control" that is "among the essential elements of a joint venture." In such a case, he said, when the transaction loses the character of a joint venture, "the general rule on bidding may then apply to govern the transaction."

Again, Vigilar found these objections something of a nuisance. "I've lived with legal opinions all my life," he said. "An opinion is just an opinion."

In a letter to Garcia, he wrote that Benpres was not willing to enter into a joint venture unless it got the usufruct to the franchise. "In exchange, however, PNCC shall receive a cash stream equivalent of

The PNCC management had initially resisted surrendering to Benpres so much control over the joint venture.

more than P4 billion in present value during the life of the franchise, without any expenses on its part."

Benpres does not find this insistence on the usufruct unwarranted. The usufruct, it said, ensures "management control" over a project that will add up to P20 billion and could cost the company money if the projected number of toll-paying motorists does not materialize.

The agreement removed from PNCC and transferred to the joint venture company controlled by Benpres the right to manage and operate the tollway. It had no precedent. A similar deal inked by PNCC with the Indonesian firm P.T. Citra did not involve a transfer of the usufruct of the franchise and did not remove from PNCC the right to manage the tollway and collect fees.

Indeed, the PNCC management had initially resisted surrendering to Benpres so much control over the joint venture. It wanted a bigger share of the company and of the revenues.

But, argued Benpres' Gonzales: "We are undertaking the risk of financing... It's not that we don't trust the financial integrity of PNCC, it's just that to finance this project, it's important that investors and lenders can rely on or financial integrity in terms of being able to execute the project, collect what is to be collected and deliver the value to lenders."

Vigilar earnestly believes that the agreement is publicly defensible. He said that the law allows the transfer of the usufruct to parts of the franchise as long as it had the president's approval, which Vigilar obtained, in the form of a May 1995 memo from then Deputy Executive Secretary Leonardo Quisumbing.

To Vigilar, the joint venture with Benpres was the only way out for a government corporation that was heavily indebted and could not seem to get itself out of a rut.

Some congressmen, however, did not agree. Both the government and Benpres took a beating in a series of hearings held by House committee on public works since November 1995.

Ironically, the procedures that were disregarded to speed up the agreement proved to be its undoing. Questions about procedural shortcuts hounded Benpres and catalyzed the ongoing House investigation that has already delayed the project several months.

Moreover, rather than hush-hushing the investigation, the alleged P200,000 payoffs to members of the House committee conducting the investigation has only focused even more attention on the supposed flaws of the rushed agreement.

It seems that in the end, the shortcuts and envelopes of cash did not pay off.

The Grandmother of all Scams

BY ELLEN TORDESILLAS AND SHEILA S. CORONEL

First published in *Manila Standard, Sun Star Daily, Manila Times, Malaya, Business World, Philippine Daily Inquirer, Independent Post,* March 18-22, 1998

This three-part series, which hit the headlines at the start of the campaign period for the 1998 presidential elections, is an investigation of probably the biggest scam of the Ramos era. It is, in a sense, also an investigation of an investigation, as it was undertaken after the Senate Blue Ribbon committee had undertaken a months-long probe into the sale of government property just off the coast of Manila Bay. While the Senate report was pretty exhaustive, it treaded carefully on the involvement in the scam of then House Speaker Jose de Venecia. It also missed out on certain key documents and failed to provide the context of the relationships that linked the various individuals involved in the transaction.

That is what this report attempted to do. Basic sources were the transcripts of the Senate hearings, which when put together were about a foot high, and the Senate report itself. Key documents submitted to the Senate were also obtained, among them letters written by officials of the Public Estates Authority (PEA), the joint-venture agreement between the PEA and the Thai company that purchased the property, and a letter written by the company that provided details of the initial payments to two local brokers who had wangled the deal. In addition, the authors were able to get access to documents that were kept from the Senate, including an agreement that assured the brokers close to P2 billion in commissions if they were able to get the government to award the contract to the Thai firm.

The challenge in this report was putting a complex and multifaceted story together. The authors spoke to most of the cast of characters involved in this scam, which ranged from high-profile politicians to brokers who worked in the shadows. From interviews with two dozen people, the writers were able to make sense of what the documents contained and also got insights into the workings of business and politics in this country.

The Amari scam is the classic East Asian "bubble" story, one that shows how corrupt dealings between officials and businessmen make for an uneven playing field for business and rob the government of much-needed revenues. The publicity given to this series cast doubt on de Venecia's suitability for the presidency, and questions about the scam hounded his candidacy.

This series won for the authors the first prize in the 1998 Jaime V. Ongpin Awards for investigative journalism.

Huge Payoffs Made to Officials and Brokers

First of Three Parts

ON Friday, April 28, 1995, George Triviño, a convicted gold smuggler with a long history of wheeling-dealing, received 31 checks totaling P300 million from the Amari Coastal Bay Resources Corp., a Thai-Filipino company that had just entered into a P1.8-billion contract with the government to buy reclaimed property off the Manila-Cavite coastal road.

All the checks were deposited into an account at the U.N. Avenue branch of the Traders Royal Bank. As soon as they cleared, on Tuesday, May 2, just seven days before the local elections, P273 million was withdrawn from that account. The following day, the balance of P27 million was drawn from the same bank.

Triviño was the Philippine representative of the Ital-Thai Development Corporation Ltd., the Thai construction conglomerate that set up Amari. According to a Senate investigation of the Amari transaction, the checks were "encashed by the sister-in-law of a high ranking leader of Congress after said checks were endorsed by George Triviño." When the Senate released its report in 1997, the chamber buzzed with the rumor that the official was House Speaker Jose de Venecia.

De Venecia emphatically denies this allegation. "The alleged withdrawal of P300 million by a sister-in-law of the Speaker from commissions paid to one George Triviño is a wild, untrue, and unfounded conjecture. For no such withdrawal ever took place," he says.

Close to a year after two Senate committees wound up their investigation of what Senator Ernesto Maceda has called the "grandmother of all scams," many questions about Amari remain unanswered.

De Venecia's role in the deal is one. President Fidel V. Ramos's possible involvement is another. The payoffs that were made to several officials in an effort to hush up the investigation of the transaction also remain carefully cloaked in secrecy.

Our own investigation shows that from 1995 to 1997, as much as P3 billion in bribes and commissions was paid by Amari to a cast of brokers, government bureaucrats and politicians, making this the single biggest scam in memory, dwarfing the amounts made in single transactions by the most avaricious of Marcos's cronies.

In the course of several months, we have interviewed some two dozen people, including several who were privy to the transaction. These sources as well as a trail of documents, many of them subpoenaed by the Senate, indicate that the following payoffs were made:

- P300 million — to George Triviño, who later turned over the amount to the politician who was his principal
- P100 million — to a Hong Kong bank account held by Triviño's principal
- P 225 million — blank checks paid to Benito Cuevo, the broker who made the connection between Amari and officials of the Public Estates Authority (PEA), the government agency in charge of the reclaimed property
- P344.7 million — paid to two ethnic Chinese brokers, Frank Chua and Benito Co, who were negotiating with an array of officials.
- P300 million — paid to various individuals and officials in order to persuade a Korean company to give up its bid for the property.

These payoffs total P1.269 billion. A large part of that amount was passed on by the brokers to their contacts in various government agencies. In addition, our sources say, close to P2 billion more was paid to various individuals and officials in 1997, after the scandal broke and the parties involved made frantic attempts to cover up the deal.

Wheeler-Dealer's Heaven

This story began in 1994, at the height of the property and stock market boom, years before the Southeast Asian currency crisis that sent fortunes crashing. Land prices were soaring then, the Manila skyline was crowded with cranes, and the high rollers in the stock market were making so much money it was obscene.

At that time, every wheeler-dealer in town was looking for an opportunity to cash in on the boom. They seldom cared about the rules and believed that everyone, even the top officials of government, has a price. In their world, connections and access to the rich and powerful are the most valuable assets. More than anything else, what counts is whom you know and whom you can influence.

The key characters who would figure in the Amari scam belong to this netherworld of wheeler-dealers. They include Benito Cuevo, the quintessential dealmaker who hangs around at the Patisserie, the coffee shop of the Holiday Inn hotel in downtown Manila. Triviño, the smuggler who told the Senate that the House Speaker was his "long-time friend." Frank Chua and Benito Co, loggers and high-stakes gamblers who can smell a business deal a mile away. What brought them together was one of the biggest deals in the era of the fast buck.

Initially, they and their accomplices and principals were to be paid P1.75 billion in brokers' commissions from the purchase by

Amari of three reclaimed islands not far from the coastal road leading to Cavite.

The islands were an accident. In the 1970s, the area was reclaimed from Manila Bay by the Construction Development Corp. of the Philippines (CDCP), the Marcos crony company that was building the coastal road. But the road was realigned, leaving three mounds of reclaimed land stranded in the bay, in the foreshore area of the towns of Parañaque and Las Piñas.

In 1981, Ferdinand Marcos tried to rescue the bankrupt CDCP by ordering the sale of several portions of the Manila Bay reclamation area, including the three islands and the site of the ill-fated Film Palace, to the PEA, a government agency he created in 1977. PEA was asked to pay CDCP P1.5 billion for the land and to assume another P1.5 billion of CDCP's debts.

Fifteen years later, in the 1990s, PEA found itself the fortunate owner of what had become prime real estate in Manila's hot property market. Although the three islands had by then become a teeming slum marooned in the polluted waters of Manila Bay, developers were quick to see the potential of seafront property just off scenic Roxas Boulevard, only a spit away from the international airport, and with a view of a world-famous sunset.

On April 28,1995, the PEA board approved the contract selling the three islands to Amari, which was awarded the Philippines' biggest real estate project ever. On July 23, 1996, Centennial City, a publicly listed company, assumed complete control and ownership of Amari through a stock swap. Centennial then made a killing in the stock market by selling the idea of a new city complete with skyscrapers, parks, a marina, a golf course and casinos that would rise out of Manila Bay.

Not long afterward, two Senate committees investigated the transaction, concluding, after four months of hearings, the government was defrauded of billions of pesos in that deal.

But the investigation was unable to find conclusive evidence of the possible involvement of a string of public officials led by de Venecia. The Senate also looked the other way as frantic attempts were made to derail its investigation.

Montano's Role

The key person in this transaction was Justiniano "Bobby" Montano IV, an aging playboy named after his grandfather, the strongman who held Cavite in thrall from the 1940s to the 1960s. In the course of the Senate investigation, Maceda pointed to Bobby Montano as "the real architect and engineer and sponsor of this deal."

Bobby is the son of retired army colonel Ciriaco "Akoy" Montano, who was the Philippine military attaché in Washington, D.C. in 1950, the year Bobby was born and also the year the young cadet Fidel V. Ramos graduated from West Point. As military attaché, Akoy Montano took care of cadets like Ramos.

When Ramos fell ill and needed surgery, Akoy Montano arranged with the U.S. defense department to get free treatment for his ward. After all, Akoy's brother Julian was married to Ramos's first cousin, and the Montanos were a large clan with a strong sense of family ties and filial obligation.

In the 1960s, when Ramos's promotion to the rank of colonel was being questioned by the commission on appointments in Congress, he approached then senator Justiniano Montano Sr., who interceded on the officer's behalf with his Liberal Party colleague, Senator Benigno

Aquino Jr. The old man Montano likes to recall this story, which is embedded in the Montano family lore.

For this is what political families are all about: a shared myth about favors traded and owed through generations of deals and compromises. It was therefore not surprising that when Ramos was seeking the presidency in 1992, the Montanos helped him, particularly in Cavite, where they retained some residual influence.

In 1993, Senator Montano went to Malacañang to pay a courtesy call on the newly elected Ramos. He brought along his favorite grandson, Bobby. Right there and then Bobby was offered a government job.

Then 43 years old, Bobby had so far had an unremarkable career. He once ran a travel agency and dabbled in real estate. He also ran for provincial board member in Cavite in 1988, but lost. Bobby was first offered a post at the National Housing Authority, his father Akoy recalls. But when that didn't work out, the position of deputy manager for special projects was created for him at PEA, and he assumed that post in July 1993. Bobby is the only PEA deputy manager so far who was a presidential appointee.

By everyone's account, Bobby Montano pushed aggressively to speed up the development of the three islands. In 1991, the PEA board had already authorized the bidding of the 157-hectare property and set the minimum bid price at P1, 680 per square meter. The bidding was scheduled in December that year, but none of the prospective buyers submitted a proper offer. The bidding was declared a failure.

In 1993 and 1994, there were other offers, but none of them were seriously considered. In August 1994, the PEA board approved a second public bidding and set the minimum price again at P1,680 per square meter, with the option to reclaim 250 hectares more, subject to a 60-40 sharing in favor of the buyer.

By this time, Bobby Montano was already scouting for a developer. He was confident that he could push this deal through. His family was close enough to the President. And Agnes Doneza Montano, the woman he had been living with, was vice-president of the Women Auxiliaries for Ramos Movement (WARM), that was formed during the President's 1992 campaign.

Bobby Montano is "the real architect and engineer and sponsor of this deal."

The WARM women were often at the Palace to entertain guests during open-house events or to fill the hall whenever Ramos had a social occasion that needed an audience. WARM members were friendly with the Palace staff and had access to the President himself. Some of them even attend press conferences, joining those who approach Ramos to have papers signed or ask for favors.

Agnes Montano is not a shrinking violet. A former Miss Gingoog, she has beauty queen looks and a steely determination to get close to the top. Indeed, she would tell friends that she helped Bobby get his PEA post. More than that, several of those we interviewed say that it was through Agnes's lobbying efforts that Bobby managed to get Malacañang approval for the Amari deal.

Typically, Bobby employed the family network to arrange the sale of the three islands. Once the word was out that he was looking for a buyer, his cousin-in-law, Aurora "Auring" Montano, a small-time real estate broker, put him in touch with Ben Cuevo. Auring was herself a member of WARM.

Interviewed by the Senate committees investigating the Amari deal, both Auring Montano and Cuevo admitted they had done business deals in the past and that it was through Auring that Cuevo made the connection to Bobby. Confronted by receipts of payments made to her, Auring admitted that she received P30.5 million in checks for making the right introductions.

Brokering for a Living

Benito "Ben" Cuevo is a cagey, nondescript man in his late 60s. He is a seedy character, the kind who spends hours at coffee shops making deals. The waiters and the hangers-on at the Patisserie, where he stops for coffee and assorted deal making nearly every morning, refer to him as the "commissioner," because that is essentially what he is known for: making commissions on all sorts of transactions.

Cuevo owns the International Merchandizing and Development Corp., a trading company through which some of the Amari commissions were coursed. Lawyer and former Cabinet secretary Fulgencio Factoran Jr., who has encountered Cuevo, describes him as the "caricature of a hustler," a man who "is a friend to everybody he can make use of." Indeed, when one of us interviewed Cuevo, she was offered a cut in the Amari deal once he had collected on still uncashed commissions from the company.

From the accounts of various people who have encountered Cuevo, as well as testimonies and documents obtained during the Senate hearings, and from an interview with the man himself, this is what we could piece together.

When Bobby was peddling the three islands around, Cuevo saw the opportunity for another commission. He contacted old acquaintances, two Chinese-Filipino businessmen who moved in the same world of coffee shop hustlers that he did.

Cuevo admits that he had done business in the past with Frank Chua (also known as Chua Hun Siong) and Benito Co (also known as Chin San Cordova), but he is vague about the details. Chua and Co are known in Binondo as buccaneer businessmen with an instinct for a fast buck. They are also inveterate gamblers who would lose millions in one night of gaming at the casino.

Both men jumped at the opportunity to be in on the three islands deal. The key was to find a big company who could develop the property. Cuevo would then bring the company to Bobby Montano, so all four of them could then skim off fat broker's fees from the deal.

The two Chinese businessmen did not have to look very far. One of their casino buddies was Manuel Sy, whose family was involved in steel manufacturing. Sy would tell the Senate that the two men asked him whether he knew of any contractor. Sy referred his Thai partner, the ethnic Chinese tycoon Premchai Karnasuta, who ran the biggest construction outfit in Thailand.

Sy and Premchai have been partners for 18 years in a Thai company called Siam Steel. Together, they put up Amari in 1994. By then, Premchai's Ital-Thai, which was founded in 1958, had grown into a multibillion-baht company that cornered the largest construction projects in Thailand and even in Burma and Laos.

Premchai had cashed in on the construction boom in fast-growing Thailand, and was building, among others, hotels, airports, power plants, and an elevated railway system in Bangkok. He was definitely big-time. Awash with cash like many other Thai companies during that period, he was also eager to spread his wings to the Philippines.

Premchai was a veteran of the rough-and-tumble world of Thai politics where, much like in the Philippines, access to top decision makers is the key. When he came to Manila on the lookout for investment possibilities, he was introduced by Sy to his casino crony, George Triviño.

Sy would tell the Senate blue-ribbon committee that Triviño was in search of a *"medyo sikat na* contractor *na may pangalan* (big-time contractor with a name)." When Triviño met Premchai, he offered to be Ital-Thai's Philippine representative and also arranged to introduce the Thai tycoon to de Venecia. The Speaker, in turn, brought Premchai to Malacañang to meet the President.

Triviño, originally Uy Han Kiat or George Uy before he took on the name of his godfather, Bicol politician Juan Triviño, was convicted of smuggling in 1969. He fled to the Dominican Republic, where he got himself a new citizenship. He later moved back to Asia and was reported to have run afoul of Singaporean authorities for illegally trading gold.

Somehow, Triviño wormed his way back to the Philippines where, like Chua, Cuevo and Co, he acted as a bridge between the underworld of crooked deals and illicit commissions and the very public klieg-light world of politics. Before long, Triviño was seen around in the company of the House Speaker whom he described in the course of the Senate investigation as an old friend, *"matagal ko nang kaibigan."*

Amari's Trail Reaches Malacañang

Second of Three Parts

SINCE the nineteenth century, discreet brokers, many of them ethnic Chinese, have played a key but often invisible role in Philippine politics. Filipino officials have relied on such middlemen to make under-the-table arrangements away from the glare of public scrutiny.

For sure, men like these take a cut for themselves, but that is the price of the connections and the maneuvers they bring into the transaction. They also provide politicians the plausible deniability the latter need if, for some reason, the deal is exposed. They are the fall guys. They take the flak.

Premchai Karnasuta, the Thai construction tycoon who heads the Ital-Thai conglomerate, was apparently aware of the importance of the brokering function, even in the late twentieth century, the era of transnational capital flows. That is why he let the well-connected George Triviño do his work.

Triviño admitted to the Senate that he helped Ital-Thai in its bid to get the contract to build the Clark airport and the North Luzon Expressway. For various reasons, both these deals fell through. Ital-Thai opted out of Clark and a related project to build a railway from Makati to Angeles City when it was clear that the Manila airport would remain the premier airport. Ital-Thai also lost the North Luzon Expressway contract to the Lopezes of Benpres.

In both cases, Triviño said he sought de Venecia's intercession. The Speaker, however, did not succeed in mustering enough support in government for the company's proposals. During the Senate investigation, Triviño also admitted that he and Premchai got as far as meeting the President twice, the first time in August 1994.

"Mr. Triviño was introduced to me as a possible investor," Ramos replied in response to our queries. "I receive or meet several of these a week and give them only the Philippines 2000 investment list."

When Premchai and his family saw the three islands along the coastal road on one of their visits to Manila sometime in 1994, the Thai magnate, eager for a project, immediately saw the potential of the property.

His business partner Manuel Sy told a Senate hearing that Premchai then asked for a meeting with Chua and Co, which Sy arranged. The two brokers, in turn, brought in Benito Cuevo, who made the link to Bobby Montano, deputy manager of the Public Estates Authority (PEA) and other PEA officials.

At that point, Triviño did not know of the deal and so was left out of the negotiations. By November 1994, the details of the deal were ironed out. Chua and Co assured Premchai that they could get government approval for Ital-Thai's purchase of the three reclaimed islands in Manila Bay.

Premchai was apparently so convinced of this that on November 25, 1994, he signed a memorandum of agreement promising that Ital-Thai would pay Chua and Co P1,250 per square meter or a whopping total of P1.973 billion for "securing the acquisition of the subject asset and the subject reclamation project."

The contract bound the two brokers to deliver a deed of sale on the property and an agreement with PEA that the three islands would be purchased by Ital-Thai at P1,000 per square meter, and that an additional 250 hectares to be reclaimed by the project would be shared 70-30 between Amari and PEA, with the latter getting the smaller percentage.

This contract, which was withheld from the Senate, provides positive proof that under-the-table negotiations between Ital-Thai and PEA took place even before the project was formally taken up by PEA, which officially received word about Amari's proposal only seven weeks later, on January 13, 1996.

The contract guaranteeing the commissions was also signed even before Amari, named after a chain of Thai hotels owned by Premchai, was incorporated on December 5, 1994. It is apparent from this contract that the two brokers had already wangled an assurance from PEA that the deal would be approved.

Why else would the extremely savvy Premchai agree to pay such a huge commission at that point? The truth was, various sources familiar with the deal told us, Bobby Montano, through Chua and Co, had assured Ital-Thai that PEA would deliver.

Presidential Approval

It was abundantly clear to Montano and the pair of brokers with whom he was negotiating that a transaction of this magnitude would move only if it had the presidential seal of approval. By then, PEA had received four other offers for the property and was basically sitting on them. The Senate found proof that Montano was transacting with Malacañang on his own, without the knowledge of then PEA general manager Amado S. Lagdameo.

On December 3, 1994, Amari wrote a letter to Ramos proposing to develop the three islands. The letter contained exactly the same conditions set out in the November agreement between Premchai and the two Chinese brokers: a purchase price of P1, 000 per square meter on the reclaimed property and a 70-30 sharing scheme on the land that was still to be reclaimed.

During the Senate hearings, Montano admitted that he personally took the letter to Malacañang. What he did not say was that it was Agnes Montano, the WARM vice president and Palace hanger-on, who made sure it got to the President. Indeed, Ramos endorsed the letter on December 13, with a marginal note that said, "To GM/ CEO Lagdameo, for study/comments ASAP, President Ramos."

That letter reached Lagdameo only a month later, but without a transmittal note from Malacañang, leading Lagdameo to conclude, when queried in the Senate, that it was probably hand-carried back to PEA by Bobby Montano.

On December 14, Montano wrote to Amari to inform the company that its proposal had been "favorably acted upon by the President by referring the matter to the PEA for immediate response." Moreover, Montano wrote, "all indications centered into the acceptance of your said offer and proposal, which under our observation are legally tenable."

On what authority did Montano write the letter? It would take a month before Lagdameo would even have a look at Amari's proposal and the President's recommendation. Montano also did not have the power to say that the transaction was "legally tenable," as this was a function of the Office of the Government Corporate Counsel (OGCC).

Ramos's role in this entire transaction remains one of the many mysteries surrounding the Amari scam. Despite the letters and Montano's own admission that he delivered Amari's proposal to Malacañang, the President insists he did not deal with Montano. "Either Montano has unusual access (to the President) or pretends to have such access," says Senator Franklin Drilon, chairman of the Senate blue-ribbon committee which investigated the Amari deal..

Ramos's role in this entire transaction remains one of the many mysteries surrounding the Amari scam.

Members of the Montano family insist it was the former. They reveal that Bobby met with the President on the Amari proposal; on at least one occasion, the meeting took place at the Malacañang golf course.

Moreover, they say that when push came to shove in December 1996, and Bobby had resigned from PEA in disgrace and was in fear of being exposed by the Senate investigation, Presidential Security Group commander and senior aide-de-camp Brig. Gen. Jose Calimlim phoned Agnes Montano at 2 a.m. to relay the message to Bobby that "we are in control. We are on top of everything."

Calimlim does not deny making the call, but insists that he merely wanted to assure Agnes and Auring Montano, who were his friends, that they should not worry despite an arrest warrant issued by the Senate. "I assured them of their safety," Calimlim recalls, adding that he escorted the women to the Manila Hotel to meet with National Bureau of Investigation (NBI) Director Santiago Toledo. "They are my friends.:.*Baka ang sinabi ko,* tell Bobby not to worry about this."

Unfortunately, the Senate investigation did not pursue Ramos's possible role. But it is clear from the Senate hearings that whether or not the President was dealing with Montano, Malacañang's blessings went a long way in ensuring the deal's approval.

Lagdameo, in his disjointed Senate testimony, admitted that "in the normal course of business, the marginal notes of the President receive immediate attention." Indeed, on January 26, 1995, barely two weeks after Lagdameo received the letter with Ramos's instructions, he informed Amari that PEA had accepted the company's offer.

When asked by senators how it was possible to approve in only two weeks a business proposal involving something as technical as land development, Lagdameo reasoned that PEA had been studying the technical issues involved in the project since 1991.

To be fair, Lagdameo, by everyone's account, was completely clueless about the back-door negotiations taking place right under his nose. It appears that he was merely following the President's instructions.

HUGE COMMISSIONS

In his testimony, Lagdameo revealed that Montano and the PEA management group assigned to the three islands were insisting on selling the property to Amari at only P750 per square meter despite a 1991 resolution by the PEA board requiring public bidding for the property and a minimum bid price of P1,680 per square meter.

It was he, Lagdameo said, who fought for raising Amari's offer from P1,000 to P1,200 per square meter. When the price of the property was raised, the brokers' share was proportionally decreased.

It is clear from the way events unfolded that Premchai was willing to pay a total of P2,250 per square meter, or P3.3 billion altogether, for the property. The brokers could split the change from whatever price they could negotiate from the government. When PEA insisted on P1,200 per square meter, the total brokers' commissions, as indicated in a receipt signed by Chua and Co, was reduced to P1.75 billion from the original P1.89 billion.

It is an eye-popping amount. If the deal were done legitimately, this money (and more, because the property was undervalued) should have gone into PEA's coffers, for doing what the agency was mandated by its charter to do: build low-cost housing for the poor. Instead, the money went into various well-lined pockets.

> The total brokers' commissions were reduced to P1.75 billion from the original P1.89 billion.

By all indications, Amari got the three islands for a song. By the admission of PEA's own officials, the cost of reclaiming land stood at P2,000 to P5,000 per square meter. While it is true that a good portion of the three islands remains under a few feet of water, P1,000 per square meter was still barely the cost of reclamation.

In fact, three other firms had offered P1,400 to P1,600 per square meter for the property, but PEA did not negotiate with them. Moreover, reclaimed land near the three islands was selling at up to P90,000 per square meter.

Yet the Amari deal was approved by PEA without much questioning from either the agency's management or board. In fact, one of the most incredible—and instructive—things about this transaction was that it passed the scrutiny not only of PEA but also of a range of government entities established precisely to prevent scams such as this.

Among the many lessons from Amari is that the check-and-balance mechanisms against corruption are flexible: they can be bent by those with the right connections and sufficient cash. The scam would have slipped right through the Senate as well, had one of the disgruntled parties in the transaction not squealed. But that is getting ahead of the story.

Adjusted Appraisals

What helped convince the PEA management and board to accept Amari's proposal were three appraisals of the property made by different companies that priced the three islands from P750 to P1,000 a square meter. There are indications that these appraisals were tailor-made to favor Amari's bid.

One firm, Asian Appraisers, had valued the property at P1,680 per square meter in 1991, yet it pulled down its estimate to P1,000 in 1995. A year later, when asked by Amari to appraise the same property, the company put a per square meter price tag of P4,500.

PEA records show that Bobby Montano contracted the appraisers. "The appraisal process was clearly flawed and designed to justify what is otherwise a flawed transaction," says Drilon. *"Talagang maliwanag, niyari nila ito* (It's clear that it was fixed)."

The records also show that PEA used the appraisals to cast aside the minimum base price of P1,680 per square meter set in 1991. Recalling previous failed biddings, PEA also decided not to auction the property, but to negotiate with prospective developers.

At this stage, PEA was seriously considering only two proposals: Amari's, which Lagdameo believed had the presidential endorsement, and that of Hyosan Prime Construction, a Korean company that had found a patron in PEA chairman Rivera.

In his speech exposing the Amari scam, Maceda alleged that Amari paid Rivera and his cohorts P200 million "to settle (their) competing claim to the property." Congress sources say that the payoff was actually P300 million and that it was given to Rivera and various individuals in Hyosan.

Part of the payoff, we were told by various sources, reached a presidential relative who had helped Hyosan push its bid. Hyosan, Senate sources say, merely held on to its bid so it could be bought out.

With Hyosan out of the way, the field was left to Amari. On April 8, 1995, Amari increased its offer to P1,100 per square meter. On the same day, Lagdameo said that PEA would accept the proposal if Amari raised the price to P1,200. On April 21, Amari agreed. Immediately, Lagdameo asked the OGCC to review the draft of PEA's joint venture agreement with Amari.

Suspiciously, the OGCC said that the joint-venture agreement was "valid and in order" in just half a day. At the Senate, OGCC assistant counsel Anthony Sison admitted that he received the agreement late morning of April 21 and finished his opinion before 5 p.m.

Sison's boss, OGCC chief Oscar Garcia, approved the opinion. Drilon recalls that when he was justice secretary, he appointed Garcia to the OGCC on the intercession of de Venecia, who was the government counsel's friend and fellow Pangasinense. Moreover, when Garcia reached the obligatory retirement age of 65 in December 1994, his term was extended by the President, who also comes from Pangasinan.

In April 1995, when de Venecia tried to stop Benpres from getting the North Luzon Expressway contract, partly by initiating a House investigation of the transaction, Garcia issued an opinion questioning the legality of Benpres' contract. After he resigned in the wake of the controversy generated by Amari, Garcia joined de Venecia's staff.

In a similar fashion, the agreement slipped through the justice department. In the Senate hearings, PEA chairman Rivera admitted that he personally delivered to the Department of Justice (DOJ) PEA's request for an opinion. Rivera reasoned that there was nothing unusual about his action, as he merely wanted to speed up the approval process.

Actually, Rivera also took with him a draft opinion approving the agreement. "They already had a ready opinion for DOJ to sign," says Drilon, who heard about it from his old staff at the DOJ. But then DOJ secretary Teofisto Guingona Jr., played it safe. The DOJ declined to render an opinion on the ground that the agreement fell within the purview of the OGCC.

"After all, the DOJ secretary is a political animal and he is an extension of the President," Drilon surmises. "It's possible he saw the President's approval in writing and felt he had to sustain the President's approval. The next best thing was to refrain from rendering an opinion."

The PEA board was swayed by a perception of Malacañang support for Amari.

The PEA board was also swayed by a perception of Malacañang support for Amari. At the Senate, board member Arturo Trinidad revealed that PEA management presented to the board a memo which said that the agreement had been submitted to and approved by the President.

"That is a major consideration insofar as the members of the board are concerned," he said. Trinidad added: "I was also concerned with (sic) my stay in the board of directors and that my questioning the position of the general manager could lead the general manager to propose that my appointment be terminated."

Another board member, Marylou Ventura, recounted: "When the board gave the authorization to the then general manager, Mr. Lagdameo, to negotiate with the Amari people, we expected that he would come back to us and spell to us for approval the terms and conditions of the JVA (joint-venture agreement). However, the JVA came to us already signed."

Lagdameo had signed the agreement on April 25, 1995 without the board's authority. The board also approved the Amari contract in record time—three days afterward.

Maceda, in the course of the Senate investigation, concluded that the rush was due to the fact that elections were scheduled on May 9, 1995, and the ruling Lakas party was anticipating a hefty donation from Amari.

The Scam Unravels

Conclusion

GEORGE Triviño, Ital-Thai's Philippine representative, was livid when he found out that the company had begun negotiating the purchase of three reclaimed islands in Manila Bay without his knowledge.

He had been kept out of the deal by the other brokers and most likely found about it from the idle talk that was circulating in Binondo. *"Sinekreto nila sa akin* (they kept it a secret from me)," he told the Senate committees investigating the sale of the reclaimed land. *"Lahat na* business *dito, kailangan dumaan sa akin* (All their business here should pass through me)."

Triviño, Senate sources say, then reported the matter to House Speaker Jose de Venecia, who had been helping Ital-Thai acquire infrastructure contracts in the Philippines.

Our sources say that sometime in the first quarter of 1995, de Venecia met in his home with Frank Chua and Benito Co, the two brokers hired by Ital-Thai to arrange the purchase of the property from the government. In that meeting, the Speaker asked the two men to work out an arrangement that would make "everybody happy."

What happened next is amply supported by documentary evidence subpoenaed by the Senate investigation. Amari, the Philippine company formed by Ital-Thai and its Filipino partners, issued to Triviño 31 manager's checks totaling P300 million from its Citibank account in Makati.

The checks, copies of which were obtained by the Senate, were signed at the back by Triviño. They were dated April 28, 1995, the same day the board of the Public Estates Authority (PEA) approved the joint-venture agreement with Amari.

Amari representatives also told the Senate that they deposited P100 million more in an account in Hong Kong, also on April 28. The money was sent by telegraphic transfer from Ital-Thai's account in Bangkok.

A footnote in the final report of the two Senate committees investigating Amari says that the P300 million was encashed by a sister-in-law of a high Congress official. Senate sources say that the official referred to was de Venecia, and the woman who collected the money just before the 1995 elections, was a sister of his wife Gina.

Senator Juan Ponce Enrile, chairman of the committee on government corporations and public enterprises, put that footnote there. He said that the information was passed on to him by a source he could trust. "I would not put it as a footnote if I had no confidence that the story was probably true," he said.

In 1995, de Venecia was in charge of the Lakas campaign at the local level, recalls former executive secretary Ruben Torres, then the party's campaign manager. Torres says he took care only of the Lakas senatorial slate and received money for this from Emilio "Lito" Osmeña, then the party fund-raiser.

The Speaker, Torres adds, raised his own funds. "De Venecia spent for the congressmen, governors, and mayors, so he spent more than we did. For him it was a strategic thing as he was preparing for 1998, *hindi siya* agree *na hahawakan ko lahat* (he didn't want me to manage everything)," Torres says.

The Speaker, however, denies any involvement whatsoever with Amari and points out that he had been cleared by an exhaustive Senate investigation. As he pointed out, "In a letter dated March 1 (1997), Mr. Triviño, the Senate witness in the Amari-PEA land probe, was emphatic in saying that I precisely refused to intercede for him in the Amari deal: 'I wish to confirm that since you refused to help me on the Amari case, despite my repeated requests, I could not extend financial assistance to you or to the ruling party then and do not intend to in the future.'"

By the time that letter was written, however, it was two years after the 1995 elections, long after the P300 million had already been released through Triviño. What Triviño was actually writing to the Speaker about this time was his attempt to get more money out of Amari.

By all accounts, Triviño is a slippery character with a checkered past. Nor does he have compunctions about turning against his patron. Conveniently used as a front for payments, he wanted a cut in the deal as well. When that was not forthcoming, he squealed.

Drilon reveals that it was Triviño who gave Senator Ernesto Maceda the basis for his Amari exposé. Triviño also furnished the senator a copy of the "Dear Joe" letter he wrote de Venecia on November 7, 1996.

In that letter, Triviño complained: "Amari cut me out of the deal after I had formulated a perfectly legitimate deal. In that deal everybody—squatters, Amari, our friends, partymates, and supporters—would have been happy."

He also warned of "dire consequences" unless Amari was pressured to "fulfill its obligations" to him. He added that he was committed to bankroll de Venecia's monthly needs "and to save up for future operations, including an airplane." He said that he had already paid the deposit on two jets. It is no secret that at that stage de Venecia was already preparing for his presidential campaign.

Our sources say that it was made clear to the Chinese brokers who had been negotiating with the PEA that Triviño was fronting for a powerful politician. Thus, in effect, the two brokers, Frank Chua and Benito Co, fronted for a string of public officials and private individuals who played a role in ensuring that Amari would acquire the reclaimed islands at a bargain-basement price.

String of Payments

It will be recalled that the total amount Ital-Thai's Premchai Karnasuta was willing to pay for the property was P2,250 per square meter. Originally, in the November 1994 agreement, this amount was to be divided this way: P1,000 per square meter as the purchase price, and P1,250 for the brokers. When PEA insisted on the price of P1,200 per square meter, the balance of the P2,250—P1,050 a square meter, or a total of P1.657 billion—went to the commissions.

Later, the total commissions were adjusted to P1.596 billion, our sources say. To save on cash, Amari also told the two Chinese that it would pay P300 million of this amount in the form of reclaimed land in the project area. The company computed the price of the property at P5,500 per square meter. The P300 million therefore translated into 54,545 square meters.

In addition, to make up for the intrusion of the politician who took P400 million of their commission, Chua and Co were promised a cash bonus of P157.84

million once the property had been developed and was to be sold.

The cash bonus, together with the P1.596 billion the two Chinese had earlier been promised, brought the total commissions to P1.75 billion, nearly equal to the price at which Amari bought the property from PEA.

Amari records show that the first payment of the brokers' commissions was the P400 million released just before the elections, on the same day the PEA board passed a resolution confirming the joint-venture agreement with Amari.

Amari records show that the first payment of the brokers' commissions was the P400 million released just before the elections.

In a letter on June 9, 1995, the day after Ramos signed the joint-venture agreement, Amari asked the two brokers to acknowledge receipt of the P400 million paid on April 28. Also on June 9, Chua and Co were paid P262.5 million in the form of 14 manager's checks from Amari's Citibank account. In addition, Amari gave the two men the following:

- 10 checks totaling P127 million and payable 60 days from the date of the letter
- 24 checks totaling P150 million and payable monthly from August 31, 1995 to January 31, 1998
- 48 checks totaling P357.36 million and payable in monthly installments of P29.75 million beginning July 1996 and ending June 1997.

By the time Senator Ernesto Maceda blasted the deal in a Senate speech in November 1996, Amari had already paid P969.7 million through Triviño, Chua and Co. Payments on postdated checks were stopped at this point.

In whose pockets these amounts eventually ended up is another of the many questions that still surround the Amari deal. There is evidence to show that some of the money coursed through Cuevo reached PEA deputy manager Justiniano "Bobby" Montano IV and his cousin Auring.

The Senate dug up a credit memo transferring P6.25 million from Cuevo's account to the account of Bobby Montano at the Pilipinas Bank branch at the Holiday Inn. Our sources say that there were other, more substantial payments to Montano, and that these can be traced by following the trail of the blank checks issued by Amari after the June 9 letter.

In a separate hearing, Auring Montano also admitted that she was given P30 million as her share of the fees: P10 million in cash and P20 million in postdated checks, which she never encashed.

We also found an ethnic Chinese hardware storeowner in Cavite who revealed, on condition of anonymity, that he was approached by Auring Montano just weeks after the May 1995 elections. In a meeting at the Holiday Inn, Auring wanted him to encash P10 million worth of postdated checks in exchange for a rebate. Auring, this source says, was accompanied by Cuevo and a Cavite politician who, he was told, needed the money as he was leaving for a trip to the U.S.

Apart from the Cavite hardware dealer, there were others who rediscounted Amari's checks. These include businessman Sy Pio Lato, believed to be the principal behind the jai-alai gambling operations in Manila, and his wife Wee Te Lato, who encashed four checks worth P45.35 million, according to records obtained by the Senate.

There were apparently several layers of payments. Chua, Co, and Cuevo were merely the conduits for a network of other wheeler-dealers. This network included a Metro Manila mayor who also demanded a share. Polly Tragico, who was Bobby's girlfriend at the time of the payoffs, told us that she accompanied Cuevo when he paid off the mayor at the Westin Philippine Plaza.

Greed Takes Over

Our sources say that the entire package of bribes includes more than the commissions paid to the brokers. Apart from the close to P1 billion paid to Chua, Co, and company, our sources say, P600 million was paid to a high official to clinch the deal. But that's not all: when the story broke out in late 1996, another series of payoffs was made, several of our sources say.

Since so many others were making millions from the transaction, Triviño should probably not be blamed for having wanted to cut his own deal. What can be gleaned from his Senate testimony and the letter he wrote to de Venecia in November 1996 is that he had proposed to Amari that he would take care—for a fat fee—of the relocation of the squatters living on the three islands.

Amari agreed but Triviño became greedy. He wanted Amari to pay him an advance of P400 million. When the company refused, saying it would deal directly with the squatters, Triviño asked de Venecia to intercede. The Speaker, however, did not.

Thus, Triviño wrote the alternately threatening and supplicating "Dear Joe" letter quoted above. He also exposed the deal to Maceda. That was when all hell broke loose. The Amari scam unraveled. The share price of Centennial City, the new owner of Amari, plummeted. There was also panic at the highest levels of officialdom.

Bobby Montano was in pieces, sources in his family say. He was forced to resign on December 10, 1996, 11 days after Maceda's exposé. After that, Bobby's lines to Malacañang were cut, says a close friend who asked not to be named.

Desperate, the friend called a congressman to tell him that Bobby was in bad shape. Apparently, the congressman called de Venecia. Not long afterward, just before the Speaker's birthday on December 26, 1994, de Venecia summoned Bobby to his home in Dasmariñas Village, Makati. Bobby lost a bit of his shakes after that.

The friend also ran to a Palace official to say that Bobby was in a state of panic. She warned that if Bobby talked, many people could be hit. That was when Agnes Montano, Bobby's wife, got the reassuring call from Presidential Security Group commander Brig. Gen. Jose Calimlim.

On the November morning the day after Maceda's speech, de Venecia was also worried enough about the consequences of the exposé to summon to his home for a breakfast meeting then executive secretary Torres and political affairs adviser Gabriel Claudio. "He was consulting me on how to handle the situation, which he said was politically damaging to Lakas," remembers Torres. *"Asikasuhin ninyo ito* (Take care of this)."

As the Senate investigation progressed, de Venecia made more determined efforts to sort things out. Sometime in February 1997, he called to his home Centennial City officials Micky M.S. Yong and Louis

Coson, and Triviño in what Drilon describes as a "family council." Yong told the Senate that the meeting was held "to clarify the problem with Mr. Triviño." Weeks later, Triviño fled the country, as did Chua and Co, who said they feared for their lives.

Stymied Investigation

Without these key witnesses, the Senate investigation was stymied from pursuing its inquiry. Amari was also not completely forthright and held back vital documents. Some of the witnesses, particularly Cuevo, lied through their teeth, even if they were put under oath.

The Senate also failed to follow the trail of the checks paid through Triviño. Although Senate investigators summoned records of Amari's bank transactions, they made no effort to check out the bank withdrawals allegedly made by de Venecia's sister-in-law and the account from which these funds were drawn.

Moreover, Drilon says, both Maceda and Enrile, who were among the toughest interrogators during the hearings, were soft on Triviño. "He was treated with kid gloves," says Drilon. *"Hindi ko maintindihan* (I could not understand it). And the thing that floored me was that after the executive session with Triviño, the following day, I see George Triviño acting as a godfather at the wedding of Maceda's son."

Irwin Maceda was wed on February 28, 1997. Apart from Triviño, the other sponsor at his wedding was de Venecia. Gina de Venecia, the Speaker's wife, is the younger sister of Marichu Vera Perez, Maceda's estranged spouse.

Not surprisingly, weeks later, Maceda issued a press statement that said in no uncertain terms, "As far as the Senate hearings on this detestable scam have gone, there is no evidence at all of Speaker Jose de Venecia's participation in the negotiations on this deal."

In the end, the Senate committees recommended the prosecution of several officials for violations of the anti-graft law, including PEA general manager Amado Lagdameo, Bobby Montano and two other deputy managers of PEA. The committees also recommended that charges be filed against 12 private individuals, including Cuevo, Chua, Co, Triviño, Manuel Sy, Aurora Montano, and several Amari officials led by Premchai.

The Office of the Ombudsman is still looking into the Senate's findings. Always one step ahead, Cuevo and Sy hired lawyer Jose Flaminiano to be their counsel. Flaminiano happens to have been Ombudsman Aniano Desierto's own lawyer when he was facing a House investigation.

Subsequent efforts to investigate the deal, such as that undertaken by the House of Representatives, a Malacañang legal task force, and a Palace committee of peers have upheld the legality of the contract and recommended only amendments to certain provisions.

Although the Senate report said the joint-venture agreement should be voided, PEA is merely renegotiating the terms of the old agreement. As far as the government is concerned, the project is still on.

What went on behind the scenes can only be speculated about at this point. One

Both Maceda and Enrile, who were among the toughest interrogators during the hearings, were soft on Triviño.

high government official told us that after the scandal broke, Amari sent a representative to presidential friend Rosemarie "Baby" Arenas to ask her to intervene with her favorite senator. The representative came with P35 million. Arenas delivered the money to the senator, who was supposedly insulted by the "small" offer. She then went back to the company representative to say that the money had been turned down, but she did not return the cash.

When asked about this at a January 1998 luncheon with journalists, Arenas denied that the incident took place. "I was never approached by Amari to talk to the senator," she said. "There's no such thing. That's one million percent wrong. May God punish me right now. Nobody offered money to anybody."

There are other rumors, including how the senator later asked to be paid in U.S. dollars an amount that came close to the nearly P1 billion the brokers had been given. The purchase of his cooperation cleaned out the company's entire dollar account. The money was stuffed in boxes and delivered to the senator's home in the dead of night.

In a way, the scam itself has become larger than life, challenging our notions of what is plausible. It becomes harder to distinguish rumor from fact. Once the payoffs are in hundreds of millions, who knows what people will do? Who among the most pious can resist the temptation? If someone told us two years ago that a company was willing to pay up to P3 billion in bribes and commissions, we would have laughed in his face. Now we are dead serious. Amari has created a new standard for thievery.

Amari has created a new standard for thievery.

Centennial Scandal

BY CHAY FLORENTINO-HOFILEÑA AND IAN SAYSON

First published in *Business World, Malaya, Philippine Star* and *Manila Times*, June 14-16, 1999; and *Abante*, June 14-23, 1999

Corruption should be the last thing Filipinos should associate with the celebration of the Centennial of the Philippine Revolution in 1998. But subsequent revelations on how the millions spent to mark the event were wasted in useless projects or discreetly channeled to the campaign coffers of the Lakas party marred the centennial celebrations. This investigation, which involved going through two cartons of documents and interviewing over 30 people in the course of several months, traces exactly how hundreds of millions of pesos were misused in the guise of celebrating a historic event.

Like the report on the Amari scam, this series of articles was written after the Senate Blue Ribbon committee had released the results of its own investigation of the Centennial. This report describes how the government mobilized all of its resources, including money from government corporations and financial institutions to raise money for Centennial Exposition. What the Senate report missed—the use of the Centennial as a cover for raising funds for the Lakas campaign—is vividly described in the first part of this story. Although this series relied heavily on documentary proof, the information provided by a whistleblower, an official who had an insider's view of what was taking place, was crucial in showing the extent to which officials of two government corporations raised money from government contractors to oil the machinery of the ruling party.

As in the Amari scam, many of the documents used in this

report came from the Senate, but a lot of them were also obtained by the authors themselves. Interviews with officials and government contractors in Manila and Angeles, Pampanga helped them fill the gaps in the story and provided background, context and information not available from the documents.

This series was a finalist in the 1999 Louie Prieto Awards.

Convenient Cover for Election Fundraising

First of Three Parts

MONTHS before the May 1998 presidential elections, the Lakas party, through campaign manager Cesar Sarino, opened a discreet, fund-raising office at the Manila Hotel where contributions to the then ruling party's campaign were accepted.

Among those who visited Sarino's office were representatives of the Bases Conversion Development Authority (BCDA) and the Clark Development Corporation (CDC), two government agencies involved in the construction of the Centennial Exposition in Clark.

Joseph Ocol, then head executive assistant to CDC president and chief executive officer Romeo David, recounted that during those visits, BCDA and CDC representatives delivered millions of pesos stashed in envelopes. The deliveries, he said in a recent interview, were made mostly in the afternoons when Sarino was present to accept contributions.

In a June 1999 affidavit, Ocol described how contractors working on the project were asked to make substantial donations to Lakas. Such contributions violate the Election Code, which bans direct or indirect contributions from companies or individuals with contracts or subcontracts with government agencies.

In his affidavit, Ocol said, "I witnessed the delivery of money by CDC and BCDA officials, as well as contractors and duty-free shop owners to a political office at the Manila Hotel." He recalled going to the hotel at least "six times" either for meetings or deliveries.

In a statement submitted to the Senate blue ribbon committee early this year, Ocol —whose position made him privy to CDC biddings and transactions involving contracts, procurements and lease arrangements in Clark—described how "everybody in BCDA and CDC then at that time was desperate in (sic) coming up with all means and money to prevent Erap from winning in the elections."

"That is why 'Centennial' was an overused word then," he added. "It was the best alibi to shortcut rules and regulations to raise money from contractors, suppliers and businessmen in order to support the candidates for the May elections."

One year after the centennial celebrations, controversy still hounds the sprawling 60-hectare Centennial Expo project, which cost the government more than P9 billion, according to investigations of the Senate blue ribbon committee. This amount is 1.7 percent of the 1998 national budget, almost equivalent to the allocation for a medium-sized government department.

After months of investigation, the blue ribbon committee discovered substandard work on some projects in the Expo site and irregularities in the disbursement of funds, but it was unable to trace where the money went and who should be held accountable. It also failed to pursue the leads provided by witnesses like Ocol who gave clues to the money trail, particularly in infrastructure projects.

Our own investigation shows that the centennial projects, which involved either support infrastructure or services for the Expo site, became a convenient vehicle for election fund-raising at the expense of the Filipino taxpayer.

Originally intended to catalyze development in both Clark and Central Luzon, the project has so far brought little tangible gains to the region. Instead, it reveals the inefficiency and extravagance of the Ramos government, which poured in billions into a project of dubious worth, while scrimping on other projects—roads, housing, etc.—that were sorely needed.

Government financing institutions were also pressured to bail out the Expo at the expense of other priorities like agriculture and housing because, officials involved in the centennial preparations reasoned, the country could ill-afford a sullied image during its first centennial.

Over 30 people involved with the Expo in some way were interviewed for this report. We examined the transcripts of the blue ribbon committee hearings and close to 30 folders containing documents submitted to the committee. Documents obtained from other sources were also used to piece together a story about government officials who were leading celebrations for the centennial while at the same time raising funds for a presidential campaign.

Financing a Campaign

Contractors and duty-free shop owners in Clark were among those tapped to help oil the Lakas campaign machine, according to Clark insiders. They were convenient targets because they had business interests to protect or were eager to make investments they could collect from in the future.

Lakas fundraisers, however, were torn between supporting Jose de Venecia Jr., Ramos's preferred candidate, and former defense chief Renato de Villa, a long-time Ramos ally.

Torn between their loyalty to Lakas and their own personal preferences, some Ramos loyalists based at Clark were forced to work doubly hard to be able to contribute to both the de Venecia and the de Villa camps. Because they had quotas to meet in such a short time, some of these Lakas supporters, according to BCDA and CDC officials, turned to the multibillion-peso centennial and other related projects inside Clark.

At the helm of both the CDC and the BCDA were former military officials with known close ties to Ramos, and who were said to be rivals for the latter's attention. CDC chief David, a retired Air Force general, belongs to the class of 1956, the same Philippine Military Academy class as then Ramos security adviser Jose T. Almonte. BCDA chairman Victorino Basco, a retired Navy captain, was in class 1957, the same class as presidential candidate de Villa.

Sometime in late December 1997, Basco and Nestor Mangio, a CDC board director who is also a Ramos ally, called for a meeting at the CDC conference room, Ocol recounted in his June 8, 1999 affidavit certified by an Ombudsman graft investigating officer.

"The purpose of the meeting was to find means of funding and helping certain presidential candidates in the coming May elections," Ocol said. "Among those who attended the meeting were CDC/BCDA director Roberto Flores, vice president (Francis) Elum, vice president Angelino Medina, manager Monina Pineda, and manager Carmelo Villacete." Ocol said he was present in that meeting. So was David, Ocol's boss, said a CDC official who was also there.

"It was agreed that money was to be raised from contractors, smugglers, duty-free shop owners, importers, lessees and buyers of disposed equipment and materials," Ocol added in his sworn statement. "The beneficiaries of the money raised from the aforementioned people were presidential candidates Jose de Venecia and Renato de Villa."

Basco denies the meeting took place or that Ramos asked him to help raise funds for the campaign. *"Mahihiya siya sa akin eh* (He would be embarrassed to ask me)," Basco said. Besides, he added, Ramos knew he was for de Villa.

But two other CDC officials named by Ocol did not categorically deny that a meeting was called. Elum said he had "heard about it" but that he was not invited, while Pineda said she could not recall it and that she could not have been invited as well because she did not belong to David's "inner circle."

Ocol however countered that Pineda was CDC's direct link to Malacañang because her husband was a "law partner" of Alexander Aguirre, who became acting executive secretary, and deputy executive secretary Renato Corona was a *ninong* in her wedding.

Money from Contractors

A month before the December 1997 meeting, Ocol said he had already learned about plans to raise money from Clark contractors for the elections.

Philippine National Construction Corporation (PNCC) vice president Ibarra Paulino, Ocol said in his affidavit, came to Clark to ask for David's help in speeding up payments to build the 14-kilometer Mabalacat-Clark spur road. The PNCC got the contract to build that road although it in turn subcontracted the project to three other firms.

Because David was not around, Ocol said he entertained Paulino, who came to Clark with his family. In the course of their drinking session, Ocol said, "I came to know about the plan of PNCC and BCDA to raise money from the contractors to support certain candidates in the coming May 1998 presidential elections."

> "It was agreed that money was to be raised from contractors, smugglers, duty-free shop owners, importers, lessees and buyers of disposed equipment and materials."

In his affidavit, Ocol said that Paulino admitted he brought "P2 million as initial 'SOP'" which he was handing over to a CDC official to ensure his cooperation. "Paulino and I had some drinks at the Holiday Inn coffee shop" where he was to meet (that) official, Ocol said in his affidavit.

When the official arrived and talked with Paulino, Ocol said he sat at another table. "I saw (with) my own eyes" a long, brown, expandable envelope being handed to the CDC official, Ocol recounted in his sworn statement. When the official left, Ocol said Paulino told him that he got assurance from the CDC official that "he will not be a hindrance to the PNCC projects in Clark."

The official denied he "ever asked Paulino for any amount whatsoever." He also dared his accusers, *"Kung totoo yang mga iyan, i-*file *ninyo sa* Ombudsman (If that's true, file a case against me at the Ombudsman's office)."

Paulino, too, denied the incident took place. "That's ridiculous. That's untrue because everything we do is audited by the Commission on Audit. We never engaged in such deals. What would we get from that when we are both government corporations?"

Also in November 1997, another former CDC senior official said contractors went to the Manila Hotel to attend informal meetings with Basco. The official said there were "not less than 10" people in one meeting held at noon, with two contractors present. One contractor handed over a P1-million check, the CDC official added.

Big Ticket Item

All in all, there are about 18 centennial-related projects funded mostly by BCDA in Clark. Contract costs total some P3.67 billion, according to the CDC and BCDA. The biggest among these projects—about a third of the total—is the Mabalacat-Clark spur road.

The project was originally packaged as a joint venture between the PNCC and a subsidiary of Benpres Holdings Corp. But because of delays in securing government approval for the project, four government firms (BCDA, CDC, CIACOR and PNCC) took over, supposedly to speed up the project in time for the Expo. BCDA and PNCC took charge of contracts and implementation, while CDC and CIACOR or the Clark International Air Corp., also chaired by David, handled administration.

Signing the documents for the project were David, BCDA's Basco, who had just moved from his post as chairman of PNCC, and another retired military officer, Col. Rogelio Luis, who assumed Basco's position at the PNCC.

Estimated by the Senate blue ribbon committee at P1.071 billion, the project was supposed to consist of two sections: the Mabalacat-Clark spur road, a four-lane 5.6-kilometer expressway from the Dau interchange to Clark; and the 8.7-kilometer Clark perimeter road that connects the spur road to Gil Puyat Ave. inside Clark and to the Centennial Expo site.

In early 1999, the current BCDA chairman Rogelio Singson stopped the construction of the spur road after it was found to be of "substandard" quality and the performance of the contractor, PNCC, was found to be unsatisfactory. By then the government had already spent more than P200 million on the project.

The suspension of the work, Singson said, was by mutual agreement since the urgency was no longer there as the centennial year was over. "BCDA would have been in the red if we had not stopped. There is no way PNCC could have finished on schedule," he added.

The Senate blue ribbon committee found that the project was tainted with irregularities, among them, illegal subcontracting by the PNCC and the absence of public bidding.

Referring to the spur road project, Willy Castor, national president of the National Constructors Association of the Philippines Inc., said, *"Malakas ang lagayan diyan* (there were big payoffs there)."

PNCC was given the P1.2-billion contract but acted like a "broker," according to Castor, because it subcontracted the project for some P628 million to three firms: R.D. Policarpio and Co., New Sampaguita Builders Construction, Inc., and Unicorn Construction Co., Inc.

> Fund-raisers also eyed duty-free shop owners who were bold enough to smuggle items out of Clark.

Sampaguita, in turn, subcontracted four other contractors to do its work, providing a third layer of contractors. This is "disadvantageous" to the government because the "contract price is jacked up with the entry of each contractor or subcontractor who will factor in his mark-up," the Senate report said.

In a letter to blue ribbon committee chairman Aquilino Pimentel in February 1999, Basco defended the lack of public bidding in the spur road project, saying that "where time is of the essence," projects may be undertaken by negotiated contract "subject to the approval of the President."

He added that since PNCC is the "sole legislative franchisee to own, operate and maintain the tollways and their extensions," subcontracting was its "prerogative." BCDA, he said in a counter-affidavit submitted to the Office of the Ombudsman in October 1998, "had no participation whatsoever" in the selection and engagement of subcontractors.

On December 15, 1997, Basco wrote Luis, giving him the "notice to proceed" or NTP for the project's second section, the Clark perimeter road. Days later, Basco would be in that meeting where he supposedly talked of the need to produce campaign money for Lakas.

Castor said that after the NTP is issued, contractors get their initial down payment to begin work. It is from this down payment that commissions given out to officials are usually taken, he added.

More Money

In December 1997, the president of Leadway Construction, a contractor for at least two centennial-related projects worth over P50 million "turned over P1 million" to a BCDA and CDC director at Woodland Resort Hotel in Mabalacat, Pampanga, Ocol said in his affidavit. The money was in exchange for the official's signature on the check payment for Leadway, Ocol said.

The official, according to other CDC officials, was said to be a close associate of then executive secretary Ruben Torres.

The official "wanted to hand me P100,000 to help him follow up the papers of Leadway," Ocol said in his affidavit. "When I refused to accept the amount, he told me, "*Kung ganoon*, I'll just donate this amount to the campaign fund of Lakas and Secretary Torres."

Besides contractors, fund-raisers also eyed duty-free shop owners who were bold enough to smuggle items out of Clark. As part of the "fund-raising" effort, Clark officials agreed to tighten security and squeeze money "from those who made money at the expense of government," Ocol said.

On February 3, 1998, police operatives

intercepted frozen duty-free goods worth P800,000 that were about to be smuggled out of Clark via the Sapang Bato gate at noontime.

The goods were inside an Isuzu van with plate USG-273, according to an "After Operation Report" submitted by Clark security and fire department manager Carmelo Villacete to David.

"Further investigation revealed that the goods are owned by one Edgar Ti," the report said, a "locator" or investor in Clark who is also president of ELT Enterprises and director of Gloria Maris restaurant.

Ti offered to settle. In his affidavit, Ocol said, "Although the goods smuggled cost only P1 million, Ti agreed to pay Villacete the P2 million because he did not want a scandal of a smuggling case against him. I personally witnessed Ti (give) the P2 million to Villacete because it was done inside my residence. He then took P100,000 from the envelope and tried to hand it to me. I refused to accept it and told him that it was against my religion." The following day, Ocol said, the money was forwarded to CDC higher-ups.

Ti's case, listed under violations of the tariff and customs code, was described as an "ongoing case" in an April 10, 1999 report of the Clark security and fire department. In another report the following month, the case was no longer part of the list.

Part of the campaign money raised by the Clark officials was eventually turned over to the Manila Hotel office, two former CDC officials confirmed. Some contractors went straight to their "solicitors," said Castor. The contributions, he said, ranged from P500,000 to P10 million, with the average donation at about P1.2 million.

It is difficult to ascertain how much was raised all in all from these operations since the transactions were made mostly in cash and left behind no paper trail. Official Comelec records of contributors to the de Venecia campaign do not show the names of these contractors either.

Only de Villa's list of campaign contributors revealed familiar names—Mangio, who contributed P1 million, businesswoman Nora Bitong who gave the same amount, and contractor Edgardo Angeles of Asia Construction & Development Corporation who shelled out P5 million.

The latter two would figure prominently in another facet of the centennial scam involving a much grander and more expensive project.

How to Build a White Elephant

Second of Three Parts

THE LARGEST amphitheater in Asia, with a seating capacity of 35,000, stands virtually unused in the middle of what used to be barren, lahar-filled land inside the Clark Special Economic Zone.

This gargantuan structure, which cost P1.2 billion to build, is called the Freedom Ring and was intended as the centerpiece of the 60-hectare Philippine Centennial Exposition.

How it got built is a story of grand plans gone wrong, made worse by poor government planning, unbridled ambition and the symbiotic relationship between contractors and public officials.

One year after the centennial celebrations, the Freedom Ring is a white elephant whose long-term benefits to the local economy are as hazy as the procedures that were followed to build it.

Envisioned to symbolize "freedom and the Philippine spirit," it is instead a monument to the power of a president to mobilize massive government resources for a project with little tangible returns.

Our investigation shows that the Freedom Ring was built by systematically shortcutting government procedures and with high officials led by former president Fidel V. Ramos and National Centennial Commission (NCC) chief Salvador Laurel irrationally insisting on the grand project even if it could not be fully funded. Although we did not uncover hard evidence of commissions or bribes being paid to these officials, the project is nonetheless reminiscent of the extravagance of the Marcos era.

That it was considered at all, particularly at a time when the currency crisis was beginning to wreak havoc on Asian economies, shows how much more monitoring and checking there needs to be done on the use of public resources. The Freedom Ring had grown well beyond the initial projected cost of P260 million. From the initial design of two hectares, the project ballooned to nine hectares.

Today the folly of a 35,000-seat amphitheater is evident in the cracks on the floors of the bleacher section as well as dust and cobwebs on the imported blue seats—sure signs that the place has been used only rarely.

Besides small conventions, the amphitheater has so far drawn one international show and a beauty contest that filled only half the performance area. Little wonder: the sellout Michael Jackson concert in Pasay some years ago drew a crowd of only 19,000, says former Bases Conversion Development Authority (BCDA) chairman Victorino Basco.

Other officials interviewed for this report, however, are hopeful the government will recoup its expenses from the conversion of the Expo site into a recreational theme park and the envisioned development of Central Luzon. But this, they conceded, will take some time.

The project is nonetheless reminiscent of the extravagance of the Marcos era.

Grand Vision

Former President Fidel V. Ramos wanted the Expo to be a catalyst for development in Central Luzon, which has borne the brunt of Mt. Pinatubo's wrath since 1991. The region's economy has remained almost stagnant and the Expo was expected to spur economic activity by building roads and bridges and attracting tourists and businesses.

P1.9 billion was initially thought sufficient for the project, but documents obtained from the Senate blue ribbon committee and BCDA officials showed that this budget increased to over P3 billion for structures on the Expo site alone, representing about a third of the amount spent for the centennial preparations.

When Ramos created the NCC in October 1993, he had already asked Laurel to be chairman. Laurel said he was chosen because of his "stature" and "sense of history" and that he accepted the post on two conditions: that he not be paid and the project be kept above politics.

Laurel said he contacted Douglas/Gallagher, a Houston and Washington-based development planning firm to do a master plan and feasibility study. The firm presented two options for the Freedom Ring in its Nov. 15, 1995 report: scheme A, costing P1.92 billion, involved a covered space; and scheme B, estimated at P1.53 billion, was for an open space.

The economy was then doing well. Still, the study advised a combination of public, private (through a "strategic partner"), domestic and international resources since the Philippine government could not afford the entire cost of the exposition. Officials did not expect to make money from the Expo since previous expos—save for the one in Taejon in South Korea—were financial failures.

Since a joint venture had better chances of making some profit after the lifetime of the Expo and the private sector could help shoulder the costs, the government looked for a business partner. But little did officials expect that projections would go awry and that relations with the partner would turn sour.

Extraordinary Arrangements

To implement Ramos's vision, a Philippine Centennial Expo '98 Corporation (Expocorp) was created as a government-owned joint venture that would later invite a private sector partner to assume majority ownership of the company.

The feasibility study rationalized this majority ownership as a way of allowing the new corporation to function as a private entity and not make it "responsible for following government contracting procedures. Such procedures would present a difficult burden on the development of the Exposition in the time available," the study said.

A Memorandum of Understanding was signed by BCDA and NCC on March 18, 1996—four months after the completion of the master plan—to pave the way for Expocorp. The agreement provided for an extraordinary arrangement when it required a government-controlled board for a private corporation.

Eleven days before the agreement was signed, NCC executive director Luis Morales had already written to Jaime Koa, president of Lilly Hill Corporation, asking him to confirm his interest in Expocorp.

A public relations man who helped in the 1992 Ramos campaign, Morales was appointed by the former president to run the day-to-day operations of the NCC. He spelled out in his letter to Koa the "Terms of Reference" of the negotiations—among them, a critical 55-45 percent ratio in the joint venture.

The private-sector partner was supposed to pour in P550 million in capital, while government was committed to put in its P450-million share for a total of P1 billion. In exchange, the partner would be extended a maximum 75-year lease of the 60-hectare Expo site and be allowed to operate whatever useful structure is left on the site.

The Terms of Reference also indicated a 14-18 month life for the Expo (from December 1997 till June 1999) and set land rentals at a rate of five percent on the gross revenue. It set November 14, 1997 as the completion date for the construction of the Freedom Ring.

Within five days of the Morales letter, Koa confirmed his acceptance and named as his partner, Nora A. Bitong, with whom he was putting up a consortium, Global Clark Assets Corporation (Global). Described as a "shrewd, sometimes abrasive" businesswoman, Bitong, according to several officials involved in the centennial project, saw the opportunity to make money by leasing Expo land.

By June 1996, Expocorp, BCDA, Clark Development Corporation and Global signed an agreement that pegged the total cost of the Expo project at P1.9 billion. The agreement affirmed the constitution of the Expocorp board, granting government nine of the 11 seats. It also required Global to pour in P123 million, with the balance of P427 million funded by way of loans, a departure from the paid up capital that the Terms of Reference had specified.

On July 15, 1996, Douglas/Gallagher submitted its final report which clearly indicated that the centerpiece of the Expo would be temporary and have a covered roof structure that would stretch about 2.7 hectares.

Using adjusted estimates by ICF/Kaiser which it hired to do costings, Douglas/Gallagher gave an estimated design budget of $9.5 million for the Freedom Ring structure and roof packages, roughly equivalent to P248.6 million at the time. While Kaiser estimates placed the total Expo project cost at P3.035 billion, design estimates were pegged at P2.25 billion.

In its final report, however, Douglas/Gallagher said, "While the Kaiser estimates are higher than the P1.9 billion budget adopted, we feel they do not adequately reflect the temporary nature of the celebratory architecture and exposition construction and, therefore, tend to maximize the general construction over the development of show and entertainment."

Laurel said the final report was disapproved and the original Freedom Ring cost estimate was "grossly inaccurate." He insisted on a permanent structure that, he stressed, had the approval of Ramos and the Cabinet. This, however, would heap disaster on a grand project already pressed for time.

Permanent or Temporary

Veldon Corporation, tapped by the Bitong group to manage the Expo project, listed two options: a temporary structure for the duration of the Expo and a permanent structure with a design life of over 20 years.

Following the Douglas/Gallagher proposal, Veldon's design brief gave an "indicative budget" of P260 million maximum for a temporary structure and asked contractors to submit a price estimate for a permanent structure as an alternative offer.

On November 27, 1996, Maj. Gen. Cesar Tapia, then Expocorp vice president for operations, wrote a memorandum addressed to Tony Gulliver, Veldon Corporation vice president for operations, telling him that Laurel wanted a permanent Freedom Ring structure.

"This is the understanding from the very start which I understand the chairman reiterated and stressed during the briefing at Manila Hotel last 21 August 1996. As the chairman said then, 'this is not negotiable.' The roof, when viewed from the air, should look like a giant Pampanga lantern," Tapia wrote.

Apparently wanting to make sure that Laurel's instructions were clear, Tapia wrote another letter on the same day and said, "The fact that a permanent Freedom Ring structure will cost more is beside the point."

The day before, Tapia scribbled a note to then Expocorp president Teodoro Peña. Quoting Morales of NCC, Tapia said Laurel wanted the Freedom Ring contract awarded before the end of November and that "Birdair of USA be the supplier/fabricator of the roof cover."

On the evening of November 28, Gulliver wrote Laurel to point out that covering the amphitheater only instead of the whole Freedom Ring would achieve a "substantial cost reduction in budget" without "any great loss of amenity to the remaining uncovered area which comprises already enclosed pavilions."

He also estimated that covering the entire Ring, all of nine hectares, would mean an additional P260 million for the roof material, excluding additional expenses for the structure. This meant spending beyond what was budgeted for the project.

But Laurel would not budge. On November 29, 1996, Tapia again wrote Gulliver, telling him that the structure "will be completely roofed." Laurel's decision, he stressed, is "final."

Laurel's specifications were distributed to four pre-qualified contractors: Asian Construction & Development Corporation (Asiakonstrukt), Kajima Construction, EEI Inc., and H.R. Lopez Construction.

Furthermore, the bid papers specified, "A quotation from Bird Air for the supplier of the roof fabric is to be included in your offer as a minimum requirement." To avoid a highly questionable closed bid, the brief said that alternate prices may be included "from other suppliers." Contractors were expected to present their design proposals by December 18, 1996.

In its design proposal, EEI Inc., one of the largest and oldest construction companies in the country, said that after extensive investigation and discussion with fabric contractors, manufacturers and structural engineers, it found the 300-meter roof of about 60,000 to 80,000 square meters of fabric area "impossible for anybody to guarantee to complete" by November 14, 1997 using the preferred fabric cover.

Even assuming that sufficient Teflon material is available, "the cost to cover the whole Freedom Ring is staggering and seems unnecessary," the EEI proposal pointed out. EEI eventually lost its bid.

Winning Bid

On December 11, 1996, Veldon said the budget needed to be reviewed and made a preliminary estimate of P1 billion. Then, on December 19, 1996, Laurel—vested with authority by the Expocorp Board—declared Asiakonstrukt the winning bidder after presentations were made on the same day.

Asiakonstrukt put in a bid of P1.165 billion for its proposed design and construct package that included Birdair as a manufacturer and supplier. Birdair Inc., a wholly owned subsidiary of the Japan-based Taiyo Kogyo Corporation, is known as a world-class builder of "tensioned membrane structures."

Bondad said it was Louis Berger, a service engineering and construction management firm that Asiakonstrukt teamed up with, which dealt directly with Birdair. It was Louis Berger too, he added, that got retired Lt. Gen. Bennett Lewis, an army

The cost to cover the whole Freedom Ring is staggering and seems unnecessary.

engineer and former classmate of Ramos at West Point, to become the project director of the Freedom Ring project.

The choice of Asiakonstrukt, however, only exacerbated the already uneasy relationship between Laurel and Veldon Corporation. The brewing tensions came to a head on Christmas eve of 1996 when Gulliver raised concerns about the conduct of the bid and exclusion of Veldon from the assessment of the bid proposals.

"We have also been aware of instances where Expocorp staff have had direct unreported communication with suppliers and contractors involved in the preparation of costed proposals. We find this unusual, disorganized and unnecessary. The instruction to evaluate and negotiate award of a P1.2 billion-peso contract in one day we cannot accept as reasonable and can in no way feel confident that our Client is not exposed to contractual chaos in the future," Gulliver said.

At around this time, Bitong was beginning to worry about the budget. She held on to her money and asked for control of the Expocorp board, while Laurel insisted that Global fully pay P550 million in equity to maintain its 55 percent share in the firm.

During the December 19 Expocorp board meeting, Laurel said that if the 55-45 percent ratio were not maintained, Expocorp as a government-controlled corporation would be "subject to inspection and audit by the Commission on Audit" and be required to follow rules and regulations on government disbursement and purchases. "This would also mean that all officials and employees of the corporation would have to reckon with provisions of existing anti-graft and corrupt practices laws," the minutes of the meeting said.

Laurel said he eventually terminated the services of Veldon because of "loss of confidence." He accused Veldon officials of arrogance and of being "anti-Filipino."

A former BCDA official however said there was talk about commissions given out but that no proof exists. Willy Castor, national president of the National Constructors Association of the Philippines, said it is common practice for contractors to get the commission they pay out to government officials from the advance payment given after the bid has been approved and a notice to proceed is issued.

By January 10, 1997, according to a confidential memorandum prepared by Basco for Ramos, BCDA had put in P200 million of its required P300-million share. The Bitong group by this time had poured in P216 million, putting Expocorp's capitalization at P416 million. But with barely 10 months to go before the targeted completion date of the Freedom Ring and a P1.2-billion contract to fund, Expocorp resources were clearly insufficient.

Ramos mustered all the powers of his office to finance the Freedom Ring.

Basco warned Ramos that Expocorp will likely "depend on the President's assistance to raise additional government contribution" to cover the estimated balance not covered by the initial budget. He anticipated funding problems given the emerging differences between Laurel and Bitong. Ramos, the following day, scribbled on the memo, "Let's stick to original plan. We need BCDA money for other projects."

But efforts to downsize the project did not work as Asiakonstrukt had already ordered the materials and advanced over P400 million. Laurel, meanwhile, was annoyed that a presidential team tasked to solve the Laurel-Bitong impasse recommended downsizing the project, and offered to resign in May 1997.

"Nakataya na ang mukha ng bayan. I had invited 14 heads of state and government. It would have been a national embarrassment. *Kahiyaan na,"* Laurel said.

For reasons mysterious even to officials close to Ramos, the former president went along with Laurel's decision and did not accept his resignation. He instead mustered all the powers of his office to finance the Freedom Ring.

The Great Cost of Saving the Centennial

Conclusion

THE Centennial Exposition in Clark was completed at the expense of other government projects that had to be sacrificed because public funds were diverted to the construction of the Freedom Ring amphitheater and the surrounding theme park.

Because of the grandiose plans for the exposition which the private sector could not fund and because money could not be found elsewhere, President Fidel V. Ramos mobilized all the resources of government—including those from five government departments, the government-owned National Development Corporation, and four government financial institutions—to raise money for the Expo.

Such diversion of funds was made possible by a budget law that is a legacy from the Marcos era. It meant that money intended for, among others, the development of an industrial estate in Leyte, the construction of roads and bridges elsewhere in the country, and the lending of public funds to socially meritorious projects such as housing and job creation, would be used to build the centennial white elephant in Clark.

"The spending for the centennial is a political judgment call," said Ramos budget secretary Salvador Enriquez. "(It may have been extravagant to some) but in my sense of value, the centennial is an important event in the life of a nation and I would go along with the President in admonishing everybody to participate."

Ramos stretched legal limits, in part to prevent an international embarrassment stemming from an unfinished centennial centerpiece. He used Executive Order 292, based on Ferdinand Marcos's Presidential Decree 1177, which allows the president to transfer funds allocated for one purpose to other uses as long as certain requirements are met.

Because of such fund transfers, the Department of Public Works and Highways (DPWH)—the department that contributed the largest share to the Expo—listed in March 245 projects under its 1998 work program that were suspended due to the non-payment of billings and the absence of cash allocations. Another 115 projects supposed to have been started under the same work program were stalled for the same reasons.

The DPWH funneled P720 million of its 1997 budget into the Expo, funding over a quarter of the Expo's construction cost of about P3.12 billion, including roadworks. The DPWH could otherwise have used this amount to construct a 72-kilometer, two-lane road or a three-kilometer, two-lane bridge, according to a public works official.

Similarly, the government-controlled National Development Corporation (NDC), which was ordered to invest in the Expo, could have used its money to invest in an industrial complex in Isabel, Leyte—a project that was not only more financially viable but would also have spurred economic activity in one of the most depressed parts of the country.

At the start of the Centennial project, Ramos had already directed the Philippine Charity Sweepstakes Office and the Philippine Amusement and Gaming Corporation to remit their equity contributions of P75 million each to the Philippine Centennial Expo '98 Corporation (Expocorp), the government-private sector joint venture in charge of the Clark Expo.

The Social Security System (SSS), Government Service and Insurance System (GSIS), Land Bank, and Development Bank of the Philippines (DBP) were likewise "encouraged to invest" by Ramos in the centennial project in February 1997.

But the project was stalled because of the conflict between National Centennial Commission (NCC) chairman Salvador Laurel and businesswoman Nora A. Bitong, head of Global Clark Assets Corp., the government's partner in Expocorp. The two officials were caught in a legal tug-of-war over equity contributions to Expocorp. and control of its board.

Changing of the Guard

While the squabbling was going on, Asian Construction & Development Corporation (Asiakonstrukt), the main contractor for the Freedom Ring, gave notice that it was going to suspend work on May 10, 1997.

In a letter to Laurel, Asiakonstrukt officials blamed Expocorp's failure to deliver the required funds. By this time, Asiakonstrukt vice president Eduardo Bondad said the firm had already spent P410 million on the project and borrowed money for it.

In March of the same year, Bitong's Global had already indicated its willingness to withdraw from Expocorp on condition that at the minimum, it would be reimbursed the amount it had put in as equity—about P216 million. NCC officials, in turn, had intimated that government "would be able to find a replacement for Global."

While the NCC was trying to find a new partner to replace Global, the Asian financial crisis was starting to rage. Potential partners either backed out or set conditions that government could not comply with.

Asiakonstrukt, according to Bondad, had "little choice" but to step in as the new partner to save its investment. It thus became both the major contractor of the Freedom Ring project and co-owner of the property.

The new partnership gave birth to the First Centennial Clark Corporation (FCCC), organized as a joint venture on September 8, 1997 with a capital of P1 billion. Like its predecessor, FCCC was initially a private corporation, with Asiakonstrukt owning 60 percent.

By then, Laurel had already found a way to fund the government's 40-percent share in the joint venture. Three months before, in a June 6, 1997 "urgent and confidential" memorandum to Ramos, Laurel suggested that NDC, a government corporation that has traditionally been used as a milking cow for losing ventures, be mobilized for the Expo.

Laurel said the NDC could either provide a loan or a loan guarantee for the centennial project or else it could come in as a major investor. He cited the NDC charter, which empowers it "to engage or invest in or extend loans and guarantees to, or enter into joint ventures with Filipino and foreign investors." His recommendation was approved by Ramos.

It was estimated that the Freedom Ring would cost P1.2 billion, while another P1.2 billion was needed to build the surrounding theme park.

With the backing of the Office of the President, NDC was practically pressured to be part of the FCCC even if financial returns were uncertain. Worse, it was clear that the heavily indebted NDC was not in a position to invest in the joint venture.

In an April 3, 1997 letter to the Department of Finance (DoF), Mariano Salazar, appointed NDC general manager in March 1997, said that NDC had accumulated "negative retained earnings of P4.84 billion" as of end-1996 because of high interest rates on government advances and on loans it obtained to rehabilitate the National Steel Corporation.

Overcoming Resistance

Salazar asked the DoF to ease NDC's debt burden and enhance its earnings potential by converting its advances from the government into equity. NDC could use the savings on interest, he argued, to fund projects that are "environment-friendly and vital to economic growth."

Later, however, NDC would seek the conversion into equity of P1.9 billion in advances and interest payments it owed the DoF. Documents show that Ramos eventually approved such conversion to allow NDC to invest P400 million in FCCC.

Thus, with Asiakonstrukt's P600 million and NDC's P400 million, FCCC was capitalized at P1 billion. But it needed P1.4 billion more. By this time, it was estimated that the Freedom Ring would cost P1.2 billion, while another P1.2 billion was needed to build the surrounding theme park.

On the heels of Laurel's June 6 memorandum, another memorandum prepared by SSS administrator Renato Valencia on June 10, 1997 proposed the creation of a new company to take over the centennial project. He also proposed the creation of a "financial consortium" consisting of the SSS, GSIS, DBP and Land Bank from which the P1.4 billion could be sourced.

In his memo Valencia also said, "I suggest that the loan be secured by RP guarantee or NDC guarantee," with the option to convert the principal and interest into equivalent leasehold rights on the same 200 hectares—inclusive of the 60-hectare Expo site—that were offered to the Bitong group.

The proposal led to negotiations that culminated with an approval by Ramos on November 17, 1997 of a decision to ask the four government financial institutions (GFIs) to lend P1.4 billion to NDC, which it would then put in as equity in FCCC. Of the P1.4 billion, P900 million was to be relent to FCCC and the P500 million invested as preferred shares and additional equity for NDC.

With three months to go before the Expo's "soft opening" in February 1998, wearing down resistance on the part of the NDC became imperative. With the NDC contributions, FCCC was transformed on February 24, 1998 into a government corporation that was now entitled to a government loan guarantee.

The final guarantee was issued only on February 10, 1998 and signed by then acting finance secretary Enriquez. Roberto de Ocampo, the previous finance secretary, had stalled although he eventually issued an initial guarantee letter in January 1998. Not long after, he quit his office to run for president.

"De Ocampo was also reluctant for NDC to enter into the venture especially since he had to issue the guarantee. It was clear that this is something that will be investigated," an NDC official familiar with the corporation's participation said.

Documents obtained from the office of Sen. Nikki Coseteng showed that de Ocampo doubted the "financial viability of the project as confirmed by the GFIs' reluctance to extend a loan for this project without a national government guarantee."

The document, quoting excerpts of an undated memorandum by Ocampo addressed to then executive secretary Ruben Torres, said: "We do not want to repeat history that the national government ends up servicing government-owned and controlled corporations' obligations as in Philphos. This corporation has substantially eroded the national government's fiscal position due to huge advances for debt servicing amounting to P35 billion as of 30 April 1997."

The NDC official said, "The Expo is the first in a long, long time that NDC entered into a project not on the basis of the merits of the venture." It also went against NDC's practice of investing in projects that demand little or no cash outlay.

The NDC official said the Expo continues to be a "problem" for them because of the no-win situation. "If we stop operations, all the more that the public will criticize NDC. But if we continue, we will be subsidizing it."

Indeed, a May 1998 study by the accountancy firm Sycip, Gorres & Velayo had suggested that NDC withdraw from the venture as soon as possible because the returns are very low. "But we can't just do that because the loan requires that FCCC has to be government owned—NDC has to pay the loan first," the NDC official said.

Additional Funds

Other departments were encouraged to participate in the Expo as well. Ramos's executive secretary, Ruben Torres, said during a Senate blue ribbon committee hearing in October 1998 that they "appealed to all government departments to put exhibits to help the Expo become successful as a showcase of our centennial."

For instance, Agriculture Undersecretary Domingo Panganiban said his department received P77 million in September 1997 through a Special Allotment Release Order (SARO) given by the Office of the President through the budget department. The amount was supposed to be spent for an exhibit in the Expo theme park.

The Department of Trade and Industry (DTI) was given "P49.4 million though it was promised P50 million," ranking DTI officials told the blue ribbon committee. The amounts were released in April and June 1998 for "trade shows."

The Department of Environment and Natural Resources contributed P75 million to pay two contractors and other centennial-related activities. The sums were released in September for landscaping and the purchase of trees and plants.

Also in September, the budget department released P237.50 million to the DPWH to build the Expo's parking space, inner roads and other related structures that had been identified as items that could not be funded by the P2.4 billion budget of the just-organized FCCC.

Fund transfers were made at the expense of other projects.

"This release is made pursuant to the handwritten instruction of the President dated August 19, 1997," the SARO said.

In March 1998, just three months before the centennial, Ramos ordered the DPWH to release another P491 million to fund the second phase of the theme park, which includes landscaping, the entrance plaza, millennium hall, Philippine pavilion, time walk and two bridges within the global city site. The amount was taken from congressional initiative allocations in the 1997 DPWH budget, Enriquez said.

All in all, the departments spent about P929.9 million, 78 percent of which was taken from the DPWH. Most of these releases were made at a time when FCCC had just been incorporated and was still a private entity. Government then was a minority shareholder yet it was already spending big sums.

Enriquez said using the budget to fund the Expo, including the other centennial-related projects, was "legal and did not involve the unlawful transfer of funds," contrary to the Senate's assertions.

Ramos and Enriquez, together with five former department secretaries, according to the Senate blue ribbon committee, failed to show or present evidence that the amount that "they funneled or caused to be funneled to the 1998 centennial celebration and its related projects had come from savings of their departments, agencies and/ or offices, or had been specifically appropriated for such purpose."

Enriquez argued that Executive Order 292 allows a realignment of funds on two conditions: there are "savings" from which the transfers will be taken, and the item to which the augmentation is being made must be an "existing item in the budget." The realignments they made, he insisted, satisfied these two conditions.

Ramos, in a press conference in March 1999, said he had issued Administrative Order 372 in December 1997 instructing departments to "save 25 percent of their budget for reserves" or mandatory savings.

"Upon this issue alone, the entire case against me and my officials dealt with by the Senate blue ribbon committee falls flat on its face," he argued.

Sacrificing other Projects

Such fund transfers were made at the expense of other projects. The DPWH, for instance, completed only 34 percent of its 1998 infrastructure program, way below the 85 percent goal it was eyeing for the year. By mid-1999, it had completed only 59 percent of its 1998 work program.

"It's a matter of policy decision," a DPWH ranking official said. "The money could have been spent on something else. It would have come handy especially when our projects slowed down due to the cash crunch, but it was the decision to finish the centennial projects."

The NDC, meanwhile, had given up the development of the Isabel, Leyte industrial project, which the DoF had recommended to enable the cash-strapped company to raise revenues. The project involves the development of the still unused part of the 400-hectare NDC property where the Philippine Phosphate Fertilizer Corporation and the Philippine Associated Smelting and Refining Corporation are located.

The NDC had planned to initially develop an additional 100 hectares in the Leyte Industrial and Development Estate (LIDE) as a site for medium and heavy-scale industries that would use the by-products of existing investors in the area. The NDC envisioned that such development "will benefit the local population as it will generate added revenue and provide more jobs."

LIDE is the only industrial estate in the entire Eastern Visayas and contributes significantly to the region's economy. The project, according to the NDC masterplan, could address some of the region's concerns such as poverty, slow pace of industrialization and lack of employment.

With the entry of a private sector partner and with NDC contributing the land, the Leyte project would have cost only P760 to P893 million, according to NDC estimates. The project, NDC calculated, would make profits after five years.

Thus, the Senate blue ribbon committee concluded, the sums spent by the Ramos government on the Centennial Expo "constitute a gross misuse and wanton misapplication of scarce government resources during a period of devastating financial crises."

The sums spent by the Ramos government on the Centennial Expo "constitute a gross misuse and wanton misapplication of scarce government resources during a period of devastating financial crises."

All the President's Men

BY SHEILA S. CORONEL AND ELLEN TORDESILLAS

These two articles on the people who surround President Joseph Estrada, either as appointed officials or as off-hours drinking and mahjong buddies, were first published in ***i***, the PCIJ's quarterly investigative reporting magazine. For this reason, they were written as magazine pieces, not in the news feature style of other investigative reports in this volume. These two articles, which were published a year apart, document the many men and women who surround Estrada and the influence they wield on his administration. Because Estrada's is an intensely personalistic presidency, these reports focus on people—their backgrounds and affiliations and their shifting clout in Malacañang.

These stories are instructive for the insights they provide on an unconventional president who has made full use of the prerogatives of his power to appoint friends, cronies and associates to lucrative government posts. He is able to do this because of the tremendous leeway the president is given to name his people to positions in the middle to the highest rungs of the bureaucracy. While Corazon Aquino and Fidel Ramos have also used this power, Estrada went overboard by appointing an unprecedented number of his friends as presidential consultants and advisers.

Estrada is also surrounded by cronies who hold no official posts but accompany the president during his late nights out. As the article, "The Nocturnal President," shows, these unaccountable individuals wield influence through their proximity to Estrada.

Both these articles relied on interviews with Malacañang

insiders who provided information on the goings-on in the Palace and the constant stream of people vying for influence in the corridors of power. Influence peddling is one of the most enduring evils of Philippine political life. These articles do not follow the exposé style of other reports in this book. What they did was describe the situation in Malacañang in an effort to make readers understand how decisions are arrived at, contracts awarded and appointments made in the highest office of the land. To do this, it was necessary to help readers grasp first, the prerogatives and the structure of the presidency, and second, the character of the man who occupies that post.

The *Pare* Principle

BY SHEILA S. CORONEL

First published in *i* Magazine, October-December 1998

JOSEPH Estrada is a casual man. He squirms in a *barong* and mumbles incoherently when asked to speak before a well-heeled crowd. He is most at home in the company of his kind: Scotch-guzzling men who grunt rather than talk, who are happiest when backslapping, wheeling-dealing and trading jokes. In short, he is the quintessential Pinoy macho: kind to his friends, cavalier with his women, and generous to his drinking buddies. He takes nothing terribly seriously, including perhaps the presidency.

Thus, when under criticism recently for appointing assorted buddies to various government posts, Estrada was incredulous, feeling that he was, again, unfairly being targeted by a trigger-happy press. Neither could his friends understand what the furor was all about. Their collective reaction was best summed up by Rolando T. Meyer, known in the movie world as a sidekick of action star and presidential pal Fernando Poe Jr. In a television interview after taking his oath as a member of the board of the government-owned casino company, the Philippine Amusement and Gaming Corp. (Pagcor), a post that carries with it some P2 million a year in director's fees, Meyer said, nonplussed: *"Weather-weather lang 'yan."*

It was a typical response. Erap and Co. have perfected this lumpen mockery of the English tongue and put it to effective use whenever they are held to account. "Weather-weather" is the *kanto* boy translation of the Tagalog *"pana-panahon,"* meaning to each his own time. What it essentially meant was this: everyone knows each administration leads its retinue to feast at the public trough. It's our turn now, so what's the fuss all about?

It was a statement that was both refreshingly honest and horribly cynical, simultaneously subversive (because it mocks elite pretensions to a *delicadeza* they never actually practice) and sensible (because if all past presidents had appointed their friends, why shouldn't Estrada?). It sums up Erap's unique contribution to Philippine public life: he translates the prerogatives of power into the language of the streets, making them seem acceptable and normal. After all, he challenges everyone, who among the most righteous have not favored their friends? Or for that matter, who among them have not cheated on their wives?

By speaking plainly, Estrada exposes the hypocrisy of political discourse, thereby depriving his critics of the moral high ground. The president does not deny his sins; he merely cracks jokes about them. On one hand, this is such a relief after the deathless denials at which politicians have become so adept. But on the other hand, the jocular, offhand way he turns conventional morality on its head and makes his version seem eminently sensible and acceptable makes no morality possible. That is why the Catholic Church and the other vanguards of public morals do not know how to react. How do you deal with a sinner who makes you laugh? Who confesses to his sins with devastating nonchalance?

Estrada translates the prerogatives of power into the language of the streets, making them seem acceptable and normal.

Charming Rascal

With Erap Estrada, what you see is what you get. He is, essentially, as he has always said, *pare*, a charming rascal who expects to get away with his rascality as he always had. In two decades of his political life, he has never been called to account: not for his association with underworld characters nor for the dubious business practices of his cohorts, not even for the murders perpetrated by his men when he was head of the Presidential Anti-Crime Commission (PACC).

For all his mumbling and bumbling, Estrada has a very sophisticated understanding of the unaccountability of power. That is why he can afford to be so cavalier. Take the simple matter of presidential advisers, consultants and assistants. Every president has them, but until Estrada took over, it was thought that Fidel Ramos had made maximum use of the system by appointing a couple of dozen cronies, colleagues and friends to positions where they were not actually of much use as advisers, but gave them an excuse to hang around the Palace, do the odd things a president needs to get done and also to display their credentials for whatever perks they were worth (everything from priority seating in concerts and restaurants to big time business deals, as in the case of Ramos adviser Emilio "Lito" Osmeña, who is believed to have used his position to advance his business interests).

Erap, after five months in office, has appointed over 60 people to such positions, so many in fact that the Office of the President has trouble keeping track of them, so many it has become laughable, like invitations to a wedding party that got out of hand. The list of presidential consultants, assistants and advisers includes some really worthwhile individuals whose talents can be put to good use, but also a lot of other hangers-on from business, politics, the movies and, Malacañang insiders swear, God knows where else.

Many of the appointments were predictable. Former racecar champion Roberto Aventajado, for example, a longtime and influential Erap aide, was made presidential adviser on economic affairs and head of the presidential committee on flagship programs and projects. Aventajado, however, is consulted on a wide range of issues, most of them only marginally economic. Among other things, he negotiated for the release of Italian priest Luciano Benedetti who was kidnapped in Mindanao. Together with the powerful brothers whom Estrada had known from his San Juan boyhood—Executive Secretary Ronaldo and businessman Manuel Zamora—Aventajado also played a role brokering the transfer of Philippine Long Distance Telephone Co. (PLDT) shares from the Cojuangco family to various interested parties.

Beyond his inner circle, Estrada awarded party favors to the likes of plastics tycoon William Gatchalian, who was appointed presidential consultant on the welfare of overseas Filipino workers and Julio Tan, the uncle of one of taipan Lucio Tan's wives, who was appointed presidential consultant on Chinese affairs. It is well known that Erap has the support of the ethnic Chinese business community. Lucio Tan was the biggest contributor to his presidential campaign. Another Chinese-Filipino contributor, wealthy Zamboanga businessman Wee Dee Ping, was made presidential adviser on Mindanao.

These posts bring with them little or no remuneration. But they have a certain cachet, especially in the business community, where the perception of closeness to Malacañang is an invaluable asset as it opens doors to contracts, licenses, tax cuts and other forms of preferential treatment from government entities. As every businessman knows, a reputation for being *"malakas"* or *"malapit sa poder"* (close to the powerful) makes many things possible in a country where politics and business are so intimately intertwined.

The president has the power to name people to 3,175 career executive positions in various government departments and agencies.

So far so predictable. The Philippine tradition, like the American one, gives the president tremendous powers to appoint members of the bureaucracy, and indeed, to create new positions as he or she sees fit. So much discretion is given the president that in the Philippines, as in the United States, the system has encouraged the large-scale use of bureaucratic appointments for patronage or as rewards to family, loyal followers and generous contributors. Such powers were even expanded during martial law by Marcos, who gave himself the power to appoint officials up to the middle reaches of the civil service. That power has not been much diminished since then; neither have Marcos's successors been chary about using it.

Thus, since 1986, despite the shift from an authoritarian to a democratic form of government, the president still has the appointive power over all members of the career executive service from the rank of provincial director or department service chief up. At the education department, this means that the president has discretion over everyone from provincial superintendents to the education secretary. He also appoints ambassadors, military officers from colonel up, justices of various courts, and a whole slew of assorted functionaries. Altogether, according to Elmor Juridico, executive director of the Career Executive Service Board (CESB), the president has the power to name people to 3,175 career executive positions in various government departments and agencies.

In addition, 2,488 positions in 60 government-owned and controlled corporations are subject to presidential approval, according to the CESB. For example, at the Social Security System, which administers billions of pesos of employee contributions, the president has discretion over 229 posts. The figure is 279 for the Development Bank of the Philippines and 374 for the Land Bank, both government banks with a history of crony lending. (Estrada, however, has given his finance minister, former banker Edgardo Espiritu, near total discretion over appointments to government financial institutions. Espiritu, in turn, has placed his banking cronies at their helm.)

Perks of Power

Excluded from the CESB's account are the non-career, contractual posts that the president and other high officials can create at their own pleasure. Also excluded are appointments to the boards of various government councils and commissions, government corporations like Pagcor, and sequestered firms like San Miguel Corp. These directorships, most of which come with generous perks, have traditionally been given as rewards to presidential cronies.

All told, presidential appointees make up about two percent of the total number of civil servants (close to 300,000 as of 1998, if teaching, medical and military/police personnel are excluded). Still, the discretion over appointments to the top and middle rungs of the bureaucracy and to corporations that have traditionally been milking cows of well-connected businesspeople endows the Philippine president with a power not enjoyed by most heads of state. In addition, the president can also wield some influence over the appointees of his appointees down the ladder of the bureaucracy, so he can, in theory, have a say in the appointments to thousands of other positions. Contrast this with Britain, where the prime minister can appoint only heads of ministries while leaving the rest of the bureaucracy virtually untouched.

It has too often been said that Philippine practice stunts bureaucratic professionalization. When so many of the best positions in the civil service are subject to presidential whim, efforts to form a professional corps of civil servants are continuously frustrated. Moreover, as appointees are beholden to political patrons for their posts, they view government merely as an employment agency, and a government post simply a reward, rather than a responsibility.

But because Estrada has a keen understanding of the prerogatives of presidential power, he doesn't really care. There is a certain in-your-faceness about the casualness with which he makes his appointments. To be sure, the choices for top Cabinet posts were made with evident care, in terms not only of appeasing the various blocs that supported Estrada's candidacy but also in terms of choosing men and women who had professional qualifications for their posts (even if they come came from the same San Juan neighborhood or the same class at the Ateneo as the president's). The notable exception is Environment and Natural Resources Secretary Antonio Cerilles, who was named largely for his role in mustering Mindanao votes for the president, rather than an expertise in environmental issues.

Below Cabinet level, however, the appointments have been a bit more helter-skelter. On the one hand, there were the concessions to the "Chinoy" business community. On the other hand, there were appointments from the Left flank, with former communist Horacio Morales heading the agrarian reform department, long-time NGO activist Karina David being appointed presidential assistant on housing and chief of the Housing and Urban Development Council, and environmental lawyer Donna Gasgonia being named presidential assistant for poverty alleviation. To the cynical, these appointments may seem like sops to the Left, but they make sense as far as the fit between appointee and position is concerned.

Others are more difficult to fathom; for example, the mingling of movie personalities and serious scholars in the same government boards. In one case, Estrada's brother-in-law Raul de Guzman, former dean of the University of the Philippines College of Public Administration, sits as a government nominee on the San Miguel Corp. board together with film producer Espiridion Laxa.

It can be said that this diversity is typical of the rainbow coalition—ranging from former Marcos cronies to former communists, from frivolous movie stars to dead-serious academics—that brought Estrada to Malacañang. This diversity is most evident in Erap's eclectic Cabinet, which is made up of individuals who are such polar opposites they cancel each other out. Such diversity in turn is a natural outcome of a party system that is rooted not in platform or ideology but in family, popularity, personality and convenience.

At any rate, the current crop of appointments also betray a mischievous, Erapesque sense of humor. For how else can one explain the little-known Rodolfo Balmori, who was appointed in September 1998 as presidential adviser on dairy, cattle and carabao development, except as the personal choice of a president whose most memorable bill as senator was one on protecting the carabao? Or Adelaida 'Baby' Magsaysay, wife of Zambales politico Gene Magsaysay, whose title simply says "presidential assistant" but whose real function, Palace insiders say, is to book dance instructors for presidential parties? Or, for that matter, one Danter Sullivan, appointed "presidential assistant to the presidential consultant on computer education"?

Supreme Dispenser of Patronage

The problem really is the presidential system itself, which is structured for such capricious use of power. The concentration of so much power in one person lends itself easily to both abuse and whimsy. As Joel Rocamora of the Institute for Popular Democracy writes, "The Philippine presidency is an extremely powerful position, even more powerful than its model, the American presidency. Because of the centrality of patronage for Philippine political parties, the most important powers of the president are his appointing powers and his control over the disbursement of government funds in a highly centralized form of government."

The misuse of the power to appoint is most obvious, because appointments are so public and the appointees are rarely shy about waving about their new credentials. If anything, Erap only brings this power to absurd heights. Corazon Aquino used it to appoint relatives and friends, including her dentist and her dermatologist who were named to the UP Board of Regents. Aquino also got carried away with the appointments, sometimes naming as many as seven undersecretaries for one department that Congress eventually passed a law limiting the number of usecs and asecs to only three each per department.

Ramos was not more circumspect, appointing so many former military officers to crucial posts that he was criticized for militarizing the bureaucracy. He was also not above creating positions for favored friends, among them Justiniano 'Bobby' Montano IV, for whom the post of deputy manager for special projects of the Public Estates Authority (PEA) was especially created. Montano would later play a prominent role in the Amari scandal, which involved billions of pesos in payoffs to various officials in connection with the sale of PEA property to a Thai real estate tycoon.

Estrada has essentially followed the same path, although this early, he has exceeded his predecessors in terms of the fancifulness of some of his appointments. He also has by far the widest range of presidential advisers and consultants, spanning every imaginable concern (a presidential consultant on fire protection, for example, and another one on APEC matters). Presidential aides say that sometimes Estrada just signs appointment papers thrust before him without much consideration of what they mean.

The worrisome thing is if Erap will be as haphazard in wielding presidential control over government finances. As Rocamora says, "Although Congress theoretically has the 'power of the purse,' the President's line item veto and control over disbursement gives him much greater power than Congress. Congresspersons are adept at allocating to themselves large amounts of pork barrel...None of these amounts, however, can be availed of unless the President disburses them."

Being in the good graces of Malacañang is crucial to maintain control over a lucrative monopoly.

Indeed, Ramos mastered the use of his veto and disbursing powers to get the laws he wanted passed by Congress. Ramos was, after all, a deliberate president with a clear vision and strategy. Estrada is cast in an altogether different mold. When queried in a press forum some months ago, he had trouble remembering his legislative agenda. The prospect clearly seems to be the whimsical disbursement of government funds, more so if Erap has trouble remembering where he put the people's money.

There are other presidential powers worth mentioning, powers that Ramos used quite well, in terms of getting the cooperation of Congress and the business community as well as lining the pockets of favored friends. These include the power to approve government contracts of above P100 million if secured through public bidding and above P10 million if awarded through negotiations.

There is also the power to intervene in business disputes and to craft policies that favor some businesses and put others at a disadvantage. Certainly, Estrada has exercised this power in the case of Philippine Airlines and PLDT. As PLDT president Antonio 'Tony Boy' Cojuangco knows only too well by now, being in the good graces of Malacañang is crucial to maintain control over a lucrative monopoly. Like his predecessors, Estrada has used the powers of his office to put the squeeze on those who have fallen from grace and to favor his own friends. The phone call he made in November 1998 to PLDT director Alfonso Yuchengco, virtually ordering the latter to give up his claim to the Cojuangco shares in favor of First Pacific, is an example of the many powers that the president has which is not spelled out in the rulebooks.

While Ramos used these powers within the broader framework of economic liberalization and reform (even as he helped out his friends), Erap merely wields it for his buddies within the broader framework of, well, friendship and a sense of entitlement to the privileges of public office. The resurrection of Estrada supporter Eduardo 'Danding' Cojuangco, who is now once again the king of beer, is certainly due in large part to the latter's support for Estrada's candidacy. And certainly, Lucio Tan need no longer worry about his P26-billion tax evasion case now that his pal is president.

In the book of quotations on Philippine politics, one of the most memorable is Senate President Jose Avelino's response in 1949 to queries about the abuse of congressional prerogatives: "What are we in power for?"

Fifty years later, the quote that will resound into the next millennium is *"Weather-weather lang 'yan."*

The Nocturnal President

By Ellen Tordesillas

First published in *i* Magazine, October-December 1999

THE meetings take place at night and last until dawn. There, views are traded, strategies prepared, and deals struck. By the time the men at the table stand up and stagger out the door, much has been accomplished that may affect the way things are done in this country.

President Joseph Estrada, of course, presides over these meetings. But more often than not, those gathered around him during these caucuses are far from being Cabinet secretaries. Rather, they are his personal friends, some of them buddies of long-standing, such as Ilocos Sur Rep. Luis 'Chavit' Singson and Caloocan congressman Luis 'Baby' Asistio, with whom, it is said, the president shares a fondness for the pleasures of the good life—gambling, alcohol and women included. Singson and Asistio, say Malacañang insiders, are among the president's most constant late-night companions.

There are other persistent hangers-on, wheeler-dealers like online bingo operator Dante Tan whose BW Resources Corp. has been accused of insider trading and manipulation of the stock market. Certainly, it would seem that ethnic Chinese businessmen are keenly aware that with Estrada, out of sight is out of mind, and are among those that a Palace insider says are fond of "slipping in when dark sets in."

Ramon Lee, a close associate of Dante Tan and an Estrada election contributor, drops in occasionally, say Malacañang sources. So does Lucio Co, the goateed owner of PureGold duty-free stores who was recently accused of being a big-time smuggler. Another fixture of the late-night tete-a-tetes is Jaime Dichavez, a fiberglass manufacturer and real estate developer who was recently involved in the corporate coup at Belle Corporation, operator of the controversial jai-alai games. Dichavez, who has no official post except as head of the Malacañang golf club, is another of the President's most trusted businessmen-friends.

Also sighted keeping Estrada company at night are presidential adviser on overseas Filipinos William Gatchalian, who has shifted from plastics to airlines and the tourism business, and Eusebio Tanco, who recently acquired the Tiwi-Makiling-Banahaw geothermal power plant from the National Power Corporation. Tanco is the brother-in-law of one of the country's biggest coconut millers, Douglas Lu Ym.

(But the most trusted—and most reclusive—of the president's friends is multimillionaire Jacinto 'Jack' Ng, owner of Republic Biscuit Corp. or Rebisco and of some hefty real estate. Ng, however, reportedly does not take too well to the night life and is rarely seen in the late-evening socials the president enjoys.)

Whatever their past with the president and no matter where they come from, these men offer the actor-turned-President a respite from the heavy demands of being the head of state. This they do by keeping him company while he unwinds over drinks; they even sing with him on the karaoke, as well as play mahjong, which could stretch these boys' nights out way past their usual quitting time if the President is losing. For the country's chief executive apparently does not take defeat at the gaming table very well.

But he takes well to recommendations and pieces of advice offered by his friends during these midnight sessions, say some government officials. Indeed, they even say a number of presidential decisions with wide-ranging implications have been reached not during the Cabinet meetings that are usually held once a month, but during the informal discussions that take place while the President relaxes with his pals, who are not exactly without business interests to advance and defend.

That, say the officials, has made for policies and appointments done on the fly, actions that come not from careful thinking and consultations with experts, but from what appear to be off-the-top-of-the-head remarks of private individuals, who may or may not have been inebriated when they made their suggestions. For example, the use of pension funds of the Government Service Insurance System and the Social Security System for corporate takeovers was the bright idea broached on one of those late evenings with presidential friend Mark Jimenez, a shadowy businessman wanted for illegal campaign contributions in the U.S. Jimenez is reportedly a mean singer at the karaoke and is an occasional "good time" associate of Estrada.

Then again, perhaps this could only be expected of a presidency in which decision-making is seemingly dependent on the interplay not so much of ideas but of the vested interests of individuals who align themselves in loose blocs. The "Midnight Cabinet" is just one among the many groups that compete for the President's attention, groups that have their respective trump cards to play whenever they feel someone else is gaining precious ground, or simply whenever they feel that the timing is right. There are no rules and no guarantees in this game, after all, and a bloc cannot hope to keep bending the President's ear for too long.

Powers behind the Throne

The Zamora brothers should know. Not too long ago, Manuel and Ronaldo Zamora were considered THE powers behind the throne. These days, however, Malacañang insiders say the Zamoras seem to be less self-assured about their clout in the Palace, less confident about their place in the power totem pole because they have so many other competitors for influencing the presidential mind.

Manuel or 'Manny' Zamora holds no government post, but he is considered to be the "boss" of the Zamora bloc. A former president of Security Bank, Manny was Mr. Moneybags of the Estrada presidential campaign. Said to be the shrewder of the two brothers, he is also the one who is closer to Estrada, who has been a friend for decades. While Manny's clout with the President remains strong, that of his brother Ronaldo or Ronnie, seems to be on the decline.

Zamora is at his best when wheeling and dealing.

The brothers' lieutenants in government include Lito Banayo, presidential adviser for political affairs, who also heads the money-making Philippine Tourism Authority; Ramon B. Cardenas, senior deputy executive secretary, who sits on the board of at least five more government corporations including the Manila Economic and Cultural Office, the de-facto embassy of the Philippines in Taiwan; and Jimmy Policarpio, head of the Presidential Legislative Liaison Office. Other known Zamora allies in the Cabinet are Finance Secretary Edgardo Espiritu; Press Secretary Rodolfo Reyes; and Antonio H. Cerilles, chief of the Department of Environment and Natural Resources.

Ronnie Zamora was also instrumental in making sure that Nueva Ecija political kingpin Edno Joson got the position of chairman of the National Food Authority. In addition, he was among those who lobbied for the appointment of former Senate President Ernesto Maceda as ambassador to the United States.

People who have worked with Ronnie say he is at his best when wheeling and dealing, a skill that is vital in politics, and crucial inside Malacañang. But Ronnie was also supposed to take care of the administrative side of the presidency for Estrada. Unfortunately, he has not exactly turned out to be a managerial whiz, prompting Estrada to turn to someone more knowledgeable in keeping an eye on the everyday workings of the Office of the President.

Then in January 1999, the President removed from the Office of the Executive Secretary the power to review contracts worth P50 million upwards after the National Bureau of Investigation implicated Ronnie Zamora's deputy, Vicente de la Serna, in the P3-million bribery attempt by a textbook agent. De la Serna was later cleared of any involvement in the bribery try, but Zamora has yet to fully recover politically from the incident.

Although he is still seen at the Palace, Manny Zamora was most probably not pleased when he lost the $750 million

PLDT-First Pacific sale to another of Estrada's friends, businessman Mark Jimenez. It had been Manny who introduced Jimenez to Estrada in the final phase of 1998 election campaign; at that point, he may not have been able to foresee where that friendship could lead to. At least, certainly not to Jimenez becoming a Palace faction all by his lonesome, someone who would be defended by the President against the other blocs.

Shifting Blocs

In truth, when Estrada assumed the presidency on June 30, 1998, political analysts reckoned that there would be only three major groups that would be fighting it out in the Malacañang snake pit. One of these had the Zamoras at the helm. Another was identified with Robert Aventajado, a longtime Estrada friend and one of the pillars of JEEP, an Estrada political organization that operated parallel to the official Laban ng Mamamayang Masang Pilipino (LAMMP) but focused on the grassroots. The third bloc was headed by former Senate President Edgardo Angara, Estrada's running mate, and the head of the Laban ng Demokratikong Pilipino (Laban), which had provided the Estrada campaign the national political network it had needed.

A year and a half later, these three blocs have lost some of their considerable clout and must now compete with the influence wielded by the President's nocturnal companions, the gritty dealmaking by Estrada's second "wife" Guia Gomez, and also the emerging power of Leonora de Jesus, chief of the Presidential Management Staff (PMS).

Certainly, Malacañang observers say that Aventajado, who was named presidential adviser on economic affairs and chair of the Presidential Committee on Flagship Projects, no longer wields the same kind of influence he did during Estrada's presidential campaign. This could be because he turned down a position that would have put him in Malacañang, where he could be in close proximity to his President-buddy. Fearing the inevitable Palace intrigues, the former racecar driver and San Juan politico opted to dabble in Mindanao issues and take charge of infrastructure projects instead.

That didn't spare him from the intrigues, however. Aventajado has ended up hounded by unsavory reports involving infrastructure projects under his committee, and Palace insiders say he has become distant from the president, an observation that the official denies. As he recently told a newspaper, "The important thing is that if I call him, he will talk to me, and if I go to Malacañang, he will receive me."

Angara, meanwhile, as secretary of agriculture, is widely acknowledged to be on the margins of power. Although he did get the agriculture post, a position promised him by Estrada, he wields no clout beyond the Elliptical Road in Quezon City, where the Department of Agriculture (DA) is situated.

Proof of Angara's diminished clout was the President's executive order transferring four major DA agencies to the Office of the Presidential Adviser on Food Security, which was created for William Dar, a little-known scientist whom Angara had chosen to warm his seat at the DA while he waited out the expiration of the one-year ban on holding government positions for those who lost in the elections. But when Dar's time was up, he tried to hold on to the position by making governors petition for his retention. When that failed, he made the President sign the executive order. This attempted dismemberment of the DA put the country's food program at risk and was thwarted only with Dar's appointment to the Food and Agriculture Organization in Rome.

Pitting Dar against Angara is seen by many as part of moves to marginalize Angara, who is believed to be nurturing presidential ambitions in 2004. In a way, these have succeeded, as Angara is no longer seen as having clout beyond the DA. Early on, he had even lost his man at the Department of Health (DOH), Dr. Felipe Estrella, whom he had endorsed as secretary. Estrella quit all too soon after becoming the subject of intrigues within the department, but not before saying he was simply too old and too tired to put up with such nonsense.

Formidable Clout

Enter the "Dragon Lady." The formidable de Jesus has been PMS chief since the Aquino administration. But while she acquired a reputation as someone to reckon with during the Ramos presidency, any clout that she had was expected to diminish, if not disappear, once Estrada and his minions came in. Instead, the opposite seems to have happened, in large part because de Jesus is competent and more knowledgeable about how the Office of the President is supposed to work than most anyone else among the Palace lightweights.

De Jesus had been drawn into the Estrada camp by the man she lives with, Ramon Abad, who was Estrada's deputy campaign manager. She soon proved invaluable to the new administration, becoming the instant guide to newcomers who could barely find their way through the maze that is the Malacañang bureaucracy.

That, however, didn't endear her to Estrada's longtime political associates who suddenly saw a new face as doorkeeper to the center of power. Palace insiders say that the reason why two agencies under the PMS last year were transferred to the Office of the Executive Secretary was because of growing wariness about her clout. The President also removed the Southern Philippines Development Authority, which oversees development projects in Mindanao, from de Jesus's plate and onto Aventajado's.

But de Jesus, a survivor of numerous power struggles, has shown savvy in choosing her allies. She maintains a close friendship with Senator Tessie Aquino-Oreta, whom the President openly calls "my favorite senator." Trade Secretary Jose T. Pardo, who is said to be Estrada's most trusted Cabinet member, is also sympathetic to de Jesus.

De Jesus also has on her side, lawyer Crispin 'Boying' Remulla, whom Estrada trusts. Now chief of the PMS's legal section, Boying is a son of former Cavite Governor Juanito Remulla, a staunch Estrada ally. In addition, the younger Remulla had lawyered for Jose Victor "JV" Ejercito, believed to be the President's favorite son. When the President removed from the Office of the Executive Secretary the power to review government contracts worth P50 million or more, it fell on the lap of the PMS section headed by Remulla.

Aside from the Zamora brothers—especially Ronnie, who has seen his political cache inside the Palace dwindle in the wake of de Jesus's rise—those who wish the "Dragon Lady" political ill are said to include the "Greenhills group" composed of the President's sisters, Pilarica, Marita, and Pat, brother Paulino and brother-in-law Raul de Guzman. Of late, de Jesus has managed to antagonize even the likes of neutral Press Secretary Rod Reyes, who was unceremoniously bumped off the presidential plane during a recent official trip to Cebu, in favor of Presidential Spokesman Jerry Barican, the PMS chief's newest Malacañang confederate.

But all of de Jesus's political friends and foes are no match in terms of clout to her most important ally, Guia Gomez, the mother of JV Ejercito and the most politically astute of the President's women companions. When Estrada was mayor of San Juan, Gomez had acted as his first lady and was known to be active in the town's politics. It is thus not surprising that Gomez is de Jesus's main connection to many of those who make up the President's Other Cabinet, which could be said to be the wild card in the Palace power deck.

Officials also have to contend with presidential friends who seem to have the propensity of making suggestions on matters they should not have any say on.

Turf Wars

There are, of course, bound to be turf wars fought by factions in any government, with the melees sometimes resulting in a skewered policy or two. But there has probably never been this many players before, and this many people who do not have official accountability but who are nevertheless participating in the business of running a country. It is bad enough that officials who should be helping the President keep order in the government are instead contributing to the disarray with all their bickering. But the situation can only deteriorate to downright chaos when officials also have to contend with presidential friends who seem to have the propensity of making suggestions on matters they should not have any say on.

To be sure, some of the advice they give may be solicited, albeit over a plate of *pulutan*. Some of them may even be well intentioned, and are meant to be no more than opinions offered to a friend who is asking for them. The problem, however, begins once the recipient takes these and without much thought assumes them to be correct. At the very least, it is a rather delusional way of making decisions, since there really is no processing of ideas that takes place. In government, it is also a method fraught with serious risks.

Former Housing and Urban Development Coordinating Council (HUDCC) chair Karina David said it best in her October 15, 1999 resignation letter to the President. Although she was actually referring to Estrada's large assortment of presidential advisers, consultants and assistants, David was making a point about the dangers of relying on people who "have no line responsibility, yet enjoy direct personal access" to the President. This could very well also describe members of his Midnight Cabinet, as well as friends who have made it a habit of hanging around the Palace grounds during the day. Wrote David: "(The) more aggressive among them can actually subvert the authority of your own line people. Not being integrated into the system, they may often give you distorted information or, worse, engage in manipulation for self-serving interests."

David did not say so directly in her letter, but it appears that she considers herself a victim of such a set-up. Four days before her resignation, she had received a call at midnight, informing her of a luncheon meeting at the Palace the next day. She was not told of the agenda. When she got there, she found a handful of movers and shakers, not all of them officials. These included businessmen Jack Ng and Jose Luis 'Sel' Yulo, both members of the nocturnal Cabinet. The officials were de Jesus, Budget Secretary Benjamin Diokno, National Housing Authority general manager Anthony F. Leynes and Wilfredo Hernandez, president of the Home Insurance and Guaranty Corp. (HIGC). Leynes is widely known in the housing industry to owe his position to Guia Gomez.

Declining Popularity

The group was soon joined by a President concerned about his declining popularity. A few days before, Pulse Asia had briefed Malacañang on the results of its survey for the month of September. The report wasn't good: the President's approval rating had plunged 21 percentage points, from 65 percent in May, to 44 percent.

It was agreed that the housing sector would play a crucial role in getting Estrada's approval ratings back up, and that David would "whip" all the housing agencies into shape. The meeting finished, David left. But as she was nearing the sentry gate, she got a call on her cellular phone informing her that PAG-IBIG head Mel Alonzo had been replaced. PAG-IBIG, a state-run housing loan agency, falls under the office headed by David. It may have struck her as odd that she had not been told beforehand of such a decision.

David marched back into the presidential residence, where the luncheon meeting had just been held and where PMS chief de Jesus holds office. De Jesus confirmed that Alonzo had been terminated. Realizing that there was no reversing the decision, David requested to allow the PAG-IBIG head to resign. Ramon Palma-Gil, a recommendee of Caloocan's Baby Asistio, a frequent late-night visitor at the Palace, replaced Alonzo.

The next day, Yulo, another erstwhile nocturnal adviser, called up David to inform her that he was faxing the Executive Order (EO) creating the Presidential Commission on Mass Housing (PCMH), with him as chair and David as member of the board. The new body essentially had the same functions as HUDCC. But the EO was not all that David's fax machine spat out; there was also an appointment of Yulo as presidential adviser on housing, a position also held by David.

In her letter, David noted that "(parallel) structures without a clear center of accountability create confusion and instability." She also said, "A shelter sector with two heads can only result in everyone working at cross-purposes, generating confusion, intrigue and suspicion."

> Parallel structures without a clear center of accountability create confusion and instability.

In addition, David observed, "Executive Orders vitally affecting the conduct of government need to be carefully studied. I was informed about our...lunch meeting only at midnight of the day before. In that meeting, there was a general agreement that we would work with the Presidential Management Staff towards the eventual reorganization of the shelter sector. There was no mention of an Executive Order. And yet one was signed in the evening of the same day. By the afternoon of October 13, despite my having raised concrete issues against many defective portions of the EO, His Excellency read a press statement that contained even more than what was in the EO."

Yulo, however, would not last even a month. He resigned soon after a newspaper controlled by shadowy Estrada pal Mark Jimenez reported that he has nine estafa cases and is the subject of an arrest warrant for issuing a bouncing check. Palace insiders say the ouster of Yulo was also on the Zamora bloc's list of recommendations to reverse the decline of the President's popularity. The list was apparently drawn up after the media outcry over David's resignation, and was meant partly as a move against de Jesus, who was seen as having a hand in the way David had been treated. But the attempt to hit back at de Jesus may have backfired. When Yulo resigned, she was named as temporary co-chair of the PCMH, together with Hernandez of the HIGC.

The anti-Dragon Lady faction, though, then waged a media blitz against de Jesus, feeding reporters and editors a story about a petition, allegedly signed by 30 people, to oust her. The tale turned out to be false.

Meanwhile, Malacañang officials say that after his approval rating dropped, the President has been waking up early, which could mean reduced sessions with his Midnight Cabinet. He has even scheduled regular meetings with his official Cabinet.

At an El Shaddai rally at Luneta earlier in November 1999, Estrada had also prayed for unity. But he may not have been referring to the bickering blocs that have made for a noisy and messy presidency. According to one Cabinet member, the President once remarked, *"Hayaan mo sila mag-away-away, para ako pa rin ang boss* (Let them quarrel so that I will still be the boss)."

The Courts

Judicial corruption is one of the most difficult subjects of journalistic investigation. This is in part because the judiciary, among all the branches of government, is the least transparent. It is true that court hearings are generally open to the public and documents submitted in the course of judicial proceedings almost always become part of the public record. But deliberations in collegial bodies of the judicial system, such as the Supreme Court and the Court of Appeals, are kept strictly confidential. So are administrative cases filed against erring jurists. Moreover, the transactions that occur outside the courtroom—between judges and litigants or between lawyers and jurists, for example—take place under circumstances of utmost secrecy. There are few mechanisms—short of impeachment or the filing of administrative cases—that compel jurists to account for their actions.

Piercing the veil of secrecy in the courts and finding evidence of wrongdoing in a judicial system that is widely thought to be inefficient and corrupt are a real challenge. The language of the law is arcane and difficult; reading court documents may be prescribed as a cure for insomnia. In addition, those who have the information that can nail down judges, such as lawyers and litigants, are often fearful of retribution from the courts. For one, jurists have the power to cite for contempt those whom they think are casting aspersions on the judiciary's integrity. Lawyers also fear that they will lose their cases if they accuse judges and justices of being corrupt. Besides, in many instances, it is lawyers who pay off judges, and they will hardly confess publicly to committing a crime.

These obstacles can daunt the most dedicated journalist. Yet it is precisely because of these circumstances that the judiciary remains among the least transparent and accountable of public institutions. The 1986 constitution made the judiciary, especially the Supreme Court, more powerful than it was in the past. The framers of the constitution thought that a powerful judiciary would act as a check on the excesses of the presidency. But as any political science textbook will say, a combination of power with little transparency and accountability is a formula for abuse.

Reporting on judicial corruption requires that journalists take a somewhat different approach in looking for evidence of wrongdoing. Our first stories on the Supreme Court were not original investigations, but were based on the studies or investigations conducted by experts or lawyers. Our first report on anomalies in the judiciary was based largely on an expert's examination of the writing style of a justice, which cast doubt on the real authorship of a decision with far-reaching effects on the telecommunications industry. That story caused the resignation of a senior Supreme Court justice. And it was written not by a court reporter but by a business journalist.

The dramatic impact of that story encouraged us to probe further. To be sure, while lawyers, litigants and even some jurists we interviewed insisted that some Supreme Court justices were receiving bribes, the trail of pay-offs was almost impossible to find. Thus, our investigations on the Supreme Court were aimed not so much at finding evidence of bribery but at examining the conduct of judges and the conflicts of interest they faced. Our subsequent reporting on the Court was more ambitious, relying on our own investigations rather than those of others.

One track of our investigations examined the public behavior of the officials of the court. Two of the articles in this section show how Supreme Court justices, by being publicly seen with litigants and lawyers with cases pending in their courts, violate the Judicial Code of Conduct, which prescribes that judges conduct themselves in a manner above suspicion. These reports also reveal the networks of intermediaries that have emerged around magistrates that are supposed to be impervious to outside influence. In particular, these investigations looked at the role of law offices run by relatives of justices or retired justices, which have been accused of peddling influence in the high court. As in probing political corruption, it is important to examine the interlocking interests—family, business and professional ties—that influence decision-making in the judiciary.

Another way we probed wrongdoing was by examining court records to see whether there was a pattern of decision-making. As the three-part investigation, "Justice to the Highest Bidder" found, a pattern of flip-flopping on decisions and of overturning precedents may be a sign not just of a lack of judicial philosophy but also of the influence exerted by pecuniary interests on a tribunal that sometimes decided not so much on the basis of precedent but on the lobbying of litigants.

A third way we went about investigating the judiciary was by doing what reporters who have probed government procurements systems have done: examine deviations from prescribed procedures, which are often a sign that anomalies are taking place. For example, the waiving of a case raffle or the unexplained transfer of a case to a particular court division to which the case was not originally assigned are signs that some behind-the-scenes deal-making may be taking place.

The field of reporting on judicial corruption is vast and relatively unexplored. The reports included in this section are initial forays into these uncharted waters. Most of our reports have been on the Supreme Court. Not enough investigation has been done on corruption in the lower courts. This is territory that is awaiting further exploration.

A Fake Ruling

BY STELLA TIROL-CADIZ
First published in the *Philippine Daily Inquirer*, January 28, 1993

This is the story that caused a justice's resignation. It is the first of several reports published by the PCIJ on the Supreme Court under the leadership of Chief Justice Andres Narvasa. Written between 1993 and 1997, these investigations took off from conversations conducted by our staff with lawyers and litigants who complained about Supreme Court decisions that they believed were biased in favor of influential lawyers or firms. These allegations were difficult, nearly impossible to document, and those who spoke to us provided little proof of malfeasance.

Stella Tirol-Cadiz, who covered the stock market for a business paper before joining PCIJ, stumbled upon this story while doing research on the telecommunications industry, which had been rocked by a Supreme Court decision that preserved the Philippine Long Distance Telephone Co.'s profitable monopoly of overseas calls. For decades, PLDT had been able to protect its turf from rivals by using its influence in Malacañang, Congress and the courts. The latest Supreme Court decision was fresh testimony to its tremendous clout. Rival firms fumed. The Court seemed ripe for investigation.

When we published this story, which is based on a study conducted by an American writing style expert on the decisions of Supreme Court Justice Hugo Gutierrez, we knew that we were only looking at the tip of the iceberg. The expert alleged that the controversial decision was written not by Gutierrez but by PLDT's lawyer. Although it was usual for judges to quote portions of lawyers' briefs, it was highly irregular for an entire decision on a case of profound importance to be written entirely by the lawyer of one of the parties.

This report, headlined by the *Inquirer*, forced Gutierrez to resign four days after its publication. It came at a time when the judiciary was being criticized for sheltering "hoodlums in robes." It was also a time when Malacañang, worried that the government stood to lose its cases against some of the Marcos cronies, was putting pressure on the high tribunal, which had been deciding in favor of the Marcos associates.

Tirol-Cadiz would later be called to testify before an ad-hoc committee created by Narvasa to look into allegations of corruption in the courts. She was grilled by Narvasa himself, who insisted that she reveal the source of this story. She refused. Taking off from this investigation, she later wrote a two-part story, also included here, on unethical conduct by Supreme Court justices.

Supreme Court Justice Faked Landmark Decision

A WELL-KNOWN American expert has alleged that a Supreme Court justice faked authorship of a controversial and important decision that preserved the virtual monopoly of the Philippine Long Distance Telephone Company (PLDT) on profitable overseas calls.

In a sworn affidavit, Dr. David Miles Yerkes, an expert of authorship of English-language texts, said Justice Hugo Gutierrez, Jr. passed off as his own a document that appeared to have been written by a PLDT lawyer.

Gutierrez, who was appointed to his post in 1982 by then President Ferdinand Marcos, is the longest serving member of the Supreme Court and is ranked next to Chief Justice Andres Narvasa.

The decision, released by the high tribunal on August 27, 1992, banned the Eastern Telecommunications Philippines Inc. (ETPI) from operating an international gateway, a channel that links local telephones to the international system. It allowed the PLDT to virtually monopolize overseas calls, which accounted for more than half of the firm's P16-billion revenues in 1991.

Gutierrez, saying that "writing styles change," denied the allegation and insisted he was the *ponente* (author) of the decision.

"I am the author of that decision and nobody can contest that," he said in an interview. "They should not include me in this war between two big firms." Noting that "somebody is spending money to discredit the court," he said "whoever wrote (the decision) is immaterial because the (issue) has to be decided by all the members of the Court."

For his part, PLDT counsel Eliseo Alampay, who wrote the pleadings in the case, said: "I find the (allegation) absurd, and I deny (it)."

The Rules of Court and the Constitution say justices themselves must write their decisions, which become part of the laws of the land. Yerkes's allegation against Gutierrez may have a wide-ranging impact on the Supreme Court and on the Philippine telecommunications industry that the PLDT has dominated for decades.

"Why would a justice allow a lawyer for one of the parties in a case to write a decision of the Supreme Court?"

If true, the allegation raises grave doubts about the PLDT's business practices, especially at a time when its dominance is under severe challenge. Yerkes's findings could also pose problems for PLDT chairman Antonio 'Tony Boy' Cojuangco, who has been accused of irregularities in his controversial acquisition of Philippine Airlines.

Yerkes's appraisal of Gutierrez's work was solicited by the lawyers of the ETPI, an affiliate of the British firm Cable & Wireless. The ETPI intended to present the expert's testimony to the Supreme Court, but sources say the company feared repercussions from the high tribunal if it made the issue public.

The PCIJ obtained copies of Yerkes's affidavit and authenticated it with the Philippine consulate in New York. Yerkes, whose testimony has been used in more than 30 civil and criminal cases in the United States, examined the decision supposedly written by Gutierrez and compared it with four of the justice's previous rulings. Yerkes also examined the writing of Alampay.

Like Fingerprints

Writing styles are as identifiable as fingerprints, said the expert. He stated in his affidavit: "Justice Gutierrez's style of writing underwent an abrupt, radical change between his four decisions dated March 31 through May 22,1992 and the date of the PLDT decision, August 27, 1992. Moreover, Gutierrez's new style of writing conforms precisely with that of the writing style of PLDT's counsel."

Yerkes concluded: "The PLDT decision looks, reads and sounds like the writing of PLDT's counsel...My explanation raises the possibility of there being bias, partiality and a lack of independence in the judicial-making process, as seen in the writing style adopted by the author of the PLDT decision."

An English professor at Columbia University and author of three scholarly books on the English language, Yerkes also examined a subsequent ruling by Gutierrez. He said Gutierrez reverted to the same writing style as the prior decisions, making the PLDT decision even more "anomalous."

Yerkes noted that in the Wenceslao Laureta case where the Supreme Court conducted a study comparing writing styles to establish authorship of documents, it affirmed that writing style is a valid, reliable means of authorship.

"Why would a justice allow a lawyer for one of the parties in a case to write a decision of the Supreme Court?" asked a prominent lawyer familiar with the facts of the case. If the allegation is true, was it because there were other considerations involved?"

"If the expert is saying that I influenced the outcome of the case, that is impossible because we vote as a collegial body," Gutierrez said. "I am just being consistent. In an earlier case, I also dissented. This became the majority decision later."

In late 1990, the PLDT asked the Supreme Court to overrule a landmark decision of the National Telecommunications Commission (NTC) allowing the ETPI to operate an international gateway. That decision marked the first time government allowed competitors into the overseas telephone market.

The PLDT case reportedly split the Supreme Court. It was originally raffled to its third division headed by Gutierrez. (The division has since been reorganized.) During a consultation meeting, the five-man division reportedly voted in favor of the ETPI and asked Justice Florentino Feliciano to write the decision.

But when Feliciano's draft was presented, several justices were said to have reversed their stand and a heated argument took place. To settle the matter, the case was brought to the Supreme Court en banc. Finally, in August 1992, the court in a decision supposedly written by Gutierrez, ruled 10-4 in PLDT's favor. The PLDT had also filed a case barring Philippine Global Communications (PHILCOM), another telecommunications firm, from operating an international gateway, but the case was dismissed on a technicality. The two firms share common directors and stockholders.

Winning Battles

Through the years, the PLDT has been able to maintain its monopoly by fighting off challenges like that posed by the ETPI. These battles have taken place in courts, Congress and government agencies like the NTC.

But while the PLDT has won most of its battles, it lost in December 1988, when the NTC allowed the Express Telecommunications Co. Inc. (Extelcom) to enter the cellular phone market. The PLDT, which had a similar pending application at the time, went to the Supreme Court to block Extelcom's entry.

In October 1990, the Supreme Court ruled against the PLDT. The decision, written by Justice Amuerfina Melencio-Herrera, criticized monopolies and upheld the NTC's power to order interconnection among telecommunications firms. Several justices have since retired and new ones have taken their place.

Gutierrez's August 1992 decision in effect reversed Herrera's ruling.

The controversy that now surrounds Gutierrez's decision could set off the most serious crisis in the Supreme Court since 1982 when all the members offered to resign after several of them were accused of lowering the passing mark for that year's bar examinations to favor a member's son.

The controversy that now surrounds Gutierrez's decision could set off the most serious crisis in the Supreme Court since 1982 when all the members offered to resign after several of them were accused of lowering the passing mark for that year's bar examinations to favor a member's son.

Yerkes, an expert in philology and linguistics, has also been involved in the investigation of writing styles and the identification of authorship of such works as the Old English classic, *Beowulf.*

He said abrupt and radical changes in style are extremely rare and that these are usually attributed to some external factor. He cited the case of American author Henry James, whose sentences became longer after he started using a typewriter.

Two Aspects

According to Yerkes, the PLDT decision differs from all four of Gutierrez's prior decisions in at least two major aspects:

The author of the PLDT decision introduced his reasons with a very brief paragraph (six words long) and then set those reasons out in sections numbered with Arabic numerals.

All four of Gutierrez's prior decisions used much longer introductory paragraphs (20 to 48 words long) and set out the reasons differently.

The author of the PLDT decision used partisan, biased language, and slang. Gutierrez normally did not.

Justices on the Dock

BY SHEILA S. CORONEL

First published in the *Philippine Daily Inquirer, The Manila Chronicle* and *Malaya*, May 31, 1993

This report is an initial exploration of a theme that the PCIJ would probe deeper into in its subsequent investigations of the Supreme Court: the influence peddling by lawyers who are relatives of high court justices. This article focuses on an administrative case filed against a Supreme Court justice, an appellate court justice, and the brother-in-law of the chief justice. Administrative cases are rarely filed against justices of the high tribunal. They are also kept tightly under wrap. The record of administrative proceedings and the actual complaints themselves are never shown to journalists. The reporting on this case was in that sense unprecedented.

The fate of this particular case, which we document in this and in two subsequent reports, shows how justices tend to protect their own. Our reports reveal that it is this clubbiness and incestuousness in both the bar and the bench that are at the heart of corruption in the judiciary.

This narrative of an administrative case against high court officials tells of how a raffle was waived and a case assigned to a presumably friendly justice at the request of the lawyer for one of the parties, who happens to be the chief justice's brother-in-law. At the Supreme Court, the case was assigned to a division of which the chief justice was a member, but he did not initially inhibit himself from the deliberations even though his brother-in-law was lawyering for one of the litigants. All of these facts are in the records of the case: the lawyer's request that the raffle be waived, the justice allowing the waiving, the assignment of the case to the chief justice's division, etc.

The case was rare in that it provided well-documented allegations of improper conduct, even if it showed no proof of actual bribery. What it revealed was the defiance of established court procedures designed to protect the integrity of the courts.

Justices Questioned about Controversial Land Case

A SUPREME Court justice, a senior justice of the Court of Appeals and a brother-in-law of Chief Justice Andres Narvasa are being charged before the Supreme Court with rigging a case involving a multimillion-peso real estate transaction.

The charges of misconduct filed against Supreme Court Justice Rodolfo Nocon, appellate court Justice Manuel C. Herrera, and lawyer Joaquin 'Bobby' Yuseco, Narvasa's brother-in-law, are among the most serious allegations ever brought before the Supreme Court concerning high officials of the judiciary.

In an administrative complaint filed by lawyers of Equatorial Realty Development, Inc., Nocon is accused of intervening, while he was presiding justice of the Court of Appeals, to waive the raffle of a case and assign it to Herrera.

Assignment of cases other than by raffle is highly irregular and prohibited by the court's internal rules. Nocon had acted on the request of Yuseco, who had written to him on behalf of Mayfair Theater, Inc.

Herrera took the case and later ruled in Mayfair's favor.

Nocon, in a memorandum to Narvasa, admitted asking the raffle committee to decide on its own. Interviewed over the phone, Nocon refused to comment until the court had resolved the case.

For his part, Yuseco argued there was nothing improper about his letter to Nocon. He accused Equatorial's lawyers of using smear tactics to win their case. "They are carrying on a campaign to malign us because they are afraid the Supreme Court would decide against them," he said in an interview.

The charges were made in late 1992, months before the Supreme Court created a committee to look into alleged wrongdoing in the judiciary.

In May 1993, the committee released findings exonerating Supreme Court justices of any wrongdoing. The committee did not take evidence on the charges against Nocon supposedly because it did not want to duplicate proceedings of ongoing cases.

Narvasa, however, failed to inform two other members of the committee that such a case had been brought before the Supreme Court, said retired justice Lorenzo Relova, a committee member.

Nearly six months after the Supreme Court second division decide to hear the administrative case, the high tribunal has yet to deliberate and decide on the charges.

"This is a test case for the Supreme Court because it involves a justice and a relative of the chief justice," says a lawyer familiar with the charges.

Lobbyists in the Court

If proven valid, the charges demonstrate the behind-the-scenes lobbying that many lawyers say happens in the courts. They also show how the networks of relationships that link lawyers, judges and justices can influence court actions and decisions.

The case highlights the role of Bobby Yuseco, a long-time law practitioner who runs a law office in Escolta. Yuseco is the brother of Narvasa's wife, Janina.

In October 1991, Yuseco wrote Nocon, the presiding judge of the Court of Appeals, asking him to "permanently assign" a case to Justice Herrera as there was a related case pending in Herrera's division.

The charges demonstrate the behind-the-scenes lobbying that many lawyers say happens in the courts.

Although Yuseco claims to have been a long-time lawyer for Mayfair, he was not officially registered as its counsel. His request could have violated the internal rules of the Court of Appeals, which require that all cases be raffled, not assigned, to justices.

Despite the possible violation, Nocon granted Yuseco's request on the very day he received the letter. A month later, he was appointed to the Supreme Court.

In the meantime, neither he nor Herrera informed the other litigants that the case had been assigned and consolidated with a related suit. Herrera took on both cases and in record time, penned two separate decisions favoring Yuseco's client.

Charges against justices are rare, partly because it is difficult to get documentary proof of alleged wrongdoing. For this reason, the Supreme Court's ad-hoc committee dismissed various charges against members of the high tribunal. But the charges against Nocon and the others included letters and other documents that seemed to have convinced the Supreme Court to ask the accused to reply to the charges. The PCIJ obtained copies of the documents.

The case began in 1978 when Carmelo and Bauermann Inc. sold two downtown Manila theaters to Equatorial Realty Development, Inc. for P11.3 million. At current prices, these two theaters are now worth about P60 million.

Mayfair Theater, which leased part of the property from Carmelo and Bauermann, contested the sale in a Manila court, arguing that it had first option to buy.

After 12 years, Mayfair lost the case in 1990 and brought it before the Court of Appeals in April 1991. The case was raffled to the appellate court's twelfth division headed by Herrera for "completion of records," a process that involves gathering the records of the case without deliberating and deciding on it.

Raffle Waived

The internal rules of the Court of Appeals require that after the records are completed, another raffle should be conducted to assign the case to the justice who will decide it. The two raffles are designed to ensure the impartiality and fairness of the decision-making process.

But before a second raffle was held, Yuseco, writing on behalf of Mayfair and its lawyer, former Supreme Court Justice Antonio Barredo, wrote to Nocon a three-page letter saying that since Herrera was already hearing a related case, both cases should be consolidated and "permanently assigned" to him.

Such a permanent assignment could have violated the internal rules of the appellate court.

But on the same day, Nocon referred Yuseco's letter to Herrera who promptly returned it to the presiding judge with a note on the routing slip that read, "No objection." Later that day, Nocon sent a handwritten note to the raffle committee: "Kindly take note of the petition for reconsideration. Justice Herrera has no objection to both cases being assigned to him."

In the end, both cases were assigned to Herrera, who quickly reversed the lower court's decision in favor of Mayfair. In the meantime, Nocon, whose nomination to the Supreme Court had been previously bypassed, was appointed to the high tribunal in November 1991.

In their replies to the Supreme Court, all three men admitted that they wrote those letters on October 14, 1991. Copies of the letters, certified by the clerk of the Court of Appeals, have been submitted to the high tribunal.

In a memorandum to the Supreme Court, Ricardo Romulo and Eduardo de los Angeles, lawyers for Equatorial, the firm that brought the property, asserted that Yuseco's role as intermediary in the case was "strange" and "suspicious." Yuseco was never a counsel on record for Mayfair and did not file any motions or pleadings on Mayfair's behalf either before or after his 1991 letter to Nocon.

"It seems Mayfair used Atty. Yuseco only for that all-important purpose: write a letter to Justice Nocon asking for the consolidation or permanent assignment (of the case) to Justice Herrera," Equatorial's lawyers wrote.

In his defense, Yuseco says he has been on Mayfair's retainer for many years and he wrote the letter because Justice Barredo, the firm's other lawyer, was ill.

Shopping for a Justice

The lawyers also alleged that Herrera's division tried to deceive them by issuing a May 14, 1992 resolution saying that the case will be raffled a second time. The second raffle never took place.

Herrera explained to the Supreme Court that the resolution was issued by the division clerk without his clearance and included an affidavit by the clerk saying the error was his.

On June 23, 1992, barely a month after two new members were appointed to the division, Herrera and two other justices released a decision on the case. Lawyers say it normally takes several months to over a year for an appellate court to release a decision.

Moreover, Equatorial's lawyers found out that Herrera wrote the decision without examining the *expediente* or records of the case. They submitted to the Supreme Court a certification from the chief of the Court of Appeals judicial records division saying that the records were not borrowed from the time the case was supposed to have been deliberated on to the time it was decided.

In his defense, Herrera told the Supreme Court that he did not need the *expediente* because he had the *rollo*, which contains the lawyer's pleadings. But in their reply to Herrera, Equatorial's lawyers claimed that the justice quoted transcripts that were not part of the *rollo*.

The behind-the-scenes maneuverings

apparently did not stop at the Court of Appeals. The case was brought to the Supreme Court and was assigned, by raffle, to the first division (The Supreme Court has three divisions).

But soon afterward, Mayfair's new lawyers, which included a son of now deceased Supreme Court Justice Leo Medialdea, asked that the case be transferred to the high tribunal's second division because there was a related case pending there. Both Nocon and Narvasa are members of the second division.

> "In our long practice of law, we have never encountered a case with so much behind-the-scene maneuvers, so much intense lobbying to shop for a particular judge or justice."

The second division accepted the case even if months earlier, it had already dismissed the related case, which called for Mayfair's ejection from the property. Mayfair's lawyers were apparently aware of the dismissal and knew their request for transfer rested on shaky ground.

In late 1992, after Equatorial's lawyers complained about the alleged anomalies, Nocon and Narvasa inhibited themselves from hearing the case. If his brother-in-law was indeed Mayfair's counsel, the Chief Justice should have inhibited himself, as is the normal practice in Court, the moment the case was brought to his division.

After the inhibition, Mayfair's other lawyer, former Justice Barredo, asked that the case be transferred again to the first division, as there were not enough members in the second division to try the case.

The Supreme Court, however, denied the request.

In a letter sent to Narvasa in September 1992, Equatorial's lawyers wrote, "In our long practice of law, we have never encountered a case with so much behind-the-scene maneuvers, so much intense lobbying to shop for a particular judge or justice."

"Such shopping for judges or justices," they said, "should never be countenanced."

Judiciary on Trial

BY STELLA TIROL-CADIZ

First published in the *Philippine Daily Inquirer* and *Times Journal*, June 3-4, 1993

While the first two reports in this section focus on how justices decided on individual cases, this two-part series examines the conduct outside the courtroom of some judges and justices. It says that jurists often meet with lawyers and litigants, many times in circumstances that are less than innocent. Such meetings violate the Code of Judicial Conduct and contribute to widespread perceptions of impropriety in the courts.

Unlike the first two reports, which were based mainly on court documents, this series was put together largely from interviews with two Supreme Court justices, lawyers, litigants and law clerks on the Supreme Court staff. For obvious reasons, these sources refused to be identified by name, but they corroborate each other and tell a consistent story of lobbying in the courts, including the Supreme Court, by litigants and their lawyers. The series also examines the brokering role played by the relatives of justices and cites an official investigation of the son of a Supreme Court justice who became notorious for his influence-peddling activities.

The second part of the series looks at what lawyers say can be done so the judiciary can repair the damage to its reputation. It examines the Chief Justice's half-hearted attempts to clean the Court's tarnished image and points out the impropriety of the chief sitting in a committee investigating judicial corruption when he is himself the subject of a complaint.

Justices Violate Code of Judicial Conduct

First of Two Parts

A LAWYER for one of the country's largest law firms helps research cases for big clients. But he doesn't just look at law books and court documents. He looks at justices: what they've been doing and who they've been seeing.

"It shames us to do it," he says, "but this is how law practice has evolved over the past years." Previously, his law firm concentrated on legal strategy—what kind of argument would appeal to which justice.

"Now it's different, you need to get information. Has the other side approached the justice? Where did the justice have lunch and who did he have lunch with? Why is he suddenly leaving for abroad?"

Interviews with lawyers from various law firms indicate a widespread perception in the legal community of corruption in the judiciary, including the Supreme Court. Such perception has been worsened by what they say are routine violations of the code of judicial conduct by jurists.

A Supreme Court justice says some of his colleagues routinely receive litigants in their offices, which is highly improper. Lawyers say they see justices at restaurants dining with parties who have cases pending before these justices' courts.

The talk of corruption is worsened by stories of relatives of justices following up cases, ferreting out confidential information from Court employees, and allegedly interceding on behalf of litigants.

In a case being investigated by the National Bureau of Investigation (NBI), a son of a former justice is accused, together with two other judges, of unfair influence and meddling in a Court of Appeals case.

"Public confidence can be eroded by improper behavior," says University of the Philippines law professor Rafael Lotilla. "As such, judges and justices are expected to willingly accept restrictions on conduct that are viewed as burdensome by ordinary citizens."

Such restrictions can be as simple as turning away visitors.

"I don't know why some of my colleagues receive visitors in their offices at the Supreme Court," a Supreme Court justice said in a three-hour interview. "As a justice, you're not supposed to do that."

"These visitors see you if they have a case or are interested in a case. They're not there to say hello. My thinking is if you don't want to be suspected of partiality, you don't see visitors."

He said the desire to remain impartial should persuade justices to stay away from social gatherings as well. "We justices are always invited and some justices love to fraternize," he said. "But the life of a justice is a lonely one. If you receive visitors in your chambers and go to parties and continue seeing old friends, what will people think of you?"

Whispering Campaigns

Such contact inevitably leads to *"ex-parte"* communication, where one litigant or lawyer manages to talk to the judge or justice without the presence of the opposing party. In the United States, such contact is illegal if the case is discussed. Some U.S. cities have laws requiring lawyers and litigants to report within 48 hours if such contact, no matter how seemingly innocuous, occurred.

Some lawyers see such communication as the first step to corruption and influence-peddling, but in the Philippines it is commonplace.

In an *Asian Wall Street Journal* story in January 1993, Supreme Court Justice Teodoro Padilla was quoted as saying that at least two justices told him they were approached by representatives of the Philippine Long Distance Telephone Co., when the company had a major case in court. Such meetings, while not illegal in the Philippines, are highly improper.

In another case involving a billion-peso industrial firm, a Supreme Court justice signed a temporary restraining order (TRO) favoring a litigant. The litigant was seen by Court employees almost every day in the justice's office before the TRO was issued.

Later, that justice officially inhibited himself from the case. But he still took part in the deliberations, according to a Supreme Court justice.

Another justice said he refused more than P1 million in grease money to favor a certain party in a major case involving trademarks. The broker who offered the bribe was a friend. This, the justice says, is the typical way parties try to reach justices.

The Supreme Court has promulgated a Code of Judicial Conduct that says a judge should behave at all times to promote public confidence in the integrity and the impartiality of the judiciary. Such *ex-parte* meetings violate a judicial canon, says a member of the committee that drafted the code.

Another source of lack of trust in the high court is the clout wielded by former justices and relatives of justices, especially sons of justices who are lawyers. Many former justices continue to be in active law practice and the relatives of justices often represent clients before the Supreme Court.

Not all sons of justices and retired jurists suffer from such criticism, prominent lawyers and Supreme Court sources stressed. But the unchecked behavior of a few, visible and influential relatives have hurt the integrity of the Court.

The Justice's Son

One such case involved lawyer Daniel Gutierrez, son of retired Justice Hugo Gutierrez. According to well-placed sources in the Supreme Court, the court en banc confronted Gutierrez on the activities of his son during the tenure of Chief Justice Marcelo Fernan.

Lawyers who know Daniel Gutierrez say he lets it be known that he could assist people with problems in the Supreme Court, thereby casting doubt on the tribunal's impartiality. Gutierrez refused to be interviewed.

In one particular case filed before the Supreme Court, complainant Wilfredo Buenaventura cites the presence of Daniel Gutierrez in the chambers of Court of Appeals Justice Filemon Mendoza as a sign of undue influence and meddling.

Buenaventura presented an affidavit of Court of Appeals employee Ramon Concepcion, who said he saw Gutierrez together with two other judges identified with the opposing party, in Mendoza's chamber on December 27, 1991, a few hours before the decision was rendered.

Justice Mendoza ruled against Buenaventura in a land case without once borrowing the records of the case, the NBI found.

The Buenaventura complaint was lodged with the ad hoc committee, which did not investigate further because it had been "moot and academic, since Justice Mendoza had already compulsorily retired." But the NBI is investigating the case for possible criminal violations of the anti-graft and corrupt practices act.

Breaching Court Secrecy

According to several Court employees, Gutierrez was also well known for following up cases in the high tribunal and talking to Court employees to obtain information about ongoing cases.

"It's a pretty slow week if he goes to Court just three times a week. He was there almost every day," said a former clerk of court of a Supreme Court justice.

The practice of "following up" cases is considered improper because of the confidentiality imposed by the high court.

To shield itself from outside influences, the Court withholds vital information, one of the most important being the identity of the *"ponente,"* or the justice assigned to pen the Court's decision on a case.

The *ponente* is tasked with studying the facts and issues of the case and recommending a position to his or her colleagues. Such is the power of *ponentes* that interested litigants try to identify them and learn their specific leanings in a case.

Among lawyers, the identity of the *ponente* is known in many cases that are pending before the Court.

One lawyer believes that the Court's notion it can keep the identity of a *ponente* secret is fiction. He thinks the practice of confidentiality should be abandoned so as not to prejudice parties who do not have similar access to the Court.

Confidentiality has been breached at the highest levels of the Court. One justice says he was shocked that his arguments during a closed door *en banc* session in a major case reached one of the parties, who sent an emissary the next day to ask him to change his mind.

He also speculates that leakage occurred at the third division when it was discussing the PLDT's petition to block a competitor's international gateway.

In that case, the entire division initially supported the position of Justice Florentino Feliciano, the case's *ponente*, to reject PLDT's petition during a Friday meeting. The following Monday, all of the justices except for Feliciano changed their position. "Somebody must have known what was discussed to have been able to reach them during the weekend," a justice speculates.

So crucial is insider information that big law offices are said to put a premium on relatives of justices. "If you look at the major law firms in the country, almost all of them have sons or daughters of justices," says lawyer Romeo Capulong, president and managing counsel of the Public Interest Law Center.

Big firms often hire a battery of lawyers that include former justices and relatives of Supreme Court justices.

For example, a serious administrative complaint alleging the rigging of a case at the Court of Appeals involved not only Supreme Court Justice Rodolfo Nocon but also the brother-in-law of Chief Justice Andres Narvasa, former Supreme Court Justice Antonio Barredo, and the son of former Justice Leo Medialdea, who all served as lawyers for one of the parties.

Can the Supreme Court Investigate Itself?

Conclusion

SOMETIME in March 1993, retired Supreme Court Justice Lorenzo Relova sought a private meeting with Chief Justice Andres Narvasa.

In that meeting, the 77-year-old former jurist questioned the propriety of Narvasa's presence in the ad hoc committee tasked to investigative charges of corruption against the judiciary.

Narvasa was not only a member of the high court, he was also one of those named in an anonymous complaint sent to all justices.

Relova indicated that it would be better if Narvasa resigned from the ad hoc committee, a suggestion that angered the chief justice who rejected the idea.

The incident, described by a Supreme Court justice, highlights how even in the ad hoc committee, there has been disagreement on the presence of a serving justice in a committee formed to investigative corruption in the judiciary, including the high court.

Relova, in an interview, repeatedly refused to comment on whether he agreed to Narvasa's presence in the committee and on whether he asked the chief justice to resign.

But sources said Relova and a few other justices apparently believed that the credibility of the investigation and the findings of the committee could be tainted by the presence of Narvasa, himself the subject of investigation by the fact-finding body.

Harsh criticism has been heaped by the media, lawyers and legislators on the 25-page report because of the perception that the committee was not independent.

Similar questions about the independence of the Supreme Court are likely to be raised if it rules on an administrative complaint filed against Supreme Court justice Rodolfo Nocon and Chief Justice Narvasa's brother-in-law, Joaquin Yuseco. The two are accused of rigging a multimillion-peso land deal. At least two Supreme Court justices interviewed by the PCIJ questioned the wisdom of Supreme Court members investigating and ruling on the actions of a colleague.

While not specifically referring to the ad hoc committee report or the Nocon case, they doubted the proposition that they could be objective judges of complaints against colleagues.

"How can they expect us to rule against a fellow justice?" asked a member of the high tribunal. "We see them and work with them everyday. Do we stop talking to them (if there is an investigation)?"

Above Reproach

Judges and justices are supposed to refrain from talking or being seen with the parties or litigants of a case. How do the rules of judicial conduct apply if a colleague is involved?

Another justice in a separate three-hour interview voiced a strikingly similar view. "It is not a good idea at all," he said, stressing the situation was fraught with problems. "I cannot sit in judgment of a colleague. *Delikado*."

The controversial case involving Justice Nocon throws that dilemma into sharp focus. The circumstances of the case raise questions on whether the Court is the appropriate body to handle such investigations.

The complaint, which was filed in September 1992, accused Justice Nocon and Yuseco of involvement in a raffle-rigging scandal.

Other parties accused in the case include a former Supreme Court justice, the son of a Supreme Court justice and a Court of Appeals justice.

The complaint alleged that Nocon, while he was presiding justice of the Court of Appeals, violated the internal rules of the court by assigning a case to a specific justice upon the request of Yuseco and former Supreme Court Justice Antonio Barredo, both of whom worked for one of the parties in the case.

Assignment of cases other than through raffle is highly irregular and is ground for disbarment.

According to a Supreme Court justice, the case was so sensitive that at least one justice refused to handle it.

A Supreme Court justice interviewed by the Center says that as far as he knows, to avoid unease in the case, a committee composed of retired justices was proposed to receive evidence and recommend action on the controversial administrative complaint.

The idea was that if the committee found basis for the allegations, it would recommend its findings to the court and the court would quietly pressure the justice to resign.

The justice said the proposed committee was transformed into the ad hoc committee after there were more reports and rumors of corruption in the judiciary. But in the end, the ad hoc committee did not tackle the administrative complaint filed against Justice Nocon and the other accused.

Relova said he was not informed of any such case during the three-month tenure of the ad hoc committee.

Narvasa denied that the ad hoc committee was originally created to hear the Nocon case. Speaking through Assistant Clerk of Court Luz Puno, he said that the case was from the beginning assigned to the Supreme Court and was not moved to any other body.

PROTECTING THE CHIEF

The ad hoc committee appears to have excluded the Nocon case because it is not authorized to "duplicate ongoing or pending judicial or administrative proceedings."

But the decision to exclude ongoing administrative cases, which affected the Nocon case, was made public in a Court statement only on March 25, 1993, two months after the committee was formed.

Lawyers question why the Nocon case was not thrown to the ad hoc committee when it would at least be more objective than the Supreme Court in dealing with a colleague.

There is only one other known case when the Supreme Court as a whole attempted to tackle issues of irregularities or corruption involving one of its members.

During the tenure of Chief Justice Marcelo Fernan, the whole court in an *en banc* session confronted now retired Justice Hugo Gutierrez about the activities of his lawyer-son, Daniel Gutierrez.

According to several sources, including a justice, the Court had received persistent reports that Daniel Gutierrez was following up cases in court and letting it be known that he was willing to help those who had problems in the Court, both considered highly irregular behavior.

"The very fact that the Court confronted a justice is significant," insisted a lawyer close to the Court. When confronted, Justice Gutierrez said he would ask his son about the allegations as soon as he returned from abroad. In a subsequent session, Gutierrez said his son had denied the allegations. The case was considered closed.

More recently, when allegations were made by an English language expert questioning the authorship of a landmark ruling on telecommunications supposedly written by Justice Gutierrez, the ad hoc committee refused to probe the allegations.

In its report, the committee said it considered the case closed with the resignation of the justice.

Lawyers say major steps in reducing corruption in the judiciary can be taken if a permanent judicial commission is created to investigate reports and complaints of corruption and irregularities.

According to sources, at least four justices favor the creation of a judicial commission independent of the Supreme Court but the idea is still strongly resisted by Chief Justice Narvasa.

A person who confesses to bribing a judge or justice is just as liable as the person bribed.

Proposed Reforms

These are among the ideas that have been proposed:

Lawyers' groups have asked the Supreme Court to form an independent commission, meaning one that does not fall under the jurisdiction of the high tribunal.

The commission must take an active role in ferreting out corruption, instead of just receiving evidence. It must have the power to investigate, to summon people and to subpoena documents.

"One problem of the ad hoc committee is that they expected to come forward with a fully developed case of corruption," says a lawyer. "The attitude should be corruption is such a great evil that the government should give the citizen every assistance to weed it out."

The commission must have the power to grant immunity. A person who confesses to bribing a judge or justice is just as liable as the person bribed, thus closing one source of information.

The commission will work hand in hand with Congress, where its findings will be sent if there is basis for impeachment.

A lawyer in Makati says: "The commission will help develop a case if there is any. I don't think Congress can take on a full time job of investigating complaints of corruption."

The Constitution strictly delineates which offenses—among them treason, graft and corruption, bribery—are impeachable.

But a Supreme Court justice suggests that even if an offense found against a justice is not ground for impeachment, it should still be brought to Congress. "Even if the offense is not impeachable, if during the course of the hearings it becomes clear that the justice nevertheless committed an offense, public pressure can then compel the justice to resign."

Justice to the Highest Bidder

BY SHEILA S. CORONEL

First published in *Manila Times, BusinessWorld, Sun Star Daily,* May 21-23, 1997; *Manila Chronicle,* May 21, 1997

This series, which won the first prize in the 1997 Jaime V. Ongpin Award for Investigative Reporting, is the logical culmination of the reporting the PCIJ has done on the Supreme Court since 1993. Building on the insights and the network of sources formed in the course of past reportage on the judiciary, this investigation probes in greater depth and with more details and examples, the charges of impropriety and malfeasance in the Supreme Court.

It cites concrete cases, this time with lawyers and litigants quoted by name, of illicit approaches to justices. It reveals the existence of a network of brokers composed of well-connected individuals who offer to fix cases for a price. These brokers include the chief justice's son and one of his best friends, both of them lawyers with a thriving practice.

This report was researched over a six-month period and was based on interviews with dozens of knowledgeable individuals, including current and former justices. Many of these sources agreed to be named, in part because the practices in the high tribunal had become rather scandalous and they had had enough. Many were convinced to go on record only if other sources were willing to be named as well.

This investigation also relied heavily on a critical examination of court decisions, in an attempt to establish some sort of pattern of decision-making. What emerged, as this series shows, was a pattern of flip-flopping on decisions and a reversal of precedents that attested not only to a lack of judicial coherence, but also to the influence of powerful lobbyists. The documents used for this report were not only court records but also records of the immigration bureau, which showed the chief justice traveling abroad almost always in the company of his lawyer-friend. We also hired a photographer who followed the chief justice around, including when he was playing golf with officials and lawyers with cases pending in his tribunal. The chief justice's social life is one of the topics examined in this report.

This investigation probed the roots of the problem, including the heavy workload in the Court, the division system which makes it easier to influence decision-making in the high tribunal, and the *ponente* system, where the author of the decision, in a collegial court overloaded with cases, almost always has the last say. The immense power given to the Supreme Court after 1986 and the high-stakes cases that were put before it made the tribunal open to more powerful temptations than ever. These and the fallibility of the individuals named to the highest court in the country formed the bedrock for corruption.

Bidding Wars in the Supreme Court

First of Three Parts

IS justice for sale?

Abraham Sarmiento did not think so. But in 1991, when he was still a justice of the Supreme Court, an attorney on his staff was invited to lunch by a former law school classmate, Danilo Gutierrez, whose father Hugo was then a member of the high tribunal.

The lunch took place at a well-known seafood restaurant, and in the course of the meal, Sarmiento's assistant was asked whether P3 million was enough to sway her boss, who had been assigned to write the decision on the Banco Filipino case. The insolvent bank had been closed by the Central Bank (CB) in 1985, and it was contesting the closure in the high court, accusing then CB Governor Jose Fernandez of wanting to take over the bank himself.

The assistant was told she would not want for anything if she helped out, but Gutierrez never made clear in whose behalf he was making the offer. Sarmiento reported the incident to the court en banc. "The Court asked Hugo to find out from his son what had really transpired," he recounted. "The son said, 'Don't believe her, she's schizophrenic.' So this was relayed to the Court."

Sarmiento inhibited himself from the case because apart from that incident, he was also a neighbor of a member of the family that owned the bank. The Court, he said, never acted on his report as his assistant refused to execute an affidavit against a former classmate.

Banco Filipino won. Among those who voted in its favor was Gutierrez who, despite the incident involving his son, did not abstain from the discussions.

In the legal community, the Banco Filipino case is considered a landmark. The stakes in this case were exceptionally high, running up to billions of pesos. It was also among the first few instances when rumors of pay-offs to Supreme Court justices began circulating in both the bar and the bench.

Although most of the discussions took place during the term of Chief Justice Marcelo Fernan, the ruling on the Banco Filipino case was released just three days after Andres Narvasa was named the country's chief magistrate.

Five-and-a-half years later, Narvasa presides over a court whose reputation has sunk to its lowest in a decade. In January 1997, the Makati Business Club asked the country's top executives to rate the performance of government agencies. They gave the Supreme Court a rating of minus 29.8 percent, just a few notches higher than transport and worse than telephone service. Ten years ago, in the euphoria that followed the Edsa uprising, the Supreme Court topped the same survey.

The high court's fall from grace is a story of how the influence of kin and cronies, the weakness of check-and-balance mechanisms, and the fallibility of officials can erode the credibility of institutions. It reveals the porousness of the structures and procedures that govern the Court, thereby allowing approaches to justices that have undermined the confidence of the legal and business communities in the judiciary.

In the last six months, dozens of lawyers, litigants, former Supreme Court justices and insiders in the current court interviewed for this article expressed profound frustration with the country's highest tribunal. It is, they like to joke, the "best supreme court that money can buy."

They paint the picture of a powerful institution prey to equally powerful temptations: As the economy grows and the stakes involved in legal disputes are higher than ever before, litigants are willing to pay a steep price for favorable decisions.

Narvasa strongly disagrees with this perception. "We know of no instance of what might be described as a 'venal or corrupt approach' to any member of the Court," he said in a recent letter in response to journalists' queries.

Discreet Approaches

True, corruption charges are difficult to prove. The approaches to justices are said to be discreet and indirect, made largely through trusted relatives and intermediaries. Moreover, the rumor mill is constantly fed by stories from litigants and an executive branch engaged in a battle of wills with the Supreme Court, which has ruled against Malacañang in landmark cases.

"I have no personal knowledge of anyone actually having been bought in the Supreme Court," said former Justice Florentino Feliciano, who retired in 1995. "When lawyers lose a case, the immediate reaction is that the judge has been bought."

But in interviews, litigants and lawyers described to us how, once high-stake cases are elevated to the Supreme Court, the parties involved maneuver behind the scenes to get access to the justices assigned in order to plead their case. While many of the justices, they said, cannot be approached or corrupted, some of them have allegedly accepted significant sums for favorable decisions.

Intermediaries—former justices, relatives of current justices, well-positioned lawyers—allegedly play a key role in these maneuvers by acting as channels for otherwise unapproachable magistrates. Our interviews have revealed the emergence of a network of brokers composed of well-connected individuals who offer to fix cases for a price.

"Some former justices and sons of justices can be retained to pursue cases," said Eduardo de los Angeles, former Philippine Stock Exchange president and senior partner in one of the country's biggest law firms, who balks at the practice. "You can tell your client or you can approach them directly yourself. Litigants continue with their lawyers and as an added facility, get some of these former justices to work incognito."

This informal network of fixers who can be approached by litigants means that while lawyers slug it out in court in big-league cases, an even more bruising battle is going on behind the scenes, as brokers try to influence justices on behalf of opposing parties. Lawyers say that the role of intermediaries is so important that often, it is a race between the parties on who gets to the most influential fixers ahead of his rival.

When former Quezon Rep. Bienvenido Marquez, for example, thought he would lose his case in the Supreme Court, he was advised by a friend, a Malacañang official whom he declined to name, to seek the help of Gregorio "Ogie" Narvasa II, a lawyer who is also the chief justice's son.

The Malacañang official claimed to be in the know about the Court, the former congressman recalled recently. "So I talked to Ogie," he recounted. "I said, whatever the terms, just tell me."

Ogie seemed interested, but two days later, said Marquez, he sent word through a common friend that he had to decline as his partner had already been hired by the congressman's rival, Quezon Governor Eduardo Rodriguez.

Asked why he decided to hire Narvasa's son, Marquez replied: "They're not good lawyers. They're just ordinary lawyers. But because his father is the chief justice, everybody approaches him."

Rodriguez apparently thought the same thing. Sources close to him say that the governor, through an intermediary, offered money so Ogie would intercede for him.

Ogie Narvasa admitted both parties approached him, but denied helping or receiving a fee from either one. It was not the first time, he said, that litigants had come to him. "All of them obviously want to win their case," he said. "They ask me what I can do. They present the problem to me. I tell them immediately, I can't do anything. I can't influence my father and I certainly cannot talk to the other justices."

"What has happened here is people have the perception that our courts can be paid," he added, "so what they do, to even the playing field, they come to see me first so that the other party cannot talk to me."

The Beer Case

Lawyers say that the higher the stakes, the more determined the approaches to justices. When former Justice Jose C. Campos Jr. was assigned to pen the decision on the "Beer na Beer" case, he was hounded by several friends he had not seen in decades, all of them interceding on behalf of tycoon Lucio Tan.

In 1988, San Miguel Corp. sued Tan's Asia Brewery Inc. for copying the size, shape and color of its famous beer bottle. In 1990, the case went to the Court of Appeals. It was raffled to Campos, who was asked to rule on whether Tan's firm was guilty of unfair competition and of infringing on San Miguel's trademark.

"What puzzled me was this," Campos recalled recently. "I have very few Chinese friends and they do not know Lucio Tan. Suddenly, one of them called me and he said Lucio Tan was in his house." The tycoon, his friend was told, wanted to meet with the justice.

Well known for his independence and outspokenness, Campos refused. Later, Tan sent word through the justice's friend that he had already spoken to the two other justices who made up the division and they had agreed to decide in the tycoon's favor.

"I was the only one who had not been talked to, and he was willing to give me double of what he gave the other two," said Campos. The two justices had been offered the equivalent of their retirement pay or roughly P2.5 million each, he said.

Antonio Ocampo, in-house counsel for Asia Brewery, denied knowledge of this incident. "If there was such an offer, either real or imagined, it didn't come from us, it was not authorized, not solicited," he said.

Eduardo Ceniza, who lawyered for Asia Brewery in the case, added, "Everybody knows Justice Campos cannot be bought. Everyone on our side knew that, so why even make an attempt?"

Campos decided against Asia Brewery and two other justices of the five-member division he headed voted with him. Months later, he was promoted to the Supreme Court, which eventually reversed his decision. Narvasa denies there was ever pressure on high court justices. But, said Campos: "They waited until I retired." The decision was dated July 5, 1993. Campos had retired three months earlier, on April 13.

"If Asia Brewery lost this case, this would have been the end for them," said Lorna Patajo-Kapunan, San Miguel's lawyer. "They would have to close their whole production line, destroy all the bottles, the molds and all their advertising materials and start from scratch."

Even at the trial court, she said, a bidding war was already taking place. She recalled being approached by a person who claimed to have been sent by the judge assigned to the case. The judge would decide in San Miguel's favor if the company gave him P3 million, the emissary said. San Miguel refused to pay, and it lost the case.

Heavy Caseload

But many times, the approaches to justices do not involve money, lawyers whom we have interviewed said. As justices have heavy caseloads, litigants approach them merely to plead that their motions or briefs be read.

Not all justices, however, can be approached. When they were in the Supreme Court, former Justices Florentino Feliciano and Isagani Cruz recalled, there were always lawyers or litigants trying to see them. "A great deal depends on the individual justice involved," said Feliciano. "I do not allow lawyers to discuss cases. The only people allowed in our chambers are members of the Court or my own lawyers."

In the Quezon election case, both Marquez and his arch-rival, Rodriguez, were actively lobbying with the Court. They also accuse each other of paying off justices.

When Rodriguez was seeking a third term as Quezon governor in 1995, Marquez tried to unseat him by charging that he was a fugitive from justice and therefore banned by the Local Government Code from public office. In April 1995, the Supreme Court defined what a fugitive was and asked the Commission on Elections to determine whether Rodriguez was one.

At this point, Rodriguez said, he was confident of winning. Although he was accused of faking the deaths of his wife and mother-in-law and then collecting on their insurance, the Court limited the definition to those who flee after being charged or convicted. The governor left the U.S. before he was charged, so did not fall under that definition.

The Rodriguez camp believes it was Marquez who approached some of the justices first. But when it seemed that the Court could reconsider its position, the Rodriguez side began to lobby with individual justices.

"In the beginning, we were not concerned with the maneuvers because we thought we would win," said someone close to Rodriguez. "But when Rodriguez thought the other side was maneuvering, he wanted to move also."

Sometime in 1995, the governor, these sources said, was approached by Evener Villasanta, a lawyer who is the chief justice's godson and golf crony. When Marquez found out, he phoned Villasanta, who was a distant relative. "I told him not to interfere in my case because I heard that he was being approached and that Rodriguez was seen in a hotel talking to him by some of my friends."

Villasanta said he was consulted by both parties on the legal issues of the case, but didn't intercede for them. Marquez, he said, approached him first. "He was the one who pleaded with me," said the lawyer. "*Sabi niya,' Primo, ako ang tulungan mo, ako ang kamag-anak mo* (He said, 'Cousin, help me, I'm the one who's related to you')."

On June 5, 1996, while the case was still pending, Marquez ran into Narvasa and Villasanta waiting for their flight to Hong Kong in the Philippine Airlines first-class lounge at the Manila airport.

Immigration records show that both the chief justice and the lawyer were on the same flight to and from Hong Kong. Rodriguez said he had arranged for Hopewell, a Hong Kong company with big investments in Quezon, to pick up the tab for rounds of golf that the two men played in the Crown Colony.

Behind the scenes, the battle heated up. In one instance, a Rodriguez aide was talking to one justice when lobbyists for Marquez were shown into the room. The aide had to hide behind the curtains, said sources close to Rodriguez.

In July 1996, the Supreme Court ruled that the governor was not a fugitive from justice. Rodriguez won by one vote. "If we didn't maneuver, we would have lost," said someone close to the governor. "Marquez was outbidded."

But despite the golf games and the approaches through his son and close

As justices have heavy caseloads, litigants approach them merely to plead that their motions or briefs be read.

friend, Narvasa voted against Rodriguez, a fact that the governor resents, those close to him say. Marquez is bitter as well. Although the chief justice voted in his favor, Marquez claimed that Narvasa actually supported his opponent by delaying the release of the decision until there was a majority vote for the governor.

"To them, it's a continuation of politics," said Saguisag, who appeared briefly for Rodriguez in the Supreme Court. "It's gamesmanship. That is their culture. Nobody loses sleep over it. Each side was committed to do what had to be done. This is a good case of how justice is administered in this country."

The High Price of Justice

Second of Three Parts

THE phone rang at an office in Makati and the senior partner of a big law firm took the call.

At the other end of the line was the head of one of the Philippines' biggest business houses. He was worried about how the Supreme Court was going to decide on the fate of one of his companies, where a big bloc of shares had been sequestered by the government and was now being contested by a determined rival.

The phone call came while this journalist was interviewing the lawyer.

"I thought we had talked with those justices already," the businessman said.

His lawyer replied: "But the other side is talking to them as well. What can we do?"

What was at stake was the future of a company that was worth several hundred million pesos. The controversy had dragged on for years, with the Court reversing itself, depending, the parties suspected, on who was paying some of the justices.

By now, the lawyer was blasé about the whole thing. "If the stakes are high and you think the other party is maneuvering, you have to even the playing field for your client," he said. "You have to pay the price."

This lawyer is not alone. All around Makati these days, lawyers and businessmen talk about the steep price of justice in the Supreme Court.

But corruption is not the only issue. Lawyers cite the Court's heavy workload, its seeming incompetence and lack of brilliant legal minds. All these, they say, combine to make a Court where laws and procedures are applied helter-skelter. They accuse Andres Narvasa, who has been chief justice since 1991, of failing to lead the tribunal toward any discernible direction or coherent philosophy.

"It's almost whimsical," said lawyer Ricardo Romulo, chairman of the Makati Business Club and head of one of the country's biggest and most respected law firms. "They seem to go every which way and I put the blame on what I discern is a lack of a consistent philosophy underlying their decisions."

Precedents, on which the entire system of law is based, are overturned with enough frequency to confound the legal profession, some of the country's top lawyers say.

"The legal system is no longer predictable and stable," said law professor and practitioner Haydee Yorac, who once served as election commissioner. "Corruption aside, there has been no effort to establish a systematic order. I have nothing against the Supreme Court overturning established decisions, nothing against reversing precedents perceived to be wrong or against the Constitution. But in most instances, they don't even cite any basis for doing so."

Narvasa brushes aside these criticisms. It is not a question of philosophy, he said in an interview, merely a matter of applying the law. In the Philippines, unlike in the United States, where "there is greater latitude in the exercise of judicial function," he explained, "what is expected of a justice is to determine what the facts are in a particular case and to apply the law to those facts... regardless of your personal feeling or your own personal philosophy."

Reversing Precedents

But some lawyers charge that decisions are sometimes tailor-made for well-connected litigants—even if they are contrary to well-established precedents and wreak havoc on the conduct of law and business, both of which rely on the predictability of rules.

"The problem for us lawyers is that the Supreme Court has now become unpredictable," said Eduardo de los Angeles, senior partner in a major Makati law firm. "Our practice was to give advice on the basis of precedent, but here we now have a situation where you can't rely on precedents. There are times the Court cites precedents only to find reasons why these are not applicable."

Such unpredictability comes at a time of economic liberalization and growth and the stakes involved in business disputes are gargantuan. In recent years, the Court has been asked to resolve disputes on land, taxes, sequestered companies, patents and intellectual property, where the amounts involved reach billions.

But the Court has failed to rule with coherence and clarity on these disputes. In December 1995, for example, it decided against the U.S. manufacturer of Lee jeans, which sued a local garments firm using the Lee trademark. Emerald Garments, the local firm, had been sewing an almost exact replica of the Lee logo on its jeans, except that it added the words "Mr. Stylistic" in small print.

By deciding in favor of Emerald Garments, the Supreme Court overturned some two dozen precedents on the infringement of trademarks. It also went against the Philippines' international commitments to honor intellectual property rights.

"That was a crazy decision," said lawyer and former Senator Rene A. V. Saguisag. "I saw the logos and there really is a confusion in the public mind. It set a very bad precedent from the standpoint of law, public opinion and our international standing."

In another case involving the sale of a large tract of land in Pasig to National Bookstore, the Supreme Court's third division chaired by now retired Justice Florentino Feliciano unanimously ruled in favor of Lim Ket Kai, the original buyer of the property.

Two weeks after that decision was made, the third division was reorganized, with Narvasa as the new chairman and two other justices as new members. A month after the reorganization, the new division cited the Lim Ket Kai case as a precedent in a decision on the First Philippine International Bank case.

But two months afterward, in March 1996, the division reversed itself. It set aside the first Lim Ket Kai decision and ruled in favor of National Bookstore.

There are similar flip-flops in sequestration cases. In January 1995, Narvasa penned an omnibus decision involving dozens of sequestered companies, which said that the government's failure to file cases against each of the sequestered firms within the six-month deadline set by the Constitution does not nullify their sequestration.

But in March 1996, the Third Division chaired by Narvasa lifted the sequestration on two companies owned by Lucio Tan—Sipalay Trading Corp. and Allied Bank—on the ground that the government had failed to file charges against them within the timetable prescribed by the Constitution.

Saying that there was a "hairline, but critical distinction" in this case, the division argued that, unlike in other sequestered companies, the government had no evidence with which to file charges against the two Tan firms.

"Frankly, I'm confused," said Katz Tierra, who has been practicing law for 30 years and is a partner in an Ortigas Center law firm. "It's rather scary. You would think, all right, this is the doctrine now, and then you read another decision and it seeks to distinguish and you can't quite grasp the distinction. So you get scared. It gets to be there are so many distinctions, it's no longer clear."

Powerful Tribunal

These charges come at a time when the Supreme Court has never been as powerful, a consequence in part of a provision in the 1987 Constitution, which expanded the high tribunal's power to review cases.

This provision was put into the Constitution by jurists like former Supreme Court chief justice Roberto Concepcion who saw how Marcos controlled the court during martial law and so envisioned a powerful tribunal that could check the excesses of an abusive executive.

The Supreme Court has the leeway to set its own procedural rules which, some lawyers say, makes it easier for some justices to revise the procedures to suit favored litigants.

At the same time, the high tribunal's own power remains virtually unchecked: Lawyers are wary about reporting ethical lapses for fear of repercussions against their clients. The only check is the impeachment by Congress of individual justices, a long and tedious process that legal experts say is almost impossible to see through.

The 1987 Constitution also gave the Supreme Court the choice of sitting in divisions of three, five or seven members each. The Court is at present divided into three divisions, each composed of five justices. A division can issue a decision with a majority of three justices voting in favor. This can be a formula for confusion.

"Sometimes, the divisions don't talk to each other," said Father Joaquin Bernas, former Ateneo president and member of the 1987 constitutional commission. "One principle may be asserted with one division and the opposite by another division."

In November 1993, for example, the third division ruled in the case of Philippine Duplicators, Inc. that commissions form part of the salaries of salesmen and should therefore be used in computing their 13th month pay. But one month later, the second division ruled the exact opposite in the cases of Boie-Takeda Chemicals and Philippine Fuji Xerox Corp: Commissions are not part of the basic salary and should be excluded from 13th month pay computations.

Apart from addling the public, lawyers and litigants say the division system makes the Court easier to manipulate. Most times, an enterprising litigant has only to approach three justices to ensure his victory.

But the process is a complex one. It first of all involves obtaining information on the Court—to which division a case will be assigned and the identity of the *ponente* or writer of the decision. Cases are raffled to any of the divisions, which then assign the *ponente*, also by raffle. Some cases, especially those that involve the modification or reversal of precedents, are elevated to the court *en banc,* which means that all 15 justices have to vote on them.

The assignment of divisions is a matter of public record, but the identity of the *ponente* is kept confidential. "A few lawyers try to find out who's the *ponente,"* said Tierra. Once they obtain that information, their "first question is 'Can I talk to this guy?' If it is guys like (Justice Teodoro) Padilla, (Hilario) Davide, or (Florenz) Regalado, then that 's it. It ends there."

GETTING TO THE *PONENTE*

The *ponente* is crucial. Most times, individual justices make up their minds based on the presentation of the writer of the decision. Given the load of each justice (over 300 cases each) and of each division (some 1,500 for all five justices), the members of a division cannot be expected to study carefully all the cases they are asked to decide.

"You study the 300 cases assigned to you," said former Justice Feliciano "and then hope that each one does the same thing for their cases." Sometimes, he added, unless they are assigned to be the *ponente*, justices cannot read all the motions and pleadings in each case.

In many cases, the majority of justices go with the *ponente's* arguments for or against a case. The first step, then, is to get the *ponente's* identity. Although this is secret, lawyers say some Supreme Court personnel sell the information for something like P2,000. Once the *ponente* is known, the approaches begin.

This is why many big law offices have a two-track practice: one track to line up the legal arguments in the case and the other to lobby with members of the Court. "The key is to get the *ponente*," said Saguisag. "Some law offices would look for a connection—a former law school classmate, a *kumpadre*, a former justice, or a former associate in the law firm where the justice used to work... The game is to look for the *katapat*, the one whom the justice cannot refuse. In a transactional society, the *katapat* has some ascendancy."

One medium-sized company, for example, put a retired justice on its retainer so he could arrange access to Supreme Court justices. "The company gives him an initial fee of P50,000 and after he contacts the *ponente* justice, our petition which is initially denied and practically a dead horse, at first impossible to revive, is suddenly given due course," the company lawyer confided in a 1995 letter to Saguisag. A separate payment was arranged for the justice, but the lawyer was not privy to the amount.

One businessman we interviewed believes he lost his case involving property worth hundreds of millions because he did not approach any of the justices. By the time he realized that his opponent was lobbying with the members of the Court, the decision had already been written.

The businessman tried to make his own approaches while his motion for reconsideration was pending before the Court. But he was told by several intermediaries, including the sons of a senior Supreme Court justice, that it was too late to change the justices' minds about the case as they were already committed to his opponent.

The businessman got as far as talking to the *ponente*. Later, through an intermediary, he offered several millions for a favorable decision. The *ponente* appeared interested, the businessman said, especially as the offer was doubled and tripled in the course of the transaction. But in the end, the justice turned it down.

"We've learned our lesson," said the businessman. "It's a bidding war. It's a business. It's a question of how much the property is worth to you, how much you're willing to pay... We were caught off guard. We should have bribed in the beginning. *Unahan na lang*."

But while businessmen can charge pay-offs as part of the cost of doing business, many lawyers are aghast. "We're very frustrated, we're helpless," said a senior lawyer in a Makati law firm. "We don't know what more to do. You can't rest if you have a case because your opponent may be maneuvering. Our ethical and moral dilemma is, you can't sit back while your client tells you, 'You must do something.' But what can you do that's ethical and moral? Our cop-out is, we tell the client, 'Do what you think you have to do.'"

Questions for the Chief

Conclusion

WHEN Andres Narvasa was named chief justice of the Supreme Court in late 1991, a banquet was held in his honor at the ritzy Greenhills residence of a well-known businessman and restaurateur to whom he was related by marriage.

Hundreds of guests were invited. On one side of the sprawling lawn were the judges, justices and lawyers. On the other side, set apart by the swimming pool, were prominent businessmen and their wives, many of them Chinese-Filipino. The party, said one of the guests, former Supreme Court justice Jose Campos, "was an omen of things to come."

A practicing attorney for over 30 years before his appointment to the Court, Narvasa, those who know him say, is a sociable man who is seen enjoying himself at parties, playing golf with a retinue of lawyers and judges, and on occasion, dining with some of Manila's most controversial personages.

Just a generation ago, Supreme Court justices were never seen in parties, hotel lobbies or restaurants where they may run into litigants or lawyers with pending cases. The idea, enshrined in the Code of Judicial Conduct, is that magistrates should "avoid impropriety and the appearance of impropriety in all activities."

The chief, however, seems to love the

company of lawyers and his big, sociable clan. In recent years, his social activities have raised eyebrows in legal circles. But what has caused greater unease is his association with relatives and friends who are believed to be lobbying with the Court.

Narvasa's brother-in-law, lawyer Joaquin "Bobby" Yuseco, has been accused in a complaint filed in the Supreme Court of approaching justices on behalf of litigants. The chief's son, Gregorio II or Ogie, who has set up a law practice that senior lawyers say is far more profitable than could be explained by his otherwise average abilities, is also alleged to be approaching judges and justices on behalf of clients.

In addition, the chief's friendship with Evener Villasanta, a lawyer with Agcaoili & Associates who plays golf and travels regularly with Narvasa, is talked about in legal circles. In Manila's lawyering community, which is incestuous and tightly knit, Villasanta has gained a reputation as a conduit to the chief.

Although he is employed by a major law firm and is known as a competent lawyer, Villasanta is said to do business on his own, most times at the Manila Peninsula Hotel in Makati where he hangs out regularly. A former president of the Philippine Bar Association, he was named by the Supreme Court bar examiner for legal and judicial ethics in 1995, to the chagrin of Makati lawyers.

Villasanta was not shy about admitting his closeness to Narvasa. "He was my *ninong*, everybody knows that," he said. "There are few people whom he trusts ... I'm like a member of the family." Theirs, he said, is a decade-old friendship, which began when, as head of the Judiciary Sports Club, he was organizing tournaments for justices and asked Narvasa, an avid tennis player and golfer, to join them.

But the lawyer denied interceding for litigants in the Court. "I play tennis and golf with other justices like (Jose) Melo and Art (Panganiban)," he said. "Some of them are my *kumpadre*... But it doesn't mean that because you're a personal friend of a justice you can influence his judgment in the Supreme Court."

Narvasa seems to show little discomfort in this state of affairs. "Relatives, friends, some politicians do occasionally presume to talk to us about pending cases," he said, "but the invariable response is a noncommittal, 'We'll see or we'll look into it,' or some such vague remark, where they are not bluntly rebuffed."

But, he assured, "all cases are decided objectively, without any extraneous consideration whatsoever, whether it be family relation, past personal, business, professional, or other association, or otherwise."

No Leadership

Narvasa's behavior has disappointed those who remember the chief justice in the heady days after the Aquino assassination when he had acquired a gilt-edged reputation as the uncompromising general counsel of the fact-finding board assigned to investigate the killing. In that role, he set out the strategy for the inquiry and pieced together an account of the murder on which the board's majority report was based.

President Corazon Aquino named Narvasa to the Supreme Court in April 1986. Taking the counsel of her advisers, mainly human rights lawyers who fought the dictatorship, she tried to restore the respectability of the Court by weeding out Marcos flunkies and naming new justices.

Today, Narvasa heads a tarnished tribunal. In March 1997, Eduardo R. Ceniza, senior partner and head of litigation in the country's biggest law firm, Sycip, Salazar, Hernandez and Gatmaytan, wrote a letter to the chief justice. "In my 37 years of practice I have never seen the image of the Supreme Court and the court system sink to such levels in the eyes of the business community," he said.

A lawyer for a major law firm points the finger at the chief. "The problem is that this Court, more than any other court, has no leadership. The chief justice has been unable to lead the Court," he said. "He wields the power of the purse, he gives the justices all their allowances, their per diems, etc. There can be no perks to the justices if he doesn't agree. The office of the judicial administrator is also under his control, so in the assignment of assistants, researchers, etc., he also has a say. But with all these, why can't the chief justice lead? He has no moral authority because his colleagues suspect him of doing all sorts of things. And vice-versa, he suspects his colleagues of all sorts of things."

The dominant view in the legal community is that corruption began with martial law, when the judiciary, particularly the Supreme Court, was forced by Marcos into subservience. With Marcos gone, many thought that the legal system would be reformed. But they were disappointed.

Today the interference comes from business interests that stand to lose billions in disputes being brought before the Court. In addition, Malacañang has also tried to pressure the Court in economic and political cases in which the Ramos administration has high stakes.

Ideally the Supreme Court should be able to insulate itself from business and political interests. But, said Senator Juan Ponce Enrile, who heads a Makati law firm: "The impression is still that decisions could be bought either because of material things or because of friendship or because of power...The Supreme Court has lost the element of being an independent arbiter of rights."

Critics put the blame partly on the appointment process. The Judicial and Bar Council picks out the candidates for justices, and the President makes the appointments based on its list. Malacañang's choices, however, have been less than inspired, with the premium placed on the potential malleability of appointees rather than on their integrity or brilliance, many in the legal profession say.

The Supreme Court should be able to insulate itself from business and political interests.

"The present composition does not make for an intellectual court," said respected lawyer and law professor Haydee Yorac.

Palace Hand

But even the Palace has become frustrated with the Court, which has decided against the government in cases like the tax evasion suit filed against Lucio Tan, the sale of the Manila Hotel to a Malaysian company and the signature campaign to amend the Constitution.

In 1993, the Palace ordered the National Bureau of Investigation (NBI) to conduct a secret probe on the Court. "Prominent lawyers admitted to me that they actually paid off," said the senior NBI official assigned to the case. But apart from what the lawyers reported, he found no solid evidence of corruption.

The Palace, said a senior Malacañang official, conducted another probe in 1995, when Narvasa was accused of delaying the release of a decision banning the resumption of jai-alai to favor his eldest son, Andres Jr., who ran the jai-alai restaurant. The chief justice was also seen dining with controversial businessman Sy Pio Lato, the jai-alai franchise holder, while the Court was deliberating on the case.

In an interview, Narvasa said the meeting took place at the retirement party of his cousin. "There were hundreds of people there," said the chief, but he was put in the same table as Sy, who was also a guest.

When the Court ruled on the case, Narvasa inhibited himself but he did not release the decision immediately. He cited a constitutional provision saying that all decisions taken by the court *en banc* should be signed by every member who took part in the deliberations. One of the justices was then ill and could not sign.

Later, however, lawyers in an impeachment case filed against Narvasa were able to dig up 72 decisions made by the Court which were not signed by all the justices.

While the whiff of scandal wafted over the Court, Malacañang offered Narvasa a graceful exit: resign from the tribunal and take up any position in government he chooses. But, said a Palace official, the chief justice refused.

"I think there is a campaign to persuade the chief to leave the Court," said retired Justice Isagani Cruz, to whom Narvasa had confided the offer. "It was an attempt to ease him out and put somebody else."

But Narvasa is digging in, displaying the same defiance of Malacañang that won him so much praise during the Marcos era. In some cases, such defiance was lauded and seen as a valiant effort to stop Ramos supporters from monkeying around with the Constitution.

Unfortunately, the charges of corruption make the Court vulnerable to pressure. Narvasa's seeming imperviousness to the damage that has been done on the Court's image has also frustrated the legal community,

Neither has Narvasa done enough to clean up the lower courts, over which the Supreme Court has administrative supervision, lawyers say. "As far as we have seen," said Eduardo de los Angeles, a prominent Makati lawyer, "the chief justice has not taken any concrete steps to reform the judiciary."

In 1993, responding to widespread accusations, including those from Vice-President Joseph Estrada, about "hoodlums in robes," the Supreme Court created a committee composed of Narvasa and two retired justices to look into the allegations.

"We won't spare anyone, no matter who gets hurt," the chief justice vowed then. "We won't hesitate to let the hammer fall."

The committee worked for two months, spoke to over 70 witnesses and came out with a report that was widely criticized in the press as a whitewash. It recommended the investigation and filing of complaints against a few judges in Makati but refused to entertain complaints against Supreme Court justices because they were "nothing but gossip."

Narvasa chaired the committee, even if, among the complaints it investigated, was an anonymous paper which accused him and his kin and cronies of corruption.

The committee also exonerated Justice Hugo Gutierrez who had been accused of passing off as his own a decision supposedly written by the lawyer of the Philippine

Long Distance Telephone Co., a party to the lawsuit he was deciding. Even before the investigation, Narvasa had already cleared Gutierrez of any culpability. In an interview, he admitted that he even tried to dissuade the justice from resigning.

Impervious to Criticism

Responding to the public dissatisfaction with the report, 11 lawyers representing the country's top law associations wrote to Narvasa, asking the Supreme Court to create an independent commission to investigate cases against incompetent and corrupt jurists. The suggestion was ignored.

Four years later, most of the Makati judges probed by the Narvasa committee are back in trial courts, though not in Makati. One judge who was investigated was even promoted.

Meanwhile, the one and only formal complaint filed against a justice directly to the Supreme Court has been consigned to oblivion. In 1993, lawyers Ricardo Romulo and Eduardo de los Angeles filed a letter-complaint against Supreme Court Justice Rodolfo Nocon, Court of Appeals Justice Manuel Herrera and lawyer Bobby Yuseco, Narvasa's brother-in-law.

The lawyers presented documents showing that, as presiding justice of the Court of Appeals, Nocon, upon Yuseco's request, agreed to forego the raffle of a case involving a multimillion-peso real estate transaction and assign it to Herrera. The assignment of cases other than by raffle is highly irregular and violates the internal rules of the Court of Appeals.

The complaint was treated by the Supreme Court as an administrative charge, which to this day has not been heard. In November 1996, a decision was issued on the real estate case, with the majority of the justices ruling against the company whose lawyers dared challenge a Supreme Court justice.

The high court's decision was based largely on the controversial ruling made by the Court of Appeals. Among the key pieces of evidence cited in both rulings was a letter from one of the parties. The two decisions omitted from the letter a crucial paragraph that would have cast doubt on the soundness of the rulings.

Seventeen years after the case was first filed at the Manila trial court, the value of the disputed property has gone up to over P400 million. But both the appellate and high courts had ruled that it be sold to the winning party for P11.3 million, the price of the property in 1978.

In the meantime, Nocon had retired. Among the last few rulings he penned was on a land dispute in which he decided against the family of one of the lawyers who filed the administrative complaint.

The lawyer filed a motion for reconsideration and tried to get Nocon to inhibit himself from the case, which had been languishing in the Court for years when it was finally decided. But the second division headed by Narvasa did not act on the motion to inhibit Nocon, saying that the papers pertaining to the inhibition had been misplaced. By the time the papers were found, the division had already turned down the motion for reconsideration.

The one and only formal complaint filed against a justice directly to the Supreme Court has been consigned to oblivion.

The Environment

The PCIJ has published over 50 investigative reports on the environment since its founding in 1989. Most of these reports probed the relationship between politics and the environment, especially in the distribution of rights over the use of natural resources. While undertaking such investigations, the Center has come upon cases of fraud, malfeasance or impropriety. The articles in this section show that the environment sector is a rich source of corruption stories.

These reports, all written by Howie G. Severino, who headed the PCIJ's Environment Desk, uncovered the abuse of power or misuse of public funds at the DENR. Severino relied a great deal on documents available from the department. Many of these documents were accessible to any reporter who asked for them, although many of them were also provided by whistleblowers at the DENR itself or by investigators who played an oversight role over DENR operations.

As is obvious in Part I of this book, corruption in most agencies providing services to the public usually takes place in the procurement of supplies and equipment and the awarding of contracts. The environment field is different. The cases of corruption reported about in this section have more to do with irregularities that arise from flawed policies, ineffective implementation of policies, the political influence wielded by powerful officials, or the lobbying of corrupt officials within the DENR.

Severino also went beyond the DENR, to look at other agencies, including the courts, in particular a Makati trial court that had consistently overturned a government ban on pesticides. He followed the trail of the trial court judge, did background checks, examined corporate papers and found that the judge was once a lawyer for a subsidiary of a major pesticide firm while his wife owned shares in another of the firm's affiliates. This investigation won for Severino first place in the Jaime V. Ongpin Awards for Investigative Journalism.

Severino used the same backgrounding methods—looking for corporate and other property records, interviewing both rivals and associates, and probing potential conflicts-of-interest —in his investigation of three successive DENR secretaries. The environment secretary has the power to shape government policy and to influence the implementation of this policy on the disposition of natural resources. He or she should therefore be a neutral arbiter of the competing demands on how those resources should be used. Thus, the PCIJ's reporting on the DENR has focused on extraneous influences on the crafting and implementation of environment policy, such as the secretary's business and political interests and affiliations. It was necessary to document these interests and connections and make the link between them and the DENR secretary's actions.

To write the other stories in this section, Severino pieced together information available from DENR documents and interviews with industry and environment officials, experts and NGOs. He tapped to the fullest the expertise in various facets of the environment that is available in the Philippines, whether it is in the public sector or in universities, NGOs, private companies and other institutions.

Environment, after all, is a complex field, and reporters find that general knowledge is rarely adequate. Experts provide not only explanations, but also insights and perspectives that are crucial in helping reporters map out the breadth and depth of their investigations. In several instances, Severino also relied on the studies or investigations conducted by others: an academic, in the case of reforestation contracts, or a DENR investigation team, in the case of fraud in a new forestry scheme.

To complete all these stories, Severino made field visits, including to such places as a reforestation site contracted to a logging company or a rubber processing plant owned by the current environment secretary to see for himself the impact these operations have had on communities and the environment.

The classic investigative reporters' tools—documents, interviews, field visits—are indispensable for probing corruption in the environment field. In addition, case studies and the establishment of a pattern of flawed decision or policymaking, are techniques that can be used for developing investigative reports. With these tools, much more can be written on corruption in the environment sector, especially in a country where the rich and powerful have traditionally viewed as part of their entitlement the exploitation, if not plunder, of the nation's natural wealth.

Flawed Men at the Helm

BY HOWIE G. SEVERINO

These investigative profiles of three environment secretaries, while not focused on corruption as such, nonetheless reveal the stakes—and the temptations—involved in the post of chief of the Department of Environment and Natural Resources (DENR). Although the three men who headed the department from 1992 to 1998 were so different from each other in training, professional inclination and temperament, all of them were hounded by charges of impropriety.

Two of them—Edelmiro Amante and Antonio Cerilles—are Mindanao politicians who were named to the post not because of their environment credentials but because they helped bring in the votes for their respective presidential candidates, Fidel V. Ramos and Joseph Estrada. Their appointments were clearly political, itself an indication of how natural resources, and the DENR, have always been looked at as part of the spoils of patronage politics. The PCIJ's reporting on the environment since 1989 has shown that this predatory view has contributed in large measure to the wanton destruction of forests and marine resources.

Severino's profile of Amante relied on corporate records to show that Ramos's new appointee owned a logging company. It examined Amante's legislative record in Congress, which indicated that he was not exactly known for his pro-environment sentiments. The writer also interviewed Amante's associates and traveled to his native Agusan to show that a man with such close ties to the logging industry could not possibly be a neutral arbiter. The story contributed to raising awareness about a little-known politician and to Ramos eventually withdrawing appointment as DENR chief.

Severino's examination of Cerilles follows much the same method: tracing the official's property records to show that he owned not a logging firm this time, but a rubber processing plant. The author followed the property trail to its logical conclusion, visiting the site of the plant, checking out its operations, and then finding out whether it had an environmental clearance certificate. It didn't—until Severino asked the DENR secretary in a television interview, and Cerilles worked on the papers in record speed, obtaining it in just days from a DENR regional official who had been at his post less than two weeks. The incident exposed Cerilles's cavalier attitude toward a vital environmental requirement, but did not have an impact on the Commission on Appointments, which confirmed Cerilles's nomination, despite media exposés on his activities and widespread NGO dissatisfaction.

Unlike Amante and Cerilles, Angel Alcala was a marine scientist with close links to the NGO community. But, as Severino's investigation showed, he issued questionable orders that allowed logging firms to cut huge swaths of forest, in violation of DENR procedures. Unlike his probe of the other two DENR secretaries, Severino did not follow Alcala's property trail. Instead, he pursued the paper trail of the permits to cut and found that they were issued by shortcutting DENR rules. They were signed by Alcala on the basis of the lobbying of a "syndicate " within the department that included the secretary's own daughter. The tragedy of Angel Alcala—an otherwise respected scientist whose tenure at the DENR was tainted by charges of irregularities—attests to the persistence of temptations in a post that comes with so much discretion over the disposition of natural resources. Often, the tempting overtures are made to officials by those they find hardest to resist: relatives, friends and long-time professional associates.

Former Logger to Become Environment Chief

First published in the *Philippine Daily Inquirer*, July 27, 1992; and *Malaya*, July 27-28, 1992

BUTUAN CITY — In this northern Mindanao city that timber barons built, former Environment and Natural Resources Secretary Fulgencio Factoran, Jr.

won't be missed.

Credited elsewhere for being tough on the timber industry, Factoran has been blamed here by loggers and some ordinary citizens alike for putting people out of work, shutting down businesses, and creating a pall of depression over Butuan, a city of 350,000.

Businessmen say over 70 percent of the local economy is based on wood industries.

The figure may be much higher in the surrounding timber areas of Agusan del Norte province.

On the outskirts of the town, the screams of sawmills used to fill the air, until Factoran blamed logging in the nation's virgin forests, and cancelled the licenses of some of the biggest logging companies in northern Mindanao.

According to Agusan del Norte Governor Eddie Rama, at least seven big sawmills have gone out of business as a result of Factoran's policies, displacing 10,000 workers and their dependents.

Enter Rep. Edelmiro Amante, Factoran's looming successor and Butuan's native son, who represents Agusan del Norte in Congress.

"Edel will help us because he understands us," says Doming Escorpeso, the production superintendent of a large plywood factory, which he says, is barely breaking even.

He and many other wood workers in Butuan see Amante's new appointment as a ray of hope for the local economy, in addition to being a cause for regional pride.

The Reality of Agusan

That may represent some agonizing choices for the 32-year veteran of Agusan politics, who is scheduled to vacate his congressional seat on July 28, 1992 to head the Department of Environment and Natural Resources (DENR). Amante will be watched closely as the implementer of Ramos's campaign pledge of "environmental protection," one of the supposed pillars of the Lakas-NUCD platform.

But he will also face pressure to give favors to a wood-dependent constituency that has repeatedly voted him into public office, but will be deprived of representation in Congress once he joins the Cabinet. He comes from a province which has no known environmental groups and whose governor, Eddie Rama, is a Cebuano who migrated to Agusan to manage one of its biggest logging concessions.

"He can't escape the reality of Agusan," said Fred Asis, a human rights lawyer in Butuan who also has timber companies as clients, "unless he is prepared to confront his people as a traitor to their cause."

Amante's constituency has included some of the biggest names in Mindanao logging—Plaza, Tupaz, Aquino, Fernandez, Calo, and Luna—not coincidentally some of Agusan's most prominent political families as well.

Some of them have not only been Amante's constituents, but clients and eventually peers in the logging industry. A few inevitably became his political opponents.

Amante's appointment has been assailed by Manila-based environmental groups for his background as a lawyer for logging companies, implying that he would favor timber licensees and give new forest concessions in his new position.

In a city dependent on wood, almost all lawyers are expected to work for logging firms. Amante joined the Luna Timber Corporation as legal counsel shortly after his graduation from Silliman University Law School in 1959. He worked for the company for more than 10 years, including a long stint setting up sawmills in Indonesia in the 1960s at a time when he was also an elected city councilor of Butuan.

By the time he was elected to the 1971 Constitutional Convention (Con-Con), Amante, who grew up in a poor Butuan barrio, was a wealthy man. Former senator Aquilino Pimentel, Jr., a fellow Con-Con delegate, recalls that published lists of the delegates' assets at the time had Amante at or near the top.

Less known to his critics, however, is that Amante himself was a logging concessionaire in the 1970s, according to family members and documents obtained from the Securities and Exchange Commission (SEC).

His brother Romanito, a radio commentator in Butuan, said that Amante was part of a group of five delegates to the 1971 Constitutional Convention who were given license to log more than 15,000 hectares in Surigao del Sur, a "gift" from then-President Marcos.

According to the SEC documents, the timber company formed to cut trees in the concession area was incorporated on September 22, 1973, the first anniversary of martial law, and named Maharlika Logging Corporation, after Marcos's legendary World War II guerilla outfit. It was renamed Summit Timber and Development Corporation several months later. Amante was a member of its board of directors and a major shareholder.

In a series of telephone interviews, the lawmaker spoke freely of his involvement in commercial logging, but said it was all in the past, and he has since been converted to environmentalism.

"I have repented. After seeing the bare lands of Agusan, I told myself that these represent the barren hopes of our people," he said. Calling himself a frustrated preacher, Amante, a Protestant, sprinkled his replies with proverbs and quotations from the Bible and John F. Kennedy, but spelled out few details of how he intended to protect the environment, pleading for time to study the issues further.

He spoke vaguely of the idea of selling "forestry bonds" to raise money for tree planting, which would be one of his priorities. But he showed little familiarity with concepts such as community forestry and ancestral domain.

He did vow to show no mercy to loggers who violate the law. He said he would mobilize NGOs and cultural communities to confront soldiers involved in illegal logging, arming them if he has to. His voice rising, he said, "The thievery in our forests must be stopped. I will catch the thieves everyday. If God and conscience are with me, how can I fail?"

He said his connections in the logging industry would be an advantage. "Since I know the loggers intimately, I can talk to them. If they violate the law, I will plead with them once. I will plead with them twice. But the third time, they will plead with me," he said.

He explained, however, that just as he

Amante spoke freely of his involvement in commercial logging, but said it was all in the past, and he has since been converted to environmentalism.

would punish erring loggers, he would "reward good loggers" who have sustainable operations in residual forests.

As congressman, he voted against the bill on the total commercial log ban, opting instead for a selective ban because "we also need trees for wood and food." He said that as environment secretary, he would stick to his position.

That alone would put him on a collision course with environmental groups such as Haribon, which harshly criticized even Factoran's policies. "Amante represents old politics, where control over our natural resources is in the hands of a favored few," said Haribon president Junie Kalaw.

With his preference for continuing the system of forest concessions awarded to mostly Manila-based businessmen, Amante would also be at odds with local communities across the country which have become increasingly outspoken on the environment, in the wake of the catastrophic flood in Ormoc, Leyte in 1991.

They and major national environmental groups comprise the lobby for a law on a total commercial log ban, which failed to pass the Lower House in early 1992 by a small margin. Amante's legislative record, from his years in the Batasang Pambansa to the last Congress, gives scant indication of a deep interest in the environment. He seemed proudest of his bills to establish tree parks in every town, subdivision and school campus in the country. He also claims to have supported the ban on log exports long before it became policy two years ago.

But his political partymates say he wasn't chosen for the post for his environmental record, but for his loyalty to President Ramos. Amante was one of the earliest supporters of Ramos' candidacy, and engineered the Ramos victory in Region 10 where the new president won by 140,000 votes over the runner-up in the region.

Attacked by Environmentalists

Since the announcement that he was headed for the DENR, Amante has been hit by a barrage of press attacks from environmentalists and political enemies. He has countered with a public relations campaign among selected columnists, and by changing some of his views on logging.

Reversing a reported statement from an earlier interview, he said in an interview that he would not review timber licenses that have been cancelled or allowed to expire under Factoran. "They are doomed, they have no chance," he said.

Interviews in Butuan confirmed the bitterness between some of the most prominent loggers in the city and Amante, who has opposed a number of them in several elections. His primary opponent in the 1992 election, Roberto Aquino, is a son of Agusan logging pioneer Jose C. Aquino, a former Amante ally and patron.

Amante has threatened to strike back at wealthy political enemies in Butuan who have been feeding newspapers with negative statements and information about him, by canceling their DENR permits once he is in power.

His critics fear that he will use the country's natural resources as carrots and sticks to consolidate his power in northern Mindanao, where he is on course to become the new political kingpin.

Close to the President and sensitive to public opinion, Amante could probably afford to ignore the wishes of the loggers in his province at this stage in his career, in order to create a national base among grassroots groups and "give power to the people," as he said he would. But getting tough on the timber industry by strictly monitoring for violations and suspending or canceling timber licenses may anger more than a few of his province-mates. This poses for Amante the greatest potential for conflict of interest.

"It would be unpopular among the grocers and hardware store owners here for Amante to crack down even on illegal logging," remarked Winston Guillen, a lecturer in economics at Butuan's Urios College. "That's where the buying power in this economy now comes from."

Amante insisted that he would not favor his home province, saying that displaced wood workers would have to find other jobs. "We will plant trees, so that there will be no end to the trees that we will harvest. The people of Agusan will be grateful when they see that it has become green once more," he said.

Other Cabinet members can try to dispel suspicions of conflict of interest by claiming to divest themselves of corporate stocks. But Amante "can never erase the doubts because he was elected by a wood-based province," said Agusan del Norte Gov. Eddie Rama. "He can't prevent Agusanons from asking for favors."

Rama added that he himself hoped that Amante will review expired or cancelled timber concessions in Agusan, such as his own Roa Industries, Inc., whose expired timber license agreement was not renewed by Factoran.

The Tragedy of Angel Alcala

First published in the *Manila Times*, June 23, 1995

ENVIRONMENT and Natural Resources Secretary Angel Alcala, whose transfer to the Commission on Higher Education was announced by President Ramos last Wednesday, signed a series of questionable orders in the weeks leading to the May 1992 elections, which allowed various wood companies to either resume logging or recover seized logs.

Despite Ramos's glowing appraisal of Alcala's performance, these orders have raised doubts about the 66-year-old former university president's competence and integrity.

Having been appointed upon the recommendation of environment NGOs, Alcala assumed his post on a wave of public approval. But the internationally recognized marine scientist has shown, at the very least, a lack of leadership and political savvy in the three years he has been at the helm of the graft-prone Department of Environment and Natural Resources (DENR).

According to sources in industry, Congress, and the DENR itself, Alcala seemed to tolerate the use of his office as the base of a syndicate composed of advisers and consultants who have been extorting from timber companies in exchange for favorable decisions.

The members of this syndicate "can cause the operation of any wood-based entity to be closed or opened almost at will," said Agusan del Sur Rep. Ceferino Paredes.

Among the questionable directives

from Alcala's office was a secret order that allowed a timber company that had been idle for the last nine years to log 10,000 cubic meters of trees, with a commercial value of about P40 million.

Another order signed by Alcala would have reactivated a logging concessionaire that had been suspended since 1978 and is located in a town covered by a logging moratorium since 1989. The lifting of the suspension was later ordered withheld by a senior DENR official.

A number of Alcala's directives contradicted recommendations made by DENR special investigators or bypassed offices that were supposed to review the draft orders.

These orders have bitterly disappointed the environmental NGOs that had strongly supported Alcala. After he assumed office, the former Silliman University president had vowed to "phase out" commercial logging concessions. But after three years in office, there has been no reduction of active timber license holders.

Before becoming DENR head, Alcala had served on the board of Haribon, the environmental NGO that has been lobbying for a total commercial log ban.

"I feel betrayed," said Junie Kalaw, the president of Haribon, of reports of Alcala's decisions favoring loggers. "It was clear that (Alcala) had made a commitment to reduce timber license agreements."

DENR officials and staff say that Alcala had been manipulated into signing the questionable orders by a small group of advisers, a number of whom are former Silliman University students whom he appointed. One of the key members of the group, these sources said, is Bing Cruz-Am, Alcala's daughter and confidential secretary.

Although the secretary himself is said to be unaware of many of the group's actions, they have reportedly taken advantage of his tendency to "trust blindly" and sign documents without fully understanding their contents.

Alcala had exhibited this trait in the past. As board member of Haribon, he signed checks without inquiring about their purpose, according to Haribon sources.

Either Honest or Shrewd

Many close observers of Alcala, however, have not decided whether he was honest but naive at the DENR, or shrewder than everyone thought and in cahoots with his advisers who engineered many of the controversial orders.

"He has been told many times about what was happening, but he ignored the advice," said one long-time colleague.

Alcala's impatience with bureaucratic details forced him to depend on advisers, and give them unusual power, those who work closely with him said.

As a scientist more at home in the field, Alcala preferred to delegate almost all the management details of his office to trusted subordinates.

Since the DENR's controversial anti-illegal logging campaign, Operation Jericho, in 1993, the Alcala era has been marked by persistent reports of corruption among the men and women he had placed in sensitive positions.

As he prepares to depart from the DENR on July 1, Alcala leaves behind a demoralized bureaucracy that had long perceived the emptiness of the secretary's reformist rhetoric.

Despite pronouncements about his bias for community forestry programs and determination to crack down on logging, Alcala signed orders that clearly favored logging companies. The grounds for many of these directives have been questioned by other DENR officials.

Nearly all of the questionable orders were drafted by Alcala's legal consultant, Joseph Cedrick Ruiz, a mayoralty candidate from Dapitan City who was defeated in the last elections.

Ruiz, a lawyer who was Alcala's student at Silliman University in Dumaguete, drafted the March 1 order that secretly authorized Siari Timber Company to cut 10,000 cubic meters of timber. Siari's logging operations, which had been suspended by former DENR secretary Ernesto Maceda in 1986, are based about 100 kilometers from Dapitan City, Ruiz's hometown in Zamboanga del Norte.

According to personnel in Alcala's office, Ruiz also asked Alcala to sign the document and then ordered it delivered by commercial courier directly to Zamboanga del Norte without going through the DENR records office. Ruiz bypassed at least two other DENR offices that should have reviewed the draft order.

Ruiz was one of the DENR officials close to Alcala named by Rep. Ceferino Paredes of Agusan del Sur as members of a syndicate in the central office, which was controlling the illegal logging trade in his province.

In a October 1994 confidential memorandum to President Ramos, Paredes included as members of the syndicate Ruiz, Cruz-Am and Edgardo Galeon, a former provincial environment officer in Agusan del Sur and now an official with the DENR's Special Concerns Office.

This claim was supported by logging industry lawyers, congressional sources and other DENR officials in separate interviews.

But Ruiz called allegations that he was part of a syndicate "old hat," and attributed them to people who "are out to get the secretary and I'm the only one whom they perceive to be the stumbling block." He also said that all the orders he drafts are "upon the instructions of the secretary."

"The secretary knows my ideals, he knows me through and through. That's why I'm here," said Ruiz.

Alcala refused to be interviewed for this article. But he has repeatedly denied the existence of a syndicate in the past, and denied the involvement of his daughter.

In response to written questions on the role of his lawyer Ruiz, Alcala wrote that (Ruiz) "functions as my confidential legal staff and acts upon my direct and expressed instructions." Alcala also assumed responsibility for granting Siari its "temporary allowable cut."

Another order that Alcala signed but has yet to release would lift the suspension on Ravago Commercial and Logging Company, a TLA that has been suspended since 1978 and whose concession lies in General Nakar, Quezon where a logging moratorium was declared in 1989. Forestry Management Bureau officials say the draft order was not channeled through their office as required by DENR regulations.

This order was also drafted by Ruiz.

Ruiz was at the center of a recent controversial incident that divided Alcala's staff, led to the transfer of some of his per-

Alcala's impatience with bureaucratic details forced him to depend on advisers, and give them unusual power.

sonnel, and sparked more rumors about the activities of Alcala's advisers.

Shortly before the May 1992 elections, two of Ruiz's colleagues—Cruz-Am and legislative consultant Valli Faith Cuevas—were seen by two clerks counting stacks of money in the lounge behind Alcala's office.

That same day, May 5, P225,000 in P1,000-notes were deposited in Ruiz's Metrobank personal account by a clerk ordered to do so by Cruz-Am. Ruiz was then in the homestretch of his campaign in Dapitan City.

Cuevas later claimed that the funds were raised by private individuals as campaign donations for Ruiz. But Ruiz denied in an interview that he ever received the money, despite being shown a copy of the validated bank deposit slip with his name on it.

The directive in favor of Siari Timber Company, which reportedly started logging soon after Alcala issued his order, was only one of a string of recent orders that benefited TLA holders and other timber firms. Some of these orders reversed recommendations made by special investigative teams formed by the DENR.

Other Questionable Orders

Among the other orders drafted by Ruiz and signed by Alcala and questioned by other DENR officials are:

- a January 31, 1995 resolution that released a large quantity of seized logs belonging to Surigao del Sur's Rexcon Farms, Inc. In this document, Alcala mentions that the company had sought the help of National Security Adviser Jose Almonte.
- an April 19 order that released logs in Aurora allegedly illegally cut by Industries Development Corporation, a holder of an industrial forest management agreement. The order contradicted a recommendation by a special DENR investigative team for the government to confiscate the logs, said to be worth about P20 million.
- an April 25 letter to Picop Resources, Inc. that authorized the logging company to "harvest the naturally growing trees in alienable and disposable areas" within its TLA. The letter erroneously cited a recommendation by Undersecretary Ben Malayang III, which clearly declared invalid Picop's license to cut trees in alienable and disposable lands.
- a 1994 order which ignored an inter-agency committee recommendation to turn over a huge forest concession in Lianga Bay to a Surigao-based federation of local officials and NG0s. Instead, the concession was granted to two handpicked cooperatives, one of which was backed by a wealthy businessman. A large Davao-based engineering company was subcontracted to do the logging. This experiment in "community forestry" became a fiasco after reports of overcutting and complaints by USAID, the project's donor.

The federation made another appeal in February 1995 to manage the concession. But Ruiz, who flew to Surigao to meet with the federation, told members "more consultation was needed," according to a forestry expert who was at the meeting. Several weeks later, Alcala extended the cutting privileges of the cooperatives.

The controversial decisions have agitated a number of DENR officials, including some of those directly working with Alcala. "It's very demoralizing," said an official who has drafted several recommendations that were reversed. "My staff work has become sloppy, and they say what's the use, our decisions will be changed anyway?"

DENR officials had been complaining for a long time that their recommendations were being reversed by Alcala upon the advice of Ruiz. But the discovery of Siari's secret permit to resume cutting after a nine-year hiatus struck some officials as a flagrant abuse of authority, because it had no supporting documents and had skipped the normal process.

In addition to bypassing several DENR offices that were supposed to review the draft order, the "temporary allowable cut" was issued without a timber inventory conducted at the site, a violation of DENR procedures.

"Blank *kami sa* Siari. We haven't seen anything," said Jose Malvas, director of the Forest Management Bureau, which is supposed to process regulatory decisions pertaining to TLAs.

Ruiz, however, claims he could not recall drafting the order and denied knowledge of the timber company. But former head executive assistant Annabelle Plantilla acknowledged that Ruiz had been requesting Siari's files since 1994.

The Siari case compelled some DENR officials to finally speak out to the media. "We thought that we were supposed to reduce the number of TLAs, and not reactivate them," said one frustrated official. "I didn't want to reach the point where I would have to point a finger at the secretary, but he has tolerated this for so long."

Documents show that Alcala finally ordered the required timber inventory of Siari's concession area only after then head executive assistant Sheila Vergara demanded that the correct process be followed.

By that time, trees had already been cut and roads built in the concession area, DENR forestry officials said. But Undersecretary for Field Operations Ben Malayang III denied this was so, adding that cutting operations need the undersecretary's approval. On the contrary, DENR regulations clearly show that regional directors can approve operations plans.

A confrontation over the Siari issue between Vergara and Cruz-Am prompted the former to offer her resignation, which Alcala declined. Instead, she transferred two weeks ago to the coastal environment program, which is in a different DENR building. Some officials said that with Vergara out of the picture, it is unlikely that anyone else around Alcala will strongly oppose questionable decisions.

Caught in a Bind, Cerilles Gets 'Midnight' ECC from the DENR

First published in the *Manila Times, Manila Standard, Philippine Star, Business World, Malaya,* and *Cebu Daily News,* November 23, 1998

LAKEWOOD, Zamboanga del Sur — Facing a bruising battle before the Commission on Appointments, Environment and Natural Resources Secretary Antonio H. Cerilles is in a bind over his own business.

Six days after it was revealed on television that his rubber processing plant here was operating without an environmental permit, the embattled former congressman was quietly issued the license by a regional official whom he had promoted less than two weeks before.

The hushed signing on October 19, 1998 of an Environmental Compliance Certificate (ECC) for the DENR secretary's rubber processing plant is almost sure to fuel the intense lobbying campaign being waged by a coalition of NGOs against Cerilles's appointment.

The upcoming congressional confirmation hearings on Cerilles's appointment are expected to be among the longest and most heated under the Estrada administration. According to a Commission on Appointments (CA) official, the complaints submitted from around the country about Cerilles are the most against a single appointee since the CA was set up in 1987.

"Allegations against other recent appointees had to do with their private lives, but the statements of opposition against Cerilles are policy-based and question his fitness for the job," said a CA staff member.

The secretary's critics are already pouncing on the revelation of the barely month-old ECC. "If he can do this for his own interests, issuing an ECC retroactively," said Atty. Marvic Leonen of the Legal Rights and Natural Resources Center, a leading oppositor, "he will not have the discipline to impose a higher standard on other, bigger businesses."

In a joint television report last October 13, the PCIJ and "The Probe Team" disclosed that Cerilles's rubber plant had been operating for at least a year without an ECC, a violation of the law. Long routinely ignored by business, the ECC requirement has been subjected to much closer scrutiny in recent years by both government and a more discerning public. Cerilles himself asserted in an interview that he had not yet signed a single ECC, as an indication of how "extra careful" he was.

Cerilles's two-page ECC was dated October 19, 1998 and signed by the DENR's director for Region 9, Antonio M. Mendoza, who was promoted to his new post in Zamboanga City only on October 9.

A copy of the ECC was faxed to this reporter only after repeated requests. According to two key DENR officials in Manila, they were not informed about its signing.

Operating the rubber plant without the required ECC was expected to be an issue against Cerilles before members of the Commission on Appointments. His hearings are scheduled to begin on December 10, 1998.

But the sudden appearance of the permit may raise just as many questions, including accusations that he misused his powers to benefit his own business. His ECC application had been pending in the DENR's region 9 office for a year and a half, back when he was still in the political opposition in the House.

"The Secretary has said that if you can allow a congressman to wait that long, how about other people?" said Ramon Paje, the DENR Undersecretary for Field Operations. "Maybe that's the reason it was fast-tracked." Paje added, however, that he did not know until this reporter told him that the ECC had been issued.

For his part, Mendoza said that some ECCs are delayed because of a lack of required submissions by the operators of the business. He explained that he signed his boss's ECC after it was recommended by a subordinate, his region's technical director, Teotimo M. Redulla, and claimed there was no significance in the timing. "Signing ECCs is one of my functions," Mendoza said, but he could not give the reason why his boss's ECC application was suddenly recommended for approval.

Rubber Plant

The Ace William Cerilles Rubber Processing Plant, named after the secretary's only child, is here in his former congressional district in Lakewood municipality, Zamboanga del Sur, on the edge of a 200-hectare rubber plantation that Cerilles also owns.

Cerilles has become a focal point for the nation's environmental politics.

In a recent visit here, this reporter observed light milky wastewater being discharged from the plant into the Buyugan River right below. The waterway flows directly into Kumalarang municipality. The rubber plant itself reeked of a strong odor akin to animal dung, supposedly the typical smell of raw rubber being dried.

Yet, according to the conditions contained in the company's ECC, the plant can only operate if it treats its wastewater on-site and if measures are in place to "prevent odor."

The secretary is presently on an extended overseas official trip. But in an interview, he first told this reporter that he didn't know whether his plant had an ECC. Then in the next instant, he said it had been issued "a long time ago" and he would fax a copy to this reporter.

It was not faxed. Members of his staff later acknowledged that there was no ECC, which was also what Zamboanga del Sur's provincial environment and natural resources office in Pagadian City said.

In the same interview, Cerilles said that he believed that "for businesses that are not critical, there is no need" for an ECC. Such a statement would signify a stunning departure from the present policy of requiring two kinds of projects to have ECCs: critical projects such as power plants and other large-scale infrastructure; and other projects in "critical areas," which include irrigated agricultural lands and other ecologically important sites.

Cerilles's plant, which appears to be a small-scale, water-intensive rubber flattening operation, lies just above layers of irrigated rice paddies. This reporter did not see more than 20 workers inside the plant, but many more could be seen outside on the plantation where Cerilles's men were planting rubber tree seedlings even in pouring rain.

Excluding enterprises like his from the ECC requirement would affect thousands of small and medium-scale businesses located in or near sensitive ecosystems and would surely raise an outcry from communities and activists concerned about the environmental impact of commercial activity.

The penalty for operating without an ECC is a fine and possibly the closure of the plant. The stakes for Cerilles could be higher: CA members, coming from both the Senate and the House of Representatives, may use Cerilles's violation of a regulation enforced by his own department to justify his removal from one of the most powerful posts in government. The DENR has jurisdiction over 16 million hectares of public land, over half of the country's territory.

Cerilles has become a focal point for the nation's environmental politics. His hearings are expected to become the main arena for progressive environmental activists trying to fight off what they see as an attempt to take control of the environmental agenda by conservative forces backing Cerilles.

Under the Ramos administration, the environmental movement had notched some significant triumphs, notably the passage of the Indigenous Peoples' Rights Act, which has recently been challenged in the Supreme Court.

Controversial Appointment

Cerilles had just finished his third term as a congressman with little experience in environmental legislation when he became President Estrada's surprise appointment to the DENR in July, 1998.

Controversial appointments and statements by Cerilles have led to the formation of one of the broadest environmental coalitions in recent years. Called Bantay-DENR, it is focused on opposing Cerilles's appointment.

Expected to support Cerilles at the CA are some of his former colleagues in the House of Representatives who are now also members of the commission, such as Faustino Dy, Jr. Cerilles has long been close to Executive Secretary Ronaldo Zamora, another former colleague in the House; Zamora's family controls the country's nickel mining industry.

Cerilles was also a campaign manager for President Estrada's LAMMP party in Mindanao.

Sources in the Commission on Appointments say that they have received an "unprecedented" 15 formal complaints against Cerilles, ranging from his proposal to build roads around forests to voting against pro-agrarian reform issues while in Congress.

One of the most critical issues among the oppositors is his lobbying for a notorious local official from his district, Cesar Sulong, to be the chair of the National Commission on Indigenous Peoples, a position that has great influence over the fate of ancestral lands nation-wide. Sulong faces a string of corruption charges stemming from his tenure as mayor of Lapuyan, Zamboanga del Sur. After protests from indigenous groups, Sulong's appointment was placed under reconsideration in the Office of the President.

The CA's committee on environment, chaired by Senator Loren Legarda, postponed Cerilles's first hearing when CA "members will have no excuse not to attend," according to a Senate source. By then, the CA expects the present large batch of appointees to have been decided upon, enabling commission members to concentrate on Cerilles.

"I will be fair," says Legarda, "but honestly, he could have a difficult time because he is such a controversial figure."

There are also some issues not previously publicized by oppositors. On a recent trip here, this reporter spoke to Subanen tribal leaders who claimed that Cerilles was using an intermediary to buy up land in areas already covered by a Certificate of Ancestral Domain Claim. Moreover, a widow, Guillerma Udal, said Cerilles had taken over her land without permission on the shore of a scenic lake in this town.

Cerilles denies both allegations. "I have enough land," he asserted. "If they want to prove that, *ipakita nila*. Anything I buy there (ancestral land), *iyo na. Kanila na* (They can have it)."

The Pesticide Rulings

BY HOWIE G. SEVERINO

First published in the *Philippine Daily Inquirer* and *Times Journal*, January 24-25, 1994

This groundbreaking investigation examines the actions and connections of a Makati trial court judge who had issued several rulings in favor of Hoechst, a German multinational, while overturning a government ban on harmful pesticides. Severino examined corporate records, court documents and minutes of Hoechst board meetings to prove that the judge who had been issuing the rulings was once a lawyer for a Hoechst affiliate while his wife owned substantial shares in another Hoechst subsidiary. Hoechst, manufacturer of Thiodan (endosulfan), stood to lose a big chunk of its market if the ban on endosulfan and other harmful chemicals were implemented.

Severino's story tells how a rich and powerful company (Hoechst is the world's second largest chemical manufacturer) has used the courts to protect its sales. Severino combined his knowledge of the environment beat and his access to environment officials, activists and experts, with a thorough search of corporate and court archives to show how a company used the equivalent of goon tactics in the courtroom to the detriment of millions of rice farmers who were using Hoechst's deadly formulation.

What Severino did was to uncover a pattern of decision-making by a judge caught in a classic conflict-of-interest situation. He also investigated a pattern of bullying corporate behavior. For example, he dug up threatening letters that Hoechst had sent to journalists, NGOs, even a United Nations agency, that had linked Thiodan to cancer and deaths.

In addition, he interviewed experts—particularly public health specialists—and combined their insights with the evidence gathered from scientific journals to put together a compelling story that has both courtroom drama and a public health angle.

This story won first place in the 1994 Jaime V. Ongpin Awards for investigative journalism.

German Chemical Giant Evades Ban on Deadly Pesticides

First of Two Parts

SINCE 1988, one of the world's largest chemical companies has been using Philippine courts to continue selling hazardous drugs and pesticides in the local market, thwarting government efforts to ban them.

According to government regulatory officials, the German multinational Hoechst AG has expanded its sales in the country by obtaining favorable court rulings from a friendly judge, intimidating state regulators with threats of legal action, and suppressing criticism of their products with multimillion-peso lawsuits against two journalists and a doctor.

"Other companies withdrew their banned products voluntarily. Only Hoechst challenged us in court. They are exhausting legal means to keep their products in the market," said Dr. Quintin Kintanar, director of the Bureau of Food and Drug, which has been trying from 1989 to 1994 to remove from the market two Hoechst drugs—Baralgin and Melubrin—containing the harmful dipyrone.

The company's legal counsel Cesar Cruz said Hoechst is only "protecting its rights because we were deprived of due process...We should welcome those who are courageous enough to dissent."

Citing findings by the U.S. Food and Drug Administration, Kintanar said that dipyrone has been known to suppress the production of red and white blood cells, affecting the body's ability to fight infection.

Lawyer Cruz argued that dipyrone's side effects are so rare that they don't justify the ban, while Kintanar counters that with available alternatives to the drug, the risks are not necessary.

But no matter how many hairs are split over the technicalities, Hoechst (pronounced herxt) has managed to keep selling dipyrone and other controversial products, despite government bans and restrictions.

Among the more notorious chemical-based items which have recently been banned by government regulators is endosulfan 35 EC, the scientific name and formulation of the Hoechst product Thiodan, one of the country's leading pesticides.

It is still widely distributed despite

government and international findings that it is a highly toxic substance which cannot be safely used in the country.

Doctors at the University of the Philippines College of Medicine have claimed that endosulfan is the country's leading cause of poisoning, with as many as several thousand poisoning cases every year. The Fertilizer and Pesticide Authority (FPA) has already tried to ban it twice.

Second Ban

Hoechst evaded the second ban on Thiodan in December 1993 when Makati Regional Trial Court judge Julio Logarta stopped the government from enforcing it. Logarta was later charged by the Office of the Solicitor General with issuing his court order "under questionable circumstances." The Supreme Court has recently ordered Logarta to suspend proceedings on the Hoechst case.

Our investigation has shown that Logarta and Hoechst legal counsel Cruz, a former Mandaluyong judge, were both lawyers for the same company, Marblecraft, Inc., in the 1980s. Logarta had also served as the firm's personnel manager.

Marblecraft and a Hoechst subsidiary are connected through their ownership structure. Marblecraft's corporate papers show that the company is now owned by Far East Bank and Trust Company, which took over the firm from its original owners. The bank belongs to holding company Far East Piggeries, which is also listed as an incorporator of Hoechst Philippines, Inc.

Both Far East Bank and Trust Company and Far East Piggeries were controlled by former Central Bank governor Jose B. Fernandez before he divested himself of his shares in 1984. Cruz's wife Librada is listed as the owner of 36.6 percent of stocks in Hoechst Far East Marketing, Inc., the other Philippine subsidiary.

Since 1992, Logarta has struck down every attempt by the FPA to ban or restrict Hoechst pesticide products. He also issued a court order in May 1992 which nearly doubled Hoechst's import quota for endosulfan, a controversial pesticide, which he claimed was the result of an "amicable settlement" between FPA officials and Hoechst. An FPA source said that the FPA agreed to the settlement after being threatened with legal action by Hoechst lawyers.

Hoechst's ability to obtain favorable court rulings has effectively prevented government efforts to protect the public. This has created fear among regulators that other firms may employ the same methods to maintain banned products in the market, and emasculate the authority of regulatory agencies.

Invoking the "due process" in court, Hoechst has demanded extensive public hearings, effectively delaying regulatory decisions while company products continue to be sold. The risk, according to government lawyers, is that these products could cause harm and even kill farmers while "due process" takes its course.

Government hospital records indicate that between 1980 and 1987, there were 4,031 reported cases of pesticide poisoning around the country, according to Dr. Lito Gapas, a health officer with Shell Philippines, another pesticide distributor.

Dr. Nelia Maramba, a toxicologist at the U.P. College of Medicine, said that endosulfan, one of the Hoechst pesticides which Logarta has allowed to stay in the market, has recently become the nation's number one cause of poisoning.

She added that, according to World Health Organization findings, there could be as many as 100 unreported poisoning cases for every one that is reported, making the actual number of poisoning cases in the Philippines since 1980 closer to 500,000. About one in seven cases are fatal, sometimes from simple inhalation or exposure through the skin.

Death by Pesticide

All pesticides, which were invented to kill pests, are poisonous to other living things. But experts say that what makes them especially dangerous in the Philippines is improper use and weak monitoring by the government. Maramba noted that some pesticides used in the U.S. by highly trained personnel using "astronaut-like suits" are handled by Filipino farmers with their bare hands.

In a well-known study published in the British medical journal *Lancet* in 1987, scientist Michael Loevinsohn found a highly significant correlation between rising death rates of rural men and women in Central Luzon and increasing pesticide use.

Many pesticides also tend to stay in the environment for a long time, and have been found to kill fish, beneficial insects and animals, characteristics which have been well accepted since American environmentalist Rachel Carson's pioneering exposé on pesticide in the mid-1960s.

With increasing evidence that pesticides may not be as important to crop production as once believed, FPA officials concluded that the known benefits from some pesticides may no longer justify their high human and environmental costs.

The only problem is they have yet to make a single ban order stand up in court. Hoechst's success in the judiciary has recharged the debate on the discretionary power of judges, and driven senior government officials to "civil disobedience" against a judge.

It has also galvanized public opinion against the company, emboldening regulatory officials to start cracking down on Hoechst's violations of the law.

While Hoechst's legal tactics have won court victories, they have also created a climate of fear, regulators say. In 1993, according to agency officials, the FPA was intimidated into granting Hoechst what in effect was an increase in its import quota for Thiodan, after company lawyers threatened to cite FPA executive director Francisco Cornejo for contempt of court. The FPA later claimed that it mistakenly believed the increased quota was the same as the old one.

Fertilizer and Pesticide Authority deputy director Nicholas Deen said that the company's threats "hang like a Damocles' sword over our heads. For example, while there is case against us, we cannot collect our government pension when we retire."

The lawsuits against the two journalists—Sophie Bodegon and Jo Calderon—and Dr. Romero Quijano of the U.P. College of Medicine, who allegedly linked endosulfan to cancer, and legal threats by Hoechst against their critics have led to a "chilling effect" on criticism of company products. The journalists and doctor were sued jointly for P22 million. In numerous interviews, experts and activists have been reluctant to name specific Hoechst products, for fear of court action.

"We have been advised by our lawyers to refrain from discussing them publicly," said Andong Hilario, an officer for Forum for Rural Concerns, a support group for farmers. Hilario received a letter in April 1993 from Hoechst lawyers threatening legal action if his organization did not retract a comment critical of a Hoechst product made by a farmer in a documentary produced by the group.

This writer was furnished a copy of the letter signed by lawyers Cesar Cruz and Jaime Padilla. Hoechst also sent written complaints to ABC-5, the TV station that aired the show, and to the United Nations Development Programme, which sponsored it.

A lawyer familiar with the lawsuits against the three individuals but asked not to be named, said that these were typical SLAPP suits, or Strategic Lawsuits Against Public Participation, which are cases filed by industry worldwide intended to "silence critics." SLAPP suits have become part of U.S. jurisprudence.

Hoechst lawyer Cruz remarked in an interview that the company filed lawsuits "so the truth will come out, and prevent wild accusations...If you have the facts, go to court, because the judicial system is always fair. It is just unfortunate that it is not obeyed by some. Where are we going if we do not follow the law?"

FPA officials hasten to add that the company and its two local subsidiaries, Hoechst Philippines, Inc. and Hoechst Far East Marketing, Inc., are also protecting more than P500 million in sales in the Philippine market.

Protecting Market Share

Hoechst AG is the second largest chemical company in the world, after U.S.-based DuPont, and is a leading drug and pesticide distributor in the Philippines.

The financial stakes for the company in its legal disputes with the government are high. An FAO official estimates that Hoechst earns as much as P300 million yearly from Thiodan alone.

According to the minutes of corporate board meetings, Thiodan accounted for 52 percent of company sales in the agro-chemical market in 1992; total sales of Hoechst agro-chemical products increased by five percent in 1992 from the previous year.

A former agriculture official said that Thiodan is the firm's lead product in that market, supporting its distribution system for a wide range of agricultural products. Thus, banning Thiodan could in effect drive Hoechst out of that market altogether.

> Banning Thiodan could in effect drive Hoechst out of the pesticide market altogether.

But while the multinational stands to lose enormous revenues, the stakes are even higher for consumers, according to government doctors. Dr. Nelia Maramba, a toxicologist at the U.P. College of Medicine, said that endosulfan, the scientific name for Thiodan, is being used by millions of Filipino farmers in ways that would not be allowed in other countries.

Few farmers wear protective clothing which would prevent poisoning through the skin. "It can cause convulsing, dizziness, vomiting, and seizures for as long as 48 hours after exposure," said Maramba, who is a technical adviser to the FPA.

The pesticide is also a favorite method of suicide, Maramba said, because of its high toxicity and wide availabilty. Health workers at a recent government seminar on pesticides in Manila claimed that endosulfan has been used for homicide, especially in domestic quarrels.

Hoechst lawyer Cruz acknowledged that all pesticides are poisonous, but "we are for judicious use."

The problem, said FPA official Nicholas Deen, is that millions of farmers are not using them judiciously, due to lack of information and a shortage of FPA inspectors, and the government ban is part of the state's duty to protect farmers "in spite of themselves."

When then Health Secretary Alfredo Bengzon tried to ban all dipyrone products in 1988 because of their possible effect on the body's immune system, Hoechst obtained an injunction from a Makati Regional Trial Court judge on the grounds that it was not given a fair hearing.

After the case was elevated to the Court of Appeals, the department and the company forged a settlement in which the government agreed to exhaustively examine scientific evidence presented by Hoechst.

This process took two years. When the Bureau of Food and Drug recommended a new ban order on dipyrone in 1990, the recommendation was sent to then-secretary Bengzon, who BFAD officials claim sat on it for the rest of his term. But in a recent telephone interview, Bengzon claims never to have seen the recommendation.

His then chief of staff, Mario M. Taguiwalo, recalled that he had sent the document to the department's legal division for rewording, where he said it got lost. So to this day, five years after the first ban order, dipyrone is still being sold, despite a new commitment from current health Secretary Juan Flavier that the drug would be withdrawn this year.

The lesson was not lost on Hoechst lawyers: get an injunction from the courts, demand "due process," and let the cumbersome bureaucracy do the rest.

Court Decisions Help Keep Dangerous Pesticides in the Market

Conclusion

A SINGLE judge in Makati has stood in the way of the government's efforts to protect the country's 12 million rice farmers from hazardous pesticides.

Government lawyers and regulators are indignant over the pattern of decisions coming from Judge Julio Logarta against state regulatory actions and in favor of petitions by a local subsidiary of a German multinational, Hoechst Far East Marketing, Inc. Solicitor General Raul Goco has questioned how a crucial Hoechst case raffled to another Makati judge ended up in Logarta's sala, and referred to Logarta as a "friend" of Hoechst lawyer Cesar Cruz.

"The decisions have been one-sided," said Francisco Cornejo, executive director of the government's Fertilizer and Pesticide Authority (FPA).

The failure of the state regulatory agency to implement its pesticide bans from 1992 to 1994 illustrates the power that a single judge can wield, and the amount of leeway he can give to a company that has taken government regulators to court.

The "banned" pesticides remain in the market despite substantial evidence that these highly toxic substances are not being safely used by farmers and that safer alternatives already exist. The government bans are being backed by scientists at the UN's Food and Agriculture Organization (FAO) and a wide range of nongovernmental organizations.

But to Logarta, the issue is simply a matter of giving the multinational its day in court. "Hoechst was granted the license to import and distribute its products, and it was suddenly stopped by the government without hearing," Logarta said in an interview. "Hoechst should be heard, and the government's claims have to be proven in court."

Legal Strategy

Hoechts's critics assert, however, that the judge's actions are part of a strategy to tie up regulatory decisions in court, while the pesticides continue to be sold. "Hoechst has found a refuge and medium in the law to realize its private maneuver for power and financial gain," remarked Senator Orlando Mercado, who has asked the judiciary to allow him to participate in a recent Hoechst case on behalf of his constituents.

Through Logarta, Hoechst has been able to counter every effort by the FPA since 1992 to ban or restrict their products, until the Supreme Court earlier this month ordered Logarta to suspend court proceedings.

In April 1992, after a lengthy review process involving a battery of experts, the Fertilizer and Pesticide Authority issued an order to ban four pesticide products, including a leading Hoechst product. All four—azinphos ethyl, methyl parathion, monocrotophos, and endosulfan's 35 EC formulation—were deemed too hazardous to be safely used by Filipino farmers, a move applauded by farmers' groups, nongovernmental organizations and the FPA.

Of the four companies affected by the ruling, only Hoechst, manufacturer of an endosulfan product called Thiodan, took the government to court.

Less than a month after its April 1992 order, the FPA was overruled by Logarta, who decided that only the FPA Board could issue a ban order. Then-FPA board chairman Senen Bacani had approved the recommendation without convening the Board.

Logarta not only overruled the FPA, but also issued a court order a week later nearly doubling Hoechst's import quota for endosulfan, one of the pesticides which the FPA tried to restrict, from 30 metric tons a month to 50 metric tons. Logarta asserted that he was only enforcing an "amicable settlement" between the company and the regulatory agency.

After another extended review period, the FPA Board was convened more than a year later. It issued a September 1993 resolution that would ban a wide range of pesticides, including brands distributed by Hoechst Far East Marketing, Inc.

Confident that it had satisfied the due process requirement demanded by the judge, the FPA gave companies the customary six-month phase-out period to dispose of inventories.

"We thought we had cured the defect of the previous ban order," said FPA deputy director Deen.

But Hoechst filed for another injunction. After being raffled to another judge, Edilberto Rosario, the Hoechst case was "consolidated" under the sala of Julio Logarta, who awarded Hoechst another injunction on December 1, 1993, stopping the FPA Board's order.

"The Board simply adopted the action of the Board chairman in 1992," said Logarta, explaining his decision and echoing the argument in Hoechst's petition. FPA officials said, however, that the reasons for banning the pesticides hadn't changed, but this time the Board followed the banning procedures to the letter.

The four pesticides which were condemned by government experts in April 1992 never left the market.

Solicitor General Goco, in a January 1994 petition to the Supreme Court, cast suspicions over how a case raffled off to another judge ended up with Logarta.

According to members of Logarta's legal staff, the rules are clear for the consolidation of cases: the raffled case can be transferred by the recipient-judge to a fellow judge already handling another case sharing "common questions of law and fact."

But in this instance, the Hoechst case was transferred to Logarta without giving the Office of the Solicitor General, the government's lawyers, a chance to oppose, which Hoechst lawyers were required by law to do.

In addition to stopping the second FPA ban order, Logarta permitted the re-entry into the Philippines of the suspended Hoechst pesticide Brestan, which goes by the scientific name triphenyltin acetate, which is even more hazardous than endosulfan, experts say.

When dissolved in water, as was commonly done by farmers to kill golden apple snails in irrigated rice fields, this pesticide can cause "birth defects, abortion, fetal weight loss, immune system damage, and severe eye damage," according to a memo to the government by Dr. Peter Kenmore, a pest control specialist at the FAO office in Manila, citing WHO and U.S. Environmental Protection Agency findings.

Logarta's decision disregarded a consensus among Philippine doctors and government experts about the need for the ban. By ordering the government not to carry out its ban, the judge cancelled the efforts of several technical committees, the FPA management staff, and the FPA Board, all of which approved the ban order.

Logarta's reason: the FPA would first have to grant Hoechst public hearings in Logarta's sala where he would hear scientific evidence from both sides. This entails a process that could last several years and would probably involve technical presentations on biochemistry, anatomy, entomology, and agricultural sciences.

"All this is a matter of evidence," said Logarta. "It is up to me to balance and make a decision."

During this tug-of-war in Makati board rooms and court rooms, the four pesticides which were condemned by government experts in April 1992 never left the market. The Hoechst product Thiodan 35 EC, one of the products given a reprieve by Logarta, is currently being used by several million Filipino rice farmers, according to experts at FAO.

"They're not even used for traditional rice pests, but to kill golden *kuhol*, which endosulfan is not registered for," said an official with the FAO's Philippine Integrated Pest Management programme.

An FPA official estimated earnings of Thiodan to be at least P300 million a year.

An internal Hoechst report stated that the product accounted for 52 percent of 1992 sales for its agro-chemical division, which increased by five percent over the previous year.

Doctors at the U.P. College of Medicine have been saying that even skin exposure to endosulfan, the scientific name for Thiodan, could lead to convulsions and dizziness. And a recent study in the U.S. reported by *Newsweek* in November 1993 showed that long-term exposure to endosulfan could be linked to breast cancer.

Flooding the Market

Ironically, despite the litigation, Hoechst has been able to flood the market with Thiodan because of its increased import quota, even offering discount rates to farmers, according to FPA director Francisco Cornejo.

In April 1993, KASAMA, a farmers' group based in Sta. Cruz, Laguna, filed a motion to intervene with the Makati RTC in the 1992 case involving the first batch of pesticides the FPA tried to ban. But the motion was denied by Logarta, who wrote that the farmers "did not have actual, direct and material interest in the case."

In an interview, Logarta said that there is nothing wrong with pesticides if they are used properly. "It's the farmers' fault if they use the pesticides improperly. *Nasa timpla yan*. These farmers are in a hurry. *Tinatapangan nila masyado*."

But to the nine-year veteran of the bench, the issue is not the effect on farmers, but whether the company was allowed a fair hearing. "I am not concerned about whether the pesticides are harmful or not," Logarta said. "My concern is due process."

"When in doubt, don't gamble with public health," said former senator and now practicing lawyer Rene Saguisag, who has followed the Hoechst cases. "Defer to the body of experts. Suppose government is right? Why resolve doubt in favor of industry?"

Despite Logarta's insistence on holding public hearings, FPA officials say that there is nothing in the law that would require them to do so. "We evaluated position papers of the company. They submitted scientific data, which we reviewed. That to us is due process," said FPA deputy director Nicholas Deen, a lawyer by training.

Hoechst's strategy of blocking the FPA's moves in court has been so effective it has driven frustrated senior officials to vow to conduct a civil disobedience campaign against the judge, a peculiar confrontation between two branches of the same government.

FPA Chairman and Agriculture Secretary Roberto Sebastian announced in a public statement that the FPA would ignore Logarta's injunction and implement FPA's ban. "If I and the entire FPA Board will be jailed in the process, so be it," Sebastian said.

"This is no longer a legal issue but a moral one."

Saguisag agreed with Sebastian's action. "This is no longer a legal issue but a moral one," said Saguisag, a former chairman of the Senate ethics committee whose advice has been sought by Sebastian. "Public welfare is at stake. The system is not working, and is getting in the way of public welfare. One layman is standing at the gate."

Logarta stressed that the courts exist

to serve the public, including industry. "Government is not perfect in making decisions. It can also be influenced. The claims of both parties have to be proven in court."

More recent events may render Logarta's opinions moot and academic. The Supreme Court in January 1994 issued a temporary restraining order directing Logarta to suspend court proceedings on the Hoechst case, and to cease from carrying out his orders allowing Hoechst to continue importing the banned products.

The order in effect cancels Logarta's injunction on the FPA ban, unless the Supreme Court changes its mind. That would give Hoechst and pesticide dealers only until May 31, 1994 to dispose of its stocks of the profitable Thiodan 35 EC.

Goco also petitioned the Supreme Court to censure Logarta for issuing decisions favorable to Hoechst "under questionable circumstances." Implying a bias, Roco described Logarta as a "friend" of Hoechst legal counsel Cesar Cruz, without elaborating.

But this writer has learned that both Cruz and Logarta served a private company, Marblecraft, Inc., at the same time in the early 1980s, which both acknowledged in separate interviews. Cruz was its corporate secretary until 1991, while Logarta left the company in the mid-1980s to join the bench, from which he is retiring at the end of this year.

Marblecraft, Inc. and the Hoechst subsidiaries were also linked through the corporate interests of former Central Bank governor Jose B. Fernandez. According to its corporate papers and corroborated by a company manager, Marblecraft, Inc. is owned by Far East Bank and Trust Company.

The bank in turn is one of the firms belonging to Far East Piggeries, a holding company that is listed as one of the incorporators of Hoechst Philippines, Inc. Both Far East Bank and Trust Company and Far East Piggeries were controlled by Fernandez, before he divested himself of his shares in 1984.

Hoechst's Philippine distribution arm, Hoechst Far East Marketing, Inc. is 33.3 percent owned by JBF Investments, Inc., another Fernandez holding company that was sold in the 1980s. Hoechst AG, the mother company based in Germany, controls another third. Hoechst's Philippine subsidiaries were founded in the 1950s.

Ombudsman Conrado Vasquez suggested that based on the circumstances, the government could have filed a motion to inhibit Logarta from the Hoechst case.

A government lawyer monitoring the case said that at this point, the Supreme Court has the choice of either dismissing the case filed by Hoechst against the government, thereby making the FPA ban stick, or transferring the case to another judge.

> The Supreme Court has been asked to censure Logarta for issuing decisions favorable to Hoechst "under questionable circumstances."

While Logarta finds himself in hot water, Hoechst is seeing the tide turning against it. After repeated setbacks at the hands of Hoechst lawyers, the FPA has finally decided to get tough, but only after suffering another indignity.

In November 1993, the FPA sent a circular to pesticide dealers asking them to submit reports on their Thiodan inventories in preparation for the ban. But Hoechst sent its own circulars to the same dealers advising them to ignore the FPA directive.

For FPA officials, that was the last straw. On December 22, 1993, they suspended the licenses of all Hoechst agrochemical products, until company executives could satisfactorily explain why they defied FPA orders. The company has been unable to import new stocks of endosulfan since November.

Barely disguising his delight at the turn of events, FPA director Cornejo disclosed that conciliatory Hoechst executives recently paid him a call, appealing for the lifting of the suspension.

With the ban on Hoechst's leading pesticide set to take effect in a few months, the company's ability to import curtailed, and its relations with the pesticide regulatory agency ruined, the chemical giant's days in the Philippine agro-chemical market may be numbered.

Hoechst's legal strategy, effective only while Judge Logarta could exercise his power, may have backfired.

Fraud in the Forests

BY HOWIE G. SEVERINO

First published in the *Manila Times, Manila Standard,* and *Philippine Star,* April 20-21, 1995

Logging is the classic environment story in the Philippines. But despite widespread public condemnation of the logging industry and its collusion with bureaucrats and politicians in the destruction of Philippine forests, large-scale and destructive logging continues. This two-part series uncovered logging in a new guise: a government scheme designed to save forests. The widespread fraud in Integrated Forest Management Agreements, the government's flagship forestry project, was discovered by investigators of the Department of Environment and Natural Resources (DENR) who found that dense forests were deliberately misclassified as "inadequately stocked" so that companies can log them. Such reclassification, done with the apparent collusion of DENR field personnel, provided companies with a cover for illegal logging. And in some cases, even after the fraud had been discovered, the DENR officialdom only looked the other way.

This article was based largely on documents from the DENR, particularly the reports of field personnel and letters and memos to and from DENR officials. Interviews with department staff provided additional information. Although it would seem that the DENR's field personnel were colluding with the companies, the oversight provided by DENR investigators uncovered the fraud. This series shows how independent investigators can be good sources of information on wrongdoing taking place in government departments. These investigators did not have to look very hard. It was fairly easy to detect the anomalies: either by field visits or by measurement of the logs taken from IFMA areas, which showed that these could only have come from dense forests.

This series was enriched by a case study of a Taiwanese company that got an IFMA in an area that was within the Agusan Marsh, a protected area because of its rich biodiversity. The IFMA would have allowed the firm to cut trees supposedly to set up a bamboo plantation within the marsh. Fortunately, an environmentalist in Mindanao alerted the DENR to the fraud. The context in which the IFMAs were granted, including pressure from the Asian Development Bank, rounded out this story of illegal logging under a new, more sophisticated guise.

DENR Program Abets Forest Destruction

First of Two Parts

A GOVERNMENT scheme to save the country's remaining forests is being illegally used to destroy them.

A widespread pattern of fraud in the awarding of Integrated Forest Management Agreements (IFMAs) has resulted in rampant tree-cutting in areas intended for forest protection, according to investigators at the Department of Environment and Natural Resources (DENR).

The IFMA system is a so-called integrative approach to forestry, one which aims to preserve uncut forests. Holders of IFMAs are supposed to cut only in forests classified as "inadequately stocked" or "open and denuded."

But DENR investigators suspect that dozens of department personnel may have connived with loggers to use the agreements as a cover for illegal logging. The field personnel classify dense forests, which should be protected, as "inadequately stocked." Loggers then proceed to ravage the fraudulently classified forests.

It is an ingenious scheme that furnishes IFMA holders with legal documents from the DENR for what essentially are contraband wood products.

According to a senior DENR official, as much as 15 percent of forest lands in IFMA areas could have been deliberately misclassified as denuded or "inadequately stocked".

But one DENR investigator says his own field inspections convince him that the "majority" of IFMA sites were misclassified. The most recent DENR data show that more than 300,000 hectares of IFMA-covered lands around the country were eligible for clear-cutting. The majority of the IFMA sites are located in Mindanao.

"It's a new strategy for illegal logging," says Leonardo Paat, a former DENR regional director who now heads the central office's Operations Control Center (OCC), a foreign-funded environment task force that coordinates the government's anti-illegal logging operations.

"The misclassification (of forest land) could not have happened without the involvement of our field personnel," Paat adds.

Since the middle of 1994, special teams dispatched by the DENR to remote sites have reported logging and clear-cutting by IFMA holders in densely stocked forests, which on paper had been described wrongly by field personnel as having few trees of commercial value.

Alcala's Suspension of Clear-cutting

DENR Secretary Angel Alcala says he was so concerned by reports of anomalies in the IFMA program that he attempted to reorganize his department in January 1995. The attempt was aborted when it met with strong opposition from the DENR rank and file.

Alcala suspended clear-cutting in IFMA sites in September 1994 while the DENR conducted an investigation. "We looked at the situation and saw that in the past there may have been misclassification of forest from adequately stocked to inadequately stocked," says Alcala. "There were errors in the field. They could have been deliberate."

The environment secretary lifted his suspension on clear-cutting in March 1995 and issued new IFMA guidelines. But he stopped short of announcing any disciplinary action or naming the officials involved in the fraud.

An official who took part in the investigations says that central office staff were too overworked to file cases against erring environment officers. At least one environment officer at the community level known to have approved the misclassification of an IFMA site was merely transferred to another office.

Ironically, IFMAs were meant to replace the notorious Timber License Agreements (TLAs), which accelerated the country's deforestation. The IFMA system was supposed to be the government's primary means for both forest protection and commercial wood production. But the numerous reports of abuse of the system seem to show that weak DENR enforcement of the rules was leading instead to the further depletion of the nation's already thin forest cover.

Under the IFMA scheme, the income from logging operations in denuded areas was intended to be an incentive for IFMA holders to protect "adequately stocked" forests within the same IFMA site.

IFMA Replaces TLAs

With the gradual phaseout of the DENR's graft-prone TLA system, the IFMA has become the government's flagship forestry program, emphasizing "management" rather than logging or extraction, with over 500,000 hectares of forest lands already covered by the scheme.

The IFMA system started as the Industrial Tree Plantation program for former logging firms in the early 1980s. With foreign support, the DENR in 1992 opened up areas set aside for tree plantations to bidders and applicants from the private sector. The DENR's latest reports show 227 corporate and individual holders of IFMAs, with a few government agencies such as the National Tobacco Administration having acquired contracts as well.

The Asian Development Bank gave

the program a push with a $25 million loan, which so far has funded only former TLA holders trying to switch to commercial forest plantations, which can grow trees, bamboo, rattan, and other forest products.

But according to an environmental consultant familiar with the project, the program will only work if the DENR carefully screens IFMA holders and monitors them closely.

"The concept collapsed almost immediately," the consultant notes, "when the DENR handed out IFMAs hammer and tongs."

The ADB's Clout

Convinced that the damage to the program was irreparable, a DENR investigative team had recommended that all IFMAs be cancelled and forest lands re-evaluated, so the program could start again with a clean slate.

But Alcala instead issued guidelines that basically reiterated the original ones, before lifting his clear-cutting suspension. DENR sources say that senior officials were getting worried about losing crucial support from the Asian Development Bank.

The ADB had objected to the suspension, explaining to Alcala in a letter in 1994 that delays in the issuances of more IFMAs would endanger a second loan earmarked for the program. The letter had also expressed concern, according to DENR officials, that the clear-cutting suspension would hinder the ability of borrowers to pay back their loans.

The lifting of the suspension cleared the way for the issuances of new IFMAs, which had stopped for seven months.

Critics of the ADB's forestry policies cite that as another example of the bank's clout. "It can make changes if it wants," says Andre Gerard Ballesteros of the NGO Working Group on the ADB, a network that monitors ADB projects in the Philippines. "But it's either blind to what is happening to the environment, or it knows and is just interested in the loan. The ADB has to decide whether it is a development institution, or just a bank."

The ADB had earlier pressured Alcala into reversing a previous decision to lift the performance bond imposed on IFMA holders.

Almonte's Influence

The fraud came to light in August 1994 when a DENR team seized almost 12,000 cubic meters of logs which had come from the IFMA site of Rexcon Farms, Inc. in Surigao del Sur. DENR documents showed that Rexcon was managing 1,079 hectares of inadequately stocked forests, which investigators said could not produce the volume of premium wood that was confiscated. The 12,000 cubic meters of wood would have increased the DENR's total haul of confiscated wood in 1994 by almost 50 percent. The logs were worth nearly P50 million.

But Alcala eventually cleared Rexcon Farms, in a resolution dated January 25, 1995, and ordered the seized wood released. In his resolution, Alcala said that Rexcon "solicited the help of Presidential Security Adviser Jose Almonte...in a last-ditch effort to persuade this Office to nullify the suspension."

Alcala quoted verbatim a letter from Rexcon citing a detailed report by the regional director of Region 10 that purportedly cleared Rexcon. But the secretary's resolution barely mentioned another report with conflicting findings produced by a central office team that investigated the company.

Sources say that Rexcon is owned by a retired military officer and guarded by former military men.

Another case involved Provident Tree Farms in San Luis, Agusan del Sur, one of four major corporate borrowers of the ADB loan funds. According to environment officials, DENR agents inspecting logs arriving in Manila's pier in 1994 from Mindanao found that the average diameter of the wood was much larger than what could have been extracted from inadequately stocked forests.

The wood was later released by DENR officials under mysterious circumstances, according to DENR Undersecretary Ricardo Umali.

Both Provident and Rexcon are still operating, according to DENR records.

Since these cases brought to light the pattern of fraud, the DENR has improved the monitoring of IFMA areas, forestry officials say. Central office teams have been visiting sites more often.

The new IFMA guidelines issued in March 1995 direct companies to submit aerial photographs of their sites as verification of the forest classification in their area plans.

But this requirement was already contained in IFMA guidelines issued in 1993, or DAO 60, and was never enforced, according to DENR officials. Regional and senior officials who signed previous forestry agreements relied on ground surveys by field personnel, who appear to be at the heart of the problem.

Boundaries drawn by field officials delineating forest resources inside IFMA sites had often been accepted by their superiors without verification, according to an environmental consultant, because of the difficulty of reaching remote, roadless areas.

Environmentalists say that this problem could have been avoided with updated resource maps which pinpoint density and location of forests. This drawing of the country's forest line was mandated by the Constitution, but which Congress has not accomplished.

Protected Area Saved from Clear-cutting

Conclusion

NEAR the tip of northern Mindanao is a marshland so rich in biodiversity that it was one of the first beneficiaries anywhere in the world of a new global fund to protect pristine areas.

But a major portion of the Agusan Marsh Sanctuary was almost stripped of its precious forest cover, after field officials of the Department of Environment and Natural Resources had fraudulently marked it for clear-cutting under a controversial forestry program.

The misclassification of parts of the sanctuary for timber clear-cutting and plantation development was only one example of what DENR official Leonardo Paat calls a "new strategy for illegal logging."

According to officials, forest lands around the country, but mostly in Mindanao, have been deliberately misclassified by poorly supervised DENR personnel under the Integrated Forest Management Agreement (IFMA) system to evade new restrictions on logging in secondary forests.

Some officials are furious that even a protected area such as Agusan Marsh, which has aroused the interest of international experts for its ecological value, was not spared from the widespread practice.

Only an alert environmental activist in Cagayan de Oro saved the sanctuary from ruin last year.

By forging an IFMA covering 4,995 hectares inside the Agusan Marsh with a Taiwanese firm, DENR officials in Agusan del Sur had paved the way for the legal denudation of one of the most productive of all ecosystems.

The IFMA would have permitted logging inside the sanctuary ostensibly to make room for a bamboo plantation to be established by Chu San Forever Fertility, Inc., a subsidiary of a Taiwan-based conglomerate.

Compromise

Chu San Forever's operations were suspended in July 1994, but were allowed to resume in December that year even after an investigation by the DENR found that the company had cleared forest land for roads without the necessary permit. Chu San representative Katherine Ng Suy-Sy says that the road was built through private land.

Katherine's father, Ricardo Ng Suy, the firm's Davao-based vice-president, appealed to various authorities, including several agency heads. In the end, the DENR agreed to a compromise that reduced the size of the sanctuary to accommodate the company's IFMA operations.

Ng Suy, who ran logging operations in Mindanao in the 1960s, the height of commercial logging, is the Filipino partner of Chu-San.

The Agusan Marsh had been delineated by the government as one of the country's ten priority protected areas, which were previously known as national parks. But according to members of the DENR investigation team, environment field officials in Agusan del Sur had misclassified a large chunk of it as land fit for plantation development.

Officials acknowledge that the Agusan Marsh's rich timber resources could have been the target of Chu San's operations, suggesting a possible collusion between the company and DENR officials in Agusan del Sur. "It was no coincidence that an IFMA was given for an area with a pure, stand of premium hardwood trees," remarks DENR official Carlo Custodio, who headed the team that investigated the anomaly. "It would have been *tubong lugaw* if the area was clear cut."

Ng Suy-Sy insists that the company's main aim in the area was to plant bamboo. But she does not deny that trees were cut. "As businessmen, we will sell trees if needed. That is part and parcel of our investment. But we replant after cutting."

Assailed by NGOs

The denudation of a protected area could add fuel to the uproar among environmental groups created by the DENR's IFMA system.

Created in 1992 and partially funded by a $25-million loan from the Asian Development Bank, IFMAs were supposed to promote the rapid production of wood and other forest products by the private sector. But critics say the IFMA system has been used by timber corporations to skirt recent restrictions on logging, with some environmentalists denouncing IFMAs as little more than the much-deplored Timber License Agreement system in disguise.

"Corporations are logging even in areas which should be left protected," says Judith Pasimio, public information and external linkages coordinator of the Legal Rights and Natural Resources Center, an NGO that has been critical of the IFMA concept.

In recent months, the IFMA system has been assailed by NGOs for allowing an IFMA holder, a former logging company called Alsons, to operate in an area in southern Mindanao claimed by a group of Ata-Manobos. Alcala suspended Alsons' operations in the wake of several killings of Alsons workers, allegedly by Ata-Manobo tribesmen who had declared a tribal war on the company. The company's suspension was lifted in March 1995.

Complaints about clear-cutting in misclassified IFMA sites had been reaching the DENR since 1994, prompting DENR Secretary Angel Alcala to suspend clear-cutting in some IFMA areas in September that year and order an investigation. "Criticism of the DENR has come from various sources, claiming that there has been widespread cutting of residual trees in IFMA lands," says Alcala.

In March 1995, the DENR lifted its suspension on clear-cutting and issued guidelines that would build in new safeguards to "prevent abuses," according to DENR Undersecretary Ricardo Umali.

However, the clear-cutting suspension had only applied to IFMA areas with both "adequate" and "inadequate" forest stocks, and not to sites such as Chu San's, which fell under an IFMA category not covered by the order.

Despite evidence of some densely forested portions, the IFMA site inside the Agusan Marsh Sanctuary had been misclassified as having "inadequate" forest cover only, according to forestry officials.

The quiet investigation by the DENR in 1994 resulted in a reduction of the area delineated as the Agusan Marsh Sanctuary to make room for Chu San, which received the IFMA in late 1993 to plant a bamboo plantation in the same site.

By removing the most ecologically sensitive areas of the marsh from the IFMA site, the DENR created boundaries separating the two that now resemble a "jigsaw puzzle," according to an official.

The DENR reduced Chu San's area from 4,995 hectares to 2,394 hectares. "Since the sanctuary has not been formally proclaimed (by the President), we decided to compromise," says Custodio.

But environmental lawyers say that the DENR did not have to compromise with the company. "If the site is found to have the wrong classification, the contract is illegal and can be thrown out," says Asis Perez, a lawyer with Tanggol Kalikasan. "Government is not bound by the mistakes of its people."

Priority Protected Area

Butch Dagondon, the president of Green Mindanao, an environmental group in northern Mindanao, had alerted Secretary Alcala in a letter in mid-1994 to Chu San's preparations for developing the marsh, which had been declared one of the country's 10 priority protected areas.

The 10 areas, which together comprise the Integrated Protected Area System (IPAS), have been targeted for substantive grants from the Global Environment Facility, a World Bank-administered fund set up as a result of the 1992 Earth Summit. These sites represent a wide cross-section of Philippine biodiversity, including marine, upland, and freshwater ecosystems.

The government, however, will only formally recognize these sites after extensive public consultations and a proclamation by the President, which may not happen for another couple of years.

Unlike other protected areas, Agusan Marsh had not been a national park before it was included in IPAS. But a panel of environment experts had decided to include it in late 1992, according to Wilbur Dee, the former director of the DENR's Protected Areas and Wildlife Bureau. "It is a unique habitat with many endemic species," says Dee.

Among the rare animals found in the marsh is the Philippine crocodile, which international wildlife experts say is in danger of becoming extinct. The sanctuary's nearly 40,000 hectares incorporate a variety of ecosystems, including dry, non-marshy areas.

According to Dee, all DENR field officials should have known where the IPAS sites were by the time Chu San was awarded its IFMA in the same area in late 1993.

According to DENR documents, Chu San was permitted by the DENR's local field officer in Bunawan, Agusan del Sur, Juan Perez, to develop in Agusan Marsh despite instructions from the DENR director in Region 10 to preserve the site. Investigators say that Alcala signed Chu San's IFMA without any of his staff checking the area against IPAS maps.

Chu San had already spent P22 million on bunkhouses, roads, bridges, and other infrastructure in the area before Green Mindanao's Dagondon discovered the Chu San's plans in the area, according to documents on the case.

Alcala's order to suspend its operations in July 1994 prompted a lobbying effort by Chu San's Ricardo Ng Suy to reopen it, including an offer to protect the IPAS site if the government could not.

In letters to Alcala, the Department of Trade and Industry, the Bureau of Investments, the Taiwanese government's economic representative in Manila and others, Ng Suy claimed that his company was ignorant of its IFMA site's status as a protected area when it was awarded the contract by the DENR's office in Bunawan, Agusan del Sur.

Ng Sung-Sy says the DENR took 13 months to process Chu San's IFMA application, during which it passed through several offices in the bureaucracy.

After the DENR compromised by dividing the area between IFMA site and protected area, Chu San was allowed to resume operations in December 1994. The company states in its official communications that it is planning to grow Machiku bamboo in order to propagate and export bamboo shoots to Taiwan, where Chu San's mother company is based.

But the DENR's Custodio, who headed the team that investigated Chu San's IFMA, says that with the area's new boundary now outside the stand of high-value trees, and the IFMA site cut in half, the Taiwanese firm may eventually decide to withdraw.

The DENR official who had originally recommended the awarding of the IFMA covering Agusan Marsh, Juan Perez, has been transferred from Bunawan to nearby Talacogon, Agusan del Sur. Neither he nor anybody else has been charged with wrongdoing.

The Theft of Reforestation Dollars

BY HOWIE G. SEVERINO

First published in the *Manila Standard, Manila Times, Philippine Star, Manila Chronicle, Today*, and *Malaya*, October 3-4, 1994; and *Abante*, October 3-5, 1994

For years, the government has spent millions of pesos in reforestation projects but the rate of reforestation remains dismal. Those who live in upland communities know that this is partly because funds intended for replanting trees have been drained by corruption and waste. This two-part series shows how logging companies and fly-by-night NGOs made money from a government reforestation program funded by a loan from the Asian Development Bank (ADB). Based on field visits to reforestation sites, interviews with forestry experts and environment officials, and the research done by a UP Los Baños professor, this series explains how ADB-funded tree-planting projects were marked by padded costs, profiteering, low tree survival rates and abandoned sites.

This series documents the latest episode in the continuing tragic story of Philippine forests. The twist in this installment is the plunder of development funds by private contractors, many of them NGOS put up by politicians, and vested interests more interested in siphoning off public money than in regreening the country. Apart from interviews and field visits, this report also relied on ADB reports, documents from the environment department, and researches done by experts at the UP, the Environment Research Division of the Manila Observatory and the East-West Center.

Foreign Funds Wasted by Private Contractors

First of Two Parts

MAGALLANES, Cavite — The bald hills of the village of San Agustin, some 100 kilometers south of Manila, look like they have been clear cut by loggers.

But these denuded slopes are actually the site of a reforestation project that was part of an international showcase funded by the largest forestry loan ever made by the Asian Development Bank (ADB).

Today, when this 73-hectare piece of public land should have already reverted to forest, its bare slopes contain little evidence that it was ever planted.

The contractor here was Pagdanan Timber Products, a logging company that made its fortune in Palawan, the country's last frontier. Near the height of the controversy over its vast timber operations in Palawan in the late 1980s, Pagdanan was given a P1.32-million government contract to plant trees here.

"They planted the seedlings, but didn't bother to pay for cleaning and weeding, so the trees died," says Jose Paiton, a barangay captain who supervised the labor during Pagdanan's three year-presence here, which ended in 1992. According to a recent study by the University of the Philippines at Los Baños (UPLB), only seven out of 100 trees planted on the site survived.

Pagdanan was one of several thousand private groups that benefited from a $240-million contract reforestation program funded by loans from the ADB and the Japanese government's Overseas Economic Cooperation Fund (OECF).

The four-year program, which officially ended in December 1993, has been proclaimed a success by both the ADB and the Department of Environment and Natural Resources (DENR) officials. They say that the program resulted in the regreening of some 170,000 hectares and an increase in rural incomes.

Plundering Reforestation Funds

But academics, nongovernmental organizations and independent analysts say the showcase reforestation project was an expensive experiment that largely failed. Although they concede some of the contracts were successful, they also cite the large profits made by corporate and other contractors on projects that after four years, yielded only a few trees.

Critics stress that the program was pushed and funded by international lenders who are now being repaid by the public.

They say that results from reforestation contracts show that the program was marked by poor government monitoring and screening of contractors, frequent abandonment of project sites, low tree survival rates, the exploitation of upland labor, minimal community involvement, and profiteering.

Some critics of the program, however, concede that many of the 11,000 small-scale reforestation contracts awarded to rural families yielded high tree survival rates. But these contracts covered only about one-third of the 178,000 hectares the DENR claims were planted under the program.

The problems were with the corporations and so-called nongovernmental organizations (NGOs) which gained control of over 10,000 contracts covering two-thirds of the area funded by the program and getting a bigger slice of the funds than the family contractors.

One such corporation was Pagdanan Timber Products. But in an interview in Manila, Pagdanan forester Manuel Labastilla claimed that the lack of rain and the unpredictable weather in Cavite caused the high tree mortality. Residents, however, say that another reforestation project in the area funded and managed by the municipal government is thriving.

Many contractors were engaged in the "disguised plunder" of public funds.

In a recent study which consolidates research findings on 33 reforestation projects in Luzon and Central Visayas, UPLB professor Antonio Contreras contends that many contractors were engaged in the "disguised plunder" of public funds.

"*Maraming yumaman sa* reforestation," says Contreras, a political scientist with a forestry background.

In the case of Pagdanan, the company made P400,000 in undeclared profits through padded costs and underpaid rural labor, according to the Contreras study.

Contreras and Conrado Marquez, Jr., a DENR official who finished a separate study this year as a graduate student at the UPLB, found that profits of contractors were an average of 40 percent of the contract, much higher than the 10 percent intended by the program. Moreover, tree-survival rates were as low as five percent in some project sites, far below the 80 percent the DENR considers an acceptable level.

In a glowing report on the project, the ADB claimed a tree survival rate of 65 percent. That confidential report, completed in September 1994, was based on inspection of project sites over a three-week period.

DENR officials themselves acknowledge that at least 10 percent of the more than 21,000 reforestation contracts forged by the government with private organizations from 1989 to 1993 were "delinquent."

Many of these groups abandoned their reforestation sites before completing their projects, according to Rudy Ungson of the DENR's National Forestry Development Office (NFDO). Ungson says many delinquent groups blamed poor weather for the deaths of their trees.

After decades of ineffectual reforestation administered by government personnel, the new program was meant to "privatize" reforestation by mobilizing the "people power" that brought Corazon Aquino to the presidency.

The loans for a fresh approach to reforestation were touted as a "model" for environmental lending, because they were designed to address both the country's ecological crisis and a shortfall in the country's foreign exchange.

The Model Fails

But the foreign funds triggered an explosion in the number of NGOs vying for larger "community contracts" of not more than 100 hectares, even though many of them were not even based in the provinces of their project sites.

From several hundred NGOs registered with the DENR, the figure grew to over 2,000 at the height of the rush to corner contracts, according to Tita de Quiros, head of the department's NGO Desk.

According to DENR records, NGOs received 2,832 reforestation contracts, with some acquiring more than one. Corporations received 172 more; but these contracts often covered more than 1,000 hectares each. More contracts were also awarded to NGOs for inspections of project sites and for specific reforestation-related tasks, such as the construction of roads. The contracts ranged from a few hundred thousand to over P10 million.

Most were awarded by DENR regional offices through negotiation, having been allowed by the Commission on Audit to eschew the usual bidding requirements owing to the urgency of restoring the environment.

But P212 million worth of contracts, or six percent of the total foreign funding, was reserved from 1989 to 1992 for the discretionary release of then DENR Secretary Fulgencio Factoran, Jr.

According to several current and past DENR officials interviewed, these contracts were used mostly to appease congressmen and senators who lobbied to have private groups given contracts.

"It was politics," Factoran said in a recent interview. "If you didn't give contracts to NGOs that politicians recommended, they could call you to hearings every single day."

He said that the groups favored by congressmen were the most notorious for not fulfilling the terms of their contracts. The NFDO's Ungson said that his office did not have figures on the exact number of contracts awarded by Factoran.

The groups favored by congressmen were the most notorious for not fulfilling the terms of their contracts.

But a DENR summary report of the reforestation program shown to this reporter showed that 43 contracts issued by the Office of the Secretary from 1989 to 1992 were cancelled for various violations, or 18 percent of the total number of cancelled contracts.

According to DENR sources, among the current or former congressmen who were most favored with contracts awarded to NGOs in their constituencies were Jerome Paras of Negros Oriental, Simeon E. Garcia Jr. of Nueva Ecija, Francisco Sumulong of Rizal, Antonio E. Bengson III of Pangasinan, and Macabangkit Lanto of Lanao del Sur.

Despite the criticism, DENR officials still claim the contract approach, which ended in 1992, accomplished its objectives. "It was generally successful if you consider the area planted," says Oscar Suguitan, the director of the DENR's National Forestry Development Office (NFDO).

The DENR reports a national tree survival rate of 76 percent for the program, higher than the ADB's claim of 65 percent. Factoran says that because of the program, the value of trees was "planted in the minds of communities."

Many private analysts, however, point out that the 76 percent survival rate was based on inspections often occurring only months after planting. Estimates of tree survival after over a year by independent groups such as the Manila Observatory and the Upland NGO Assistance Committee range from 24 to 50 percent.

"But even a 50 percent survival rate would mean a regreening of about 800 trees per hectare," says the NFDO's Ungson, who has monitored the outcome of the contracts.

"That's like saying the cup is half full.

We're saying it's half empty, or maybe three-fourths empty," says Rev. Peter Walpole, SJ, the head of the nongovernmental group Manila Observatory's Environmental Research Division, which specializes in the study of critical watersheds.

DENR officials attribute some poor results to factors beyond the control of contractors, such as late congressional approvals of government budgets, which delayed payments to the field.

The Stampede for Reforestation Dollars

Conclusion

FOR at least the next two decades, Filipinos will be paying for a $240-million reforestation project that critics say has largely failed.

Academics and nongovernmental organizations accuse the Asian Development Bank (ADB) of pushing a flawed, expensive and over-ambitious project on a weak government bureaucracy.

The Bank conceived of the program, got the Japanese Overseas Economic Cooperation Fund (OECF) to pay for half of it, and convinced Philippine officials to implement it.

The government grabbed the project because it was in a foreign-exchange crisis. The ADB offered a $240-million loan that was regarded as an innovative way of infusing badly needed dollars into government coffers in exchange for a commitment that the equivalent in pesos would be spent for reforestation.

Bank officials admit that the reforestation program has had certain "shortcomings," but they also credit it for the pioneering reforms it initiated in reforestation, such as the involvement of the private sector and NGOs.

But former Ford Foundation Philippine representative Frances Korten says the program was badly conceived, resulting, she wrote in a paper prepared for the East-West Center, in "the lack of community preparation, the reliance on one short-lived tree species, the lack of contractor training, the late payments, and the corruption."

She adds that to pay for the loan, the government might be compelled to intensify the extraction of natural resources in order to raise foreign exchange, thus unwittingly contributing to further environmental damage.

Rather than empowering well-meaning private groups, the four-year contract reforestation project also opened the gates to an unexpected stampede of corporations and instant NGOs wanting to plant trees.

Critics have assailed the program for the feeble monitoring that allegedly encouraged profiteering and the non-completion of projects. "The government assumed that everyone who wanted to plant trees had good intentions," says Antonio Contreras, a professor at the University of the Philippines in Los Baños (UPLB) who conducted a recent study of the reforestation program.

From a few hundred, the number of NGOs accredited with the DENR ballooned to over 2,000 after the contract reforestation program began in 1989, according to Tita de Quiros, head of the DENR's NGO Desk.

That figure was trimmed in 1992, which was also the final year of the program, to less than 1,000 after screening requirements were tightened, de Quiros says. In the past, anyone registered with the Securities and Exchange Commission could qualify as an NGO.

Thus, wrote Korten, the contract reforestation scheme bred a large number of "fly-by-night" NGOs formed by individuals who simply wanted reforestation contracts and had no commitment to poverty alleviation or environmental restoration.

Delinquent Contractors

Of over 21,000 contracts awarded to rural families, NGOs and corporations, at least 2,100 are delinquent, say DENR officials. Of these, only six cases have been filed by the government in court, reveals Rudy Ungson, the DENR official in charge of investigating erring contractors. No contractor has yet been found guilty.

DENR officials admit that the program was just too large. *"Kulang ang tao namin* (We lacked the manpower)," says Ungson, who reports to the DENR's National Forestry Development Office (NFDO) which administered the program. "We were overwhelmed by the number of projects that had to be inspected."

Neither did ADB make any effort to audit where its money went and provide controls against abuse, says Contreras.

ADB officials counter that the system provided for its own checks and balances. "That's why the NGOs were involved," says Nihal Amerasinghe, a manager of one of the ADB's agricultural divisions who handled the reforestation loans. "They did the auditing."

Yet, in a confidential report on the program, a four-person ADB mission credited the DENR for effective monitoring of tree survival and reliable inspection reports. That mission, however, spent only three weeks inspecting project sites and visiting implementing agencies.

Amerasinghe adds that since the ADB did no auditing of how the money was spent, his only knowledge of delinquent contractors was from "what we read in the newspapers." He acknowledges that "there were thousands of contractors, and a few could have skipped by."

Nevertheless, he defends contract reforestation as an improvement over "reforestation by administration," the previous system where DENR personnel did all the work, resulting in a paltry 15,000 reforested hectares every year up to 1987, a feeble effort to offset deforestation which was then occurring at about 150,000 hectares a year.

In contrast, he claims that since 1989, private contractors reforested about 100,000 hectares annually. This figure, however, is higher than the yearly average of 45,000 hectares claimed by the DENR for the contract scheme.

These figures are contested by the

The contract reforestation scheme bred a large number of "fly-by-night" NGOs formed by individuals who simply wanted reforestation contracts and had no commitment to poverty alleviation or environmental restoration.

Manila Observatory's Environment Research Division, which estimates, based on site inspections and field reports from other groups, that the average tree survival rate is only 24 percent for community and corporate reforestation contracts. This means there could be few trees left standing in areas the government claims to have been covered by contracts.

The UPLB's Contreras even found some projects containing as few as five live trees for every 100 that were originally planted.

Community Approach

Community reforestation under the program was implemented mostly by NGOs. Many of them were based in areas far from the project sites, according to both critics and DENR officials.

The DENR reports an official tree survival rate of 76 percent nationwide. But officials acknowledge that this rosy assessment was based on inspections that took place as early as one month after planting.

The most successful projects were the 11,000 contracts given to rural families living in project sites of not more than five hectares each. These family contracts generally yielded positive results, according to Contreras, with high tree survival rates and low levels of profits and labor exploitation.

When the loan agreements with the ADB and the OECF were signed in 1988, according to government and Bank officials, the reforestation program was supposed to be a showcase for "privatizing" government forestry projects.

For the previous three decades, the government had virtually monopolized reforestation efforts in the country. The DENR admitted in the late 1980s that the results had been dismal.

"This was the first time that NGOs were significantly brought into a national program," says the ADB's Amerasinghe.

But critics say the new system was not much better, because it allowed so-called "fly-by-night" reforestation NGOs and unscrupulous corporations to receive foreign funds.

ADB's confidential report on the project itself admitted that "most problems of poor performance and contract cancellation" lay in "awarding contracts to untested and poorly organized ad hoc groups carrying the NGO label."

Bank officials are apparently dissatisfied enough about the experience to overhaul the reforestation approach again for a new $100-million environmental loan to the Philippines. This time the ADB is requiring reforestation funds to be channeled straight to resident communities with less NGO involvement.

Despite the claims of achievement, the ADB is abandoning the contract reforestation scheme in favor of its new "community approach," which started in 1993 in six pilot areas.

The new system allowed so-called "fly-by-night" reforestation NGOs and unscrupulous corporations to receive foreign funds.

NGOs are involved only in organizing communities for reforestation, after which 25-year land tenure and technical and financial support are given by the DENR to residents.

This program is supposed to address the lack of provisions in the previous program for long-term maintenance.

This emphasis on communities seems

consistent with ADB's much-publicized "spring cleaning" announced in early 1993. ADB President Mitsuo Sato explained at a press conference that henceforth communities would be more involved in Bank-financed project implementation, and the institution would break away from the "approval culture" which led to unsuccessful projects.

Such vows however have failed to appease some of the Bank's critics. "They have the audacity to say that 'this did not work so let's try something else,' but they're not writing off the loan," says Walpole, of the Ateneo's Manila Observatory who has presented his complaints to Bank officials. "We forget that they're a bank. They only want their money back."

Walpole says that the approach was wrong because the objective was simply to provide for the country's timber needs and create upland ground cover. "Reforestation does not directly contribute to biodiversity and the whole range of non-timber forest products," says the Jesuit ecologist, who has traveled extensively in upland areas in Mindanao.

He explains that a more effective method called "assisted natural regeneration" promotes the growth of naturally occurring seedlings by clearing the cogon grass around them. Upland residents can be given "community forest management agreements" and trained to practice this form of forestry. According to DENR records, less than 100 contracts have been given for this purpose.

In contrast to contract reforestation, the UPLB's Contreras says, the government's more promising but underfunded Integrated Social Forestry program, which allowed farmers to grow food along with trees and gave 25-year tenure to participants, is dying.

Since the program was devolved to local governments in 1992, Contreras explains, local officials have tended to assign trained social foresters to supervise mining concessions, which generate more public revenues than reforestation sites.

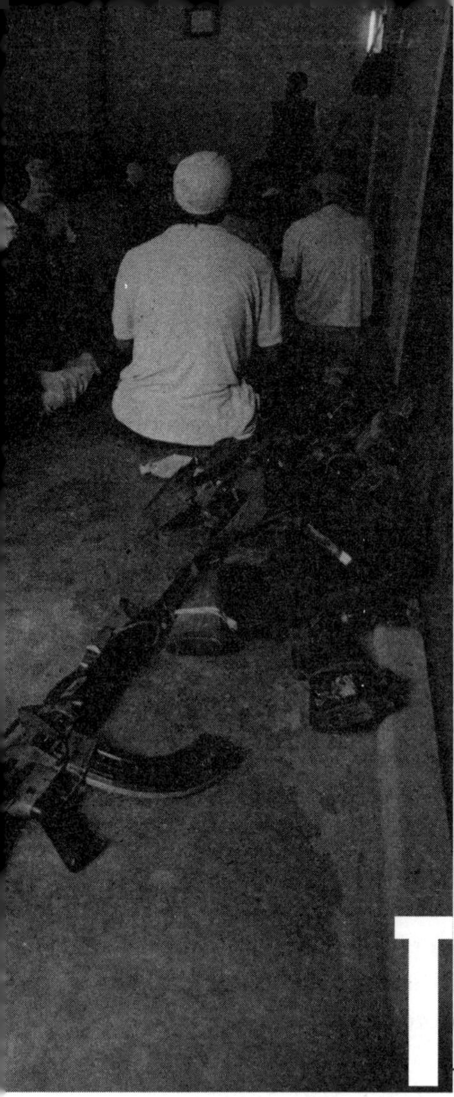

Local Governments

The issue of corruption in local governments is one that deserves far more investigation than the press is currently giving. The three articles in this section barely scratch the surface. The devolution of powers and resources since the enactment of the Local Government Code in 1991 means that local governments have much more clout and much more money now than in the past. The potential for abuse is therefore also greater.

The techniques used to investigate the three articles in this section are as varied as the topics the authors have chosen to write about. The investigation of *jueteng* in a Pangasinan town was based largely on immersion and loosely structured interviews with residents, officials and the gam –

bling lord and his network of collectors known as *cobradores*. That series took somewhat of an anthropological approach in its attempt to describe the worldview and the cultural roots of this illicit numbers game. But it also probed the layers of protection that gambling gets from police and civilian officials.

In contrast, the three-part series on corruption in the Autonomous Region of Muslim Mindanao (ARMM) took a more journalistic approach by examining government records and conducting structured interviews with officials, academics and NGOs. The authors used the typical "follow the money" method as they set out to discover where the enormous amounts allocated to ARMM from the national coffers went. As in corruption at the national level, they found that the trail ended in the pockets of officials. They also followed the trail of appointments to the ARMM bureaucracy and found, similarly unsurprisingly, that most of the appointees were related to politicians and were members of entrenched political clans.

The last article uncovered similar links in explaining why a government environmental agency policing fishpens on Laguna de Bay was being harassed by Rizal officials. The report discovered that many officials were either owners of fishpens on the lake or were otherwise connected with the lucrative fishing industry. This is by no means an atypical case. The control of natural resources by local officials who also use the powers of their office to perpetuate such control is an area ripe for investigation, as are conflicts of interest in local governance.

Jueteng Country

BY THE PHILIPPINE CENTER FOR INVESTIGATIVE JOURNALISM
AND THE INSTITUTE FOR POPULAR DEMOCRACY
First published in *Today, Malaya, Abante, Philippine Star,* and *Manila Times,*
December 4, 1995

This is a story without a paper trail. Because *jueteng,* a popular numbers game, is illegal, and the gambling lords who run it operate in a gray area where they don't register their operations, pay taxes or get a business permit, it is impossible to get documentary proof of the game's reach and network. This investigation relied solely on extensive interviews with government and police officials in one Pangasinan town, the town's gambling operator, and the network of people in his employ. Through these interviews, this study paints what is probably the most detailed and insightful portrait ever done of *jueteng's* grassroots base and the layers of protection by elected officials and the police that shield the gambling operation from the force of the law.

This report takes a case study approach to explain why *jueteng* persists despite attempts to stamp it out. Instead of going for the big picture of illegal gambling in the entire Philippines, the series focuses on *jueteng* in one municipality, putting together a careful and nuanced explanation of the ties that bind the local gambling lord to politicians, the police, even the parish priest. This report shows how gambling proceeds fund political families and enable them to engage in what the article calls "development patronage," largesse in the form of roads, chapels, and other favors given to the community.

Rather than reporting exposé-style, this article aims to make readers understand *jueteng* as a social phenomenon, not just an illicit activity. In the end, it does not matter who the gambling lord is (in fact neither he nor the town he operates in is named in this report). What matters is that the reader begins to understand the complexity of *jueteng* and how closely it is woven into the fabric of local life.

The techniques that were used in this report were more those of the social scientist rather than the journalist. They involved immersion in the life of a town, understanding the way local people interacted with gambling, and attempting to grasp the worldview of *jueteng*. At the same time, the report also drew strength from a journalist's persistence with following the trail of a story and having a nose for what is newsworthy.

This report won the second prize in the 1995 Jaime V. Ongpin Awards for investigative journalism.

Illegal Gambling has a Grassroots Base

First of Three Parts

SOMEWHERE in Pangasinan — Despite a high-profile congressional investigation and President Ramos's strident pronouncements against illegal gambling, *jueteng* is alive and flourishing here in Pangasinan, his home province.

Sonny G., a *jueteng* operator who monopolizes the illicit numbers game in a town in the heart of this province, attests to this. Every day he collects P160,000 to P200,000 from *jueteng* operations in his medium-sized municipality.

Sonny keeps 20 percent of the take—about P1.2 million monthly in net profits, after deducting expenses for operations. The rest—about 80 percent or P4.8 million every month—goes to an elaborate, multi-tiered structure of protection that has kept *jueteng* thriving not only here, but in many other parts of the country. (For obvious reasons, we cannot use Sonny's real name or identify the town where he operates. But this series is based on extensive interviews with him, his network of operators, local officials and residents of his town.)

Protection money goes to the military and the police, the mayor, barangay captains and their *tanod,* Sonny admits. Some of it goes out in the form of "donations" to key persons in the town, including Sonny's relatives and friends, even the parish priests, who ensure that *jueteng* operations here are smoothly run.

Sonny himself comes from a political family whose members have been at the helm of this town since 1945 and whose campaign coffers have been enriched by *jueteng* funds. The grassroots-based *jueteng* structure is also a ready-made political machine: village *cabos—jueteng* supervisors—often double up as ward leaders.

Such a symbiotic relationship between illegal gambling operators and those who man the law-enforcement apparatus of the town—a relationship that has lasted almost as long as *jueteng* has been in existence—illustrates how deeply embedded the illicit numbers game is in local politics and culture.

It also shows how, despite an administration that sees *jueteng* as a threat to the State, the game will likely persist. *Jueteng* is a variation of a numbers game held during festivals in ancient China. It dates back to the Spanish colonial era and was introduced to the Philippines by Chinese traders.

Jueteng's tenacity is best demonstrated here, in this thriving modern municipality, where the game's grassroots base, the largesse it bestows on grateful inhabitants and the *inteligensiya* or protection money it gives to the town's most influential patrons ensure its continuing success.

Protection starts at the grassroots, at the level of the barangay. To safeguard his daily operations, Sonny shells out contributions for the barangay captains of the town. This money is used for village projects, for "special occasions" like fiestas, or for filling up the *capitan's* campaign kitty during elections.

Policemen patrolling the barangay are likewise given a regular *tong* or bribe, says Sonny. If a *cobrador* or *jueteng* collector is arrested, Sonny's *cabos* (supervisors to whom the collectors report) bail him out and treat arresting officers to a meal or "night-out" at the local beer garden.

At the municipal level, protection is no big problem. Sonny's first cousin is the mayor. In fact, Sonny often "rents" local policemen to protect the game against possible competitors and other law-enforcement agencies. Bodyguards in uniform accompany Sonny in his regular drinking bouts.

These bodyguards say that *jueteng* money allows police chiefs to augment their very small operational expenses. It replenishes a station commander's petty cash and is often used to purchase office supplies and gasoline for police vehicles.

Dealing with the Law

Sonny's biggest headache are the national law-enforcement agencies. Raids are usually conducted during visits of higher officials or as proof of the effectivity of an anti-gambling campaign. Raids also occur when a station commander is reassigned. The raid is a subtle indicator of a "change of management" that requires new negotiations over the "terms of protection."

Most times, Sonny is adequately forewarned of a raid by his "friends" within the police force. Oftentimes, instead of resisting, he encourages his *cabos* and *cobradores* to get themselves arrested. It is easy to bail them out afterwards, and a few arrests are enough to satisfy the "higher-ups" and cool hotheads at the national level.

The anti-gambling campaigns can be quite a nuisance. It was easy, Sonny reveals, during the pre-martial law days, when one bribed only the provincial commander who took care to "discipline" overzealous and idealistic officers who ran after the *jueteng* operators. Before 1972, says Sonny, *jueteng* operations were small and localized, "*paunti-unti, sentimo-sentimo ang pinupusta* (it was small-time, the bets were in the range of only a few centavos)."

But the character of protection changed with the change in the pattern of *jueteng* operations. In the past, winnings were limited by collections. In the 1970s, regional gambling lords entered the scene. *Jueteng* became more exciting as potential winnings increased.

In Pangasinan, Sonny and his operators say, Gusting Roxas of Tarlac started to dominate *jueteng*, driving away or co-opting small-time operators. The regular draw or *"bola"* for the whole province was held elsewhere. In areas dominated by Gusting, the *bola* took place in San Miguel, Tarlac. For those areas that were dominated by certain police generals, the *bola* was held in Laguna.

The entry of the regional lords coincided with the integration of the police with the military. Gambling operators were forced to give regular bribes not only to the police commander but to various police and military units. *"Intelihensiya ang nausong salita dahil sa dami ng* intelligence unit *mula sa pulis at iba't ibang batalyon ng AFP na lumalapit at humihingi."* says Sonny. *"Iba ang pagju-jueteng ngayon, dati iisa lang ang kailangang malagyan, ngayon napakarami ang dapat mabigyan* (*Intelihensiya* became the operative word for bribes, because of the many military and police intelligence units which proliferated, all of them wanting a cut. It's a different ballgame now—in the past, all you had to do was pay one person. Today you have to give to so many)."

Lucrative Career

Sonny G. discovered a lucrative career in *jueteng* in the early 1970s, just before martial law. Prior to this, his main source of income was cuts from lucrative contracts he was able to get through his relatives in the municipal and provincial capitols.

Sonny comes from a political family that had been involved in the power struggles of Pangasinan since 1945. On the side, he enjoyed gambling. At first, his grandfather, who was then the incumbent mayor, scolded him for his involvement with *jueteng*. But an uncle prevailed on the old man: "If our family does not control *jueteng*, others will. Besides the earnings could be channeled to projects for the development of the municipality."

With the downfall of Marcos, the situation became more complicated. With the death of the aging *jueteng* operator, Gusting Roxas, other regional gambling lords rushed into Pangasinan. Sonny and local officials here say that Bong Pineda, who recently starred in a congressional investigation on *jueteng*, used his connections in Malacañang to make major inroads in all provinces of Central and Northern Luzon.

With his political and military links, Bong Pineda became a major competitor of Pangasinan gambling lords, says Sonny. Many *jueteng* operators were driven out of business or operated under Bong Pineda through a system of royalties. The exception was this town where Sonny's first cousin, who inherited the municipal mayorship from his grandfather, ensured the *jueteng* lord's survival.

"Kundi pinsan ko ang may hawak ng jueteng sa bayan na ito, walang jueteng dito (If my cousin didn't control *jueteng* in this town, there would be no *jueteng* here)," the mayor of the town says he told police officers sent by Bong Pineda.

Faced with the mayor's tenacity, the provincial law-enforcement officials backed off. Later, some of them figured that dealing with, rather than going against, the mayor could be more lucrative. They could now collect *intelihensiya* from both Bong Pineda and Sonny G.

The raids would of course continue, as Sonny G. at that time did not have backers in Malacañang, he says. National and

Manila-based police and military units would hunt down his operations.

His followers say that Sonny's *jueteng* operations are of the renegade, guerrilla type. *Bolas* were often conducted at the back of a Pajero or Hi-Ace Van. And he was not the sole operator in the town. For a time, there were several operations, often confusing the town's *jueteng* aficionados.

But the existence of several operations created a free market for *jueteng*: collectors could choose the *cabo* that offered the best deal. In the end, Sonny's *cabos* prevailed over the others.

They had transportation (tricycles, motorcycles or bicycles) to make the rounds of the different *cobradores*. Another important factor was the trust that Sonny was able to establish through his family's political network. Sonny also gave extra monetary "incentives" for *cobradores* and *cabos*.

Sonny says that his business peaked with the change of administration in 1992. As Bong Pineda's Malacañang backers fell from grace, so did his monopoly over national connections. Other gambling lords entered the game, providing "alternative" channels of protection. One of them, reveals Sonny, is an engineer named Sanchez, who appears in Rep. Roilo Golez's list of *jueteng* lords. Sanchez collects royalties from local operators and ensures their protection from national and Manila-based law-enforcement agencies.

The *jueteng* lord is often cloaked with an aura of mystique and power over the police forces. However, in reality, he is not omnipotent. Protection is a reciprocal engagement based on a negotiated process between various gambling lords, incumbent officials and law-enforcement agencies. Shifts in the patterns of power between these officials cause changes in the patterns of *jueteng* operations.

Sonny was able to survive these shifts. A major reason for this survival is his affiliation with a political family that had ruled this municipality for several decades.

Police and Politicians Protect Jueteng

Second of Three Parts

SOMEWHERE in Pangasinan — The intimate relationship between *jueteng* and politics is best demonstrated in this town where the local *jueteng* lord comes from the same family that has controlled municipal political office for several decades.

The family has been able to survive various regime changes—from the pre-Marcos era to martial law to the Aquino and Ramos administrations—through a combination of deeply entrenched familial and *compadrazco* linkages with various barangay officials, patronage, and skillfully built alliances with provincial and national officials.

Jueteng is also part of the family's political arsenal. Since the 1970s, the clan has been able to use the earnings and the grassroots network of the illegal numbers game to perpetuate itself in power .

Politics here is intertwined with the *jueteng* structure. The gambling network, based on a hierarchical system of *cabos* (supervisors) and *cobradores* (collectors), does more than collect bets or deliver winnings. It is also an A-1 source of up-to-date political intelligence and a ready-made machinery for election mobilization. In addition, *jueteng* money contributes not just to campaign coffers but to a social welfare fund administered by the political family.

Sonny runs a network of over 2,000 *cobradores* or collectors who go around the villages to collect bets of as low as P1 each. Each *cobrador* has a quota, at least P100 worth of bets every day. The collectors form groups of five to ten *cobradores* called PLOPs. Efficient PLOPs get a share of their collection for operational expenses like paper, pencils and transportation.

Each PLOP reports to a *cabo,* a supervisor who gathers the collections. Sonny has 80 to 90 *cabos* under his command; they are trusted individuals who have earned a reputation in their communities for being able to deliver efficiently and honestly. Trusted *cabos* get either a regular salary or percentage from the collection, regular incentives or bonuses, social security in the form of emergency loans, and protection from the harassment of law enforcers.

The *cabos* in turn report to a table manager, who supervises the draw. At the top of this hierarchy is Sonny, the town's *jueteng* lord.

This grassroots-based network is crucial to the game. Unlike casino gambling which earns from prohibitive entrance fees and high stakes, *jueteng* depends on a large number of bettors, no matter the amount they bet. The odds in *jueteng* are high: a bettor chooses two numbers from 1 to 37. The winner gets the pot if he chooses the right pair of numbers from one of 1,369 (37 x 37) possible combinations. *Cabos* and collectors ensure the lucrativeness of the game by taking as many bets as possible.

Sonny put his *cabo-cobrador* machinery at the disposal of his first cousin, the mayor who ran for re-election in May 1995. Through the *jueteng* network, the candidate was able to check on the implementation of backroom political deals between himself and his allies. He also used this machinery to monitor the shifting loyalties of barangay captains and ward leaders and to keep track of the vote-buying rates and schemes of his rivals.

But the *jueteng* network is not like a military command. The *cabos* and the *cobradores* often have mixed loyalties, and they may choose to be slack in their obedience to the gambling lord.

Source of Patronage

To Sonny's family, however, *jueteng* is more than just a political machine, it is also a source of funds. Sonny nets up to P1.2 million a month from *jueteng*. Part of the proceeds goes to a nightspot in Dagupan City that imports the latest "models" from Metro Manila. (This nightspot however, did not become lucrative, as Sonny's brothers and bodyguards often monopolized the "models," depriving other patrons.)

But a significant amount of the funds also goes to "development patronage." *Jueteng* money has been used for livelihood and infrastructure projects. It is also given out as *abuloy* (donations to the needy) and used in the construction of community artesian wells and basketball courts and a host of other donations expected of a political family but not provided for in the regular municipal budget.

Sonny, in fact, invested part of his profits in the cementing of a chapel. The parish priest had asked him for help to cement the stairs and the walls. But Sonny felt that it would be better to include the floor of the chapel, which of course pleased the parish priest all the more. The priest had no moral qualms about this. In fact, he had won several tens of thousands from a *jueteng* draw held in 1994.

Jueteng money is also an important source of election capital. In the 1995 elections, when the family's rival spent P1 to 2 million to buy votes in the last three days of the campaign, Sonny's cousin topped the offer, thanks to *jueteng*.

Equally important, *jueteng* funds are a source of political maneuverability and allow the family to remain fiercely independent from pressures of provincial and national politicians. Sonny G.'s political family does not have any large corporations or extensive landholdings. The family's lifestyle is much more akin to that of the middle to upper-middle class in Metro Manila.

But during elections, the family prefers not to depend on contributions from provincial or national politicians. In fact, the clan decides to support a candidate not on the basis of how much he is willing to contribute, but on cunning and careful political calculations of his prospects for victory.

Money contributed by candidates is often respectfully returned, say members of Sonny's family. This reputation not only increases the family's political stock, it also makes for a subtle way of doing politics, where loyalties are established on a more long-term basis. Supporting a candidate without financial incentive marks an open debt that can be paid back in a much better way once that candidate has won. The family knows that *utang na loob* is a stronger bond than money that has been exchanged for services delivered, clan members say.

Jueteng funds also serve as a safety net for the family. With continually flowing gambling money, it can readily replenish exhausted coffers after an election. As one member of Sonny's staff explained, "*OK lang gumastos nang malaki sa panahon ng eleksiyon, puwede naman bawiin ito sa jueteng pagkatapos ng eleksiyon* (It's okay for us to spend during an election, because we can always recoup our losses once *jueteng* profits come in)."

The Downside of *Jueteng*

But despite its political advantages, *jueteng* has its pitfalls. For one, it has been used by rivals to cast the family in a bad light. Although Sonny's family has managed to prevail against challengers, it does not always get its way.

Sonny himself is the best example. He recently ran for local office, but despite his access to *jueteng*'s money and its grassroots network, he lost the election, a defeat which local pundits attributed to a weakening of the family's influence in certain areas.

There are also limits to expanding *jueteng* beyond the municipality. This is often circumscribed by relationships with mayors in adjoining municipalities. *Jueteng* requires an intimate relationship with the incumbent mayor. It cannot survive in an area dominated by a hostile mayor, unless of course, the *jueteng* lord has more powerful connections to the congressman, governor, or provincial commander.

Jueteng tends to be on the side of the incumbents, says Sonny. In cases where there is a strong opposition, the *jueteng* lord usually invests in both. The politics of acquiring support from a *jueteng* lord is quite simple: a strong opposition candidate need only intimidate the gambling operator and warn of more effective anti-*jueteng* campaigns if he wins.

In rare cases, the *jueteng* lord may

choose to suspend operations during the campaign. This sends a clear signal to the incumbent that the *jueteng* lord is withdrawing support. More often, however, the *jueteng* lord would invest in both. Anyway, the politician will never know whether his rival also got a similar if not bigger amount, says a family member.

Sonny's familial affinities put him in a better position than other gambling lords in Pangasinan. However, even if powerful family connections allow gambling lords of his type to maintain impenetrable beachheads in towns like this one, they are also beholden to higher loyalties.

The term "*jueteng* lord" is therefore in a sense a misnomer, for the logic of *jueteng* and the countless negotiations its leaders undertake with politicians and law-enforcement officials is just part of the process of contesting claims to leadership by various political families. The *jueteng* lord is not omnipotent: these engagements and negotiations limit his power.

But, ironically, they also ensure his survival. These relationships are the main reasons why *jueteng* in Pangasinan has survived a series of anti-gambling campaigns launched by the national government.

There is another reason for *jueteng*'s impenetrability. This has to do with the "culture" of *jueteng*. It is also this "culture" which predisposes *jueteng* toward engagement with politics.

Jueteng is Embedded in Local Society and Culture

Conclusion

SOMEWHERE in Pangasinan — *Jueteng* here is an entrenched social system that is grassroots-based. Unlike other numbers games, the *cobrador* literally knocks at people's doorsteps to solicit bets. Bettors do not have to travel all the way to a retail outlet. Winnings are also delivered straight to their homes by the *cobrador*.

Jueteng is a game whose outcomes are in the realm of the familiar. *Jueteng* aficionados are the next-door neighbor, the *sari-sari* store retailer, the tricycle mechanic, etc. Winning in *jueteng*, unlike other forms of gambling, is tangible. One's next-door neighbor wins, not someone from a distant province announced over the radio.

The game is also perceived as harmless because of the low amounts involved: a P1-bet can take in anywhere from P400 to P1,000 in winnings. *Jueteng* is also seen as some form of community charity. Villagers shell out spare change to aid the neighborhood *cobrador* who engages in *jueteng* to make ends meet. The *jueteng* operation and its extensive grassroots staff of indigents and the idle underemployed have been compared to a social welfare agency.

At the grassroots level, one reason for *jueteng*'s permanency is its ability to reaffirm community bonds and community notions of trust and *pakikipagkapwa* or neighborliness. The betting transactions are natural occasions for community gossip. The *cobrador* doubles up as the town crier, updating fellow citizens with the latest sex scandal, political intrigue, personal tragedy or lucky break.

Betting on *jueteng* is an expression of

Filipino magic-realism. Folkloric notions of *malas* and *suwerte*, of good and bad luck, permeate the betting transaction. Bettors look for lucky signs from dreams, from a sibling's birth date, or a combination of symbolic premonitions. Betting involves the ability to interpret supernatural forces and powers that influence the natural order of things.

Betting also indicates the bettors' own power to harness these forces by choosing the right combination and the right time to bet. In other words, Filipino betting is not just a question of fate. It is the choice of a deliberate set of actions by the bettor to act on a lucky hunch.

The *Diskarte* Psychology

In essence, *jueteng* represents a reciprocal relationship between conscious choice and the unpredictable winds of fortune. This is embodied in the concept of *diskarte.*

Diskarte means careful calculation in the face of given circumstances. Its success depends not only on the bettor's own skill but also on the character of the *cobrador* accepting the bet. Trust is an important part of the bettor's calculation. The fate of a *cobrador, cabo* or an entire *jueteng* network in a community hinges on trust and goodwill.

Diskarte is built into the game itself. A bettor can choose any combination of two numbers between one and 37. The lucky pair is drawn, and the winnings depend on how much and on which numbers other competitors have bet.

Diskarte is also expressed in the countless negotiations revolving around *jueteng*, transactions that are built on trust and goodwill. A bettor places his bet as part of a social ritual that revolves around the fate of the latest winner, the latest community gossip, intrigues in government, and the interpretation of *anuncios* or supernatural premonitions of a winning combination.

This ritual reaffirms the bettor-*cobrador* relationship. *Jueteng* does not involve receipts, the implication being that it revolves on a bond of trust stronger than any piece of paper.

Trust is an important part of the qualification of a *cobrador* and/or *cabo.* Woe to the former, if he or she is associated with cheating and lack of transparency. In other words, the mediator is as important as the bet he mediates. And community residents are quite meticulous about the credentials of their *cobrador*es.

A *cobrador* is selected on the basis of the following:

- Clan Credentials. He or she comes from a family of *cobradores.* Usually the former *cobrador* retires due to old age or sickness, and his or her children inherit the "career."
- Active Recruitment. The potential recruit is highly trusted by the community. *Cabos* usually target those in charge of collecting *abuloy* or donations for sick community members or for the funeral expenses of a neighbor.
- Walk-ins. On other occasions, an enterprising youth may actually walk in and volunteer to be a *cobrador.* Usually, their training ground would be experience in other forms of betting that involved extensive "community visitations."

From the point of view of the people, therefore, what makes *jueteng* legitimate is linked to the notions of trust and community goodwill attached to the betting transaction.

Network Based on Trust

Membership in a *jueteng* network requires no written contracts. Relationships are built on trust. Entrants to the system are not required to submit written bio-data. What they need are endorsements from trusted members of the network.

In business terms, *jueteng* here is a medium-scale industry with a gross revenue of P6 million monthly. There are no formal management systems or written contracts, only countless informal negotiations. Ironically, these relations are mediated by an element of trust-distrust. The complex structure and negotiations of *jueteng* are not only about making the game work or earning lucrative profits; it is also about managing mistrust.

Jueteng is one of the least transparent of all gambling games. And there is a strong element of tension permeating the game. One reason is illegality and the inconvenience of arrest. But the other reason is the possibility of cheating.

Sonny is a master of this. In the past, he used to maneuver the winning combination in order to please his great-grandmother, a *jueteng* aficionado, during her birthdays. Unfortunately, his great-grandmother's servant got wind of the pattern and bet on the same combination. Of course, Sonny found out and fired the servant, accusing her of abuse of trust.

But Sonny says this was an exception. He claims that as a rule, he ensures that the draw is open to all *cabos*. *Cobradores* and even favored bettors are welcome to watch the proceedings. There are strong countervailing factors against cheating, he claims. A gambling lord with a reputation for cheating loses mass support for his game, suffers a decline in bets, and makes himself vulnerable to takeovers by other *jueteng* lords muscling into his stable of *cabos* and *cobradores*.

Altogether, these factors—protection, community goodwill, tradition, personalistic negotiations and mutually beneficial exchanges—make *jueteng* popular. In addition, the elaborate organization of the *jueteng* network and the game's limited transparency add to its allure. But it is these same factors that predispose *jueteng* toward its intimate engagement with politics.

From the point of view of good governance, public order and the rule of law, however, *jueteng* is illegal. But from the point of view of the Pangasinan politician, the protection of *jueteng* by public officials is just one of many transactions—among them the apportioning of public works contracts and other sources of patronage—which are arrived at through complex political negotiations and shifting alliances. Like these transactions, *jueteng* is embedded in the dynamics of clan politics, political patronage and *diskarte*.

Jueteng lords have often been compared to the Sicilian Mafia, the Colombian drug lord, or the Kuomintang warlord. But perhaps reality is less conspiratorial than what these images suggest. *Jueteng* leaders take into account the factors that shape any political family's intervention in politics: electoral traditions, the language of patronage, access to national and regional powers.

Sonny survives not because he has some omniscient power over the politicians, but because he knows how to play the game of politics. He, too, practices *diskarte*.

Like political families, *jueteng* depends on grassroots support. Like politicians, *jueteng* lords are adept at tapping community notions of trust, familiarity, and goodwill. Take away the grassroots, and both *jueteng* and politicians fall like a house of cards.

Datu Politics in Muslim Mindanao

BY MARITES DAÑGUILAN VITUG AND ERIC GUTIERREZ
First published in the *Evening Paper, Manila Standard,* and *Sun Star Daily,* September 4-6, 1996

This examination of the Autonomous Region in Muslim Mindanao (ARMM) provides documentary proof of corruption, waste and nepotism in the workings of the autonomous government. Obtaining employment lists from the Civil Service Commission and ARMM, the authors discovered a bureaucracy bloated by appointments of relatives and townmates of ARMM officials. They also found evidence of the diversion of funds intended for infrastructure projects.

Budget records yielded figures on the large amount of public funds spent on ARMM—about P1 billion for every province. The writers traced where this money went and found that most of it went to "pork barrel," discretionary funds given to ARMM officials who promised a lot but delivered little. They found corruption was exacerbated by a sluggish and inept bureaucracy incapable of exercising the basic administrative functions required to run a government. ARMM residents have to suffer from the slow delivery of social services that is the consequence of this ineptness.

This series, written just before secessionist leader Nur Misuari was elected ARMM governor, shows in graphic detail the intractable problems that the new autonomous government would face. It also looks at the strange mix of former guerrillas and traditional politicians that would make up the new ARMM government, which was voted into office with the help of the patronage doled out by the ruling Lakas party in Manila. This report relied on employment records, documents from a congressional inquiry, academic studies and interviews with ARMM officials, Moro leaders, academics and representatives of Mindanao NGOs.

This article was a finalist in the 1996 Jaime V. Ongpin Awards for investigative journalism.

Misuari Faces Big Headache

BY MARITES DAÑGUILAN VITUG

First of Three Parts

COTABATO CITY — When Nur Misuari takes over the leadership of the Autonomous Region in Muslim Mindanao (ARMM) in September 1996, he will find himself at the helm of an organization tainted by charges of corruption, internal wrangling and waste.

Created after a 1989 plebiscite held to determine the scope of an autonomous region for southern Philippine Muslims, which was provided for in the 1987 Constitution, ARMM today is an administrative unit that is saddled with an oversized, demoralized and mostly inept bureaucracy staffed by people hired for their political connections and family ties rather than their skills.

It is also paralyzed by the wrangling over money among the governors of the four provinces that compose the autonomous region and the members of the Regional Legislative Assembly (RLA). The prized pot is a P615-million annual subsidy from the national government, most of which goes to pork barrel projects for ARMM officials.

In the six years since its creation, ARMM has received generous infusions of funds from Manila. According to our estimate, each of the ARMM provinces gets P1 billion a year from the national government, including internal revenue allotments, congressional initiative allocations and countrywide development funds.

But ARMM—the poorest region in the country, with the worst social services—has little to show for this money. In addition, millions of pesos worth of funds remain unaccounted for, according to Commission on Audit reports.

Indeed, the problems besetting ARMM are so monumental that they are bound to challenge even the most efficient administrator. When he takes over the autonomous region this month, Misuari will find his hands full with a legacy of patronage and graft bequeathed by his two predecessors.

Bloated Bureaucracy

Currently at the helm of the autonomous region is Governor Lininding Pangandaman, a Lakas politician from Lanao del Sur, who has inflated the ARMM bureaucracy to more than 19,000 employees.

Thus, ARMM, which administers four provinces with a combined population of two million people, has more personnel than national agencies covering the entire country. Data from the Civil Service Commission show, for example, that as of December 1995, the Department of Agrarian Reform had 16,429 employees and the Department of Agriculture, only 13, 231.

ARMM's "bloated bureaucracy, filled with non-performing political appointees" has been cited as one of the region's most severe problems in a policy study done by the Office of the Presidential Assistant for Mindanao.

Apart from political connections, family ties determine appointments in ARMM. About 15 of the key officials are related to Pangandaman. His wife Ester, three nephews, 11 cousins and in-laws hold important positions, despite a provision in the ARMM law that bans nepotism. Lists from the CSC and the Office of the Regional Governor show the posts held by members of the governor's clan:

- Alim Pangandaman, regional chief of staff
- Ester Pangandaman, executive assistant
- Pangaga Pangcoga, regional executive secretary
- Camar Pangandaman, assistant regional executive secretary
- Amer Pangandaman, director, intelligence security service
- Agakhan Pangandaman, chief, security division
- Bamra Pangandaman, chief, property division
- Paisalin Tago, director, finance and budget management service
- Ansani Pangandaman, officer-in-charge, Lanao extension office
- Metalicop Unda, DENR secretary
- Macaling Saligon, DECS assistant secretary
- Jarmila Makakua, DOH secretary
- Ali Macalawi, DOLE secretary
- Soraya Pacasum, DSWD secretary
- Cadar Omar, SPDA regional administrator

Soon after Pangandaman assumed office in 1993, the CSC found that six of his appointments had violated the anti-nepotism provision in the ARMM law, congressional transcripts show. The violation was exposed in a privilege speech in Congress by Rep. Hernando Perez.

The House committees on Muslim affairs and civil service held public hearings where the CSC disclosed its findings of nepotism. Pangandaman's defense was that he appointed only competent and qualified people. Although he clearly violated the law, no sanctions were meted out. The ARMM law penalizes nepotism with dismissal from office.

The appointment of relatives and townmates—Pangandaman is from Masiu, Lanao del Sur—has demoralized many in the ARMM government. "Many of the civil servants are not properly tapped because of favors given to the family and political patronage," says ARMM Vice Governor Nabil Tan.

In 1993, Alim Pangandaman, the governor's nephew and then ARMM assistant executive secretary, told the House committees that some of the questionable appointments were made only for the transition period. Indeed, after the Perez exposé, the governor replaced a few of his most controversial appointees.

But, in his first few months in office, he put his relatives himself in charge of two of the most graft-ridden departments in the region: his son-in-law was named officer-in-charge of the public works department while another relative became caretaker of the Department of Environment and Natural Resources.

Officials of the current ARMM administration defend Pangandaman by blaming former ARMM governor Zacaria Candao who did not make any formal turnover of assets or inventories to the new governor. Pangandaman had to put his own people in charge of sensitive departments before the losses increased, the governor's allies say.

Candao, who is now governor of Maguindanao, does not deny this since, he says, he did not concede defeat in the 1993 elections. When Pangandaman took over, many of the ARMM's office equipment were missing, including vehicles. Pangandaman says he inherited a literally empty office.

Centralizing Power

Pangandaman is also faulted for centralizing powers in his office. He has found himself involved in turf battles with other officials who accuse him of monopolizing everything, from appointing personnel to various departments to allocating the national subsidy.

Some of the ARMM secretaries, a recent study found out, have complained of lack of power to appoint the employees of their own departments. Many of the personnel report for work with appointment papers already signed by Pangandaman.

Trouble erupted a few years ago when the governors declared they wanted to secede from ARMM because they felt their powers were diminished. They were unhappy with their share of the P615-million annual subsidy that was allocated by the national government for ARMM's first five years of operation.

Lanao del Sur passed a resolution saying they wanted to get out of ARMM. Maguindanao, Tawi-Tawi and Sulu, Rep. Nur Jaafar said in a privilege speech in 1994, also expressed a similar sentiment.

During Candao's term, the P615-million subsidy was divided equitably among the governors of Sulu, Tawi-Tawi, Maguindanao and Lanao del Sur. Under Pangandaman, the office of the regional governor controls the money with each of the 21 members of the regional legislative assembly getting his/her share of P12 million. The provincial governors have been left out.

Pangandaman defends the arrangement as more conducive for "rational and wiser spending." Rather than distribute the funds to the governors, the entire chunk could be used to fund projects in the region.

"We don't like the leadership of ARMM," says Lanao del Sur Governor Mahid Mutilan. "They usurped the power of provincial governments. Virtually, we lost control of our provinces." Mutilan complains that heads of line agencies coordinate with the regional offices rather than with the governors and that they have been bypassed in identifying provincial projects on which the subsidy should be spent.

Ideally, the governors, who are members of the regional planning and development board, have a say in the choice of projects. But the board is dominated by members of the Regional Legislative Assembly who are with Pangandaman's party, Lakas-NUCD. Mutilan says their recommendations are not heard. Most of the governors have stopped attending board meetings. Candao admits he has been the only governor present in these meetings.

ARMM Vice Governor Tan, known as a reform-driven and development-oriented politician, has also been bypassed by Pangandaman, even if they belong to the same party. Tan does not recall any quarrels they have had. But he has not been consulted on appointments to the Cabinet and neither has he been given any projects. "He (Pangandaman) isolates me," Tan says. "He does not communicate to me."

Sukarno Tanggol, a professor at the Mindanao State University in Marawi who has studied ARMM extensively, says Pangandaman is very turf-oriented. Tan's isolation is part of the process of "overcentralizing" the governor's powers.

Absence of Competence

The ARMM leadership has also been criticized for its administrative ineptness. In 1994, Lanao del Sur health officials went on a weeklong sit-down strike to protest the delay of their salaries.

The event dramatized the phenomenon of late salaries common in the entire ARMM. "It may seem like a small thing but it demonstrates administrative ineptness and fiscal inefficiency which destroy the credibility and integrity of ARMM," Tan says.

Tanggol, in his doctoral dissertation on ARMM for the UP College of Public Administration, looks at delayed salaries as one of the problems that accompany a heavy and unqualified bureaucracy. Unnecessary appointments have strained ARMM's resources. The law that created ARMM provided for the creation of nine regional departments. But today, there are 25 regional departments and agencies in ARMM. The obese regional structure, Tanggol says, accounts for the sluggish behavior that makes for organizational incompetence.

Not only that, ARMM employees have had to resort to loan sharks who advance their salaries at 20-percent interest a month. Usury has thrived in ARMM offices because of official ineptness. As a result, employees have become victims twice over, first of the bureaucracy and second, of usurers.

The Office of the Regional Governor, Tanggol found out, is partly to blame for salaries that are usually delayed a few months. "The executive branch uses allocated funds for other purposes. Having appointed too many temporary or contractual people, the chief executive has this problem of where to charge their salaries. One mode of solving this problem is to use appropriated funds," Tanggol wrote in his dissertation, now published into a book, *Muslim Autonomy in the Philippines: Rhetoric and Reality*.

Tanggol also reviewed the ARMM Cabinet and their staff and found that many of them "lack technical competence." For example, DPWH Secretary Nasrodin Makabinta was Engineer II at the DPWH in Manila before becoming executive assistant at DPWH ARMM in 1993. Soon after, he was promoted to DPWH ARMM secretary. Makabinta, according to his bio-data provided by the Civil Service Commission, got a civil engineering board exam rating of only 71.85 percent, barely above the passing grade of 70. He hails from Masiu, Lanao del Sur, Pangandaman's hometown.

"Giving way to family, cronies, personal considerations is more pronounced here (than other parts of the country)," Tanggol says in an interview. "In the process, they (appointing powers) do away with merit and qualifications."

A Culture of Corruption in ARMM

BY ERIC GUTIERREZ
Second of Three Parts

COTABATO CITY — For the past five years, the four provinces composing the Autonomous Region in Muslim Mindanao (ARMM) have been linked to the national government by huge infusions of money.

Unfortunately, ARMM has little to show for this money. It remains the poorest region in the country, with literacy and income levels lower than all other areas in the Philippines. The bulk of national government subsidies for the region has been spent on infrastructure where the opportunities for graft for the Moro elite abound.

Since 1991, ARMM received from Manila P615 million a year to run its operations. Apart from this, Internal Revenue Allotments (IRA)—or the share of national taxes—are released every year to the region's four provinces, 83 municipalities and 2,128 barangays. In 1996, for instance, IRA for Lanao del Sur and Maguindanao added up to P749 and P603 million respectively, figures from the Department of Budget and Management show.

In addition, each of ARMM's seven congressional districts gets P12.5 million in Countrywide Development Funds (CDF) as well as varying amounts from Congressional Initiative Allocation (CIA). In 1996, ARMM's seven representatives were given a total of P255.26 million in CIA.

The regional governor also enjoys discretion over various funds transferred from national government agencies. In 1991, when the ARMM structure became regular, the Office of the Regional Governor received P364 million in such funds, a study on ARMM shows.

Combining these resources, each province in ARMM receives more than P1 billion in revenues yearly from the national government. This is above the revenues raised locally by local governments and projects funded by senators and the President's Social Fund.

But there is little evidence of these sums being wisely spent. The recently released Human Development Report of the United Nations Development Program (UNDP) shows that ARMM is at the bottom of the heap. It has the lowest per capita income and functional literacy rate in the country.

ARMM has the lowest life expectancy among all the regions (55.3 years in 1994). In fact, it is the only region where life expectancy went below 60 years of age. The national average is 66.9 years.

The UNDP report further showed that average local government expenditures on social services was low in two ARMM provinces, Maguindanao and Sulu, with P1.82 and P4.75 per person per year, respectively. Neighboring Lanao del Norte, which does not belong to ARMM, spent P62.88 on social services per person each year. There are no available statistics on the two other ARMM provinces—Lanao del Sur and Tawi-Tawi.

These figures indicate that infrastructure projects took the lion's share of public spending in ARMM. Social services like education, primary health care, water supply, nutrition and family planning suffered. Significant amounts have also been lost to corruption.

Corruption Charges

The first two ARMM administrations have been accused of tolerating corruption; charges have been filed against some officials, but none of them have prospered. Among those charged in the Office of the Ombudsman were then ARMM Governor Zacaria Candao's public works secretary Datukan Guiani and his environment and natural resources secretary Lanang Ali.

In 1993, *Mindanao Cross* editor Jaime (Bong) Guayco wrote an exposé about "the fathers of graft and corruption in Mindanao." He accused Candao's associates of "making a killing in construction deals, the barter trade, and usurious lending that victimized ARMM employees."

Guiani subsequently sued the journalist for libel. Guayco was imprisoned for four days, but the libel case was dismissed a year later.

Corruption was noted by NGOs as well. One of them, the Cotabato-based Moro People's Resource Center, cited corruption as the major reason for the slow delivery of social services in the region. It quoted from a 1992 Commission on Audit (COA) report which said that of 294 infrastructure projects inspected, 213 worth P49.54 million were not yet implemented at the fiscal year's end.

COA also reported excessive disbursements of funds: a film production on drug abuse which cost P1.89 million; charter of planes with no purpose stated; unliquidated cash advances; unnecessary hiring of consultants; and the disbursement of P25.876 million worth of confidential funds through cash advances. Local papers reported in January 1994 that Department of Agrarian Reform employees accused ARMM officials of "converting office supplies into instant cash."

An aide of ARMM Governor Liningding Pangandaman admits that corruption takes place in ARMM agencies. Aside from the usual kickbacks in public works projects, key Pangandaman aides like his son Nasser, former regional executive secretary, have been accused of facilitating the issuance of permits to transport illegally cut logs.

But these have remained accusations. Even COA auditors, it is said, are intimidated by the threat of retaliation from those accused. A review of past COA reports shows that many infrastructure projects in ARMM have not been physically inspected because of the peace and order situation.

A 1993 audit on Lanao del Sur, for example, said that auditors "could not render an opinion on the financial operations of the province because of the absence of records and unavailability of inventories."

Pork Barrel

The Regional Legislative Assembly (RLA), the law-making body of ARMM, is an expensive institution where P7.3 million is spent for every bill and resolution passed, a study by Mindanao State University professor Sukarno Tanggol shows.

Apart from this, the RLA is better known for measures allocating pork barrel. Among the first laws passed by the RLA was Regional Act No. 5, which prescribes that a portion of the P615-million national government subsidy be allocated for "projects which shall be identified, proposed and implemented in consultation with the regional assemblymen of each district."

The subsidy has been transformed into the local version of the national CDF. But since there are other key players involved in the region's decision-making, a *modus vivendi* for sharing the seed money emerged.

Projects funded by the national subsidy are classified into district, provincial, and regional impact projects. District impact projects totaling P265 million are placed under the discretion of the regional assemblymen. Each legislator could identify P12 to P13 million worth of projects for his or her district yearly. The Assembly Speaker had a bigger share of P25 million.

During the first ARMM administration, Candao provided each provincial governor P50 million for provincial impact projects or a total of P200 million. The remainder went to the regional impact projects under his office. This arrangement was changed by Pangandaman who did away with allocations for provincial impact projects. Instead, he centralized under the Office of the Regional Governor the P150 to P350 million allotted for regional impact projects every year.

Pangandaman defends the move, saying all he wanted was a "more rational and focused use of infrastructure funds. It is the only way to create impact."

"Our infrastructure projects are the monumental achievements of this administration," Pangandaman says, referring to the newly opened road linking Lanao del Sur to Cotabato and the Lake Lanao circumferential road still under construction. "These roads are strategic to this region's economic development," he beams, "and will definitely improve the flow of goods to and from ARMM. "

The first ARMM administration started the Ramos highway but ran out of funds and time. Pangandaman, with President Ramos breathing down his neck, had to complete the road. That is why some sectors of ARMM, including the Moro Islamic Liberation Front (MILF), credit Ramos, rather than Pangandaman, for the highway.

It is easy to see why ARMM officials favor infrastructure projects over social services. First, road and similar projects are visible. Secondly, they also provide opportunities for graft. Pangandaman, ARMM politicians say, favored one Manila-based contractor for ARMM projects so that local contractors rose up in arms. In early 1994, they arranged to have the field manager kidnapped "to embarrass and anger Pangandaman," says Lanao del Sur Governor Mahid Mutilan.

Mutilan claims he helped rescue the engineer. "All local contractors were called to bid but even before the bidding started, it was already awarded to a Manila company," he recalls.

Failure in Planning

Vice Governor Nabil Tan argues that there is no problem with spending large amounts on infrastructure "for as long as the projects complement and support each other to maximize use and efficiency." But complementation does not happen, he says, because of failure in planning. "It all depends on the politician making the recommendation," he points out.

Maguindanao chief executive and first ARMM Governor Candao admits that projects are not aligned with the Master Plan for Development of ARMM. "There is no planning at all," he says.

Much of the problem comes from the shortcuts made in the process of allocating money. The regular procedure is for local governments to submit a list of priority projects to their respective planning and development councils. The councils align the lists based on priorities and the

Master Plan, draft a package and submit recommendations to the proper legislative bodies for appropriation.

In the case of ARMM, the main body tasked to do this work, the regional planning and development board is not functioning as intended. The chief figures in the board are the regional governor and vice-governor, four provincial governors and seven members of the RLA. Ultimately, it is the governor and his allies in RLA, who form a majority, who have the final say.

A Mindanao State University historian, who wishes to remain anonymous, says that it is unfair to judge local Moro politicians using Manila standards. "The concept of the state is not well-developed in these areas. That is why people find more security in their clan or in their *datus*. Thus, government becomes an alien structure imposed by Manila. Using public funds and equipment for private use may be seen not as criminal acts, but as the normal and logical exercise of the authority of the *datu* or politician in dealing with an alien authority," he explains.

"Given the instability in the region, these local leaders, whatever limitations they have, provide the only visible semblance of governance in an impoverished and volatile region," argues the historian. "The biggest challenge is how they can be trained and transformed from being local bosses to development managers."

Can Misuari Reform Moro Politics?

BY ERIC GUTIERREZ

Conclusion

COTABATO CITY — Alvarez S. Isnaji is one of the four most senior generals of the Moro National Liberation Front (MNLF). He is a member of the "Batch 300," the first group of MNLF guerrillas who trained abroad in the 1970s, and was the principal architect of the MNLF's attack on Jolo in 1974, which triggered the massive air and naval bombardment of the proud Islamic town.

The burning of Jolo by Philippine troops is now seen as an important turning point in the Bangsa Moro struggle. Today Isnaji faces another milestone in his career as revolutionary. He is standing as a candidate for the Regional Legislative Assembly (RLA) of the Autonomous Region in Muslim Mindanao (ARMM), in a ticket led by MNLF chairman Nur Misuari.

Isnaji is one of seven ranking MNLF members who compose the 21-person slate supported by Malacañang. The ticket also includes eight Lakas-NUCD politicians and six other politicians chosen jointly by the MNLF and the administration party.

It is a slate as unwieldy as the compromises that the MNLF has been forced to make since it signed a peace agreement with the government in July. And it symbolizes the difficulties that Misuari and the MNLF face as they deal with the realities of Moro politics.

As the long-standing symbol of Moro resistance, Misuari is expected to reform an ARMM bureaucracy that has been plagued with corruption, ineptness and waste. To do so, he will need a capable Cabinet and a reform-driven and development-oriented regional legislature when he assumes office on September 30, 1996.

But such a team may already have been compromised by the deals Misuari has entered into with the ruling party, Lakas-NUCD, and with the region's traditional politicians.

For instance, his most immediate problem will be getting seven MNLF candidates into the Regional Legislative Assembly. Already, this appears doubtful: these politically inexperienced guerrillas are being pitted against some of the most entrenched Moro politicians who are backed by powerful political clans.

Political observers here are also worried that Misuari, once elected ARMM governor, will choose members of the ARMM Cabinet based on political connections and debts of gratitude, rather than qualification and competence.

The Real Battle

The election next week of Misuari and incumbent RLA Speaker Guimid Matalam for ARMM governor and vice-governor, respectively, is assured. No strong candidates are running against them, and they have the full support of the Lakas machinery.

The real contest is in the race for seats in the RLA. The Lakas-MNLF coalition has fielded a complete slate for all three seats in each of ARMM's seven districts. The MNLF has only a third of those seats. Apart from Isnaji, its candidates are:

Anni "Abdul Sahrin" Ahlul, who was a second year student at the Philippine Military Academy when he defected to the MNLF in 1971. As chief of the MNLF's military intelligence, he has sat across the negotiating table with his former PMA classmates who are now officers of the armed forces.

Alhabsi M. Hassan, who as the MNLF's propaganda chief, aired broadcasts on the clandestine MNLF radio station from different locations in Sabah, Malaysia. He has been assigned to the MNLF foreign office in Pakistan and was the Sulu information chief during the 1986 peace talks with President Corazon Aquino. He is now a secretary of the joint cease-fire committee.

Zenaida P. Bubong, who heads the Bangsa Moro Women's Committee and is a veteran field official of the MNLF, is married to Commander Narra, a legendary guerrilla chief who heads one of the largest MNLF camps in mainland Mindanao.

Kabilan G. Sema, who is running in Maguindanao's first district, is the vice-chairman of the support committee on defense. He is the brother of MNLF secretary-general Muslimen Sema.

Hussein "Pusing" B. Mohammad, who was also one of the first foreign-trained MNLF commanders, is now a member of the MNLF general staff.

Omar "Marco" A. Taher, who was a field political officer of the Bangsa Moro Armed Forces, is running in Lanao del Sur.

The MNLF is pinning its chances of victory on the Lakas bandwagon. Most of its candidates are not actively campaigning as they are more preoccupied with wrapping up the peace agreement. On the other hand, some of the region's most entrenched traditional politicians are throwing everything they've got into the race.

Fifteen incumbent assembly members, all backed by established political clans are running for reelection. In Lanao del Sur, a regional secretary and relative of ARMM

Governor Liningding Pangandaman is running. A prominent lawyer who is the brother of the incumbent second-district representative is also running along with a member of the Dimaporo clan. The opposition Laban party is fielding three lawyers in the race.

These candidates not only have the backing of their families behind them, they have also been dispensing patronage, through the sponsorship of public works projects, for at least the last three years.

In Maguindanao's first district, the current provincial governor's eldest brother, Abdulkadir "Peping" Candao, is leading a complete Laban slate. In the second district, Laban has likewise fielded a three-member slate, all of whom are relatives of the other candidates.

In Sulu's first district where the Tulawie and Loong clans hold sway, three Tulawies and two Loong relatives—a cousin and a brother of Governor Tupay Loong— are running. The patriarch of the prominent Anni clan of Sulu—former congressman and governor Indanan Anni—is leading the Laban slate for the province. All the major political clans of Tawi-Tawi have fielded their respective candidates.

For these candidates, inclusion in the Lakas-MNLF ticket is the biggest assurance of victory in the ARMM elections. But the regional chairman of the opposition Laban party, Maguindanao Governor Zacaria Candao, is upbeat over his party's chances. "We'll give them a run for their money," declares Candao, who has built a coalition with the Islamic Party of the Philippines (IPP) and has fielded an 18-member slate to the RLA. The IPP is said to enjoy the support of the Moro Islamic Liberation Front.

Family ties are definitely playing a role in the campaign. Politicians talk about "controlled votes" under the sway of the major political clans. ARMM Vice-Governor Nabil Tan, for instance, concedes that he will not get a solid Tausug vote behind him if he were to run for governor because half of Sulu's voters are controlled by his family's rivals—the Loongs and the Tulawies.

Tawi-Tawi, Lanao del Sur and Maguindanao have their equal share of families lording over territories and acting as gatekeepers to key voting communities. Whether the MNLF can break through this hold or else gain the support of the clans remains to be seen.

Even in the Lakas-NUCD and regional government offices, officials are not confident all MNLF candidates can make it, despite the administration's support. A veteran politician said, "They're up against an established political machine and Laban has already given way by not fielding a candidate against Misuari."

He added, "Lakas can exact compliance from the mayors and governors in supporting Misuari and Matalam, but it is an entirely different story in the RLA elections. Besides, it will be these mayors, and not the MNLF, who will herd in the controlled votes and who are expected to field precinct watchers on election day."

Strange Bedfellows

Aside from embracing *trapos,* MNLF candidates now also find themselves allied with politicians who were once their bitter enemies. For example, two "Magic Eight" leaders in Sulu are running on the Lakas-MNLF ticket. The "Magic Eight" was a group of MNLF commanders who surrendered to Marcos in the 1970s and was used in the campaign against the MNLF.

Thus, the Lakas-MNLF slate has become an odd assortment of Muslim elite and traditional politicians (*trapos*), MNLF guerillas, and even former Moro fighters who have defected to the military's side. This ticket is more than capable of packing the campaign with guns, goons, gold, and also a fourth "G"—genealogy.

For the past weeks, Lakas secretary-general and House Speaker Jose de Venecia, along with other major Lakas politicians, have been crisscrossing the ARMM provinces and have visited Nur Misuari's main guerrilla camp in Timbangan, Sulu. On August 11, 1996, local politicians and MNLF leaders alike were on hand to receive campaign funds from de Venecia who arrived in Jolo with his party on board two Lear jets.

MNLF leaders are uneasy about the strange alliance. A top leader commented sarcastically that "we have just completed our transition to being *trapos* (traditional politicians)." Banker and economist Abraham Iribani, head of the MNLF peace panel secretariat, defended the action by saying, "We have no choice. These are the realities of elections in the Philippines and Lakas *is* the ruling party."

Concerns are being raised that not only the RLA, but also the incoming regional Cabinet, will be packed by traditional politicians (*trapos*). Should this happen, Nur Misuari may find himself constantly negotiating with a *trapo*-controlled assembly to get the legislation he needs, as he presides over a *trapo*-dominated Cabinet. "It is going to be the biggest challenge to his leadership," says incumbent ARMM Vice-Governor Nabil Tan.

The Cotabato-based Moro People's Resource Center (MPRC) worries about a *trapo*-controlled assembly. "Nur may have to eat his share of pork," says MPRC Executive Director Wahab Guialal, warning about what may lie ahead for the MNLF-led ARMM administration.

The MPRC fears that an RLA dominated by traditional politicians may again fail to discuss the most sensitive issue in Moro politics—land and ancestral domain claims. "Land is the root cause of the Mindanao problem and continues to be potentially explosive," argues Guialal. "It is at the core of Christian opposition to the peace agreement as it may mean freeing land controlled by settlers for Muslim or *lumad* (indigenous peoples) claimants." Misuari has given his assurance to Christian leaders that due process will be observed.

Guialal adds that *lumad* communities, such as the Tirurays of Upi town are increasingly becoming insecure about Muslim and Christian incursion into their lands. "These are groups which have no representation at all in the regional nor in provincial legislative bodies. And their problems have never received the needed attention from Muslim or Christian *trapos*."

It will not be easy. Those observing the MNLF remain guarded about the future. Says Mohaghir Iqbal, chairman of the public information commission of the Moro Islamic Liberation Front (MILF): "As revolutionaries we have been trained to destroy. The challenge is if we can learn to build in the coming months." After September 9, 1996, addressing that challenge falls squarely in the hands of Nur Misuari.

The Governor's Revenge

BY HOWIE G. SEVERINO
First published in *i* Magazine, July-September 1997

This is the story of the woes of the Laguna Lake Development Authority (LLDA), which incurred the ire of Rizal officials for its attempts to regulate the number of fishpens on the lake. The LLDA was evicted from its office by its landlord, the Rizal provincial government, and it received death threats from the Rizal governor's men. The reason, this report discovered, was that the governor and several of the mayors were themselves either fishpen operators or had links with the fishing industry on the lake.

This report was based on interviews with LLDA and Rizal officials and on environmental studies done on Laguna de Bay. The author also followed the trail of the Red Sea Corp., a big fishpen operator, and found evidence that the company was owned by the Rizal governor. The evidence included photocopies of checks for the company's fishpen fees, which were signed by the governor himself.

This article documents a typical case: in many areas of the country, exploitation of natural resources is controlled either by politicians or by businessmen with close links to them. It therefore becomes the reporter's task to uncover and expose these links. But the story of Laguna Lake is more than just one of a tussle between an environmental agency and entrenched politicians. It is also one of the conflicting claims on Laguna Lake by fishpen operators, local fishermen, factories, and Metro Manila water agencies, which plan to tap the lake to provide water for the capital. There is no way to meet all these claims, and this story goes beyond corruption and the abuse of power to the politics of resource use.

Showdown in Laguna de Bay

IT was, from the sound of the meeting's tape recording, a typically heated confrontation between government regulators and agents for a fishpen corporation trying to extract a permit from the bureaucracy.

But officials of the Laguna Lake Development Authority (LLDA) knew this was no ordinary argument with the regulated. Facing them on June 19, 1997 were official representatives of their landlord, the provincial government of Rizal. And they had come to argue on behalf of Red Sea Corp., which operated a large fishpen allegedly owned by the governor of Rizal province, Casimiro Ynares, whose office was only one floor below the LLDA's.

After the agency refused to give in to the demands of Ynares's men, its electricity was cut off and bomb threats came through the telephone. Two weeks later, the LLDA was finally evicted by the governor from the offices it had been occupying for the past several years.

That encounter and its aftermath capture in a nutshell the risks of refereeing the intense, often violent competition to exploit Laguna de Bay, Southeast Asia's second largest lake and soon to be a vital source of Metro Manila's drinking water. But the incident also displayed the new confidence—some say arrogance—of local government officials who resent the presence of the referee, an LLDA that has powers over a lake basin encompassing nine cities, 60 towns, 21 river systems, 8,000 factories and 15 million people.

The agency's efforts in recent years to crack down on illegal fishpens and pollutive factories in the basin reflect government's growing desperation over the nation's water crisis as much as it does the increasing clout and seriousness of environmental authorities.

The LLDA is accustomed to pressure tactics employed by fishpen operators, but the incident that led to its eviction was particularly brazen. Trying to persuade agency officials to release a permit to stock Red Sea's 50-hectare fishpen with *bangus* fingerlings, a gruff voice on the tape identified as that of a member of the Governor's staff, Leon Mendoza, could be heard saying, "*Alam ninyo naman kay Gob ang nilalakad namin* (You know this is for the Governor)."

A softer voice belonging to LLDA division chief Adelina Santos-Borja could be heard explaining the procedures to Mendoza, who then raised his voice. "*Kaya bang bigyan o hindi kaya* (Can you give it or not)?" he growled, referring to the stocking permit. After a faint response from Borja, Mendoza warned, "*Maghanda-handa na kayong lumayas dito* (Get ready to get out of here)!"

Less than an hour after the confrontation, the LLDA's lights went out. Then the agency's employees were told of a bomb threat and were evacuated.

That was the last day they held office

in that building. In the next several days, bomb disposal experts failed to find any evidence of bombs, but the LLDA staff was still prohibited upon orders by the Governor from entering their offices. Provincial government staff claimed the agency was refused entry for its workers' own safety. By early July 1997, Governor Ynares ordered the LLDA to leave, saying the provincial government needed the space for other offices.

Whose Fishpen?

The agency has since moved to its underused facility in Calauan, Laguna, more than two hours away from Metro Manila. LLDA officials assert that their eviction was in retaliation for their refusal to grant a permit to Red Sea, which LLDA records show had illegally built part of its fishpen in the way of the lake's navigational lane.

Governor Ynares insists that the LLDA was asked to leave to make way for other provincial offices. "I don't own a single fishpen," he says. "My relatives, my friends have many, but not me."

Red Sea's corporate papers do not list Ynares among the incorporators. But his man Leon Mendoza is clearly audible on the tape referring to Red Sea's fishpen as the governor's.

Moreover, the company's fishpen fees are paid for with the governor's personal checks, as evidenced by photocopies that we have obtained. In a telephone interview, Atty. Joey Mendoza, a lawyer for a fishpen operators' association and Leon Mendoza's nephew, said that Red Sea does indeed belong to the governor.

Asked who owned it, Leon Mendoza himself denied that Red Sea was Ynares's. But he added that it was owned by the Alcantaras. Ynares's wife is an Alcantara. He angrily warned this reporter not to mention his name or the argument with the LLDA. "This matter is closed," he said.

The LLDA's forced transfer to Calauan, Laguna posed an enormous inconvenience for more than 100 staff members of the agency, many of whom now have to commute daily from Metro Manila. But its actions risk worse consequences.

In addition to the bomb threats called in by telephone, the LLDA has received handwritten death threats. Demolitions by agency personnel of illegal structures on the lake have sometimes involved violence, on one occasion by a local government staffer who allegedly kicked a worker helping tear down a governor's fishpen. LLDA officials also seem to spend an inordinate amount of time in court, trying to fight off attempts by fishpen operators to get judges to grant restraining orders against the LLDA.

Courtrooms are not the only places agency officials are finding themselves in these days, as revealed in a paper written by acting LLDA General Manager Carlos Tomboc Jr. In the paper, Tomboc narrated that shortly after he assumed his post in March 1996, he was called to the chamber of the "second ranking member of the Lower House" and asked not to proceed with the demolition of an illegal fishpen owned by another prominent politician. (Tomboc did so anyway, accompanied by 50 policemen and coast guard personnel.)

Beleaguered Agency

All this should come as no surprise, considering the political magnitude of the LLDA's task. With a good harvest of *bangus*, fishpens—giant corrals of netting attached to long posts embedded in the lake's silted bottom—can generate millions of pesos in revenues for owners who are already wealthy and often well-connected. Among them are generals, judges, elected officials, and prominent media personalities, most of whose names cannot be found in the corporate papers. But as in the case of Red Sea, lackeys following up permits freely drop the real fishpen owners' names.

They wield power not only as rich capitalists and influential people, but also as major food producers, providing Metro Manila with nearly a quarter of its fish requirements. "The lake stabilizes the fish supply in the country," says Chuck Crisanto, former lake manager in the late 1980s.

Fishpen operators are by no means the only significant players in the lake, where the competition for its use gives new meaning to the environmental concept of "multiple stakeholders." For most of history, Laguna de Bay has been what academics call an open access resource, owned by no one but used and abused by anyone. All of 90,000 hectares, it has mostly been a wild frontier of brackish water and water lilies where the law's presence in the form of police and coast guard is much more sparse than on land. In the 1980s, according to a former lake administrator, New People's Army guerrillas in pump-boats were said to roam the lake, robbing other boats for their motors in an innovative way to raise funds.

Today, private armies guard some of the bigger fishpens, ready to shoot poachers. Many of the latter come from the ranks of several thousand small-scale fishers living along the shores who are irate about huge areas cordoned off from subsistence fishing. Ironically, fishpens were introduced in the lake by the government in the 1970s to boost the fish production and income of small fishers. Some of them have formed cooperatives that have been granted fishpen and fishcage permits, while many others have continued fishing in the open waters for indigenous species such as *ayungin*, *biya*, *kanduli* and *dulong*.

And then there are the so-called "divers," poachers who make a living stealing from the big fishpens by cutting them open below the surface and shooing fish into a submerged net attached by rope to a distant pump boat. Even retired Philippine National Police chief superintendent Mariano Filart, a fishpen owner, has reportedly been victimized by this operation.

Fishing is only the best-known use of the lake. Some of the richest farmland in the country source their irrigation water from there, lakeside municipalities have been reclaiming shore areas and turning them into real estate, and industry uses lakewater to cool machinery and regards the lake itself as a sink for wastewater.

Most importantly, before it was privatized, the Metropolitan Waterworks and Sewerage System (MWSS) had been planning to make use of the lake as a source of domestic water. According to various sources, Ayala Alabang Village, where President Ramos's family resides, is the first community to pipe in its drinking water from Laguna de Bay after treatment.

Tough Referee

All agree that the water quality has to be improved drastically before it can be consumed in households. For that to happen, the LLDA must continue to be a tough referee and to receive the kind of political support it currently gets from the Department of Environment and Natural Resources (DENR) and local officials like Laguna Governor Joey Lina, who has disciplined his own subordinates for building illegal structures called *kulong-kulong* on the lake.

In recent years, factories spewing waste into the lake have started to feel the growing arm of environmental enforcers. More companies have been either suspended or closed in the last two years than in the LLDA's previous 20. In 1996, workers at Cosmos Bottling Company in San Pedro, Laguna were ordered by managers to link arms and barricade their premises to prevent LLDA personnel from padlocking it for violations of pollution standards. The same Cosmos factory has since redeemed itself by becoming part of a LLDA pilot program to charge companies for using the lake as a wastewater dump.

Since the LLDA became an attached agency of the DENR in 1994, after years of being under the Office of the President, its bias has clearly been for the protection of the lake, rather than fish production or income generation, despite the hefty fees collected by the agency from fishpen operators. From a high of 33,000 hectares of fishpens in 1992, this area is now down to 6,000 hectares, aided substantially by Typhoon Rosing in November 1995 that destroyed many of the structures on the lake.

The LLDA, a government corporation known as a "super agency," wields a sweeping mandate over the Laguna de Bay basin that has also allowed it to experiment with fresh approaches to pollution control. These include an environmental users fee system, which taxes factories for dumping even small quantities of wastewater into the lake and provides an economic incentive to reduce pollution to zero. The concurrent system of pollution standards only penalizes establishments beyond a certain level of wastewater emission.

Perhaps even more worrisome than organic effluents is the heavy metal contamination, including mercury and lead, which has been found in the lake water. Authorities are not yet alarmed by current levels, but scientists warn of the accumulation of toxics in the fish we eat.

Powerful Fishpen Operators

By far the most contentious issue on the lake is the enforcement of fishpen standards, including the confinement of structures within a recently delineated fishpen belt. It was not industry, after all, but an alleged fishpen operator in power that managed to drive the LLDA from its base in Pasig City. Fishpen operators have rallied at LLDA offices and repeatedly taken the agency to court for what they deem to be excessive red tape.

The Local Government Code of 1991 unleashed the fury of local officials who believed their new powers over municipal waters gave them authority over their part of the lake. Town mayors in Rizal eager for greater municipal revenues from fishpen permits challenged the LLDA's jurisdiction in a celebrated legal dispute that reached the Supreme Court, where the local governments eventually lost in 1995. The LLDA has fought back, filing charges with the Ombudsman against Taytay Mayor Godofredo Valera who allegedly operated an unregistered fishpen and tried to misrepresent it as a cooperative.

Fishpen owners attack LLDA operations as a threat to Metro Manila's food supply. "There seems to be a hidden agenda to eradicate fishpens," says Atty. Joey Mendoza, counsel for the Kapisanan ng Tao at Lawa sa Laguna de Bay, which includes fishpen operators and has a pending case against the LLDA. "They want to clear the lake so it can be used for Metro Manila's water."

LLDA officials admit that is the

agenda. But it is far from hidden, having been pushed since the 1980s, when the national government already saw the potential of the lake for domestic water use. Of all the competing uses of the lake, its preservation as a source of drinking water is now paramount.

"We are now entering a crisis of water," says LLDA chief Tomboc. "In the next few years, the worst crisis will hit Metro Manila and Calabarzon. Where will we get water for industry and domestic use? We have already shifted the major function of the lake from fisheries to domestic and industrial water supply."

Tomboc, who has a doctorate in forestry and rose through the ranks at the DENR, has been the recipient of death threats. He has had to change his home telephone number and vary his routes. And yet, if he stays at the LLDA, his headaches may just be beginning. When the national government does decide in the next several years to start treating lake water for domestic use and piping it into the congested, parched communities south of Manila, the LLDA will have to block the saltwater of Manila Bay from entering the lake via the Pasig River.

But that would disrupt the chemical action that clears the water and allows sunlight to enter the depths, triggering the photosynthesis process that produces the phytoplankton organisms that fish feed on. In essence, using the lake for domestic water could eventually kill the fishing industry.

The environmental situation of the metropolis and its surrounding provinces has almost reached the point where such a painful trade-off between food and water is necessary. "We can import fish, but we cannot import water," Tomboc says emphatically.

"We have a critical water situation," says Atty. Mai Flor, the executive director of the Presidential Task Force on Water Resources Development and Management. "Our only source of surface water now is Angat Dam (in Bulacan), and that is being shared with agriculture and (electric) power. So many people now are extracting groundwater through deep wells that saltwater intrusion is happening. Soon that source will be gone."

Optimism about the water crisis has flickered with the privatization of the MWSS, with consumers hoping that the Ayala and Lopez conglomerates can quench the thirst of millions. Antonio Aquino, the director for corporate affairs of the Ayalas' Manila Water Company, cautions that Laguna de Bay will need a lot of work before it can be pumped for domestic use, with perhaps the greatest challenge being the growing populations along the lakeshore without septic tanks.

Among the MWSS priority projects inherited by the Manila Water Company is the plan for a Rizal Province Water Treatment Plant, which is currently being re-evaluated. If approved, that can supply Rizal's eastern towns with 150,000 cubic meters of Laguna de Bay water per day within three years, according to Aquino.

But that may well depend on whether the LLDA succeeds in establishing some semblance of law and order on the lake, and persuading the powerful fishpen owners to sacrifice their economic interests for the greater good. Rizal Governor Casimiro Ynares, who so abruptly sent the LLDA packing from his building, may have to forfeit his fish to relieve his thirsty province.